D0850681

THE POETRY OF HART CRANE

BOOKS BY R. W. B. LEWIS

The American Adam
The Picaresque Saint
Trials of the Word
The Poetry of Hart Crane

The Poetry of
HART CRANE
A Critical Study

R. W. B. LEWIS

GREENWOOD PRESS, PUBLISHERS
WESTPORT, CONNECTICUT

Library of Congress Cataloging in Publication Data

Lewis, Richard Warrington Baldwin.
    The poetry of Hart Crane.

    Reprint of the ed. published by Princeton University
Press, Princeton, N. J.
    Includes bibliographical references and index.
    1. Crane, Hart, 1899-1932--Criticism and interpreta-
tion. I. Title.
[PS3505.R272Z74 1978]   811'.5'2   77-25520
ISBN 0-313-20059-9

For Nathaniel

Preface

THE PREMISE of this book, though nowhere else do I state it so unguardedly, is that Hart Crane is one of the finest modern poets in our language, and one of the dozen-odd major poets in American history. But this is a premise, not a thesis; I do not attempt to prove the unprovable. My purpose is simply to follow the development of Crane's poetry from the apprentice poems written around 1916 to "The Broken Tower," completed within a relatively few weeks of his death in 1932. I have tried to chart the career of Crane's imagination—of his vision, his rhetoric, and his craft. I have sought especially to relate those elements, as Crane consciously and sometimes defensively related them, to the Anglo-American Romantic tradition: in particular, to the work of Blake, Wordsworth, Keats, and Shelley in England; and of Emerson, Whitman, Melville, and Emily Dickinson in America. Late in his short life, Crane remarked to Allen Tate—who, Crane said, had "posit[ed] *The Bridge* at the end of a tradition of romanticism"—that "a great deal of romanticism may persist—of the sort to deserve serious consideration, I mean." The subsequent work of Wallace Stevens, with that of the proliferating heirs of both Crane and Stevens and the ever-mounting critical interest in Romantic writing, suggest that Crane's rather wistful contention was sounder than he could have dared to hope.

This is a long book, and no doubt it should have been longer. The excursions into cultural history—notably in Chapters Three, Eight, and Nine—seemed to me quite necessary journeys, undertaken to show the many affinities between this seeming poetic sport and whole clusters of figures and imaginative tendencies of the near and more remote past. But as to the poems themselves, there are a certain number that I do not even mention, much less gloss.

More important, there are a good many images, lines, and stanzas over which I might have paused longer—not in exclamatory admiration (though this has often been hard to suppress), but in an effort to find interpretative language for the burgeoning implications they contain; implications which either I have felt forced to pass by, because of space, or which have edged their way into my consciousness too belatedly. As a single example, let me take a phrase I once thought of adapting for my title: "spindrift gaze," in "Voyages II." It is not enough to observe, as I do in Chapter Six, that "spindrift" is a Melvillian word meaning "spray-swept," and that the image is visually precise. It has all too recently occurred to me that what Crane is describing is the *impeded* or *misted over* as well as the searching visionary glance; that this notion too has its discoverable antecedents in Wordsworth; and that such a partly beclouded vision is almost the main subject of Crane's best poetry, as it is the characteristic property of the poet himself. But a book possibly twice as long would be needed to take account of all these significant enchantments. And in any case, my intention is to open, not to close, the discussion of Crane's achievement.

I have included a modest amount of biographical material, little of which cannot be found in the biographies by Philip Horton (1937) and Brom Weber (1948), and perhaps none of which will not be found in John Unterecker's forthcoming book. The materials I have drawn upon have to do entirely with Crane's productivity, with the ebb and flow of his creative energies and the conditions which subdued or diverted or released them. Upon occasion, too, these materials have been indispensable aids to interpretation. The figure that emerges—the man *and* the poetic voice—is, I suppose, less bedeviled, less emotionally and verbally violent, indeed less self-destructive, than has usually been thought. But it is the figure that, over half a dozen years of mental association, I have come to recognize.

As to other critical studies of Crane, I have frankly learned more from those writers with whom I most strenuously disagree—writers like Allen Tate, R. P. Blackmur, and Yvor Winters, who have variously indicted Crane for dissipating an immense talent out of wilfulness, strategic wrongheadedness, or bad Romantic habits—than from those who have praised him without qualification. More frankly yet, I gave up reading criticism about Crane several years ago. I am sure that I have, thereby, missed some astute and helpful readings, and worse yet I must have laboriously repeated what others have said earlier and better. But it did seem to me increasingly that what I was reading in articles and explications had almost nothing to do with my own experience of the volume of poems that lay open on the other side of my desk. One exception is L. S. Denbo's *Hart Crane's Sanskrit Charge* (1960), an analysis of *The Bridge* with which, as will be evident, I am also in some disagreement, but which has taught me many things. Another is Thomas A. Vogler's essay on *The Bridge* in the *Sewanee Review* (Summer 1965). Other sources of insight or provocation are mentioned in the text.

Given my own encounters with Crane criticism, I think I may be confident that no one will agree with all my readings of the poems. But it may well be that some will disagree with all of them; for my best hope has been to attain a degree of consistency in interpretation—in the identification of theme, in the analysis of poetic method, in the assessment of spiritual aspiration in the various works. Whether I have succeeded or not, the task should not be beyond the possibilities of criticism; for Crane's poetry itself reveals an extraordinary consistency.

The more I think about that poetry, the more I find it characterized by two remarks of Emerson, both appearing on the same page of *Nature*. The first is this: "The invariable mark of wisdom is to see the miraculous in the common." The second is Emerson's comment on the need to satisfy "all the demands of the spirit": "Love is as much its demand as perception. Indeed neither can be perfect without the other." In poems as early as "Meditation" (1917 or thereabouts) and somewhat later in "Chaplinesque," and in almost everything he wrote from "Faustus and Helen" (1923) onward, Crane was concerned with the spiritual needs of vision and love, with making manifest their fused power through the remarkable resources of his art, with enacting their miraculous and transfiguring effect upon the common and often discordant and repellent ingredients of life. Even *The Bridge,* for all its length and complexity, can be seen as a vast enlargement of the theme so regularly sounded in the lyrics—the theme of the visionary and loving transfiguration of the actual world. If, as eventually I do, I claim for Crane the role of the religious poet par excellence in his generation, it is because such a combination of love and vision seems to me to partake indisputably of the religious imagination. "And so it was," Crane wrote in "The Broken Tower"—"And so it was I entered the broken world / To trace the visionary company of love." Crane's journey through that broken world and his effort to heal and transform it by poetry are the subject of this book.

A book that takes as long to write as this did incurs many debts along the way, and one of the pleasures of completing the work is the opportunity to acknowledge them.

I am grateful to Professors Newton P. Stallknecht and Horst Frenz for inviting me to give a seminar on *The Bridge* at the School of Letters, Indiana University; and to the late R. P. Blackmur both for permitting me to offer a Christian Gauss Seminar at Princeton University on the same subject, and for the headiest kind of intellectual stimulation over many years. My sincerest thanks are due to the American Council of Learned Societies for a generous grant over the year 1962-1963, as a result of which I made the first substantial progress on the writing of the book. To Smith College, I am beholden for the honor of giving the Jacob Ziskind Memorial Lectures in 1966—lectures for which I drew upon (and was consequently able to improve) my Chapters Eight, Nine, and Twelve. I was fortunate, in addition, to be able to try out some of my ideas about Crane in public lectures at Brown and Columbia Universities, and at the Universities of Virginia and Pittsburgh.

Among the many individuals to whom I am indebted for counsel, information, and suggestions, I should like to mention Daniel Aaron, Glauco Cambon, Malcolm Cowley, Charles T. Davis, Ralph Ellison, Richard Ellmann, Paul Fussell, Jr., John Hollander, Philip Horton, Robert Lowell, Norman Holmes Pearson, Mrs. Vivian Pemberton, Alan Trachtenberg, John Unterecker, and Brom Weber. I should make special mention of Harold Bloom, for patiently working through a number of Crane's early poems with me, and for guiding me with much vigor through the domain of Romantic poetry; of Peter J. Conn, for his careful proofreading of the manuscript and for many helpful stylistic and interpretive comments; of Kenneth Lohf, curator of the Special Collections of the Columbia University Library, for his unfailing assistance in making accessible Hart Crane's worksheets, and for placing at my disposal his invaluable bibliography of Crane's published and unpublished writings.

A much abbreviated version of Chapter Three appeared in the Summer 1963 issue of the *Massachusetts Review;* and virtually the entire chapter in *Learners and Discerners,* edited by Robert M. Scholes (University of Virginia Press, 1964). About four-fifths of Chapter Seven appeared in the Spring 1966 issue of the *Massachusetts Review*. I am grateful in all cases for permission to reprint.

The definitive edition of Crane's poetry, edited with annotations by Brom Weber, was published as *The Complete Poems and Selected Letters and Prose of Hart Crane.* This is the text I trust any reader of this book will have on hand. In almost all my quotations, I have adopted the wording, spelling and punctuation as established by Mr. Weber. I gratefully acknowledge permission to quote from *The Complete Poems and Selected Letters and Prose of Hart Crane,* Black & Gold Library, $5.95, Liveright Publishers, New York. I am grateful again to Brom Weber for permission to quote from *The Letters of Hart Crane, 1916–1932,* copyright © 1952 by Brom Weber, reprinted in 1965 by the University of California Press. Quotations from the unpublished Hart Crane materials owned by the Columbia University Libraries are made with the permission of Columbia University.

The person to whom this book is dedicated is not yet quite as old as the critical enterprise itself; I look forward to the time when I can explain to him how much and often how knowingly he contributed to it. But as always the largest, most joyful and least repayable debt is to his mother.

RWBL

Yale University
December, 1966

Contents

THE ESCAPE FROM IRONY

CHAPTER ONE

Geographies

IN DECEMBER 1919, when he himself was twenty, Hart Crane remarked about two recently acquired friends that one was "classic, hard and glossy," while the other was "crowd-bound, with a smell of the sod about him, uncouth. Somewhere between them," he went on in the self-deprecating manner then characteristic of him, "is Hart Crane with a kind of wistful indetermination, still much puzzled." [1] By circumstance and temperament, Crane was almost always "somewhere between" the variously opposing elements that made up his early life and nourished his creative powers. Carl Sandburg noted one of the unlikely combinations in him when he referred to Crane, with a kind of jocose shrewdness, as "the Cleveland Rimbaud." But the opposites between which Crane moved were even larger and more widespread than that; and perhaps the best way to identify Crane during the first two decades or so of his brief life is to trace his actual and imaginative movements among the most important of these opposites—to chart as it were the multiple "geographies" of his early career.

He stood, for example, somewhere between his incompatible and eventually, in Crane's own word, "sundered" parents. The marriage between Grace Edna Hart of Chicago and Clarence Arthur Crane, an increasingly successful manufacturer of chocolate candy and founder of the Crane Company in Cleveland, ended in divorce in 1916. "I don't want to fling accusations, etc., at anybody," Hart Crane wrote his mother several years later, "but I think it's time you realized

---

[1] *The Letters of Hart Crane,* edited by Brom Weber (New York, 1952), p. 27. All quotations from Crane's letters are taken from this volume. Except in special instances, page references will not hereafter be given.

that for the last eight years my youth has been a rather bloody battleground for yours and father's sex life and troubles." On the whole, he sided with his mother in the marital warfare: at least to the extent of dropping his first baptismal name, Harold, and of signing his publications with his second name, his mother's maiden name, Hart.[2]

Throughout most of his life, he remained, or rather tried to remain (Mrs. Crane did not always make it easy) close to his mother. And it is worth remarking that, insofar as Crane's epic poem of 1930, *The Bridge,* does invoke the epic convention of the child's search for the parent, it is mainly in terms of the son's search for the mother. Still, as the tough-spirited letter just quoted indicates, Crane was anything but a mother's boy. He was neither effeminate nor maternally smothered, nor was he unable to see his father in a reasonably clear light. Long after the divorce, he wrote that "Probably the truth"—about Clarence Crane—"consists more moderately in the estimate of him as a person of as many good inclinations as bad ones"; and he could even admire his father's business achievements. "Things are whizzing," he reported with detached amusement in 1919, "and I don't know how many millions he will be worth before he gets through growing." In any event, his parents provided the youthful Crane with an unforgettable experience of the violence of feeling and the failure of communication to which the relation between man and woman can be susceptible, and with the knowledge that each party to the struggle may be equally culpable.

Domestic upheavals in the Crane household also affected, in part, the literal geography of Crane's apprentice years. He was born, in 1899, in the small northern Ohio village of Garretsville, near the Pennsylvania border. In 1903, the family moved to the somewhat larger and nearby town of Warren; but in 1908, the boy was rushed to his grandparents'

[2] Beginning with the poem "Echoes" in the October 1917 issue of the New York periodical, *The Pagan.*

home in Cleveland after Mr. and Mrs. Crane had explosively separated and the latter had been carried, in a state of collapse, to a sanatorium. A precarious reconciliation followed, and Hart Crane lived and went to school in Cleveland from 1908 to 1916. Then, in December of 1916, after the divorce, Crane felt free to go east to New York City, there to attempt a start on a literary career. He was back in Cleveland for a few months in 1918, taking a job first in a munitions plant and later in a shipyard—with some vague notion of helping the "war effort." By the end of that same year, he went again to New York. This second eastern venture lasted until November 1919, when Crane was persuaded by his father to return to Ohio and work in Mr. Crane's Akron store. He was soon transferred to the Crane factory in Cleveland; and when one speaks of Hart Crane's "Cleveland years," it is primarily the period from early 1920 to early 1923 that is meant. He quit working for his father in April 1921, but he stayed on in his grandmother's house during a nine-month jobless interval and later while working for the advertising firm of Corday and Gross. The Cleveland years ended in March 1923, when Crane had completed what was in every respect the major turning-point of his creative life, the three-part poem "For the Marriage of Faustus and Helen," and left Cleveland to settle permanently in or near New York.

Not surprisingly, Crane felt himself psychologically and culturally somewhere between the Middle West and the East as he shuttled back and forth, over the years, from one to the other. During his first stay in New York, he was very much the big-eyed ambitious young man from the western provinces—boasting to his mother about meeting "one of the principal literary figures in America," [3] but telling his father that he seemed to have lost his identity in the big city and

---

[3] Padraic Colum. In her memoirs, Mary Colum, who does not like Crane's poetry but who was interested in the young provincial personally, recalled that he pronounced the word "manly" as though it were spelled "mainly."

that he was "vainly trying to find [it] somewhere in this sea of humanity." Back in Ohio, however, he found that he had become half an easterner, and his letters sometimes bristled with distaste for the vulgarity and hypocrisy by which he felt surrounded: the poem "Porphyro in Akron" (published belatedly by *The Double Dealer* in September 1921) is a rueful account of his situation. At the same time, he had a congenital affection for the rustic and a sympathy for small-town life, balancing those qualities against the ambiguous allure of the metropolitan. This is one implication of the description of his two friends, cited earlier. The hard and classic one, Matthew Josephson, was an intellectually sophisticated resident of Manhattan; his "uncouth" opposite was Sherwood Anderson, whose tales of secreted emotions and lonely strivings in just such a small Ohio town as Crane had known—*Winesburg, Ohio*—Crane, in a reverent review (1919), called "the Bible of the American consciousness."

There was indeed a strong and steady pastoral strain in Crane's imagination. He is sometimes taken as the type of the twentieth-century city poet; but when he inspected the eastern urban scene, Crane—like another fellow Midwesterner, his contemporary Scott Fitzgerald—tended to cast upon it a glance at once western and astonished; and a glance, too, again like Fitzgerald's, that sought to convert that crowded and mechanized setting into a dream of natural purity. Some of his most remarkable lyrics, moreover, enact precisely the escape from the city's oppressions to the inspiring freshness of the hills and the sea: "Passage," for example, and "Repose of Rivers"; and the pastoral retreat westward is a dominant counter-theme in *The Bridge,* where it is salted with phrases borrowed ironically from Shakespeare's most greatly conventional pastoral romance, *As You Like It.*

So imposing a name as Shakespeare's brings us to the question of Crane's actual literary enthusiasms and affinities in his beginning years. Here once more we observe a sort of dialectical geography, as Crane's attachments moved (to

6

put the case oversimply) between Europe and America; or, to take two individual names as cultural symbols, between T. S. Eliot and Walt Whitman. Those were perhaps the chief poets around whose work and influence the critical battle waged most vigorously when Crane reached New York in 1916; and it was his direct experience of the battle rather than any formal education which was decisive for Crane. He never quite finished high school; and though he contemplated enrolling in some special courses at Columbia University and even tutored for a while in the summer of 1917 to prepare himself, Crane eventually abandoned the notion and turned instead, as he told a friend, to "pursuing the old course of self-culture." [4] No American writer ever pursued that course—so significantly typical *of* American writers from Melville and Whitman onward—more persistently and rigorously than Hart Crane; and he did so at a time and in a place where literary doctrines buffeted one another in an enormously stimulating anarchy of opposites.

Out of the welter of would-be new influences that palpitated on the New York literary scene in those years, two of the many periodicals can be taken as expressive of the major contending forces—*The Little Review* that, under the direction of Margaret Anderson, moved from Chicago to Manhattan in 1917; and the *Seven Arts,* founded in 1916 by Waldo Frank, Van Wyck Brooks, James Oppenheim, and Paul Rosenfeld. The former propagated the European aspect,

---

[4] Though Crane was mainly self-educated, the notion that he was a sort of cultural sport, emerging from a wholly unlettered family background, is quite groundless. Mrs. Vivian Pemberton, of the Kent State (Ohio) English Department, is making a study of Crane's forbears and relatives; she reports that the Crane family (as against the Harts) had evinced for several generations a strong love of literature and of things artistic. Hart Crane's great-uncle, Frederick J. Crane, for example, was a poet or poetaster in the wake of Longfellow, and he enjoyed reciting his own verses and those of the American Fireside Poets in the Crane Household. Clarence Crane liked to recite long passages of Shakespeare. The Cranes, in short, were recognizably late nineteenth- and early twentieth-century Midwestern Americans in their devotion to the arts.

7

especially French *symboliste* poets like Laforgue and Rimbaud, and those English-language poets, Pound and Eliot in particular, who were absorbing and reflecting that aspect. The *Seven Arts* was all in the American grain: a magazine, as a French admirer, Romain Rolland declared, "in which the American Spirit may seek and achieve consciousness of its nature and its role"; behind it, Rolland heard "the elemental voice of a great pioneer . . . your Homer: Walt Whitman." The opposition established will be readily recognized as another and perhaps more than usually meaningful version of a recurring American phenomenon—the periodic clash between the adherents of European literature and those who are driven to assert an essentially indigenous tradition. Somewhere in between was Hart Crane, moving with determination, much puzzled perhaps but also much exhilarated.

"I'm afraid I don't fit in your group," Crane said to one of the embattled *literati.* "Or any group, for all that." As a person profoundly concerned with the craft of poetry, Crane was drawn to the kind of writing that appeared in *The Little Review,* to its habitual ironies and large erudition, its deft indirections, its articulated sense of the sheer complexities of modern experience, and its resourceful efforts to revitalize the language of poetry in order to give voice to those complexities. But humanly and emotionally, Crane was not much less drawn to the forthright native idealism of the *Seven Arts,* even though he was for a time hesitant about its stress on the "national consciousness" and wondered aloud, in commenting on Waldo Frank's *Our America* (1919), whether writers like Dreiser, Anderson, and Frost had not achieved their successes rather through a "national *uncon*sciousness" (italics added). As a matter of fact, Crane had a good deal more in common with the American literary tradition—at least as represented by Melville, Whitman, Emerson, Thoreau, and Emily Dickinson—than he was yet aware, or than anyone could have been aware at a time when it was not yet understood that an American literary tradition existed.

The *symboliste*-Eliot aspect, however, was in the ascendancy in Crane's early creative years, and it reached its peak in 1920 and 1921—which is one reason why certain critics of the Eliotic persuasion sometimes limit Crane's accomplishment to the work of that period: "Praise for an Urn," "Black Tambourine," and a few others. The verbal hardness of these poems, their use of ironic literary allusion, their clear cadences and firm grasp of moral complexities—all this could be admired by the party in fashion. And the poems are indeed thoroughly admirable; Crane learned many invaluable lessons from what we may loosely call the *Little Review* school. But other aspects were always present, not only to Crane's creative purposes but also to his critical sense. And here let it be said that Hart Crane was one of his generation's soundest and most staunchly independent judges of poetry. He was quick to follow up a suggestion, and he was perhaps lucky to receive such radically different suggestions from such different sources; but his responses were entirely his own. "There," he said about Wallace Stevens four years before the appearance of Stevens's first volume, *Harmonium,* "is a man whose work makes most of the rest of us quail." And if in the writing of these years he usually restricted himself to the brief intensities of experience, he was hospitable in his reading to work of every kind of comprehensiveness. In February 1920, for example, he was "deep in Baudelaire's *Fleurs de Mal,*" but a month later he was absorbed in Stendhal's *The Charterhouse of Parma;* in July, he was telling Gorham Munson about his enthusiasm for "our Henry James," for James's *The American,* some short stories and his letters, and within weeks he was immersed in "the polyphonic prose" of Conrad's *The Nigger of the Narcissus;* before the summer was out, he had read *Moby-Dick, The Possessed* ("one of the most tremendous books I've ever read"), and *The Brothers Karamazov* ("even better"). "Dosty," as Crane took to calling him, was "the greatest of novelists" and "the nearest type to the return of Christ that there is record of."

But it was one particular kind of poetry that gradually took dominance in Crane's artistic consciousness, something considerably larger and older than the American aspect I have mentioned and which it included. Its ascendancy followed certain psychological experiences during the year 1922, to be considered later; and it was much affected by Crane's excited reading of S. Foster Damon's massive study of the poetry of William Blake.[5] Crane was always given to listings of writers he admired: for example, of various "English old fellows that are a constant challenge," as he wrote Allen Tate in May 1922—"Donne, Webster, Jonson, Marlowe, Vaughan, Blake, etc." But it was the tradition represented by "Blake etc." which ultimately obtained Crane's deepest allegiance: the Romantic tradition in both its English and its American phases. To this, everything Crane had so valuably learned from Eliot and from the poets whom he had met through Eliot became subordinated and adjusted. The easiest single descriptive adjective for the poetic tradition in question—at least as it was absorbed and modified by Hart Crane—is the word "visionary."

I should be glad to use the word "religious" to define the kind of poetry Crane came most to honor and to write—except that, in Crane's case, the word "religious" is peculiarly beset with semantic and historical difficulties; we shall need, later, to make a number of distinctions before we can usefully employ it. In 1930, in a grateful acknowledgment of a favorable review of *The Bridge* which had emphasized "the essential religious motive" in it, Crane said: "I have never consciously approached any subject in a religious mood." But that is only an example of the semantic problem; in context, it is clear that Crane feared the word "religious" might imply some wrong kind of Messianic impulse in his

[5] See the letter to Gorham Munson in (apparently) late August 1922.

poetry. Using the word more laxly, though not, I think, irresponsibly, one can as accurately say that from 1922 onward Crane never approached a subject in anything *but* a religious mood. With considerations of this kind, anyhow, we arrive at the last and most important of the geographies by which I have been trying to locate and identify the emergent poet. I mean, here, what we might call the geography of the spirit—the two worlds, the world of the actual and the world of the ideal, between which Crane's imagination moved, as his talent developed, with ever stronger determination and confidence.

We get an early clue to Crane's attitude in this crucial area from a comment he made about Christian Science. His mother had drifted toward Christian Science when Hart Crane was still a boy,[6] and after the divorce from Clarence Crane, she took it up wholeheartedly. Her son allowed her to believe that he, too, espoused it—because, he told a friend in May 1919, "she seems to depend on that hypocrisy as an additional support for her own faith in it." He admitted to having been "very much interested in Christian Science" at one time, and still found in it an amount of "efficacy"; but only as a psychological attitude. "As a religion, there is where I balk. . . . What it says in regard to mental and nervous ailments is absolutely true. It is only the total denial of the animal and organic world which I cannot swallow."

When Crane later began to talk and write about the actual and ideal or the "quotidian" and the "abstract"—rather than about the organic, animal, and mental—his fundamental convictions about a hierarchy of "worlds" and his evenly distributed affirmation of the value and reality of each had not changed. One primary movement in "For the Marriage of Faustus and Helen," in "Voyages," and in *The Bridge,* as well as in several of the shorter poems discussed below in Chapters Five and Seven, is a "graduation from the quotidian into the abstract," to borrow Crane's phrase about "Faustus

[6] Professor John Unterecker says: probably in 1900, though he has not found any explicit reference.

and Helen, Part I." It is expressed variously as a movement from the temporal to the timeless, from the ironically irreconcilable to the perfectly harmonious, from the divided to the united, from the hot and crowded to the cool and solitary, from the physical to the spiritual. Because Crane's poetic gaze was fixed so often and so intently upon the transcendent and timeless sphere, he may properly enough be called a visionary poet. But the label would be utterly misleading if it carried any suggestion of a "denial of the animal and organic world," of the actual and the quotidian. For just as he traveled literally between Middle West and East and just as his literary loyalties shifted back and forth more spaciously between the American and the European, so his moral and spiritual loyalties commuted between the two grand dimensions of consciousness and (in Crane's belief) of existence.

Crane was, or rather he became, a poet of powerful visionary impulses who at the same time, both as a man *and* as a poet, was a thoroughgoing devotee of the things of this world. Both as a man and as a poet, Crane entered at an early age into an enduring love affair with life itself, this actual life. Like most love affairs, this one could at times become almost unbearably intense, and it was susceptible to alternating fits of ecstasy and exasperation, to an alternating sense of fulfillment and of despair. But it was an affair that really did endure—if only because the life that often betrayed him in the fact could always be redeemed in the poetry. Crane was not a death-haunted author of death-conscious poetry, any more than he was, in the usual meaning of the phrase, a tragic poet. That false stereotype, as I shall insist on more than one occasion, derives from a muddled view of his life, a consequent misinterpretation of his poetry and a series of misleading associations with some of his genuinely tragic-spirited contemporaries.

Crane instinctively felt about the actual world that he should risk the experience of it, and report his findings;

though he knew that it was not his human or poetic business, as it were, to wallow in the actual. The distinction was not, to be sure, always held to. During the Cleveland years, even as Crane's creative excitement mounted, the sheer pace of his behavior quickened. It was then that he began to consume large quantities of red wine, and that he engaged in his first homosexual love affair. He almost never—at least at this time—showed any symptoms of remorse for such conduct, except when these matters interfered with his writing. Critics of a Protestant mentality have attributed to Crane and to his poetry a guilt he simply did not feel; Crane obviously *enjoyed*—that, as Elizabeth Hardwick has remarked approvingly, is the only word for it [7]—both his wine and his affairs with young men. And out of one of the latter, he was to write "Voyages," perhaps the most beautiful love poetry in modern American literature. The fact was that Crane remained immune to that profound sense of human sin that, under the auspices of T. S. Eliot, was providing an indispensable corrective to the flabbily optimistic progressivism of the day, and that was having in some important respects so beneficial an effect upon Anglo-American writing. Crane's attitude to his own conduct was of a piece with his attitude to the fallen world in which it occurred. In both cases, as he put it in "Lachrymae Christi," Crane favored:

> Not penitence
> But song. . . .

It was William Blake among others (later it was above all Emerson and Whitman) who helped Crane discover how to arrive at that impenitent song. One had not only to *see* the actual in all of its fallen condition, but to see *through* it; to see an ideal condition in the same glance, and to see the actual thereby irradiated. One of Blake's couplets in particular was cherished by Crane as the true, if negative, formulation of the problem:

[7] *A View of My Own* (New York, 1962), pp. 10ff.

We are led to believe in a lie
When we see *with* not *through* the eye.

It was a question of vision: of somehow seeing the two different worlds at one and the same time; but countless writers over the centuries have attested to the overwhelming difficulty of the question—no one more poignantly than one of Crane's American ancestors, Emerson, who said that the trouble with "this double consciousness of ours" was that the two halves of it never "meet and mingle," never "measure each other." In this regard, too, Crane was lucky; or to use an older vocabulary, he was touched by something like grace. It happened early in 1922, and of all places, in a dentist's chair. There, as Crane later described it, "under the influence of aether and *amnesia* my mind spiraled to a kind of seventh heaven of consciousness. . . . I felt the two worlds. And at once." The experience served to release the visionary genius latent in what had until then been a very fine but a relatively earth-bound poet; and Crane moved on into the larger phases of his career, where it was his sustained purpose to show in poetry the two worlds meeting and mingling, the dimensions of consciousness measuring one another.

CHAPTER TWO

Poetry and the Actual

CRANE'S DEVELOPMENT from apprentice to genuine poet may be measured by comparing a poem of 1917, "Annunciations," with "Black Tambourine," written early in 1921. Crane said about the latter, some months after it had been published in the New Orleans *Double Dealer,* that it had become for him "a kind of diminutive model" that at least "point[ed] a direction"; and we cannot do better than follow his lead. "Annunciations" is short enough to quote in its entirety:

> The anxious milk-blood in the veins of the earth,
> That strives long and quiet to sever the girth
> Of greenery. . . . Below the roots, a quickening shiver
> Aroused by some light that had sensed,—ere the shiver
> Of the first moth's descent,—day's predestiny. . . .
> The sound of a dove's flight waved over the lawn. . . .
> The moans of travail of one dearest beside me. . . .
> Then high cries from great chasms of chaos outdrawn—
> Hush! these things were all heard before dawn.

As even a hasty reading will show, this is a very odd combination of the muted and the headlong: the faint and painful quickening-into-life of nature and the human psyche and possibly, in some vague way, of the cosmos in general (with the murky hint of a Christian implication in the title)—all this conveyed in a series of runaway anapests. The combination reflects faithfully enough the two chief influences—Wilde and Swinburne—that Crane had to escape before he could arrive, as he unmistakably did in "Black Tambourine," at an idiom and a melody of his own.

The first of Crane's poems to see print (in the New York *Bruno's Weekly,* September 1916) was indeed a tribute to

Oscar Wilde and took as its title Wilde's identification as a numbered convict in Reading Gaol: "C 33." In it he spoke of Wilde as weaving "rose-vines / About the empty heart of night," and attributed to him a "penitence" leading to "pain"—"and with it song of minor, broken strain." Nothing could be less congenial to Crane's natural poetic impulse than a minor, broken strain, unless it be the wistful whispering that pervades the diction of the poem—or the motif of painful remorse. In all of this we recognize at once the borrowed melancholy of the aspiring young. The more expansive rhythms of Swinburne did not serve him much better, as "Annunciations" indicates; one line in the latter, "Then high cries from great chasms of chaos outdrawn" reminds one indeed of Swinburne's entertaining self-parody "Nephelida" ("Gaunt as the ghastliest of glimpses that gleam through the gloom of the gloaming," and so on). In a curious allegorical ballad composed about the same time, however, Crane deployed that rushing meter to a slightly more pleasing effect.[1] "The Moth that God Made Blind," as it was called, is interesting because of the promising flicker of its imagery, but even more because of its subject: it is the first time, so far as I know, that Crane dealt with the question of poetic vision.[2] This poem tells, in four-line

[1] This poem is included in Brom Weber's new edition, for Doubleday, of Crane's poetry. In January 1916, Crane wrote his grandmother that he was "grippingly interested in a new ballad of . . . six hundred lines"—perhaps an early reference to "The Moth," which, however, was happily kept to forty-two lines.

[2] Since the above was written, Kenneth A. Lohf has made available a group of Crane's early and hitherto unpublished poems, in a pamphlet called "Hart Crane: Seven Lyrics" (New York: The Ibex Press, 1966). These were written between 1916 and late 1918; and the last and by far the best of them, "Meditation" not only engages the theme of vision, but does so in a way that astonishingly anticipates the visionary thrust of much later work. The poem consists of three six-line stanzas, each with a rhyme scheme of aabbcc. It begins:

> I have drawn my hands away
> Toward peace and the grey margins of the day.
> The andante of vain hopes and lost regret
> Falls like slow rain that whispers to forget. . . .

stanzas with alternating rhymes, of a race of moths whose eyes were too weak to look upon the "gorgeous" world about them by day, and dared open their eyes only in moonlight. But then a moth was born totally blind, and yet by recompense equipped with unusually strong wings. One day he ventured to fly up toward the blazing sun—and vision was suddenly granted him:

When below him he saw what his whole race had shunned—
Great horizons and systems and shores all along.

Inevitably, though:

> A little time only, for sight burned as deep
> As his blindness before had frozen in Hell;

his wings wither; he falls and disappears. In a final stanza, Crane underscored the obvious: his eyes, too, "have hugged beauty and winged life's brief spell," but now his eyes are dim and his hand withered.

"The Moth that God Made Blind" may have been one of the poems Crane read to Matthew Josephson, when they met in the office of *The Little Review* on West 16th Street, early in 1919. Josephson, anyhow, pronounced the poems that Crane did read to him "old fashioned" and "Swinburnian" and at once set to giving Crane a course of literary instruction that hastened the process of Crane's liberation

---

And it ends:

> I have drawn my hands away
> Like ships for guidance in the lift and spray
> Of stars that urge them toward an unknown goal.
> Drift, O wakeful one, O restless soul,
> Until the glittering white open hand
> Of heaven thou shalt read and understand.

Mr. Lohf observes that the second line above was adapted for "Faustus and Helen I"; and it can be added that the whispering slow rain will be heard again in "My Grandmother's Love Letters." But the last stanza contains strung-out versions of motifs that would recur, highly animated, in *The Bridge*—especially in "Ave Maria" and the "Sanskrit charge" passage in "Cape Hatteras." "Meditation" almost certainly post-dates "The Moth that God Made Blind" by a year or so.

from the Edwardians.[3] As a matter of fact, the process had already begun. A year before, in July 1918, Crane had dispatched a letter to *The Little Review*, replying briskly to a critic who had lumped Baudelaire and Joyce with Wilde and Swinburne "as rivals in 'decadence' and 'intellect.'" On this occasion, Crane pretty much rejected Wilde and Swinburne: Wilde because he amounted to little more than a "bundle of paradoxes"; Swinburne because his poetry was limited to "beautiful" but "meaningless mouthing." In praising Baudelaire and Joyce for their "penetration into life," Crane was moved to call *A Portrait of the Artist as a Young Man* "aside from Dante . . . spiritually the most inspiring book I have ever read. It is Bunyan raised to art, and then raised to the ninth power." [4] The Bunyanesque "Moth that God Made Blind" was thus a token of the future, as well as an act of piety toward the past. For all its Swinburnian trappings, we detect in it the same myth of the ill-fated but admirably daring flight of Icarus which had provided a central symbol for the artist in Joyce's novel.

According to Crane's biographers, the process had started earlier yet. In 1917, during his first New York stay, Crane had a number of useful sessions with a former Warren, Ohio neighbor, the painter Carl Schmitt—sessions aimed precisely, as Philip Horton has put it, at "breaking down the formal patterns" of Crane's apprentice verse. Crane's progress in this regard—that is, in his handling of meter and rhyme— was in no way an unfamiliar one in the history of poetry; but it was in every way important, for later, in his best work, Crane could sometimes get out of sheer metrical pressure an amount of communicable "meaning" that a very different kind of poet might get from a classical literary allusion. It was a progress from the employment of metrical conventions that were dead or dying or, for Crane, irrelevant; through

[3] Josephson, *Life Among the Surrealists* (New York, 1962).
[4] Brom Weber, *Hart Crane* (1948), pp. 402-403. The Dante reference was fashionable bravado. Crane almost certainly did not read Dante until after he had published *The Bridge*.

an exploratory wandering in the open field of free or un-patterned verse; to the firm possession of a metrical scheme which, though conventional and dating from at least the early seventeenth century, Crane could freshen and re-vitalize until it became the exact musical realization of his personal idiom—the very music of his saying. These three stages are evident in sets of poems written, conveniently enough, at two-year intervals; "Annunciations" and "The Moth that God Made Blind" in 1917; "Forgetfulness" and "My Grandmother's Love Letters" in 1919; and, in 1921, two poems handsomely characteristic of Crane's first really accomplished phase, "Black Tambourine" and "Chaplin-esque."

As against the muffled gurgling and dubious rhymes of "Annunciations," "Forgetfulness" has an unplanned and thoughtful air:

Forgetfulness is like a song
That, freed from beat and measure, wanders.
Forgetfulness is like a bird whose wings are reconciled,
Outspread and motionless,—
A bird that coasts the wind unwearyingly.

Here, in this amiably youthful poem, a release from con-ventional metrical control is itself a source of metaphor; not only is it exemplified in the poem, it is the very subject of the poem. But even in the passage quoted, Crane did not wander "freed from beat and measure" for long; the last line has a quite regular stress, if a soft one. The same kind of free wandering interspersed with soft regularity is appar-ent in the poem addressed to his grandmother, Mrs. Eliza-beth Belden Hart:

There are no stars to-night
But those of memory.
Yet how much room for memory there is
In the loose girdle of soft rain.

> There is even room enough
> For the letters of my mother's mother,
> Elizabeth. . . .

This was much better; but such gently melodic musing was not Crane's natural bent. He began to hit his metrical stride, and he knew it, with "Black Tambourine":

> The interests of a black man in a cellar
> Mark tardy judgment on the world's closed door.
> Gnats toss in the shadow of a bottle,
> And a roach spans a crevice in the floor.

In the letter quoted at the start of this chapter, where he cited "Black Tambourine" as a diminutive model for future work, Crane said that he was trying "to work away from the current impressionism." The context indicates that he meant by "impressionism" the then popular experimentation with the poetical random, with non-meter and non-sense. "I may even be carried back into 'rime and rhythm,'" he continued. "I grow to like my 'Black Tambourine' more, for this reason, than before." Almost the whole story of Crane's prosodic development up to 1921 is represented in the change of a single line in the above stanza: from

> Mark an old judgment on the world

(in the worksheet) to

> Mark tardy judgment on the world's closed door.

A rhyme has been thereby introduced; and the rhythm, shaking off its original looseness, braces itself into the grave, distinctive beat that the poem deserves.

The change also importantly enhanced the poem's diction and hence its content: the added words "tardy" and "closed door" are indispensable to the final version of "Black Tambourine." It is of course impossible to talk about a poet's purely technical resources, as I have seemed to do, without considering his language; and without considering

POETRY AND THE ACTUAL

the subject or the reality which all those elements seek to bring into being. Once he came into his own, Crane—to borrow R. P. Blackmur's fine remark about Melville (whom Crane in this as in other ways so much resembled) —"habitually used words greatly." [5] It was because he did so that he needed to employ ever more forceful rhythms: a peculiar adaptation of the most literally dramatic of English metrical forms—the blank verse of Elizabethan and Jacobean drama (and especially perhaps of John Webster)—converted, often though not always, into vigorous four-line stanzas with strong alternating rhymes. As to language itself, Crane made his way haltingly from the conventional through the unpatterned to the intensively personal, in a manner similar to but more difficult than the metrical process.

For the most part, the language and phrasing of "Annunciations" are either conventional in the bad or lifeless sense ("the veins of the earth," "one dearest beside me"); or they are merely discrete. The latter is the more serious flaw. The milk-blood, the greenery, the roots, the light, the moth, the dove, the moans, the high cries: these have perhaps a logical connection and can all be imagined as belonging to the same place and time; but they have been invested with an insufficient *poetic* connection. We are moved from one item to the next by decree, rather than by the irresistible creative energy of the language. Crane grew acutely aware of the problem. In a review of Maxwell Bodenheim's book of poems, *Minna and Myself* (in February 1919), [6] Crane pointed out that Bodenheim's "poems are often little heaps of images in which the verbal element is subordinated, making for an essentially static and decorative quality." "Little heaps of images" is a fair description of many of the poems Crane wrote during the intermediate stage, once he had gotten away from conventionality in the choice and arrangements of words; and in these poems,

[5] See the discussion of "At Melville's Tomb" in Chapter Seven.
[6] Weber, *Hart Crane,* p. 404.

too, "the verbal element"—Crane seems to have meant by this the design-making power of which words are capable—was unduly "subordinated." Crane was in fact detained longer by the question of verbal pattern than of metrical pattern; the flirtation with free verse was relatively brief, as we have seen, but he struggled for years with verbal scraps and isolated images, seeking to fit or force them together into various wholes. This was due in part to the habit he had at some time acquired (as had many other poets before him) of beginning not with a story or an event or even, occasionally, with a discernible subject, but merely with an image, a cluster of words, a line or two that had struck his fancy.

In January 1921, for example, he wrote Gorham Munson that "my sum poetic output for the last three months" was "two lines—

'The everlasting eyes of Pierrot / And of Gargantua,—the laughter.' Maybe," he added, "it is my epitaph, it is contradictory and wide enough to be. But I hope soon to turn it into a poem. . . ." The poem in which the lines were first used is Crane's most astonishing effort at the enforced combination of scraps: a thirty-two-line poem of uncertain versification, called "The Bridge of Estador." [7] As it turned out, this was a kind of storeroom for themes and images of poems to come. It is the first overt treatment of that visionary search for beauty which would motivate the action, two years later, of "For the Marriage of Faustus and Helen"; and it offers the first vague use of the major

[7] Research by several hands has yet failed to come up with a source of the name "Estador." In the poem, of course, it is a place of visionary fantasy; but one is curious whether Crane borrowed or simply coined the word. Brom Weber has hazarded the guess, in conversation, that Crane may have heard it or something like it from his friend Harry Candee, in the latter's reports on his travels in the Far East. It has a naggingly familiar sound, perhaps because it punningly suggests the Gateway to the East—e.g., to Cathay. In his ecstatic letter to Waldo Frank in 1924, about a newly begun love affair, Crane wrote that he and his lover would "take a walk across the bridge to Brooklyn (as well as to Estador, for all that!)."

symbol of *The Bridge*. It throws into proximity, without at all managing to yoke them together, such eventually familiar images as these:

> High on the bridge of Estador
> Where no one has ever been before,—
> I do not know what you'll see,—your vision
> May slumber yet in the moon, awaiting
> Far consummation of the tides to throw
> Clean on the shore some wreck of dreams. . . .
>
> But some are twisted with the love
> Of things irreconcilable,—
> The slant moon with the slanting hill:
> O Beauty's fool, though you have never
> Seen them again, you won't forget.
> Nor the Gods that danced before you
> When your fingers spread among stars.
>
> And you others—follow your arches
> To what corners of the sky they pull you to,—
> The everlasting eyes of Pierrot,
> Or, of Gargantua, the laughter.

Brom Weber, who made this poem available, has noted that lines four to six were reworded into "At Melville's Tomb"; that seven and eight turn up almost intact in Part I of "Faustus and Helen"; and that lines nine and sixteen and seventeen, originally independent jottings, were thrust into "Praise for an Urn." There are also clear anticipations of the ironic attitudes and cadences of "Chaplinesque" and "Locutions des Pierrots" in the passage; and the dancing gods of line twelve are perhaps rehearsing for their much wilder performance in Section II of *The Bridge*. Against the latter work as a whole, the charge has often been leveled that it is little more than a display of exciting but incompatible fragments. The charge can hardly withstand a sensible reading of *The Bridge;* but as regards "The Bridge at Estador" it is instructively correct.

"Oh! it is hard," Crane lamented in the letter about "Black Tambourine." "One must be drenched in words, literally soaked with them to have the right ones form themselves into the proper pattern at the right moment." So, in all simplicity, the immense challenge was stated. Crane felt that in a poem of July 1921, called "Pastorale"—which he regarded as "thin, but rather good"—the verbal miracle had occurred. It is true that in this unstressed and dusky meditation on the passing of time, the words do drift toward each other, and the atmosphere is thickened a bit by a mildly incantational tone, to the extent that the poem has a character if not a shape. But "Pastorale" seems limp when set beside the work from which it probably derived, Emerson's "Days." Crane's poem ends with the poet's scornful address to himself:

> 'Fool—
> Have you remembered too long;
>
> Or was there too little said
> For ease or resolution—
> Summer scarcely begun
> And violets,
> A few picked, the rest dead?'

Emerson's final lines sound the same self-accusing note of opportunity lost; but at the same time, they bring to fulfillment the verbal pattern that winds through the poem like the very image it composes—that of days (the "daughters of Time") marching silently across the horizon, offering each man such gifts of life as he is able to take:

> I, in my pleachéd garden, watched the pomp,
> Forgot my morning wishes, hastily
> Took a few herbs and apples, and the Day
> Turned and departed silent. I, too late,
> Under her solemn fillet saw the scorn.

Not until "Black Tambourine" did Crane arrive at so resolute a diction.

If in "Black Tambourine" the right words did in some modest (or, as Crane said, "diminutive") way "form themselves into the proper pattern at the proper moment," it was in part because the poem's subject induced them to do so. Before inspecting the verbal activity of this little landmark in Crane's career, we should pause over the question of Crane's subject matter and the sources of it, especially since it has sometimes been maintained that he did not have any subject matter, but only a highly charged rhetoric.[8] According to Northrop Frye's recent and influential argument, the poetry of any composition comes out of the traditional structures and devices of poetry itself, that is, of other poems; by implication, however, the immediate subject of a poem and the peculiar slant of its perception come out of the poet's own experience.[9] From this viewpoint, we might say that both the poetry *and* the subject in works like "Annunciations" were untimely ripped from existing literature. Beginning with "My Grandmother's Love Letters" and "Garden Abstract" in 1920, Crane turned much more to his personal experience and sense of life as sources of creative material; and—it was a matter of degree, but of considerable degree—"Black Tambourine" was more graspingly personal yet.

Probably nothing in English is more ambiguous than the word "experience." Talking about the relation between feeling and thought in poetry, T. S. Eliot once remarked— in a much-quoted but, when one thinks about it, rather singular and revealing sentence—that at one and the same

[8] For example, Edmund Wilson, reviewing *White Buildings* in May 1927, felt that Crane possessed "a great style," but that it was a great style "not merely not applied to a great subject, but not, so far as one can see, to any subject at all" ("The Muses out of Work" in *The Shores of Light,* 1952).

[9] *The Anatomy of Criticism* (Princeton, 1958). The immediate subject, be it noted, not the general or universal subject toward which it may grow: the death of Lincoln, in Whitman's "When Lilacs Last in the Door Yard Bloom'd," for example, and not that poem's larger theme of death and poetry.

time, a man may "fall in love or read Spinoza"; and that in the best kind of poetry, these two dimensions of experience—the emotional and the cerebral—were wholly fused. Eliot, of course, was then making a subtle case for the *im*personal as against the personal element in poetry; but one can easily imagine that Eliot could during the same period fall in love and read Spinoza; as one imagines that Wallace Stevens might have fallen in love and read or even listened to the Harvard lectures of George Santayana. For both poets, that is (though much less so for Stevens), a systematic body of thought, including a view of the nature of reality and a theory of knowledge, could in all honesty be a part of their individual experience and hence a source for their writing. Hart Crane fell in love periodically; but for better or worse (I am not disposed to say that it was for worse), he did not at the same time read Spinoza or Santayana—or any other writer of formal philosophy or theology.[10] He read imaginative literature; in particular, as the years went by, an increasingly definable group of poets—including (in chronological order) Donne, Webster, Blake, Keats, Whitman, Melville, for a time Baudelaire, Laforgue, and Rimbaud; and his contemporaries, especially Eliot. Crane had at his poetic disposal no sort of systematic interpretation of the universe, neither an inherited one nor (like Blake's) a privately assembled one. What he did have was his experience of actual life and his experience of poetry, both the reading and the writing of it. And that, in a sense, is what "Black Tambourine" is about.

It is a poem about the American Negro in the modern world that becomes a poem also about the American poet in the modern world—and about the destiny of poets generally.

---

[10] The exception may be the *Dialogues* of Plato, which Crane began to read with great care in 1915-1916, underscoring some of the passages. The alleged importance for him of other "philosophers"— Nietzsche, for instance, and P. D. Ouspensky—is considered briefly in Chapter Four.

The interests of the black man in a cellar
Mark tardy judgment on the world's closed door.
Gnats toss in the shadow of a bottle,
And a roach spans a crevice in the floor.

Aesop, driven to pondering, found
Heaven with the tortoise and the hare;
Fox brush and sow ear top his grave
And mingling incantations on the air.

The black man, forlorn in the cellar,
Wanders in some mid-kingdom, dark, that lies
Between his tambourine, stuck on the wall,
And, in Africa, a carcass quick with flies.

When he wrote "Black Tambourine," Crane was himself
hobnobbing with Negroes in a cellar—Negro chefs and
waiters, in fact, in the basement of his father's tea-room
and candy shop in Cleveland; he was also busy composing
an article on Sherwood Anderson in which he expressed
the hope that Anderson might some day "handle the Negro
in fiction." [11] Crane's feelings, however, were mixed. A
Negro had been dismissed by Mr. Crane to make room for
his son; and, as Philip Horton tells us, "It became a
certainty in [Crane's] mind that his father wished to make
a humiliating comparison by this move." Crane associated
himself, and by extension the modern poet, with the Negro,
as victims of a comparable persecution and exclusion; the
world closed its door equally on both—such, anyhow, had
been Crane's experience. The chances are, however, that
Crane had never formulated the matter with any such
clarity prior to writing the poem; and more than likely,
"Black Tambourine"—to quote again from Blackmur's essay
on Melville—was "an adventure in discovery."

[11] This was a review of Anderson's *Poor White* for the *Double
Dealer*. "I would like to see Anderson handle the Negro in fiction.
So far it has not been done by anyone without sentimentality or
cruelty, but the directness of his vision would produce something new
and deep in this direction." Weber, *Hart Crane,* pp. 408-11.

The connection between Negro and poet comes un-mistakably into being—and via the technique of indirection Crane was learning from both Eliot and Whitman—when the black man of stanza one is quietly juxtaposed to the archetypal poet and fabulist Aesop in stanza two. The black man is physically surrounded by gnats and roaches; Aesop is poetically surrounded by those animals through fables about whom he expressed the highest truths about man ("mankind was his care," Crane had written in a line he later deleted), and his grave, somewhat like the black man's tomb-like cellar, is littered with animal remains. Even the "mingling incantations" that Aesop bequeathed to an implicitly deaf world link ironically with the black man's tambourine in stanza three; and as a result of such clustering suggestions, the language of the final lines can scarcely help but refer at once to Negro and poet. Even after finishing "Black Tambourine," Crane did not know as much as the poem itself knows. He described it to Munson as "a description and a bundle of insinuations bearing on the Negro's place somewhere between man and beast," and said that "the value of the poem is only, to me, in what a painter would call its 'tactile' quality,—an entirely aesthetic feature." But the poem's aesthetic feature greatly enlarged upon the initial subject; and out of the urgency of his personal feelings plus his newly achieved ability to release and then control the energies of language, Crane in "Black Tambourine" created a complex and living image of multiple victimization.[12]

The verbal element, as Crane called it elsewhere, is dominant here. I have mentioned the revision of "Mark

[12] It is an image that in part resembles and anticipates the one elaborated in Ralph Ellison's novel *Invisible Man* (1952) and already denoted in Ellison's title: the Negro as psychologically invisible to the rest of mankind; and at the same time as representing that crucial portion of man's humanity which is invisible to himself. Crane's poem may have been at the back of Ellison's imagination when he was writing the book; he tells me, anyhow, that he remembers reading Crane's poetry during those years.

an old judgment on the world" into "Mark tardy judgment on the world's closed door." This was a move toward Crane's characteristically compressed line, in which, by packing the rhythmical space with "positive" (as against neutral) language, Crane could allow words to exert their maximum effect upon each other. Meanwhile, what began as almost a sociological report ("Black Tambourine" is the most overtly socially minded of Crane's lyric poems) becomes, in the musical sense, transposed by the supple play of allusion. Perhaps the most telling example of the poem's verbal element is the final phrase, "a carcass quick with flies." "Carcass" is used to designate the body of an animal; and also the body of a human being, when a human is regarded as an animal. Normally, moreover, it means the body of a dead animal. The central human figure in "Black Tambourine" is made to resemble an animal corpse, attacked by flies, not only because the world sometimes regards him so (when it does not regard him—Negro and poet—in the stereotype of a tambourine player); but also because, within the poem, the black man's cellar is conjoined with the poet's grave, to the point that the gnats and roaches that swarm about the living figure seem like flies buzzing at a corpse. It is just possible that a closing twist of meaning is intended, one that would accord with slight hints earlier in the poem; namely, that the Negro-poet, however brutally treated, is nonetheless alive—"quick"—after all.

· I I ·

Crane was on the whole a sharp-eyed judge of his own writing. When he erred, it was rather because he was overly modest than otherwise, and sometimes, as with "Black Tambourine," because he was insufficiently aware of what his imagination had built for him. But his modesty only increased in proportion to his accomplishment, as indeed it should have done with so ambitious, devoted and ever-more knowing a poet. Late in 1921, he wrote Munson that "I am not at all satisfied with anything I have thus far done, mere shadowings, and too slight to satisfy me." The remark followed Crane's invocation of such huge literary names as Donne, Webster, Marlowe and Ben Jonson, as well as moderns like Laforgue and Eliot; and Crane might well feel that his work *to date* was shadowy by comparison with the poets mentioned. Even so, it was a hard saying for a man who had followed "Black Tambourine" with "Chaplinesque," and had, before that, written several durable if more lightly toned items—including "My Grandmother's Love Letters" and "Garden Abstract," not to mention some still slighter poems that Crane was willing, later, to gather up into *White Buildings*.[13] I shall reserve discussion of "Chaplinesque" until the next chapter. The other two titles mentioned deserve some limited comment here.

"My Grandmother's Love Letters" is itself a love letter of sorts. Crane was deeply attached to his grandmother, "that dear old lady," and he only feared that in seeking the necessary distance to express his feelings in verse he would make her seem "too sweet or too naughty." The creative problem here was part of a more general one— how to convey any emotion in a "suitable personal idiom." Against the then current belief in "impersonality" in poetry, and the then current tone of wry or witty detachment, Crane knew that he risked sounding, as he said, "silly and sentimental" when he attempted to articulate a strong personal emotion. Long after he had written "My Grandmother's Love Letters," Crane could remark to Munson that "I have never, so far, been able to present a vital, living and tangible,—a positive emotion to my satisfaction. For as soon as I attempt such an act I either grow obvious or ordinary, and abandon the thing at the second line." In the poem in question, Crane provided himself at the end with a protective and fashionable self-irony, as though to wave away the whole emotional enterprise:

[13] "In Shadow," "North Labrador," and "The Fernery."

30

> And so I stumble. And the rain continues on the roof
> With such a sound of gently pitying laughter.

Crane would have to get beyond such irony and gain command of some of the great conventions of love poetry before he would be able—in "Voyages," especially—to present the vital and living emotions that were so essential to his poetic substance. Nonetheless, "My Grandmother's Love Letters" has an unstrained charm and an unsentimental sweetness rare enough in Crane's writing at any stage; and one turns back to it, at times, with a kind of relief after the demanding intensity of the later works.

The introductory lines, already quoted in this chapter, ease into a reflection on the infinitely delicate question of spanning the long period between his grandmother's past—her letter-writing youth—and her present white-haired old age:

> Over the greatness of such space
> Steps must be gentle.
> It is all hung by an invisible white hair.
> It trembles as birch limbs webbing the air.

The human or external subject is quietly complicated by an internal or creative one; the actual and the artistic conjoin, as, in one way or another, they do in most of Crane's early poems. In the present case, there is a sort of lingering urgency; for if Crane can compose the poem (or song) about his grandmother that he wants to, if he can harmonize her past and present through the resources of art, he can then touch directly upon her intimate reality:

> And I ask myself:
>
> 'Are your fingers long enough to play
> Old keys that are but echoes:
> Is the silence strong enough
> To carry back the music to its source
> And back to you again
> As though to her?'

The poetic trick is turned even in the doubting of it, for the doubt is crucial to the accomplishment; which may be why this poem, too, was an "adventure in discovery" for Crane, or, in his words, that it held an "adventuresome interest" for him. The qualities of fragility and evanescence —of the fading letters, the grandmother, of memory, of personality, and of human relation—these qualities which set the poet's task are just the ones that are made present in the poetry.

They are present in the very gentleness of the "steps" by which the poem moves forward. They are present in the liquidity of the language, in the rhymes and murmuring internal rhymes, in the peaceful stretch and recoil of rhythm; and they are present especially when the very question about spanning the temporal space is answered by descriptive allusions that do in fact span it—successive allusions to age and youth, to an invisible white hair and to trembling birch limbs. The faint smile of apology at the conclusion is comparably double in nature: an artistically successful acknowledgment of his own youthful condescension and his inevitable failure—

Yet I would lead my grandmother by the hand
Through much of what she would not understand;
And so I stumble. . . .

"Garden Abstract," written early in 1920, is a love poem of a different order. This is a poem not of a grandson's ironically tender regard for his grandmother, but of a young girl's erotic and total surrender to nature. The experience is direct, and in it innocence is at once inflamed and unsullied by passion:

The apple on its bough is her desire,—
Shining suspension, mimic of the sun.
The bough has caught her breath up, and her voice,
Dumbly articulate in the slant and rise
Of branch on branch above her, blurs her eyes.
She is prisoner of the tree and its green fingers.

Crane told Matthew Josephson that "Garden Abstract" was "a highly concentrated piece of symbolism, image wound within image"; and the contemporary reader is likely to hurry past any alleged actuality (say, an actual tree with actual branches and apples) to confront an array of sexual elements and experiences thereby symbolized, especially when he is reminded that the first English edition of Freud's *A General Introduction to Psychoanalysis* appeared in America at just the time Crane was writing the poem. The sexual aspect is—for the psychologizing reader —happily compounded by the fact that the human figure in an earlier version was presumably a male:

> The apple on its bough
> Is my desire,—
> Shining suspension,
>
> Mimic of the sun.
> The bough has caught my breath up,

and so on. Crane, indeed, may not have been aware of the "phallic theme" in such lines until Josephson pointed it out;[14] and his final version may well represent what Stanley Edgar Hyman has called "the Albertine strategy"— an author's strategy for projecting his homosexual impulses in the guise of heterosexual ones.[15] But such speculation, elsewhere valuable and fascinating, does not tell us much about "Garden Abstract," or else it tells us the wrong thing.

There is little evidence that Crane, then or later, read any of the works of Freud. The symbolism of "Garden Abstract" is beguilingly transparent, rather like the pre-Freudian stories of D. H. Lawrence (as against the too knowing, clinically Freudian quality of some of John Steinbeck's tales):

[14] See letter to Josephson, March 15, 1920; Weber, *Letters*, pp. 35-37.

[15] As Proust is assumed to have done in the figure of Albertine Simonet; see Hyman, *The Promised End* (New York, 1964). Crane more than once in his very early poems shifted from his own speaking voice to the third-person portrait of a girl.

And so she comes to dream herself the tree,
The wind possessing her, weaving her young veins,
Holding her to the sky and its quick blue,
Drowning the fever of her hands in sunlight. . . .

Crane's imagination, like that of so many predecessors, knew what Freud argued scientifically: that trees and branches and apples are dream-symbols of male sexuality; that rising, climbing, "the act of mounting"—I am here quoting Freud—are "indubitably symbolic of sexual intercourse"; and that "the rhythmic character of this climbing is the point in common between the two" (that is, between climbing and the sexual act) "and perhaps also the accompanying increase in excitation—the shortening of breath as the climber ascends." One notices how the *poem* ascends, verbally and visually and emotionally: "caught up . . . rise . . . branch on branch above her . . . to the sky"; and a competent recital of "Garden Abstract" might suggest an increase in excitation and a shortening of breath, to what we may take as the moment of release—"Drowning the fever of her hands in sunlight"; after which, we experience vicariously the post-coital lassitude of the final two lines. At the same time, a competent reading would have to suggest a good deal more.

If "Garden Abstract" is in one perspective a symbolic sexual act, it is also, in Crane's phrase, a piece of "pantheistic aestheticism." It gives us the rapturous aesthetic experience of physical nature; and in doing so it gives us a real tree, a real bough, a real apple, a real wind, a real sun—and a real girl. Lionel Trilling has remarked with witty exasperation on the contemporary American assumption that it is somehow "subliterary" to think of any object in a literary work "as an actuality." [16] But the girl's yearning for an

---

[16] Mr. Trilling's example is the American student's habit "of speaking of money in Dostoievski's novels as 'symbolic,' as if no one ever needed or spent, or gambled, or squandered the stuff." *The Opposing Self* (New York, 1955), p. 93.

apple gleaming on a bough, her rising excitement as her gaze travels upward through the branches, her identification with the tree, her dream-like enjoyment of the wind upon her, her loss of awareness of past or present in the ecstasy of the moment: this is an experience which many people must be lucky enough to remember.

And just because the poem is so vividly concrete, it takes on the dimension of a modest archetype, a created entity susceptible of many meanings, emotionally valid within many contexts: as it could hardly do if its content were restricted to the sexual. Crane was blessed with an archetypal imagination, though up to this time (1920) it had lain half-dormant. But as we step back a little from "Garden Abstract," the garden in it becomes any garden where nature can be felt to the quick of body and spirit—and any garden thus celebrated in poetry. It associates in our mind with the much more famous garden of Andrew Marvell, even if Crane's poem quite lacks the sophisticated learning by which Marvell invested his own garden with mythological stature. It even, perhaps—though this was clearly not a conscious intention—becomes the first of all gardens where the first woman was tempted by the first of all apples. But if so, it retells that old story in a way, typical of Crane, to suggest that innocence is rather confirmed than betrayed by the event.

·III·

"Praise for an Urn," written nearly two years after "Garden Abstract," is in most respects the main achievement in this, the first distinguishable phase of Crane's career. It was written at a time when that phase was coming to an end: in the first days of 1922. Within weeks, Crane would be at work on "Faustus and Helen." Much of the poem's strength and its sustained coherence come from the fact that here, more than ever before (except possibly in "Chaplinesque"), Crane was treating his subject—the death

35

of a friend—via the conventions that had regularly attended this subject in English poetry. The individual experience and the personal relation receive a knowingly familiar treatment, but in a thoroughly original idiom. "Praise for an Urn" is an elegy which at every moment remembers the genre to which it belongs. The untimely death of the poet's gifted friend leads the poet, as in most notable elegies of the past (one need only cite the best known, that of Thomas Gray), to meditate on what endures and what does not endure, and particularly on the transience or permanence of art, the mortality or immortality of the artist. At the same time, Crane's now-maturing skills of phrasing and cadence seem to gather themselves in something like a major effort. The language is firm and trimmed, and exactly placed; the cadence is the surest Crane had yet managed—steady, appropriately undramatic, and never monotonous. Because of all this, "Praise for an Urn" establishes with utter clarity the "inviolability" of a certain human relation, despite every adverse circumstance; and, in its finality, it also speaks for the inviolability of a certain kind of relationship generally. In this regard, the poem probably represents the furthest reach of Crane's previsionary work.[17]

"Praise for an Urn," is also, like "Black Tambourine," an instructive exercise in the biographical approach to Crane's poetry.

[17] The word "inviolability" is borrowed from Allen Tate (*The Man of Letters in the Modern World*, p. 292), who makes a comparable point about "Praise for an Urn" and its "place" in Crane's career from an exactly opposite critical viewpoint. "The hard firm style of 'Praise for an Urn,' which is based upon a clear-cut perception of moral relations, and upon their ultimate inviolability," writes Mr. Tate, "begins to disappear when the poet goes out into the world and finds that the simplicity of a child's world has no universal sanction. From then on, instead of the effort to define himself in the midst of almost overwhelming complications—a situation that might have produced a tragic poet—he falls back upon the intensity of consciousness, rather than clarity, for his center of vision. And that is Romanticism."

It was a kind and northern face
That mingled in such exile guise
The everlasting eyes of Pierrot
And, of Gargantua, the laughter.

His thoughts, delivered to me
From the white coverlet and pillow,
I see now, were inheritances—
Delicate riders of the storm.

The poem was written for a certain Ernest Nelson, a Norwegian immigrant and sometime poet and painter whom Crane had come to know in Cleveland during the last months of Nelson's life, in the fall of 1921. Crane called him "one of the best-read people I ever met," and spoke of his "wonderful tolerance and kindliness." Hence, in the poem, the Scandinavian's "kind and northern face," and hence too the "exile guise": Nelson was an exile, not only as a Norwegian in America, but as a would-be artist forced by ill-fortune (as Crane also reported) "into prostitution of all his ideals." "He was one of the many," Crane went on, "broken against the stupidity of American life in such places as here. I think he has had a lasting influence on me." Those sentences give most of the substance of the second stanza: where Nelson's thoughts, presented over the months from his sickbed and deathbed, now seem to Crane to be spiritual legacies ("a lasting influence"); delicate gifts of mind that survive or ride out the storm of American life and of Nelson's own final illness.

Such clues, from Crane's letter and his biographers, do help identify some of the raw content out of which the poem was made; though we should be careful about the reference to the coverlet and pillow. To one correspondent, who had evidently surmised a sexual relationship, Crane replied: "There were no accouchements there at all. Not even temptations in that direction. It is, or was, entirely 'platonic.' " But the main point, of course, is that the most striking lines in the first two stanzas—the mingling imagery

THE ESCAPE FROM IRONY

of Pierrot's eyes and Gargantua's laughter—had been jotted
down and then incorporated in "The Bridge of Estador,"
as we have seen, many months before Crane first met
Nelson. They had originally nothing to do with Nelson
(Crane thought of them, indeed, as his own epitaph); and
they seem to apply but slightly to the real-life Nelson, who,
as described may have been Pierrotic but was anything but
Gargantuan. They enter the poem not as documentary facts
but as contributing to a poetic adventure: a pattern-in-the-
making of vital contrasts, within which a particular death
finds its large and serious meaning. The pattern—and, as
I have said, it is in the best sense conventional—comes into
full view in the next three stanzas, which also begin with
an image carried over from "The Bridge of Estador" and
made active:

> The slant moon on the slanting hill
> Once moved us toward presentiments
> Of what the dead keep, living still,
> And such assessments of the soul
>
> As, perched in the crematory lobby,
> The insistent clock commented on,
> Touching as well upon our praise
> Of glories proper to the time.
>
> Still, having in mind gold hair,
> I cannot see that broken brow
> And miss the dry sound of bees
> Stretching across a lucid space.

The stanzas unfold a sinewy dialectic with which the
tone keeps perfect pace. There is first the memory of
romantic moonstruck exchanges on the theme of endurance:
on the extent to which a person may survive after death,
if only in the insights he bequeaths to others. The theme
had been heralded by the reference to Pierrot: for Pierrot
was associated traditionally and in Crane's mind with the
moon and with the creative imagination (as we shall

notice when we come to "Chaplinesque," where the moon
has almost the same function as it has here). But the
moonstruck Pierrot was also a somewhat sad and foolish
fellow, and his presence in "Praise for an Urn" lends in
advance something sad and foolish to those hopeful guesses.
The folly of such appraisals of the human spirit and its
potentialities, such "assessments of the soul," is thereupon
confirmed by the crematory clock, whose insistent comment
is registered in a tone suddenly gone hard, regular, severe.
The clock's comment is its own relentless ticking, its impersonal reminder that nothing endures the passage of
time—

> Touching as well upon our praise
> Of glories proper to the time.

These are the firmest, one might say the most upright,
lines Crane had yet written: too much is happening in
them for adequate analysis. We have the impression that
the clock has been making a dry, legalistic address—
about its own absolute authority—in the course of which
it touches, in passing, upon another matter: on the futile
habit of bestowing praise upon present splendors and
achievements. About these mundane glories, it remarks
coldly and briefly: *sic transit gloria mundi;* or, to stay closer
to Crane's phrase, *sic transit gloria temporis.*

"Still," Crane continues; and yet; nevertheless. The
human note comes back into the poem. His friend's visible
substance may be wasted; insofar, time has proved its
power. But with Nelson's "gold hair" (always for Crane
a symbol of spiritual as well as physical beauty) in his
mind's eye, he refuses to see the actual and broken brow—
broken, we recall, "against the stupidity of American life."
The following two lines hold their meaning tightly con-
cealed; only a reckless ingenuity would pronounce upon
them with assurance. But they are, I venture, a statement
about hearing parallel in construction and import to the
preceding statement about seeing; such alternation of the

two key senses—taken as ways of understanding reality—
would be increasingly common with Crane. As he will not
see the broken brow, but only remember the former (and
in memory, the continuing) beauty, so he deliberately
"misses" the "dry sound of bees"—the hoarse, meaningless
droning, perhaps, to which his friend's once eloquent voice
has been reduced, but will remember only the lucidity. And
so:

> Scatter these well-meant idioms
> Into the smoky spring that fills
> The suburbs, where they will be lost.
> They are no trophies of the sun.

The final stanza concludes Crane's contradictory effort at
once to acknowledge and to evade the defeat inflicted by
time. The idioms are both the ashes of his friend and the
poetic lines that attempted to praise them; both the friend
and the lines were well intentioned, even if neither finally
came to much. Let both be scattered and lost amidst the
obliterating smoke of spring. But the word "spring" with its
connotation of flowering and rebirth inevitably works against
"smoky" and "lost"; the idioms are perhaps seeds that will
give rise to another life. Anyhow, they will at least be lost;
the urn that contained them, now empty, will be no trophy,
no prize silver cup, for the sun. The sun, thus appearing so
late in the poem, draws to itself everything that has been
opposed to the cluster made up of the moon, Pierrot, intimations of immortality, the gold hair, the lucid space. It stands
for the domain of the actual, the temporal, the mortal and
transient; and it is robbed after all of the symbol if not the
fact of its triumph. What was at stake was a human relation;
and that has indeed been demonstrated as inviolable—has
been made inviolable by verse.[18]

[18] "Praise for an Urn" can thus be added to the poems examined
so fruitfully by Cleanth Brooks in *The Well-Wrought Urn* (New
York, 1947). Both Mr. Brooks's essays and the poems they treat shed
a good deal of indirect light on Crane's elegy.

Crane had met Ernest Nelson through one of Nelson's fellow workers in a lithograph company, a fifty-year-old painter named William Sommer—"this *great* Bill Sommer," as Crane called him. Sommer was of a Gargantuan rather than (like Nelson) a Pierrotic temper, and the Gargantuan side of Crane responded to him with gusto. They ate and drank together in zestful abundance; they boxed together; and they read endless poetry, listened to contemporary music, and talked for long boisterous hours about painting and the other arts. More than any other figure, Sommer contributed to the sheer animation of Crane's "Cleveland days." [19] In the summer of 1922, after a Sunday visit to Sommer's studio in Brandywine Valley, outside of Cleveland, Crane wrote a poem called "Sunday Morning Apples."

It represented a pause in his season's occupation, for at the moment of composition Crane had already pretty well completed the first two parts of "Faustus and Helen." "Sunday Morning Apples" mediates as it were between the earlier poetry, which we have been considering, and the visionary lyric which succeeded it. In content, it is a summation, almost an abstract, of the themes that had hitherto preoccupied Crane: primarily, the subtle and shifting relation between art and the actual—the latter seen as physical nature—and with something of the direct experience of nature recorded in the "garden" poem. At the same time, it reveals a peculiar energy of language more characteristic of the work to come: not only strength of language, of which Crane had been a

[19] Crane tried with indifferent success to interest influential friends in New York and elsewhere—Sherwood Anderson among them—in Sommer's work. The usual comment was that Sommer was not sufficiently original; about which Crane wrote violently to Gorham Munson: "God DAMN this constant nostalgia for something always 'new.' This disdain for anything with a trace of the past in it." "Nostalgia for the new" is a shrewd phrase to describe the blindered avant-gardism that has always been one feature of the American day; but against it, of course, one must place Crane's growing conviction (hinted at, interestingly enough, in the very same letter of January 5, 1923) that Eliot suffered from an excessive nostalgia for the old.

young master for several years, but something more mysterious though not less recognizable—an interior dynamism, as though some latent force in words had been awakened and was thrusting hard, upward and outward. An external sign of this is the succession of words like "reared," "bursting," "defiance," "runs," "straddling," "madness," "explosion." But those words constitute a sign rather than a source. Partly, it is the rhythmic placing of such words, and their sound. But partly it is because "Sunday Morning Apples" offers the first notable instance we have yet seen of what would become one of Crane's poetic signatures—his technique of soldering in the heat of language and meter the two dimensions of the physical and non-physical, the concrete and the abstract.

The poem moves between nature and art as "Praise for an Urn" did between transience and endurance. The opening lines speak of nature providing the artist (Sommer, that is) with "those purposes / That are your rich and faithful strength of line." Then, however, looking at one of Sommer's paintings in the studio, Crane sees in it something more than fidelity to nature.

> But now there are challenges to spring
> In that ripe nude with head
> > reared
> Into a realm of swords, her purple shadow
> Bursting on the winter of the world
> From whiteness that cries defiance to the snow.

This is the art that does not so much imitate nature, faithfully, as outdo it; to borrow a familiar phrase from Shakespeare, it "adds to nature." But more of the Shakespearian passage should be quoted as the best available gloss on Crane's poem. It occurs in the fourth act of *The Winter's Tale.*

> *Perdita:* For I have heard it said
> There is an art which in their piedness shares
> With great creating nature.

Polixenes: Say there be.
> Yet nature is made better by no mean
> But nature makes that mean. So, over that art
> Which you say adds to nature, is an art
> That nature makes.

"Sunday Morning Apples" proceeds as though to exemplify the lesson of Polixenes. After inspecting the ripe nude, whose head rears up among the sword-like splashes of paint and whose purple shadow bursts more spectacularly than spring fruit upon the world's winter, Crane moves on to what we at first take to be another painting but what turns out to be a natural event:

> A boy runs with a dog before the sun, straddling
> Spontaneities that form their independent orbits,
> Their own perennials of light
> In the valley where you live
>
> > (called Brandywine).

This is the "art that nature makes." A boy and a dog, running at dawn in Brandywine Valley (and snapped in a second, so to speak, by the mind's camera-eye), miraculously contrive their own setting and symmetry, their own pattern of light and shadow. They compose an artistic masterpiece: but a masterpiece that is not only happening in actuality; it is a happening characterized not by artifice but by spontaneity. It is the very essence of the boy's and the dog's experience that they inhabit—more actively, as they run, they "straddle"—a world that is spontaneous, *un*contrived, free. The word "independent" reinforces the notion, as does the word "perennials": a more attractive way, I take it, of saying "dailynesses." The boy and the dog suggest in their running that for them the sun's first appearance is every morning a fresh encounter. This is what nature offers the artist, whose task it then is to capture on canvas both the beauty of the natural design and the sense of the unplanned which is a part of it.

But "Sunday Morning Apples" goes beyond the traditional and on the whole classical dialectic it has seemed to be rehearsing, and thus serves us as both a recapitulation and a foreshadowing. The interplay of art and nature, or art and the actual, is familiar enough, as is the apparent acknowledgment that art must ultimately submit to that art that "itself is nature." At the same time, however, the poem suggests that such submission is in fact art's way of making an interpretive addition to nature. I do not want to press too hard or oversubtly upon so minor a poem. But phrases like "straddling spontaneities" and "perennials of light" (which can scarcely be matched in any earlier poem) do not point to actualities inhering in nature; they rather indicate what the creative imagination sees and does when it *looks at* nature. The phrases release, as it were, the secret of the natural scene, and formulate it: as Crane then implies his artist friend does with the apples in his still life: "I have seen the apples there that toss you secrets." The formulation transcends nature even as it transcends logic; for spontaneities, one may well feel, are just the kind of thing that cannot be straddled. But the phrases quoted are the first clear instances of what Crane would later call the logic of metaphor. This was already becoming a chief instrument of Crane's visionary imagination as it exercised itself not in description but in the act of transfiguration.

CHAPTER THREE

Chaplinesque

ABOUT no poem before "Faustus and Helen" did Hart Crane have as much to say in his letters as "Chaplinesque," and no work satisfied him more. It was written over a relatively few days in early October 1921; and on Chirstmas Day, after Crane had heard from Gorham Munson that it had been published in the Paris-based magazine *Gargoyle,* he expressed an almost ceremonial gratification. "Your letter provided me with rich materials for a kind of Christmas tree, at least as thrilling as any of remotest childhood memories," he wrote. "Names and presences glitter and fascinate with all kinds of exotic suggestions on the branches. I can be grateful to you for the best of Christmas donations." Crane had more cause to celebrate than he guessed, for in perspective, "Chaplinesque" encompasses more and holds a far more richly varied interest than Crane could possibly have known.

It is, for one thing, an even better poem in itself than Crane appreciated, or than his puzzled friends could make out. It is the most *finished* of all the early poems that depict the posture or status of the poet in the modern American scene; it brings to fruition aspects of this theme—so obsessive for the early Crane—that elsewhere, for example in "Black Tambourine" and "Porphyro in Akron," remain either congested or diffused, and in either case only partly realized. The poem is a fine product because it issues from still greater depths of Crane's archetypal imagination, his creative intuition of the great recurring images through which poetry has always made its determining statements about human life. The archetype in the present instance is that of the clown: that is, of the poet as clown, or more exactly, as I shall want to suggest, of the poet, perhaps of Everyman, as Fool. This figure has a long and shifting his-

45

tory, some of which I shall want to glance at in order to press my claim for "Chaplinesque," but very little of which was in fact known to Crane. At the same time, in thus presenting his poetic self as a clown of sorts, Crane voiced part of the essential mood of his literary epoch. Better: "Chaplinesque" did as much as any one short poem can do to establish a mood; and the subsequent projections of the artist as comedian, by Stevens, by Cummings, later yet by Nathanael West and Henry Miller, tend to thicken an image and an atmosphere introduced in their generation by Hart Crane. Finally, "Chaplinesque" warrants special attention among the writings of Crane's first phase just because, on one level, it is a product of the comic spirit.

It is also a product of the rueful spirit; it marks the moment of Jules Laforgue's most pervasive influence, and of Eliot's: the moment when Crane was most tempted toward the tone of witty and ironic self-derision. Crane's journey close to and his instinctive evasion of that particular shoal is a significant part of his story. His comic sense was an oddly compounded one, but it contained too large a fund of sheer high spirits to be seriously deflected by the Laforguian kind of irony; this, too, must be emphasized, in view of the long-standing and essentially misleading clichés about a tragic, wasted, and bedeviled life.

"Chaplinesque" was written soon after Crane had been enthralled by Charlie Chaplin's film, *The Kid*. He announced at once to Munson that "comedy has never reached a higher level in this country before," and that Chaplin was "a dramatic genius" of "the fabulous sort." Despite such stated enthusiasm and despite the poem's title (Crane's titles were not always so helpful or so cogent), the first readers quite failed, as Crane said, to " 'get' [his] idiom" in it. This must have cost him a grimace or two, for he was sure that in "Chaplinesque" he had hit closer to his own idiom than ever before; while the necessary elusiveness of the poet in the contemporary world was the poem's very subject—that, and the hidden, tenuous rewards of the poetic life.

We make our meek adjustments,
Contented with such random consolations
As the wind deposits
In slithered and too ample pockets.

To one correspondent, who was apparently unable to identify the voice speaking in those lines, Crane explained carefully that he had been "moved to put Chaplin with the poets [of today]; hence the 'we' "; in *The Kid,* he added, Chaplin had "made me feel myself, as a poet . . . 'in the same boat' with him." The comedian's film gesture thus becomes a metaphor of the poet's shy strategy:

For we can still love the world, who find
A famished kitten on the step, and know
Recesses for it from the fury of the street,
Or warm torn elbow coverts.

That passage and the one which immediately follows were paraphrased by Crane in a dogged but noteworthy account to his friend William Wright: "Poetry, the human feelings, 'the kitten,' is so crowded out of the humdrum, rushing, mechanical scramble of today that the man who would preserve them must duck and camouflage for dear life to keep them or keep himself from annihilation."[1]

The very poetry ducks and camouflages, hugging its vulnerable tenderness to itself, as the poem continues:

We will sidestep, and to the final smirk
Dally the doom of that inevitable thumb
That slowly chafes its puckered index toward us,
Facing the dull squint with what innocence
And what surprise![2]

---

[1] To Munson (in a letter of October 6, 1921), Crane related "the symbol of the kitten" to that " 'infinitely gentle, infinitely suffering thing' of Eliot's." The allusion is to Eliot's *Preludes,* where "some infinitely gentle / Infinitely suffering thing" curls like a kitten around "the thousand sordid images" of a dying epoch.

[2] The stanza contains the first of Crane's numerous echoes of *Moby-Dick:* specifically, here, of the passage in Chapter CXXXIII ("The Chase—First Day"), where the whale thrusts its head under

With almost any of Charlie Chaplin's films in mind, we can immediately assign the "inevitable thumb" to the city cop who looms up so persistently, hand upraised, to block the little tramp, though Charlie manages to skip or sidestep past him for a while with an ingratiating smirk. But when the digital allusion leads from "thumb" to "index," another kind of prohibition enters the poem, the kind a poet has to dally or sidestep: the prohibition of, or turning thumbs down upon, the publication and the reading of certain books, as in the Catholic Index.[3] The figure of the poet, the would-be producer of books in modern America, is the alter ego of the slippery, impoverished, and obscurely outlaw tramp. The poet, too, must seek refuge for his insufficiently nourished sensibility from the fury of contemporary life. He must protect his small creations from the "dull squint" of a suspicious and forbidding public; and to that end, must invent poetic ways to sneak and slide around the obstacles to creative activity. He may, for instance, wear in his verses a disarming smirk and air of innocence, as though to assure the philistine reader that he, the poet, is neither serious nor dangerous. "Chaplinesque" is wreathed in just such a smirk, for it is not only an example of ironic self-deprecation, it is a defense of it, and of the poet's need to have recourse to its protection.

"And yet," Crane insists,

> And yet these fine collapses are not lies
> More than the pirouettes of any pliant cane;
> Our obsequies are, in a way, no enterprise.

---

the *Pequod,* "shook the cedar as a mildly cruel cat her mouse," and *"dallied* with the *doomed* craft" in a devilish manner (italics added). Here as later the echo is almost entirely verbal, carrying little if any of the original substance with it. See the discussion of "Repose of Rivers," pp. 213-14 below.

[3] Censorship was on Crane's mind. He was outraged at the reported censorship of *The Kid.* "What they could have possibly objected to, I cannot imagine. It must have been some superstition aroused against good acting."

If, like many of his literary ancestors and especially like Herman Melville, Crane was aware of the falsehoods into which cultural circumstance, as well as the very nature of poetic discourse, might seem to force a poet, he nonetheless affirms that the tactic of verbal trickery and the pose of self-abasement ("these fine collapses") only conceal, and do not violate, the truth perceived. Crane's affirmation is a characteristic effort to evade even the image of ironic evasion, and the subsequent word "obsequies" represents that effort in its most compressed form.

Over this word we may instructively linger. "Obsequies" has come to mean funeral rites, and given Crane's reference to "annihilation" in the letter quoted above, one might easily suppose that "Chaplinesque" is ultimately a poem about death: that the doom the poet-clown seeks to postpone is nothing other than death itself; and that the inevitable thumb, the puckered index, and the dull squint add up to a grim portrait of death personified. On the other hand, one might no less easily suppose that what Crane really meant was "obsequiousness," and that "obsequies" is simply an example of a muddled and ignorant use of language. But it is always a sounder policy with Crane to assume that he knew what he was doing in his selection of words; his poetry is a singularly dangerous trap for the critically proud or unwary. In the present case, such muddle as there is comes from medieval Latin, and Crane has not repeated it, he has cunningly exploited it.[4] The original Latin word *obsequium* meant servile compliance, but that meaning eventually got confused with the word *exsequiae,* which does refer to funeral ceremonies. Out of these two initially quite unrelated Latin sources, Crane drew a word with a

---

[4] Crane's Latin was small, but it existed. He studied it in school and returned to it periodically thereafter; that is, he returned to Latin poetry, Catullus especially and perhaps Virgil; Seneca is quoted to good effect at the head of "Ave Maria" in *The Bridge*. Authoritative evidence about his careful study of individual Latin words— *obsequium,* for example—is lacking either way.

packed and paradoxical significance. Part of the poem's context, from "meek adjustments" through "smirk" to "fine collapses," serves to reinvest "obsequies" with its etymological meaning of obsequiousness; another part, "the doom" and "the inevitable thumb," gives it its familiar contemporary sense of death and burial. In a single word, under intense contextual pressure, Crane thus says or suggests that the self-demeaning compliance the contemporary world demands of the poet or of any sensitive being would, if submitted to, lead only to utter spiritual death.

But the poet's enterprise is neither compliance nor death. His true enterprise is revealed in the final passage of "Chaplinesque," when the enforced smirk of daytime experience becomes "moonchanged" into a kind of holy laughter:

> The game enforces smirks; but we have seen
> The moon in lonely alleys make
> A grail of laughter of an empty ash can,
> And through all sound of gaiety and quest
> Have heard a kitten in the wilderness.

Again, a physical image inspired by Chaplin symbolizes a poetic experience: an experience of beauty that is implicitly religious, or, at least, chivalric in nature. Crane knew that both Chaplin and his poem about Chaplin might appear to some to be sentimental: "Chaplin may be a sentimentalist, after all," he agreed (in another letter to Munson), "but he carries the theme with such power and universal portent that sentimentality is made to transcend itself into a new kind of tragedy, eccentric, homely and yet brilliant." This was the mode of transcendence Crane aimed at in his closing lines, and which, in my view, he achieved: in a hauntingly melodic vision of the moon transforming a slum-alley ash can into a silver chalice—of the visionary imagination seeing in the jungle of the actual a vessel of supernal beauty.

But such a moment is as rare as it is precious; the main burden of "Chaplinesque" is still the image of the poet as a shabby and antic tramp, a meek-faced comedian on the run.

This was the culmination (poetically speaking it was the perfection) of a series of prior images by which Crane had advanced toward artistic maturity by assessing the value of art itself in the face of a derisive, indifferent, or bluntly hostile world, and by appraising his own performance. In the interesting mishmash, "Porphyro in Akron" (winter 1920), he had made his point in a manner flagrantly reminiscent of Eliot by juxtaposing present ugliness with past beauty, the actualities of Akron ("a shift of rubber workers" pressing down South Main Street at dawn, townspeople "Using the latest ice-box and buying Fords") and the story of Porphyro, who steals in "with heart on fire" to awaken and escape with the maid Madeline in Keats's "The Eve of St. Agnes." The original Porphyro succeeded valiantly, despite a horde of "hyena foemen and hotblooded lords"; but the contemporary Porphyro, who is reading "The Eve of St. Agnes" nostalgically in his hotel room, is ignominiously defeated by a noisy, materialistic, and utterly uninterested citizenry. In Akron, Porphyro-Crane reads aloud Keats's image of the moon and its magical effects:

> Full on this casément shown the wintry moon,
> And threw warm gules on Madeline's fair breast,
> As down she knelt for heaven's grace and boon. . . .

But he is denied the moon; and his longing to awaken his own fair Madeline, the spirit of poetry itself, seems, under the circumstances, merely ludicrous:

> But look up, Porphyro,—your toes
> Are ridiculously tapping
> The spindles at the foot of the bed.

> The stars are drowned in a slow rain,
> And a hash of noises is slung up
>   from the street.
> You ought, really, to try to sleep,
> Even though, in this town, poetry's a
> Bedroom occupation.

Thus, Crane felt, was the contemporary poet made to look absurd by a hash-slinging environment. In "My Grandmother's Love Letters" his best creative efforts were attended by slow rain, the rain that does not so much echo an oppressive world as comment upon his own creative inadequacy, with its "sound of gently pitying laughter." It is the kind of wordlessly sardonic comment the crematory clock would offer in "Praise for an Urn," "touching," as it does, "upon our praise / Of glories proper to the time." The image in "Black Tambourine" had been a good deal more brutal. There the poet had been associated with the Negro, and, like the Negro, treated alternately as a subservient, tambourine-playing entertainer and as a sort of animal. But probably the most succinct and probing identification of his poetic self before "Chaplinesque" was contained in these lines:

> "The everlasting eyes of Pierrot
> And of Gargantua—the laughter."

The face so composed of contrasting comic traditions was of course a mask of sorts, a protection against further indignities, and "Chaplinesque" gives final articulation to the poet's felt need to adopt just that face of comedy. But Crane's comic sense was natural enough, and it constituted a more sizable portion of his temper than is sometimes acknowledged. His efforts to be explicitly funny in verse tended to be almost embarrassingly bad, but he possessed another quality of humor, a tough and toughening amusement which did not spare the so-called dilemma of the modern writer. He was fully aware that there was something preposterous as well as painful in the situation; and something preposterous, too, in the general condition of man amid "the rushing, mechanical scramble of today." He had a ready perception of the lunatic aspect of human conduct and sometimes gave voice to it in the most athletic of obscenities. At such moments he saw himself belonging in good part to the comic tradition of bawdiness and gusto, to the tradition of writers like Petronius, Rabelais, Cervantes, and Mark Twain, whom he had been reading with great relish (especially in 1919) and whom he named in a letter telling Gorham Munson that the latter was "too damned serious."

> Humor is the artist's only weapon against the proletariat. Mark Twain knew this, and used it effectively enough, take *1601* for example. Mencken knows it too. And so did Rabelais. . . . The modern artist has got to harden himself, and the walls of an ivory tower are too delicate and brittle a coat of mail for substitute. . . . I pray for both of us,—let us be keen and humorous scientists anyway. And I would rather act my little tragedy without tears, although I would insist upon a tortured countenance and all sleekness pared off the muscles.

Crane, it is not too much to say, passed his apprenticeship not only by writing poems about poetry, as young men have always done, but by refining his own specific if complex feeling that the entire poetic enterprise was in one perspective ludicrous to the point of being clownish, and in another serious to the point of being sacred. He came into his own when he was able to see himself, and perhaps any other modern poet, as "a clown perhaps, but an aspiring clown"— a description registered in "Chaplinesque" a year before the poem in which those phrases actually occur, Stevens's "The Comedian as the Letter C." The nature of the achievement is indicated, even explained, by some of the mingling contradictions just observed: the "fine collapses" and the "grail of laughter" in "Chaplinesque"; Pierrot's eyes and Gargantua's laughter; the "humorous scientists" (in the letter above) and the "tortured countenance"; clownishness and aspiration. The presence of these fertile contradictions in Crane's mind and imagination, in his letters and in his poetry, shows how remarkably Crane, though only half-knowingly, had come into tune with one of the major traditions of Europe from what he regarded as a provincial hinterland.

·II·

The pirouetting clown in "Chaplinesque" is taken first, of course, from the little tramp invented by the Anglo-American comedian, Charlie Chaplin. But in the range of his wistful aspiration and in the mythic overtones of the final stanza (with its hint of the grail-quest), he is also the figure revered in France as Charlot—a personality saluted in French writing many times before "Chaplinesque," and twice by the surrealist poet Louis Aragon; a *persona,* a myth incarnate, a great illumination of the age, and (as someone said) the creator of "a sublime beauty, a new laughter."[5] This was not exactly Charlie Chaplin, it was a Gallic enlargement of him; the screen image of Chaplin underwent a great extension in the Parisian imagination. The French identified Charlot by grafting a native comic tradition to the original character, and both Charlot and the native tradition were made known to Crane in letters from abroad.[6]

The tradition was that of the clown known most recently in France as Pierrot. Chief among the literary contributions to that tradition had been the twenty-three "Pierrot poems" in a volume of verse called *L'Imitation de Notre Dame La Lune,* by the twenty-six-year-old poet, Jules Laforgue; it was published in 1886, the year before his death. The lines converge. In the fall of 1920, Crane acquired from Paris volumes of the poetry of Laforgue, Arthur Rimbaud, and Charles

[5] Cf. Glauco Viazzi, *Chaplin e la critica* (Bari, Italy, 1955). Even Signor Viazzi's enormously detailed checklist of poems, articles, essays, and books about Chaplin in many countries and languages is not complete. The discussion of Chaplin in Europe and America was one of the cultural phenomena of the twenties and thirties, and perhaps no single volume could appraise all of it.

[6] Matthew Josephson in particular reported to Crane from Paris about the French fascination with the American cinema, which meant, as Josephson said, the films of Chaplin. The letter he quotes, however, as possibly stimulating "Chaplinesque" is dated some months after the poem was written. Josephson, *Life Among the Surrealists* (New York, 1962), pp. 123-26.

Vildrac. During the following summer and with help from more expert linguists, Crane translated three of Laforgue's sixteen "Locutions des Pierrots" ("Speeches," perhaps "Soliloquies," "of the Pierrots"; Laforgue sometimes spoke of Pierrots in the plural, as though they constituted a specific class, like the American beatniks). A few months after that, when Crane came to write "Chaplinesque," he produced a remarkable fusion of images: his own image of the poet as tenderly comic and his own portrait of Chaplin; the Charlot of French commentary and the Pierrot of Laforgue; a portion of Whitman's comic hero; and something far older than any of these. The result is a figure of profoundly representative significance.

The immediate predecessors of Laforgue's Pierrot were two pantomimists of genius—Jean-Gaspard Deburau, who began to perform in a Parisian cellar known as Théâtre des Funambules in 1830, and Paul Legrand, who followed Deburau in the same little establishment in 1847. These two artists between them offered Jules Laforgue (and other poets, Gautier and Verlaine among them) a comic profile comparable in its poetic value to the one Chaplin supplied for Hart Crane. But what should be emphasized is the radical transformation effected by Deburau and Legrand upon the formerly conventional European clown. The conventional character was introduced into France by visiting Italian players in the early seventeenth century, and was known variously in Italy and France through the centuries as Pagliaccio, Pedrolino, Arlecchino, Harlequin, Giles, Pierrot, and so forth. He was primarily a figure of robustious farce. He was usually a servant, and a boisterous and self-assertive one. He was also, so to speak, the butt of Eros; cuckolded himself, he was constantly duped in his clumsy efforts to cuckold others, though he was possessed of a vein of vulgar common sense to offset his customary blockheadedness. But Jean-Gaspard Deburau, a person of a melancholy and even suicidal temperament, invested that traditional

55

bumpkin with his own quality of hard-earned, stoical self-control; Paul Legrand (in Enid Welsford's account) completed the metamorphosis of Pierrot by "introducing pathos and mystery into the character of the once rollicking clown." [7] By mid-century, Charles Baudelaire was noticing with surprise that the French Pierrot had become "pale as the moon, mysterious as silence, supple and mute as the serpent, long and lean as a pole" in contrast with the typical English clown who continued to be the old knockabout figure who "enters like a tempest, falls like a bale, and shakes the house when he laughs." [8] To adopt the phrases of Hart Crane, the everlasting eyes of Pierrot had, in France, quite replaced the laughter of Gargantua; and the dolorous figure with the painted smile had become a fact of French culture.

But in a sense Deburau and Legrand, and following them Laforgue, were reaching behind the Franco-Italian *clown,* who was mainly a Renaissance creation, to recover elements of the medieval *fool*—with a crucial difference, to be noted. The word "fool" is even more comprehensive and various than the word "clown"; it is a very complex word indeed, and its "structure," in William Empson's meaning, has a very complex and dialectical history. [9] For our limited purposes, however, we can apply the formula of Mr. Empson: since in the medieval view "all men are fools in the eyes of God," so the type of fool was exactly "Everyman in the presence of God." The human fool, so ridiculous and even contemptible to human eyes, was just the way any man, Everyman, looked when inspected by the Creator. As motleyed jester, as invented figure in poetry, drama, and impromptu festivals, the fool was a device for commenting on power, wealth, and intellect in an otherwordly perspective, one which allowed the comment to sound not only like precautionary good sense, but like humbling echoes of God's wisdom. He was, at the same time, a vehicle for acknowl-

---

[7] *The Fool* (New York, 1961), p. 310.
[8] *Ibid.,* p. 312.
[9] *The Structure of Complex Words* (Norfolk, Conn., 1952), p.107.

edging and celebrating those non-rational and antinomian aspects of human nature that a culture always suppresses or undervalues at its peril.

Some such concatenation of ideas seems to have turned up again, with a dialectical twist, in the nineteenth century, exemplified diversely by poets like Laforgue and Mallarmé, and by painters like Cézanne and then later by Roualt, Picasso, and Chagall. Those artists projected clown-figures who are not eccentric and socially peripheral objects of mirth, but modes of the modern Everyman. Alluding to the painters just named, Wallace Fowlie has remarked that "as all women were in the painted Virgin of the Italian Renaissance, so all men are in the painted clown of modern France." [10] The clown so widely and modernly represented thus became once more the old-time fool who commented on the established power of the day, upon a rationalistic, heartless, belligerent, scientific, and industrializing society. But only rarely can the modern fool be seen as Everyman in the presence of God. He is much rather Everyman confronting the absence of God, Everyman as he peers through a materialistic culture at an increasingly absurd universe in which he recognizes his own being—the human being itself—as irredeemably clownish. Examining this development, Father Martin D'Arcy has concluded somberly that the clown of modern painting and poetry bears "a pitiable resemblance to that of man crucified but without grace. The would-be hero (the image of God) is covered with grease paint, and exhibiting himself before a faceless audience in a play without meaning, without even the wisdom of the child, and certainly without its innocence." [11] A clown perhaps, but a dismal and a joyless one.

And finally, in the wake of the European Romantic movement, with its habit of filling out the picture of Man with the picture of the Creative Self, the modern clown is not

[10] *The Clown's Grail* (London, 1947), pp. 114-15.
[11] "The Clown and the Philosopher," *The Month* (London), January 1949, p. 8.

only a transformed, melancholy image of Everyman in a senseless world; frequently he is also an image of the artist. In the world's view, he is a laughable entertainer; in his own view, he has a voice of sadness, even despair, muffled behind his clownish make-up. Such, anyhow, is one of the defining tendencies of *L'Art Pierrot* of Jules Laforgue.

The Pierrot whose "asides" we overhear in *L'Imitation de Notre Dame La Lune* is the earlier Deburau-Legrand figure unhappily beset by contradictions and especially troubled by the mysteries of sex. His is a condition helplessly divided against itself, mocking what it longs for, delicately despising what it has. "I am nothing but a lunar playboy," he confesses, "making circles in ponds." The moon for Laforgue was a sort of hollow unreality, a Romantic convention carefully emptied of meaning; in dedicating himself (in the volume's title-phrase) to an "imitation of Our Lady the moon," he is in fact deliberately accepting a career of nullity, even as he is carefully blaspheming aspects of the Christian tradition. Meanwhile, a natural fastidiousness of conduct is constantly betrayed by the erotic impulse, upon which in turn Laforgue's Pierrot takes his malicious and self-defeating revenge. He is still the butt of Eros; he complains about his lady's "perverse austerities," nurses a "divine infatuation" for Cydalise, and "fishes in troubled water / For Eve, Gioconda and Dalila" (the phrases quoted are in Hart Crane's translation). For recompense he reflects: "Yes, they are divine, those eyes! But nothing exists / Behind them! Her soul is a matter for the oculist." He scoffs at the notion of a woman "taking herself seriously in this century," and notices with exaggerated surprise that the lady has begun to weep.

At moments like this, Pierrot is Man in the sense of Male, caught up in the endless and debasing round of sexual cross-purposes, a fact which annoyed Jacques Rivière, who remarked that "that *idée fixe* of (Laforgue) is really exasperating. After all . . . there are so many other things." But as Warren Ramsay has pointed out, "if a poet happens to be a romantic, even a late-blooming and ironical one, the misunderstanding between the sexes may stand for other apprehensions, the one between the poet and society, for example." [12] Pierrot's amatory difficulties have an air of actuality, and one feels that if they could have been overcome, he might have been consoled for the parallel difficulties, the felt foolishness, of the artistic effort. But they are also no doubt a bitter-comic representation of Pierrot's relation—that is, the relation of the artist in Laforgue's generation—to the "perverse austerities" of the modern world, a world he at once courts and denigrates, a world which may claim to love him but has not the wit to understand a word he says. Both the dim-sighted world and an imagined lady are present in the artist-lover's report: "She whispered: 'I am waiting, here I am, I don't know . . .' Her gaze having taken on broad lunar ingenuousness." [13] The skeptical and hesitant Laforguian figure is less mysterious and pathetic than the clown of Deburau and Legrand, but it reveals a vein of wistfulness that cynicism never quite excises. His frustrated love affair with the world could provide a paradigm for Hart Crane's more touching, more joyful, and more fertilely moon-struck image of the clown-poet who can still love the world, thwarted as he may be by its heavy-handed hostility.

The paradigm, however, came to Crane at first through the mediation of T. S. Eliot and (less so) of Ezra Pound. As an

[12] *Jules Laforgue and the Ironic Inheritance* (New York, 1953), p. 189. I am especially beholden to Mr. Ramsay's chapter on Laforgue and Hart Crane.

[13] Translation by Henri Peyre in *The Poem Itself* (Cleveland, 1962). Part of Professor Peyre's commentary can be quoted as a very apt summary of the whole development I have been discussing: "The poet (the artist in Mallarmé and Picasso) sees himself as a clown whose profession it is to entertain, but whose white-faced mask expresses longing for the one consolation against the senselessness of the world: feminine tenderness. . . . But the feminine declaration of love for him alone and forever . . . arouses his most waggish banter" (p. 63).

undergraduate at Harvard, Eliot had discovered Laforgue in Arthur Symons' book, *The Symbolist Movement in French Literature,* and had written a number of poems that he himself located *"sous la ligne de Laforgue."* Eliot was for some years intrigued to the point of obsession (as he much later acknowledged) by a number of elements in Laforgue's work, including Laforgue's ironical manipulation of older legends and stories like those of Parsifal and Hamlet; [14] he was, however, perhaps especially drawn to the Pierrot poems, to their verbal and rhythmical innovations, and to the rueful imagery he could find in them—imagery which represented the modern sensibility hesitating and bemused among the perplexities, erotic and otherwise, of modern life. Something of this hovers in such Laforguian poems of Eliot as "Conversation Galante," "Portrait of a Lady," and "La Figlia che Piange"; it reaches full statement in "The Love Song of J. Alfred Prufrock," "the great example of the Laforguian poem in English," according to Malcolm Cowley.[15] Here the lover's wistfulness is less contaminated by self-defense and his gesture even more ineffectual than in Laforgue; Prufrock accepts his role not as Prince Hamlet, but as a Polonius who is only a step away from being the court's comic relief—

> Full of high sentence, but a bit obtuse;
> At times, indeed, almost ridiculous—
> Almost, at times, the Fool.

This is obviously a portrait of the artist as well as the confession of a lover; if the capitalized word "Fool" suggests

[14] See Leonard Unger's long essay, "Laforgue, Conrad and T. S. Eliot," in *The Man in the Name* (Minneapolis, Minn., 1956).

[15] "Laforgue in America: A Testimony," *Sewanee Review* (Winter 1963). Mr. Cowley lists the following characteristics as peculiarly Laforguian: "the urban background, the timidly yearning hero . . . the self-protective irony, the bold figures of speech, the mixture of colloquial and academic language, the rhythms that might be those of popular song, and the rhyming couplets serving as refrains." Most, though not all, of those characteristics can be detected in Crane's "Chaplinesque."

momentarily some paradoxical superiority in either role—
as in the medieval Fool of Love—it is not, I think, a hint that
long survives.

Eliot introduced Ezra Pound to Laforgue around 1914.
It was the expressed enthusiasm of the two writers for the
French poet that drew so many youthful American *literati*
to Laforgue after the war when, as Malcolm Cowley has
recalled, "The complete works of Jules Laforgue gathered
dust" on almost every mantelpiece in Greenwich Village.
Back in Cleveland, in 1920, Hart Crane was moved to send
to Paris for several volumes of Laforgue, and he felt at once,
as he wrote Allen Tate, "a certain sympathy with Laforgue's
attitude," his attitude, presumably, toward the follies and
dilemmas of the poet and the lover in modern times. In any
case, Crane's sympathy was sufficient for him to translate
three of the sixteen *Locutions des Pierrots*.

Each of the three is a combination of complaint, taunt,
and plea addressed to or concerning some young lady:
some "Vaillante oisive femme" in Laforgue's phrase; in
Crane's, some "prodigal and wholly dilatory lady." When
Crane's versions were published in the *Double Dealer* in
1922, he added a note saying "A strictly literal translation
of Laforgue is meaningless. The native implications of his
idiosyncratic style have to be recast in English garments."
He remarked defensively to Allen Tate that "no one ought
to be particularly happy about a successful translation,"
and that he only did these "for fun." In fact, Crane's
"Locutions" are less translations than (to borrow the Nietz-
schean word of which Crane would have approved) they
are transvaluations of the original; as such, they have an
unexpected interest. For one thing, Crane sometimes used
the line structure of Laforgue's verse simply as a frame
within which to practice his own brand of language: "la
lune-levante de ma belle âme" (literally, "the moonrise
of my handsome soul") thus provides the occasion for
Crane's "the orient moon of my dapper affections." But
more important, as even that single example suggests, what

Crane was really doing was to diminish, very nearly to expunge, the irony that everywhere permeated Laforgue's poetry and his vision. To focus on the key symbol, Crane restores substance and value to the disempowered moon.

The process can be best illustrated via the third of the "Locutions." In Laforgue, this begins:

> Ah! sans lune, quelles nuits blanches,
> Quel cauchemars pleins de talent!
> Vois-je pas là nos cygnes blancs,
> Vient-on pas de tourner la clenche?
>
> Et c'est vers toi que j'en suis là.
> Que ma conscience voit double,
> Et que mon coeur pêche en eau troublé
> Eve, Joconde et Dalila!

Crane renders the lines as follows:

> Ah! without the moon, what white nights,
> What nightmares rich with ingenuity!
> Don't I see your white swans there?
> Doesn't someone come to turn the knob?
>
> And it's your fault that I'm this way.
> That my conscience sees double,
> And my heart fishes in troubled water
> For Eve, Gioconda and Dalila!

An almost fundamental change is effected at the outset when, "without the moon," Crane experiences "nightmares rich with ingenuity" against Laforgue's "cauchemars pleins de talents." Instead of Laforgue's polished irony, which quietly drains the force out of every allusion, Crane offers a direct, if packed, statement about the creative imagination. For Crane, unlike Laforgue, still believed in the moon, and in the power it symbolized, the power, as he would say in "Chaplinesque," to make "a grail of laughter of an empty ash can." So believing, he could feel the struggling nightmare of the moon's absence, the ingenuities contrived to overcome its loss. Beneath Laforgue's surface there is also, of course, considerable seriousness and some anguish, but by and large, he seems to play—very skillfully—with the adversities of poet and lover, while Crane gives back to them their exigent reality. And by so contending with, by measuring himself against, the most ironical of modern European poets (all in the guise of translation), Crane's emotional honesty as well as the peculiarities of his genius forced him to take a first step away from irony itself, or beyond it. For a writer of his temperament, no step could have been more necessary at the time.

This is not to say that in his "Locutions" Crane pursued a uniform course, or that he was uniformly successful. He failed, on the whole, in the matter of rhythm. Laforgue's rhythms were themselves devices of irony, and in them his ironic attitudes found their perfect tone, almost a mono-tone; [16] but "confronted by the relaxed rhythms of Laforgue," as Warren Ramsay has observed in *Jules Laforgue and the Ironic Inheritance,* "Crane is technically ill at ease." He was at least ill at ease when he attempted to simulate the original rhythm, rather than to transform it. One plainly hears Crane's natural impulse toward a stronger, more exclamatory and dramatic statement being hampered by a line like: "And it's your fault that I'm this way"; whereas in the original ("Et c'est vers toi que je suis là"), the sounds fall into place smoothly enough. The restraining influence of Laforgue can also be heard in Crane's poem "My Grandmother's Love Letters"; it produced a rather debilitating effect in "The Bridge of Estador": "I do not know what you'll see,—your vision / May slumber yet in the moon." Even there the Laforguian elements—tone, image, cadence—were of undeniable value to Crane as he groped after his own idiom and music. Crane's involvement

[16] Though perhaps less so than one might suppose, Malcolm Cowley, in the article cited (in note 15 above), has pointed out what few of the early American Laforguians realized: Laforgue's dependence upon popular songs and children's chants.

with Laforgue was a significant chapter in his career; to have maintained it, however, would have proved fatal.

But of this there had, in fact, been little chance. Throughout his Laforguian phase, Crane had been a good deal more vulnerable than, say, Eliot had been to diametrically opposite poetic persuasions, including a diametrically opposite comic image. Eliot could beautifully absorb and be absorbed by Laforgue because the latter's witty self-deprecation could add salt to Eliot's incipient and, as it would develop, profound strain of Christian humility. But while Hart Crane was congenitally modest, and although he too took on for a while the mask of self-derision, there was in him no great tendency toward Christian humility—not, in any case, toward that dark Jansenistic kind that Eliot stood for. Unlike Eliot, Crane was always responsive to the poetry of braggadocio. In his view, the doleful eyes of Pierrot were intended not to replace, but to blend with the laughter of Gargantua. In somewhat simplistic literary terms, the spirit of Jules Laforgue mingled in Crane's imagination with a spirit at once more robust and more American, to which we can give the name of Walt Whitman.

He was aided in this regard by his own ignorance. Certain educated friends, Crane wrote Tate in 1922, had lamented the fact that he (Crane) had been taken to Laforgue "without having placed [him] in relation to most of the older 'classics,' which I haven't read. . . . Nonetheless, my affection for Laforgue is none the less genuine for being led to him through Pound and Eliot than it would have been through Baudelaire." Inevitably, he missed some of the implications of Laforgue's references—the accretions his moon, his swans, and his ladies brought with them from earlier French poetry. But for the same reason, Laforgue was a more easily displaceable burden for Crane than for Eliot; two years after the letter just quoted, Crane would allude deprecatingly to "the consciously-contrived 'Pierrots' of Laforgue," and two years after that, more harshly yet, he would describe Laforgue's general attitude as a sort of fastidious whimper. There are, to be sure, clear echoes of Laforgue as late as *The Bridge,* especially in the sad, erotic play of "Three Songs," when Laforgue's image of the poet "fishing in troubled water / For Eve, Gioconda and Dalila" can be heard (transvaluated, as always) in the sound of names falling "vainly on the waves / Eve! Magdalene! / Or Mary, you?" [17] meanwhile, there had been all along another powerful elment at work in Crane. If he knew rather less than his educated friends about the French literary tradition, he knew or perhaps guessed rather more about the American. "Chaplinesque" participates in a specifically American comic tradition. It is one that takes its principal start with Whitman, a tradition that, given fresh impetus by Hart Crane, has progressed to the point where it is probably the most vital aspect of American writing at the present day. Crane's place in this development illustrates as well as anything could his great talent for projecting images not only forceful but roundly representative: a talent that makes him, on balance, the most immediately communicative of twentieth-century American poets.

·III·

The poet-hero who announced his appearance amid the eccentric typography of the Preface to the 1855 *Leaves of Grass* was a comic figure of an already thoroughly familiar sort. He was, in fact, a vast verbal enlargement of the *persona* known for more than half a century as the Yankee. The latter, like the clown of the older European comedy troupes, was by convention a comic servant; and, as Daniel

[17] Mitchell Smith, a graduate student at Yale completing a dissertation on "the Age of Laforgue" in American poetry, tells me that there are a surprising number of Laforguian echoes and borrowings in a poem as late as "Cape Hatteras" (written in 1929). I have not yet detected them; but it is a fair presumption that Laforgue might turn up anywhere in the later part of *The Bridge* when—as in the "nasal whine of power" section of "Cape Hatteras"—Crane is resorting to vigorous parody.

Hoffman has remarked, he "first walks on the stage as the rustic Jonathan in Royall Tyler's famous comedy, The Contrast"[18]—a play (1797) in the sub-plot of which the native American type is given a provisional profile by "contrast" between his honest if slow-witted sturdiness and the simpering affectations of another servant named Jessamy. It was by just such contrasts with the Europeanized personality that the first recognizable New-World character got itself defined; and if, in the comparison, the American looked oafish and ignorant, he also seemed stalwart, morally pure, and sometimes surprisingly shrewd. The shrewdness and the purity eventually separated, and (Mr. Hoffman has traced this for us) the confidence man and the uncouth crusader would pursue separate or embattled careers through decade after decade. On the whole, however, we may take as *the* Yankee that virtuous dolt who stumbled untainted through villainies and temptations from the late eighteenth century on.[19] It was this figure that Whitman brought to full scale, and upon which he worked certain key and magical transformations.

Whitman, indeed, had an even more pronounced effect upon the American comic hero and the tradition in which that hero flourished than Laforgue did in France; and it is worth remembering that just as Hart Crane had been reading and translating Laforgue's Pierrot poems prior to writing "Chaplinesque," so Laforgue had been reading and translating Whitman prior to *L'Imitation de Notre Dame La Lune*. Laforgue was perhaps more interested in Whitman's metrics than in his substance, but the two aspects cannot at all be divided; for Whitman, no less than for Laforgue, rhythms were an essential part of the comic posture and utterance. The clownish figure in Whitman's poetry is, in fact, less a persistent human character than a

[18] *Form and Fable in American Fiction* (New York, 1961), p. 46.
[19] In fiction such a character can be followed from, say, Brockden Brown's *Arthur Mervyn* (1797) up to and beyond Thornton Wilder's classic version, *Heaven's My Destination* (1936).

hovering presence, and a presence felt above all in the play of language and twist of meter. The human character comes through clearly enough in the 1855 *Preface:* boastful, naïve, adventurous, a bit uncouth, and a brash lover of all creation: the Yankee as comical culture hero. In the earlier European manner, he "enters like a tempest"; and in the American manner, he is identified in all his differences from poets of other countries. The animating motif in the 1855 poems is at many moments antic and bizarre, the figure we watch and listen to is given to sudden fits of clowning; a nose-thumbing irreverence and an impish desire to shock alternate with Whitman's peculiar erotic religiosity and his moods of rapture and awe. Even so death-haunted a poem as "The Sleepers" is interrupted by a shriek of comic horror ("O for pity's sake, no one must see me now! . . . my clothes were stolen while I was abed"). Still, the comedy is even more centrally a matter of technique.

It is Whitman's language that performs the function of clown, and no one put the case more precisely than Whitman himself. "Considering language, then, as some mighty potentate," he wrote in an early prose passage, "into the majestic audience-hall of the monarch ever enters a personage like one of Shakespeare's clowns, and takes possession there and plays a part even in the stateliest ceremonies. Such is Slang, or indirection. . . ." Most of Whitman's long-debated verbal inventions belongs to his comic purpose; his statement to Traubel in the late days at Camden that "I sometimes think the *Leaves* is only a language experiment" is almost exactly parallel to his statement during the same period that "I pride myself on being a real humorist underneath everything else." [20] Nor was the allusion to Shakespeare's clowns merely vague, or grandiose, for Whitman's comedy of language proceeded in a manner very close to Shakespeare's comedy of action. In Shakespeare,

[20] Richard Chase, in *Walt Whitman Revisited* (New York, 1955), has given the best account of Whitman as a comic poet.

the comic dimension provides an indispensable corrective by parodying the serious or tragic element so as to cast the latter in an ambiguous—hence a truer—light. In Whitman it is not simply the slang, it is the audible slang in the midst of "the stateliest ceremonies" of speech that provides the comedy. We hear not only "blab" and "chuff" and "drib" and "hap" and "lag" and "swash" and "yawp," we hear those blunt verbal bullets as they ricochet off the stately and pretentious sides of words like "presidentiad" and "cartouche" and "ambulanza" and "imperturbe" and "lumine" and "sonnambula." If we add to this the coiling unconventionality of Whitman's rhythm, with its capacity to leap or to relax, to startle or assuage at will, we are close to the heart of Whitman's comedy—or perhaps to any authentic comic verse.

But there is another exceedingly significant aspect to Whitman's comedy, one that comes into prominence in the late 1850's. In the poems of 1855 and 1856, both human nature and the creative enterprise were subjected to a sort of cheerful curative mockery only occasionally darkened by real doubt. In the 1860 edition, a new note appeared: new, that is, in Whitman and in American poetry, but remarkably similar to the note struck earlier in France. Whitman's comic sensibility, while not less prevalent than before, had deepened into a mysterious and melancholy sense of his own moral and artistic inadequacy. Some of the 1860 poems reflect a dolorousness like that of the French pantomimist, some a half-buried suicidal impulse like that of Jean-Gaspard Deburau, and some a sense of creative frustration which anticipates Laforgue. Pierrot joined Gargantua in these poems, and the junction is nowhere more impressive than in "As I Ebb'd with the Ocean of Life." Here, in a poem largely about psychic and artistic annihilation, Whitman introduced a supreme example of the poet's self-derision: an image of the poet and all his works mocked by what Whitman called the Real Me:

Withdrawn far, mocking me with mock-
    congratulatory signs and bows,
With peals of distant ironical laughter at every
    word I have written,
Pointing in silence to these songs, and then
    to the sand beneath.

The Real Me was Whitman's "Oversoul," his divine muse.
In the lines quoted, we have Whitman's version of the poet
as fool, the poet as Everyman in the presence of his special
God; of the way the most ambitious of human efforts looks
in the mocking perspective of divinity.

Hart Crane presumably came to Whitman, as all too
many readers have come to him, from the wrong end;
via the aggressively prophetic and patriotic and "cosmic"
chants behind which the best of Whitman lay hidden till
recently, and on the basis of which Whitman earned a
quite unjustified reputation for humorlessness. But Crane
was always a tough-minded judge of poetry, and no less
of Whitman's poetry. "You've heard me roar at too many
of his lines," he reminded Tate in 1930, "to doubt that I
can spot his worst, I'm sure." Knowing and roaring with
laughter at Whitman's most inflated lines, Crane also, in
the course of time, got to know and to revel in the authentic
Whitman: the "Cape Hatteras" section of *The Bridge*
(written in 1929) is permeated with borrowings from a
dozen of the finest lyrics Whitman ever wrote. Crane's
imaginative association with Whitman seems to have grown
abruptly with the first conception of *The Bridge* in 1923.
But it also appears that at some earlier stage Crane was
infected, in the secretive manner of poetic influence, by
Whitman's conception of the poet as something between
a comedian and a divinity (a conception that was especially
pervasive in Whitman's writing before the Civil War).
Even in "Chaplinesque" there is a sort of implicit capering,
almost a bumptiousness, a quality that for lack of a better
adjective and to distinguish it from the Gallic irony that

it pushes against, we can only call American; which, for Crane at this time, is the same as to call it Whitmanian.

The matter is interestingly beclouded by Whitman's diversity, including the diversity of his comic spirit. The force of Whitman's example is equally felt in another account of the poet as clown, one much longer and more intricate than "Chaplinesque" and completed a year after Crane's poem: "The Comedian as the Letter C," by the most cultivated of Whitman's literary grand-nephews, Wallace Stevens. But here the example works to a different effect. At one moment in this lengthy mock-epic, its wandering, undersized hero, Crispin, is observed stopping "in the dooryard of his own capacious bloom." That echo of Whitman's most famous poem nearly defines the comic essence of Stevens's work, for it is as though Stevens were openly setting his own frustrated efforts beside Whitman's great achievement, as though Whitman himself were Stevens's Real Me, and a power audible in the background who mocks Stevens "with distant ironical laughter at every word" Stevens had written. The poetic effort whose failure is comically narrated is an effort to do what Whitman had done: to render in poetry the hard, resistant, and multiple reality of America. The surface of Stevens's poem is preternaturally alive with verbal comedy of a recognizably Whitmanian kind: an extraordinary interplay of the stately, the colloquial, the boldly invented, the bizarre, the imported. But the story told in that dazzling language belongs to comedy of a different but equally familiar order, the comedy of ruefully admitted defeat, the mask of witty self-deprecation.

"The Comedian as the Letter C" is, among other things, an ironic autobiography, the poet's unsparing history of his own consciousness and how it got that way: a satiric version, so to speak, of "Song of Myself." It is the story of a poet who began, as many American poets did begin around 1900 (when Stevens, born 1879, reached his majority) by writing "his couplet yearly to the spring," by writing

"poems of plums," by affecting an air of "decorous melancholy" and the pseudo-exotic ("cloak of China, cap of
Spain, imperative haw of hum"). One thinks of those triple-
named versifiers (like Edward Clarence Stedman) who
ruled the poetic fashion at the turn of the century. "Maya
sonneteers," Stevens calls them: poets who despite the
splendid native birds available "still to the night-bird"
(nightingale) "made their plea, / As if rasberry tanagers
in palms, / High up in orange air, were barbarous." Stevens's
young hero commits himself to the native and the barbarous
to escape from the "stale intelligence" of "his fellows," and
to scrawl "With his own quill, in its indigenous dew." And
it is here that Stevens refers to him as "a clown perhaps,
but an aspiring clown."

The aspiration to abandon the stale or irrelevant European
tradition, and to face up poetically to twentieth-century
America is not ignoble. It takes the structural form of a
voyage from the coast of France to Eastern America:
"Bordeaux to Yucatan, Havana next, / And then to Carolina.
Simple jaunt." The journey from the Old World to the
New is shaped in epic style. It is cast deliberately in the
mold of the classical literary epic: the departure from the
Old World, the difficult and dangerous sea-crossing, the
tentative landings and fresh adventures, the arrival at the
site of the new home, the effort to found a new society
and a new culture. But the aspiration is also clownish,
and the outward structure mocks the inner journey, which
is a journey of poetic awareness and attitude, an attempt
to cross over from the genteel to the vulgarly alive, from
the artificial to the real, and from one aspect of the self
to another. In "The Comedian" that effort fails, as it had
historically failed with certain other poets, if not in fact
with Wallace Stevens. Those "young Harvard poets," as
George Santayana would say retrospectively, "hadn't enough
stamina to stand up to their country and describe it as a
poet should. . . . Being educated men, they couldn't pitch
their voices or find their inspiration in that strident so-

ciety." [21] Thus for the hapless Crispin, despite his good intentions:

> America was always north to him,
> A northern west or western north, but north,
> And thereby polar, polar-purple, chilled
> And lank, rising and slumping from a sea
> Of hardy foam, receding flatly, spread
> In endless ledges, glittering, submerged
> And cold in a boreal mistiness of the moon. . . .
> It was a flourishing tropic he required.

Confronted by that northern, chilled, lank, slumping, flat, misty landscape, Crispin's tropical spirit is defeated. He yields to mere domestication, and after beginning on his adventure "with a green brag," he concludes "fadedly . . . as a man prone to distemper," "Fickle and fumbling, variable, obscure, / Glozing his life with aftershining flicks."

If Stevens did not personally conclude with such fading and fumbling, it was because he adopted the strategy that Santayana (in the letter quoted) wisely observed as the only strategy capable of handling the stridencies of America in verse—that of satire. More cunningly still, Stevens not only treated the native actualities satirically, he satirized the poetic effort to treat them at all. He mocked both the discordant world and the poet in relation to it. He assumed for a time the only role that made survival possible, the role of the poet as comedian; and only after having done so could he go on, some years later, to the complex serenities of his extraordinary middle-age and old-age writing. In "The Comedian" even Santayana's reference to the poets' trying to pitch their voices amid the American noise is ironically anticipated in Crispin's decision to find "a new reality in parrot-squawks." But the central symbol is the poem's hero himself.

[21] Letter to V. F. Calverton, November 18, 1934; quoted from the Calverton papers (New York Public Library) by Daniel Aaron, in his introduction to Robert Herrick's *Memoirs of a Citizen* (Cambridge, Mass., 1962), p. vi.

Crispin is as fruitful a choice for Stevens as Pierrot had been for Laforgue and Charlie Chaplin for Hart Crane; or for that matter, the Yankee had been for Whitman. Like Pierrot, Crispin belonged originally to the Italo-French comic traditions, especially to the Commedia dell'Arte; and like both Pierrot and the American Yankee, he was initially a comical servant. But Crispin's clowning had never consisted in entering like a tempest and falling like a bale. He had been a far more canny and urbane person; his comic pattern had been to hurry back and forth, with a sort of adroit desperation, between two different and incompatible masters, trying without their knowledge to serve as valet to both at once. The Crispin of Wallace Stevens is the French valet transplanted and made into a clownish American poet, just as in the poem's "plot," Crispin leaves the French port and winds up somewhere on the North American continent. But the new Crispin gets caught in the same old predicament. He must once again try to serve two masters, or to do justice to two very different dimensions. The latter are given a variety of names in the poem: Europe and America, north and south, and so on, but they are primarily the two poles of Stevens's continuing dialectic. They are the imagination and the real, and their chief symbols here are those familiar Romantic ones, the moon and the sun. Even as he arrives in North America and inspects its "Arctic moonlight," Crispin, longing for the sun, realizes that his poetic and spiritual voyaging must always be "An up and down between two elements, / A fluctuating between sun and moon." The lines are a summary account of almost the whole body of Stevens's poetry. But here, in "The Comedian as the Letter C," the venture is made to seem merely hazardous and ridiculous; and Crispin in that poem appears as the Buster Keaton of poets.

Mention of that splendid silent film comedian can remind us again—as "Chaplinesque" reminds us—that the comic image in literature during Hart Crane's generation could draw much from its counterpart on film. Along with the evasive buffoonery of Chaplin, there were such brilliant figures as Buster Keaton and Harry Langdon, who also knew how to intermix the mirthful with the pathetic, a fragment of Gargantua with a portion of Pierrot. After them came Harpo Marx, whose comic genius rivaled Chaplin's, and who, like Crane's Chaplin, managed to skip by the hefty obstructions of officialdom and still love the world. These were only at several removes images of the artist. They were chiefly images of modern man sprung loose in an utterly random and yet mysteriously hostile universe, a universe in which persons, and more importantly somehow, *things* conspired against the individual whose "only ally" (as Frank Capra once said about Langdon) "was God." [22] The silent comedians (their achievement greatly aided by silence) comprised a sizable and enduring element in the history of modern culture; they are easily recognizable as the predecessors of the hurrying hero in American fiction since the Second World War; they have been acknowledged as contributing significantly to the European "theater of the absurd." But within the narrower confines of literature itself, it was e. e. cummings, after Crane and Stevens, who did most to advance the comic view of both man and artist, to suggest indeed, as he did in a play of 1928 called *him,* that it was because he was a man, that the artist was a comedian.

In *him,* the dominant metaphor becomes strict, and the contemporary American artist is presented almost literally as a circus clown, a member of the Ringling Brothers troupe. *Him* is a wonderfully bewildering combination of farce, surrealism, sex and its various perversions, poignancy, dream (both old-fashioned and Freudian), political and cultural satire, and tough stuff. It borrows something from Pirandello's exploitation of the very notion of theatrical make-believe, and it looks forward, especially in the grave vacuities of the three choral Miss Weirds—the Misses Stop, Look, and Listen —to the early plays of Ionesco. The play's subject, as the

[22] *Agee on Film* (New York, 1958), p. 14.

hero "him" explains about his own play to the heroine "me,"
is "the sort of man—who is writing a play about a man who
is writing a sort of play"; a satirical tail-piece to Romantic
narcissism. But the focus throughout is on the nature of the
artist, and here, a year before Charlie Chaplin's film *The
Circus,* the artist shows up as a clownish acrobat.

In a number of lyric poems, then and later, cummings
radiated a comic spirit alternately robust and wistful, coarse
and tender, Rabelaisian and Pierrotesque, a series of sur-
rogates for the aggressive or sensitive imagination. His proud
dream-horse, moving smooth-loomingly through the clut-
tered city streets, is one such; so is the little lame balloon-
man; so, in the more vigorous mode, is cummings' Buffalo
Bill, that handsome man, "who used to break onetwothree-
fourfive pigionsjustlikethat!" In *him,* the definition includes some of Buffalo Bill's daring, but the rodeo is replaced
by the circus, the clowning is more emphatic, and the accomplishment less assured. Reading the hero's palm, the
second Miss Weird (Miss Look) tells him accurately: "Your
favorite planet is Ringling Brothers"; and "him" rephrases
Wordsworth to declaim oracularly, "Barnum thou shouldst
be living at this hour."

"Damn everything but the circus," he cries impatiently.
He means: damn every account of life, modern life, except
the one that sees it as a circus; that is why the world needs
Barnum at this hour. In a note on the original dust jacket,
cummings said that his play was intended to represent the
realm where doing and dreaming interact: not the meaning
of life, but its being, the thing itself. Toward this aim, the
play in its final act dissolves "reality" altogether into a circus,
complete with freaks and sideshows and fortune-tellers and
barkers. It is within this perspective on modern experience
and behavior that the artist is identified. "The average
'painter' 'sculptor' 'poet' 'composer' 'playwright,'" says
"him" to "me" contemptuously, "is a person who cannot
leap through a hoop from a galloping horse, make people

laugh with the clown's mouth, orchestrate twenty lions." But the true and superior artist can do just those things, or has to attempt them; he must try—given the frenetic expectancies of the modern audience—to be simultaneously daredevil, clown, and lion-tamer. "Him" is more recklessly ambitious yet. "Imagine," he continues, "a human being who balances three chairs, one on top of the other, on a wire, eighty feet in the air with no net underneath and then climbs into the top chair, sits down and begins to swing. . . . I am that." Carried away by his image, "him" continues into pure fantasy: he imagines that three chairs are kicked away, and that the artist resides thereafter on top of three impalpable "facts." He does not stay there long. The very formula of his profession requires that he shortly plunge into the sawdust, to the infinite excitement and delight of his audience. For his three facts are the facts that he is an artist; and yet he is a man; and so, his unlimited aspiration mocked by his humanity, he is a failure.

·IV·

The confession is made without bitterness. There is in it, instead, a surprising amount of pure joy, along with an accent of gaiety. In his *Six Nonlectures* of 1953, cummings provided his own gloss on the "three facts" of *him* in a characteristic spray of polysyllables, contending that " 'an artist, a man, a failure' is no mere whenfully accreting mechanism, but a givingly eternal complexity—neither some soulless and heartless ultrapredatory infra-animal or any un-understandingly knowing and believing and thinking automaton, but a naturally and miraculously whole human being—a feelingly illimitable individual, whose only happiness is to transcend himself, whose every agony is to grow." That "feelingly illimitable individual," whose actual limitations are countered and overcome by a passionate urge toward self-transcendence, resembles the person celebrated by cummings in "My Father Moved Through Dooms of Love." But he will hardly appear to resemble some of the other figures in the comic tradition I have been examining: the deeply melancholy Deburau; the Pierrot, at once self-deriding and malicious, of Laforgue; the ebbing Whitman of 1860, mocked from afar; the minuscule Crispin, his bravado all faded, of Stevens. One might well conclude that the really significant development in the comic mode, both at home and abroad, over the past century or so has been the deployment of comedy as a way of registering artistic and human defeat, and the use of the clown-figure as a means of living with despair. And yet a note of something more than sheer endurance ("I laugh that I may not weep"), a note implying an unexpected victory of sorts—victory over all the forces that try to make life and art impossible—a note even of positive joy, these too are inherent in the comic tradition, and are part of the clownish profile. They are audible, of course, in the last lines of "Chaplinesque," and we may now return to them for a final assessment both of the place of that poem in Crane's personal career and for the insinuations it contains about a large potential change in the modern consciousness.[23]

On a personal level, Crane adopted the mask of comedy in his poem to the same end that Stevens did in "The Comedian as the Letter C": simply as a device for poetic survival in a society that despised art or a world (an America) not susceptible to it. But the comic role reaped unexpectedly large rewards for Crane, both in his career and within the poem. It was just because he accepted the role of comedian that the joint figure in "Chaplinesque" arrives at a sort of sacred vision:

[23] The clown-image could be usefully traced beyond its appearance in *him* through a good deal of contemporary fiction—Nathanael West's *The Day of the Locust* and Henry Miller's *The Smile at the Foot of the Ladder,* to name only two titles. I did so trace it, in a limited way, in an earlier version of this chapter (see *Learners and Discerners,* ed. Robert Scholes; University of Virginia Press, 1964).

The game enforces smirks. But we have seen
The moon in lonely alleys make
A grail of laughter of an empty ash can.

Those lines constitute the first memorable example of the imaginative act hinted at in the close of the preceding chapter: the act of transfiguration, the act by which a poetic vision transforms the object it contemplates, by seeing (in a phrase of Emerson I shall much later return to) the miraculous in the common and the near at hand. Crane's major development, moreover, is here in small: from the enforced smirk to the grail of laughter; from the comic spirit to the religious spirit; from clownish consent to overwhelming visionary affirmation. "Chaplinesque" is in this sense the touchstone of Crane's early career; there is an organic continuity between it and the poem he began to write four months after its publication, "For the Marriage of Faustus and Helen," a poem in which the irony still present in "Chaplinesque" becomes altogether transcended. At the same time, on a level higher and broader than the personal, "Chaplinesque" contains insinuations (one dare not use a stronger word) remarkably far-reaching for so brief a poem.

They are insinuations about an epochal overturn in cultural and spiritual history, and their flickering presence in "Chaplinesque" is due to Crane's skill, compounded of literary awareness, spontaneous intuition, and sheer luck, in fusing several different and even contradictory comic traditions. The nineteenth-century French clown, mournful and agile, is reanimated in "Chaplinesque" through the immediate influence of Laforgue and Eliot, but he is reanimated in tonalities that at the same time recover a good deal of the medieval Fool of which the French Pierrot had been a scrupulously truncated version. With some assistance from both the bumptious and the self-doubting Whitman, and with even more assistance from his own archetypal imagination, Crane at once Americanized and transvaluated the clown of Laforgue by a poetic method at once ironic and ritualistic. The resulting figure does participate in the long-standing modern view of art as derided and humanity as debased, but he also participates in a much more ancient view. In his very shabbiness and clownishness, as he submits to the transfiguring moon, he represents for a second that moment just prior to an immense inversion of values whereby the humble shall be exalted, the foolish become the source of wisdom, and the world shall renew itself by honoring the ridiculous, the disgraced, the outlaw.

If there is one event above all others that is truly significant in European and American literature in the past few decades, it is something of just that sort. It has been marked by a continuing exploration of the lowest of the low to find and expose elements of the highest of the high, to dig in the human debris for intimations of mythic grandeur or of sancity.[24] This is what happens so fleetingly in "Chaplinesque" when the little tramp suddenly makes out by moonlight, in the actual and spiritual slums of the modern world, the holy grail in an empty ash can; it was to happen again on an incomparably larger scale in *The Bridge.* It is a feat of the visionary imagination by a poet for whom *la lune* really was, once more, *Notre Dame,* an object to be imitated, revered, and trusted. But the grail is "a grail of laughter," and it is by an extension of comedy that Crane's own bedraggled Harlequin becomes again the Fool of Love in the presence of grace. Just so, in medieval romance, it was the most clownish and uncouth of King Arthur's knights, Sir Percival, who was elected to discover the sacred vessel and fulfill the aspiration of the age.

[24] Cf. Northrop Frye's seminal discussion of "ironic literature" in *Anatomy of Criticism* (Princeton, 1958), and the way the "ironic" mode tends to move back cyclically toward myth.

CHAPTER FOUR

"For the Marriage of Faustus and Helen"

A THREE-PART POEM of roughly 140 lines, "For the Marriage of Faustus and Helen," occupies a key position in Crane's career suggestively similar to that of *Endymion* in the career of John Keats. Like *Endymion,* "Faustus and Helen" is the poet's first venture into the long (or perhaps one should say the longer, the more deliberately ambitious) poem, after a number of masterful but carefully restricted short lyrics. More importantly, the venture itself is, in both cases, the very motif of the poems resulting. Sir Sidney Colvin's summary of *Endymion*—a "parable of the poetic soul in man seeking communion with the spirit of essential Beauty in the world"—applies readily enough to "Faustus and Helen"; though Crane's poem is less a parable, with distinctive narrative ingredients, than a prayerful meditation. The search of Endymion ("the human soul, the poet, or the poetic imagination," in the words of W. J. Bate) [1] for Cynthia, the moon-goddess and representative of ideal beauty in Keats's poem is to a telling extent re-enacted in the search of Crane's Faustus ("the symbol of himself, the poetic and imaginative man of all times," as Crane explained) for Helen (the symbol of an "abstract 'sense of beauty' ").

I do not present this fundamental similarity as evidence of poetic influence, though some influence may exist. But what is more striking is the archetypal nature, not only of Crane's

---

[1] *John Keats* (Cambridge, 1963), p. 172. At innumerable points in this magnificent book, what Professor Bate has to say about Keats, his life and his poetry, sheds direct light on the career and poetry of Crane. The parallels are sometimes awesome. I am also indebted to Professor Bate for reminding me of the remark quoted above from Colvin.

poem, but of his poetic development—something that, for me at least, contains an insinuation about *the* poetic career as such, and the phases it seems inevitably to pass through. There are, of course, major differences between Keats and Crane generally, and between *Endymion* and "Faustus and Helen" in particular: differences of idiom and of method, and larger ones of the dialectical movement characteristic of each poet. There are also further deep affinities—especially in the shared idea of the poetic construct, any poetic construct, as an instance (as Crane once put it) of "power in repose" [2]—that I shall want to come back to. Meanwhile, let me simply stress the turning-point—the poetic breakthrough, if you will—comparably achieved by the two poems. For Crane, the turning-point was so radical and complex, and raises so many questions about his technique and his temperament, his habitual procedure and even his "philosophy," that I shall allow myself to linger over "Faustus and Helen" a good deal more than, in another perspective, it might seem to deserve.

Crane apparently hit upon the general notion of his poem in April 1922, when he was still living in Cleveland and working for the advertising firm of Corday and Gross: "inventing metaphors for water heaters and sundry household conveniences" as Horton puts it; a *métier* by no means unrelated to "Faustus and Helen." By the middle of May, he had painfully written a nearly final version of the first twelve lines of Section I; but then, in his usual manner, he abandoned that section and went on to Section II, which he finished with unexpected speed in early June. Returning to the first part, he made (he told Munson on June 18) "a good start on it," but he was beginning to have doubts "about the successful eventuation of the poem as a *whole.*" The doubts persisted. He was able to feel on August 17 that the first part was "about right now" (though the stanza beginning "The earth may glide diaphanous to death" was not added until

September); and he could even show a few lines of Section III ("Corymbulous formations of mechanics" and so on). But six weeks later, he proposed issuing the two completed sections as independent and unconnected poems, the first to be called "For the Marriage of Faustus and Helen," and the second "The Sirens of the Springs of Guilty Song." [3]

As the concluding section came slowly into being, however, the work began to reveal to its author an at least sufficient harmony. "I've just about finished the last part," he remarked on January 20, 1923; and by February 7, he was confidently describing the poem's overall structure to Waldo Frank and pointing out "a few planks of the scaffolding." In short, "Faustus and Helen," like many of Crane's shorter writings, grew out of a curiously haphazard and seemingly piecemeal method of composition. But though there are rough patches along the way, the poem moves—it begins, progresses, and ends—with a kind of splendid clarity. It is the product without question of a shaping power that is at last fully in command, a power that bends the individual sections into a most compelling design.

Crane himself, on the rational level, was not very clear about the nature of that design; and the compositional fits and starts probably reflect a certain gap between a firm imaginative grasp and a degree of rational confusion. I have already remarked that, when Crane erred in his appraisal of his own poems, it was more often than not because he underestimated his achievement. His comments on "Faustus and Helen" and his outlines of it suggest that he never quite realized what he had done. He was enormously excited by the feeling that he was doing, that finally he had done something, very big; and the excitement became almost uncontrollable when Allen Tate and Waldo Frank contended (according to Crane's report) that he had proved himself the greatest American poet then alive with "Faustus and Helen,"

[3] This temporary decision led to grotesque publishing confusion. See Horton, *Hart Crane* (1937), pp. 137ff.

and when Gorham Munson added "the astounding assertion that the poem was the greatest poem written in America since Walt Whitman" (which, by the way, it very well may have been). But while at work on it, he explained glutinously to Munson that his poetic purpose was "to evolve a conscious pseudo-symphonic construction toward an abstract beauty that has not been done before in English." He alluded elsewhere, and more cogently, to the "graduation from the quotidian into the abstract" in Section I, and he implied in his retrospective summary for Frank that Section III ended in a restatement of that same "graduation."

All this is misleading. "Faustus and Helen" is more truly and profoundly Platonic than Crane understood (though I do not mean to suggest any direct Platonic influence, nor, as I shall say, that of any other formal metaphysic). It does indeed move to the rhythm of an ascending dialectic, moves from a poetic definition of the visible and temporal world— as experienced, say, in the Cleveland of 1922—to a vision of a world of timeless beauty. But then, just as in Plato's *Republic* myth the philosopher's mission brings him back down into the dim cave of the actual, so in "Faustus and Helen" the poet and poem turn of necessity downward to confront and to celebrate the here-and-now. "For the Marriage of Faustus and Helen" is not only a prothalamium for the wedding between the poet and ideal beauty; it is also a song for the reconciliation and marriage between two dimensions of existence. Its continuing subject, indeed, is nothing other than the visionary redemption of this actual world; and in this respect it is a vast expansion on the brief thematic hint at the close of "Chaplinesque," when the empty ash can was transformed for an instant into a grail of laughter.

Section I transcends the realm of time, of "bloodshot eyes" and "troubled hands" to conclude in a hymn of "praise" for Helen (ideal beauty) and her realm of "hourless days." But Section III, hence the poem as a whole, ends with a magnificent imperative in which everything that had earlier been transcended is re-entered, accepted, eulogized:

Distinctly praise the years, whose volatile
Blamed bleeding hands extend and thresh the height. . . .

Those first four words deserve to be put into italics. More than anything else Crane ever wrote, they announce his fundamental attitude toward the world man lives in, and his own mature conception of the profession of poetry.

·II·

"Praise" is perhaps the key word in the poem, and "Faustus and Helen" is in one perspective an autobiographical work. It declares the mood of praise that Crane was everywhere voicing in his letters during the months of composition, and that he was erecting into a first principle, even the prime subject, of poetry. It was at this time—over the months in 1922—that Crane turned decisively away from the kind of poetry that he recognized as dominant among his contemporaries: the poetry, as he called it, of "humor and the Dance of Death" (by "humor," meaning Laforguian irony and Eliotic wit). He told Allen Tate to follow the "upward" direction evident in one of Tate's recent poems; and he went on: "Launch into praise" (an obvious early version of the "Faustus" phrase just quoted). "*You* are the one who can give praise an edge and beauty, Allen. You have done so well in a couple of damnations, that I feel confident in you." "I cry for a positive attitude," he exclaimed to Charmion Wiegand in January 1923. "When you see the first two parts of my 'Faustus & Helen' . . . you will see better what I mean."

In March, with "Faustus and Helen" completed and *The Bridge* stirring almost violently in his imagination, Crane wrote Munson that he had "lost the last shreds of philosophical pessimism during the last few months," and that he felt himself "quite fit to become a suitable Pindar for the dawn of the machine age." Remarks like those no doubt sounded

willfully immature to most of Crane's literary colleagues, as
they explored and proclaimed the cultural death that had
visited or was about to visit the waste land of the age. Forty
years later, when one has perhaps been sufficiently exposed
to every mode and degree of "philosophical pessimism,"
such remarks may strike us instead (they strike me) as invigorating and restorative, and as being grounded in a decidedly arguable estimate of the fundamentally hopeful and
praiseworthy condition of things.

They were, of course, grounded as well in more personal
elements. Crane's mood of praise, here as always, emanated
from the simple sense of his own creative capability; he regularly transferred to the external world his alternating confidence and despair about his own abilities. But in the
present case, there was a prior cause for his feeling of immense creative potential. It now appears probable that the
immediate source of Crane's shift of spirit was something
like a mystical seizure—of the sort that, according to his
biographers, Whitman also underwent one morning in the
early 1850's, that led rapidly to the 1855 *Leaves of Grass* and
that Whitman recollected tranquilly in the fifth section of
"Song of Myself":

I mind how once we lay such a transparent summer
                    morning. . . .
Swiftly arose and spread around me the peace and knowledge
                    that pass all the arguments of the
                    earth,
And I know that the hand of God is the promise of my own,
And I know that the spirit of God is the brother of my own,
And that all men ever born are also my brothers, and
                    the women my sisters and lovers,
And that the kelson of the creation is love.

Crane may have had that passage and the experience behind
it in mind when he told Munson, in the letter about "philosophical pessimism," that "I begin to feel myself directly
connected with Whitman . . . in currents that are positively

awesome in their extent and possibilities." Crane's own experience, as he described it, was more purely visionary and egocentric than Whitman's; it was more a matter of the radiated consciousness, and it was less charged than Whitman's with the sense of the human family, of the universal binding power ("kelson"—a line of jointed timbers) of love, and the intimate presence of the Godhead. It soon gave rise, however, to the Whitmanian conviction that, as Crane put it, "in the absolute sense the artist *identifies* with life," and the corrolary belief that "we must somehow touch the clearest veins of eternity flowing through the crowds around us"; to some extent in "Faustus and Helen" and to every extent in *The Bridge,* it led to a passionate search for the Godhead.

The event took place in January or February 1922; and this is Crane's account of it, to Munson, in June of that year:

> Did I tell you of that thrilling experience this last winter in the dentist's chair when under the influence of aether and *amnesia* my mind spiraled to a kind of seventh heaven of consciousness and egoistic dance among the seven spheres—and something like an objective voice kept saying to me—'You have the higher consciousness—you have the higher consciousness. This is something very few have. This is what is called genius'? A happiness, ecstatic such as I have known only twice in 'inspirations' came over me. I felt the two worlds. And at once. As the bore went into my tooth I was able to follow its every revolution as detached as a spectator at a funeral. O Gorham, I have known moments in eternity. I tell you this as one who is a brother. . . . Today I have made a good start on the first part of 'Faustus and Helen.'

"I felt the two worlds. And at once." This experience stimulated by anaesthetic, Crane later sought to repeat through the stimulus of alcohol—and not, as it seems, altogether ill-advisedly. Philip Horton, in his fine discussion of this aspect of Crane, quotes William James on the power of alcohol to arouse man's "mystical faculties": "Sobriety diminishes, discriminates, and says no; drunkenness expands, unites and says yeas. It is in fact the great exciter of the Yes function in man."

It is also, of course, an exciter of the negative function and can arouse man's pugnacious and destructive faculties as well as his mystical ones. On the whole, though, it did intensify Crane's yea-saying impulse, for a number of years anyhow; even if Crane might have pondered Emerson's admonition on the subject. In "The Poet," Emerson, after citing the ancient belief that the poet writes "not with the intellect alone but with the intellect inebriated by nectar" and after observing that "this is the reason why bards love wine, mead, narcotics, coffee, tea, opium, the fumes of sandalwood and tobacco," goes on to argue that "never can advantage be taken of nature by a trick," and reminds us of Milton's saying that "the lyric poet may drink wine and live generously; but the epic poet, he who shall sing of the gods and their descent into men, must drink water out of a wooden bowl."

But the new or visionary quality in "Faustus and Helen" and the poems that followed it was not only the result of a mystical experience and the product of an "intellect inebriated by nectar." It also reflected Crane's growing escape from his artistic bondage to T. S. Eliot and Laforgue. Crane's relation to Eliot was both contradictory and continuing. He once said that he had read "Prufrock" twenty-five times, "and things like 'Preludes' more often"; after an initial disappointment with *The Waste Land,* he went on, as he acknowledged, "to read and re-read" it incessantly; *The Bridge,* conceived in part as an answer to *The Waste Land,* echoes it at several turns. But at a relatively early stage, Crane sensed a fundamental difference between Eliot and himself, an urgency to escape from Eliot's "overwhelming question" and the Prufrockian and waste-land moods that characterized Eliot's poetry in those years. It was something more than the ambitious restiveness of a somewhat younger generation, though it partook of that. Crane put it as honestly as he knew how in a letter to Munson, in January 1923, when "Faustus and Helen" was nearly done. The passages have been quoted frequently, but they should be placed in context here:

You already know, I think, that my work for the past two years (those meagre drops!) has been more influenced by Eliot than any other modern. . . . There is no one writing in English who can command so much respect, to my mind, as Eliot. However, I take Eliot as a point of departure toward an almost complete reversal of direction. His pessimism is amply justified, in his own case. But I would apply as much of his erudition and technique as I can absorb and assemble toward a more positive, or (if [I] must put it so in a skeptical age) ecstatic goal. I should not think of this if a kind of rhythm and ecstasy were not (at odd moments and rare!) a very real thing to me. I feel that Eliot ignored certain spiritual events and possibilities as real and powerful now as, say, in the time of Blake. Certainly the man has dug the ground and buried hope as deep and direfully as it can ever be done. He has outclassed Baudelaire with a devasting humor that the earlier poet lacked.

After this perfection of death—nothing is possible in motion but a resurrection of some kind. Or else, as everyone persists in announcing in the deep and dirgeful *Dial,* the fruits of civilization are entirely harvested. Everyone, of course, wants to die as soon and painlessly as possible. Now is the time for humor, and the Dance of Death. All I know through very much suffering and dullness (somehow I seem to twinge more all the time) is that it interests me to still affirm certain things. That will be the persisting theme of the last part of "F & H" as it has been all along.

The moments of joy were, as we see, odd and rare, punctuation marks in periods of "very much suffering." But Crane's chief assertion—that "nothing is possible in motion but a resurrection of some kind"—should no more be attributed to sheer personal temperament than the death-consciousness that it repudiates and that Crane was perfectly willing to assume to be "a very real thing" for Eliot. At this moment, in fact, Crane was not making a statement primarily of personal inclination, but a prediction of sorts about an inevitable curve in cultural attitude and literary expression—toward a freshened awareness of "certain spiritual events and possibilities." In his own generation, it was Crane himself who followed such a curve.

He did so in part, as the passage hints, by shifting his poetic allegiance from Eliot to William Blake: though not at all the Blake whose essential failure—because he lacked "a framework of accepted and traditional ideas"—Eliot had regretfully made public in a brief essay of 1920. It was much rather the poet Crane encountered, in September 1922, in S. Foster Damon's impressive critical study *William Blake: his Philosophy and Symbols.* Crane had apparently begun to read Blake as early as 1917—"You know how much Blake has always interested me," he said to Munson, in commenting on Damon's book.[4] But in the latter, by which Crane confessed he was "especially thrilled," Crane could find the poetry he had been looking for: a supreme example of the visionary imagination, and poetry which looked at once into and through the immediate and visible world; highly personal poetry in a highly personal idiom which at the same time projected a majestically hopeful myth of world history.

·III·

Affirmation was indeed "the persisting theme" of "Faustus and Helen." Yet paradoxically the affirmative impulse was

---

[4] Horton writes that Mrs. Crane gave her son "the works of William Blake in the summer of 1917"; Horton, *op.cit.,* p. 49. It seems impossible to determine just what edition and versions of Blake's poetry Crane owned or had access to. In connection with several of Crane's visionary lyrics and even more with *The Bridge,* one would like to know how much of Blake's "prophetic books" Crane had the opportunity to read.

almost undermined in advance by devices at the start of the poem that reflected Eliot's continuing influence. The point is worth laboring a little. Crane had not fully perceived the way in which Eliot's "erudition and technique" were inseparable from that very sense of cultural and spiritual decay that Crane was bent on denying, that they had been developed to convey that sense and could not readily be applied "toward an opposite goal." In another letter of this period, Crane accused Eliot of believing that "happiness and beauty dwell only in memory." This was of course a serious reduction of Eliot's attitude (though we remember that he was talking about the Eliot prior to "Marina" and "Ash Wednesday"); even so, Crane could not have altogether grasped the fact that Eliot's erudite quoting from the great literature of the past was a technique for suggesting, by ironic juxtaposition, some portion of that belief. If he had, he would not have begun his anti-Eliotic hymn of praise to the present world with so Eliotic a gesture—a title that recalls Marlowe's *Doctor Faustus* and a long quotation from Ben Jonson's *The Alchemist,* items which seem at first glance to pose a familiar ironic comparison between past splendor and present degradation.

As to the figures named in the title, once he had selected them, as Brom Weber remarks, "Crane redeemed himself by immediately disregarding them." There are few if any vibrations of Marlowe in the poem; and Faustus and Helen are, in Crane's explanation to Frank, "the symbol of myself, the poetic and imaginative man of all times," and the symbol of an "abstract 'sense of beauty.'" A careful reading of Scene XIII in *Doctor Faustus,* where Helen is magically conjured up, would only muddle the reader of Crane's poem; far from wanting to offer Helen "one inconspicuous orb of praise," as Crane's Faustus does, Marlowe's wants the lady to be his paramour and finds heaven in her thoroughly physical embraces. The epigraph (from *The Alchemist,* IV, 5) is more bothersome yet.

> And so we may arrive by Talmud skill
> And profane Greek to raise the building up
> Of Helen's house against the Ismaelite

and so on for five more lines packed with names of Old Testament figures and Biblical exegetes. A number of ingenious explanations suggest themselves, both of the relevance of the Jonson passage and the effect it produces when conjoined with the titular reference to Marlowe. But the fact is that the Jonson passage is pure Jabberwocky. In the play, it is spoken by Dol Common, a lively whore with a talent for chicanery, who is pretending to a religious fit as part of a scheme to gull Sir Epicure Mammon, a gentleman of awe-inspiring erotic fancy. The confusion is compounded: for the Jonsonian scene is a flamboyant parody of the meeting between Faustus and Helen in Marlowe's play. Crane thus confronts us with a bewildering complex of ironies as headnotes to a poem the whole drive of which is to get beyond irony.[5]

The poem itself is more self-sufficient and less devious than those headnotes might lead one to expect. Its initial difficulty is due in part to a language that is often doing several things at once, and sometimes pointing in more than one direction at a time. Then, too, there is the poem's structural method, what Joseph Frank might call its "spatial form"—whereby the full import of a word or phrase is bestowed retroactively by the later appearance of a nourishingly correlative or a suggestively opposite word or phrase. "The baked and labeled dough" in the poem's second

[5] Crane may have kept the lines for their rhetorical exuberance; it was Jonson's "verbal richness" that Crane most admired when he began to read him in the fall of 1921. For the rest, the satirical nature of the Jonson play undercuts any theory one might concoct—about the joint image of the poet as magician-alchemist, for example (in "Faustus and Helen," the poet is not a conjurer anyhow, but a spiritual seeker); the two references to Helen; the combination of religious and secular knowledge, "Talmud skill" and "profane Greek"; the hints about some secret, ancient, universal language, and so on.

line, for example, must wait thirty lines for "the white wafer cheek of love" to give it final meaning (an image of spiritual flabbiness)—even though mental doughiness is conveyed at once, and even though the immediate context invests "dough" with its slang meaning of money (hence an image of the money-grubbing temper).

All this has to do with what Crane, several years later, would call "the logic of metaphor" and would describe as "the so-called illogical impingements of the connotations of words on the consciousness," and the "combinations and interplay" of such connotations "in metaphor." In Section I of "Faustus and Helen," metaphor is the transporting agent on the journey enacted from this everyday world to a world of absolute beauty. If we let our logical faculty relax for a while, and if we permit the connotations of the words in the opening stanzas to impinge freely on our consciousness and to combine and interact—what we will then experience is the poetic creation of a world: this world.

It is a world which is crowded and confused (multitudes, stacked, numbers, crowd) but where relationship is lacking (divided, partitioned; by later implication, fragmentary). Its voice is vulgar and contradictory ("Smutty wings flash out equivocations"); its spirit is dully unchanging, back-ward-looking, cliché-ridden (accepted, memoranda, stock quotations). It is, in fact, a world that has become one huge stock market; or better, a world that Crane's poetry skillfully transforms into a huge stock market, as the business-office references to stacked partitions, memoranda, and stenographic smiles lead into the Wall Street idiom, to stock quotations (a phrase which does double duty), num-bers, margins, curbs, and corners. This is Crane's original way of releasing a large historical insight. Contemporary America has become a stock-market culture, and in "Faustus and Helen I" we see the process in action.

The movement from that world to the realm of Helen is not abrupt; it is rather, in Crane's phrase, a steady "graduation from the quotidian." Even in the thick of the quotidian, the mind, normally assailed by equivocations of smutty wings, sometimes feels itself "brushed by sparrow wings"; the imagination stirs to those "spiritual events and possibilities" that Crane spoke of to Munson. Such higher possibilities are "rebuffed" from the main walks of life; they inhabit the margins of life, its curbs and corners (those otherwise Wall Street words likewise doing double duty).[6] And in the evening, they retreat—and we follow them in imagination—into a place ("somewhere") that, though not yet Helen's world, is a partial version of it, a promise and an indication. It is "virginal perhaps" rather than smutty; if not integral, it is "less fragmentary" than the partitioned and divided setting of the usual day; as against the "baked" feeling of the asphalt world, this evening world is "cool." And from its vantage point, the journeying spirit can catch a glimpse of the home of ideal beauty:

There is the world dimensional for
those untwisted by the love of things
irreconcilable.

I hear a slight stress on the word "there." "*There* is the world I seek, that other dimension of experience that is accessible to anyone not wedded to the equivocal, not committed to unresolvable conflict as the truth of life and thought; to anyone who does not find irony to be the one true mode of expression."

·IV·

The lines about "the world dimensional" are sometimes cited as evidence of the sizable influence upon "Faustus

[6] In *A Defense of Reason,* Yvor Winters reports that he had first taken the word "numbers" to refer to the faceless abstractions of modern life; but that his final reading has the word referring back to the sparrow wings. I see no reason not to accept both readings; here (as with the word "obsequies" in "Chaplinesque") more than one context gives more than one meaning to a word.

and Helen" (and perhaps on the lyrics that followed) of *Tertium Organum,* a turgid work of mystical philosophy by the Russian speculator, P. D. Ouspensky. The claim seems to me improbable, on both particular and general grounds. *Tertium Organum,* which became available in America in 1920, was undoubtedly fashionable in some American literary circles in the early 1920's and inter-mittently thereafter. But for one thing, most of the sentence just quoted was as we remember composed early in 1921 as part of a grab-bag poem, "The Bridge of Estador"; and this was apparently some time before Crane had heard of Ouspensky's book, even if we accept Weber's conclusion that Crane had the book in his hands "before the end of 1921 at the very latest, if not earlier." The best evidence is that *Tertium Organum* was on Crane's shelf in late 1921 and that Crane glanced at it, as one does, but that he did not really look into it for more than a year. It was not until mid-February of 1923—when "Faustus and Helen" was finished—that Crane wrote Tate: "I have also enjoyed reading Ouspensky's *Tertium Organum* lately." I see no reason not to take Crane's subsequent statement literally: namely that Ouspensky's "corroboration of several experi-ences in consciousness that I have had gave it particular interest." "Corroboration" sounds like the right word: and of personal experiences, one assumes, like that undergone in the dentist's chair when Crane "felt the two worlds. And at once."

In Philip Horton's deft summary, Ouspensky's "concep-tion of the spiritual decay of humanity under two centuries of scientific materialism and the imminent emergence of a new order of consciousness," along with his "view of art as the beginning of wisdom and the artist as visionary"— all this could appeal mightily to Crane and to the New York friends upon whom he later urged a reading of Ouspensky. But Crane's own enthusiasm was short lived. When those same friends went on to adopt the bizarre discipline of the Ouspenskyite Gurdjieff, who brought his mystical and conversionary dances to America in 1924, Crane signed off at once. He found the "Hindu antics" ridiculous, and he withdrew from the whole business so completely that his friends became, as he would recall, "hermetically sealed to my eyesight," while he himself was left by them "to roll in the gutter of my ancient predispositions." Crane's most important dispositions were always toward poetry, and not to mystical flailings nor to any mode of philosophizing, however he might be momentarily diverted by the splurging arguments of an Ouspensky.

The important fact is that there was virtually nothing in *Tertium Organum* that Crane could not find—had not already found—in the poetry of William Blake, or in Blake's younger Romantic contemporaries, or in Whitman or (expressed yet more suitably for his purpose, as I shall argue) in Emerson.[7] Blake can stand, here, for that entire tradition, and one reason for quoting Horton's summary of Ouspensky is that it applies so well to Blake—in Crane's phrase, Ouspensky "corroborates" Blake. The purpose that came into view with "Faustus and Helen" was defined by Crane, in April 1923, by means of a quotation from Blake's *Jerusalem* (from "To the Christians"). Crane had been talking about how one might arrive at a knowledge of "the essence of things," when such essences are not to be found in the physical mass and bulk of things, but "are suspended on the invisible dimension." We get at them, Crane proposed, in the manner recommended by Blake:

> I give you the end of a golden string
> Only wind it into a ball,—
> It will lead you in at Heaven's gate,
> Built in Jerusalem's wall.

[7] See Chapter Eight, below. I do not want to be misleading: if Crane had clearly read in Blake, Wordsworth, Keats, Shelley, and Whitman by the time he wrote "Faustus and Helen," he had almost as clearly read very little of Emerson.

This is the way of poetry, and it indicates the way of the criticism of poetry: which must re-wind the "golden string" of metaphoric language, and so follow the imagination into its own heavenly kingdom. But it is not the way of philosophy, and here is the nub of the more general issue.

Crane, as he insisted time and again, was simply not responsive to systematic philosophic thought, not versed in it or attracted by it; and he did not regard the articulation of philosophic thought as any part of the poet's function. To those who either demanded that he acquire a metaphysic or who imputed one to his writings, Crane tended to reply, as he did with much cheerful pugnacity to Yvor Winters, after Winters' review of *White Buildings:*

> If you knew how little of a metaphysician I am in the scholastic sense of the term, you would scarcely attribute such conscious method to my poems (with regard to that element) as you do. I am an utter ignoramus in that whole subject, have never read Kant, Descartes, or other doctors. It's all an accident as far as my style goes.

That was in May 1927. A year before, Crane, in a letter to Munson, had made an ambitious effort to state his theory of the relation between poetry and knowledge. "In so far as the metaphysics of any absolute knowledge extends," he wrote, "poetry . . . is simply the concrete *evidence* of the *experience* of a recognition (*knowledge,* if you like)." Poetry, he went on, "can give you a *ratio* of fact and experience, and in this sense it is both perception and the thing perceived." That is to say: it can be both the fact, whatever the fact might be—let us say, the existence of God—and the concretely expressed experience of that fact. Crane felt that one should not ask more of poetry than a ratio of that kind. One should not ask the poet to confront directly the problem of God's existence. Poetry does not "logically enunciate such a problem or its solution"; it gives instead "the real connective experience, the very 'sign manifest' on which rests the assumption of a godhead."

Granted such views and intentions, Crane did not pore often or late over volumes of philosophy. He did read the *Dialogues* of Plato, probably more thoughtfully and carefully than any other philosophic writing. What he honored in Plato was "the architecture of his logic," the "harmonious relationship" of his statements "to each other." "This grace," he said, "partakes of poetry." [8] But for Plato, Crane pointed out, grace was subordinate to rational inquiry, and even, for example, Socrates' demonstration of the dialectical ascent to beauty was a rational excursion and not transferable to poetry; he felt that Plato was quite right, in his own view, to banish the poets from the republic. For the rest, Crane shows only peripheral and temporary contacts with unsystematic or "poetic" fragments of philosophizing: a brief, minor interest in Ouspensky; something of Nietzsche but not much (bits of *The Birth of Tragedy* drift in the neighborhood of "Faustus and Helen III" and Lachrymae Christi"); [9] conceivably some pages of William James. Some sort of philosophical and theological scheme may and very likely should be used (with tact) to illuminate Crane's poetry, as long as it is remembered that Crane's poetry was not composed to illuminate *it*. For real sustenance, Crane went not to philosophy or theology but to poetry; not to the work of the intellect but to the work of the imagination —earlier evidence of *"the experience* of a recognition."

What was being recognized, in Crane's case, was not only a timeless reality, but the connection between such a reality and the temporal world. From "Faustus and Helen" on, Crane's poems were what he called them: "connective experiences," the experience being visionary and the connections being established by the resources of poetry. If this

[8] *Letters,* p. 238 (March 17, 1926).
[9] In the April-May 1918 issue of *The Pagan,* Crane published a little defense of Nietzsche against the charge of being the founder of "Prussianism" (Weber, *Hart Crane,* pp. 401-402). L. S. Denbo, in *Hart Crane's Sanskrit Charge,* pp. 12-14, finds a more sizable element of Nietzsche in Crane's poetry than I do.

were what people meant by "metaphysical poetry," Crane was willing to accept the label. In the letter to Winters, Crane said:

> Since I have been "located" in this category by a number of people, I may as well go on alluding to certain (what are also called) metaphysical passages in Donne, Blake, Vaughan, etc., as being of particular appeal to me on a basis of common characteristics with what I like to do in my own poems, however little scientific knowledge of the subject I may have.

With poets like "Donne, Blake, Vaughan, etc."—to whom one can add Keats, Shelley, Melville, Whitman, and one or two others—Crane in part intuited an existing tradition, and in part created a tradition with which he could affiliate. In drawing upon that tradition, Crane inevitably drew upon some of the philosophical ingredients—primarily a loose and shifting Platonistic strain—reflected in it: but it was always the poetry that affected him.

This is something one may admire, regret, or simply observe. In our time, when intellectual systems are in such great and serious demand, the absence of a solid conceptual framework behind Crane's poetry has been unduly regretted, while the presence of a potent and resourceful poetic tradition has been insufficiently observed. I suspect that the majority of poets have proceeded pretty much the way Crane did, and have found their bearings in earlier poetry rather than in formal philosophy or theology. There is much to be said for Northrup Frye's flat contention that no poet ever, really, "takes over" a ready-made system of ideas; [10] though it goes without saying that some poets are born into a luckier culture than others. But we may have been misled by the immeasurably influential example of T. S. Eliot, who visited upon other poets and upon a whole generation of readers a profound and thoroughly valid belief in his

[10] In "Wallace Stevens: the Realistic Oriole," *Fables of Identity* (1963).

personal requirement of an orderly intellectual scheme wherewith to assess in poetry the "futility and anarchy" of the age. For Crane, in any event, there was coherence enough for *his* needs in the tradition of visionary poetry.

· V ·

The reference to "the world dimensional" in "Faustus and Helen I" is followed by an image of the poet, coming home of an evening in a streetcar, suddenly envisioning Helen "across the aisle." "The street car device," Crane told Frank, "is the most concrete symbol I could find for the transition of the imagination from quotidian details to the universal consideration of beauty—the body still 'centered in traffic,' the imagination eluding its daily nets and self consciousness." But the symbol is unsatisfactory. The phrase "lost yet poised in traffic" is enough to define an incipient vision, with "traffic" reinforcing the implications of "stacked" and "multitudes"; the streetcar, as an *actual* means of transportation, is a rhetorical confusion. The transition desired is better effected by the contrasts that begin to burgeon and intertwine: contrasts involving Helen's physical aspects taken as symbols; her smile, her eyes, her hands, her body. Helen's "half-riant" expression (an unlucky Whitmanism) replaces the artificial "stenographic smiles" of stanza one. Her "eyes across the aisle" flicker with "prefigurations," as against the "million brittle, bloodshot eyes" of the finite world; and, also as against that mob of eyes, the poet will bend upon Helen "a lone eye. . . . One inconspicuous glowing orb of praise"—a lone eye, perhaps, because the other eye remains fixed upon the lower realm.[11] The hands of Helen contrast with the "troubled hands" that

---

[11] Horton (*op.cit.,* pp. 115-16) tells of Crane's interest in Jacob Boehme's theory that with the true mystic the right eye "looks forward into eternity while the left eye looks backward into time." Crane's friend Lescaze had made a sketch of Crane which gave a similar impression.

press toward her; and her body is seen in a moment of ecstatic sexual sublimation above "the body of the world" as it weeps in the dust.

In short, as the vision of Helen comes into view, the actual world reveals by contrast its qualities of ugliness and desperation. For now it is morally and spiritually measured ("counted") by the emerging figure of Helen. Now her hands can

> count the nights
> Stippled with pink and green advertisements.

So measured, the world of offices and finance, later of "steel and soil," appears shrouded in a darkness lit only by advertising signs. It appears troubled; it is morally compromised and psychically wounded ("this bartered blood"). It is fallen and anguished:

> the body of the world
> Weeps in inventive dust for the hiatus
> That winks above it, bluet in your breasts.

The world's body weeps because, in the hiatus between Helen's breasts that winks far above the world, it recognizes the hiatus between the actual and the ideal—and longs to close the hiatus through love. It recognizes, too, the remote but complete experience of love Helen herself is undergoing, as her own body seems exalted in a sort of celestial orgasm:

> Reflective conversion of all things
> At your deep blush, when ecstasies thread
> The limbs and belly, when rainbows spread
> Impinging on the throat and sides.

In the compact summary of "Faustus and Helen" which Crane sent Munson in January 1923, he indicated that this is the phase of "Love" in the first section, following those of "Meditation" and "Evocation" and leading to the final phase of "Beauty." Helen has undoubtedly become a figure of intense love-in-action, and of a love that transforms reality; yet such concrete eroticism may seem to accord ill with the ideal and hence presumably bodiless or at least virginally pure figure the poem is moving toward. But Crane has not lost his poetic way. For one thing, the goddess who moves in and out of "Faustus and Helen" is a recognizably traditional being; she resembles, for example, the goddess in Keats's *Endymion,* as Harold Bloom has described her: a "contrary Goddess . . . both virginal and wanton"; [12] a figure, in short, who corresponds to the inseparable and contradictory desires of man. In "Faustus and Helen I," there is even a hint of carnal frivolity about her. The verb "winks"—following "half-riant" and in contrast with "weeps"—startlingly suggests the erotic mockery which, in "Voyages II," the god-like and moonward-bending sea (that "great wink of eternity") would direct upon the limitations of human love. For another thing, it is a significant part of Crane's intention to body forth the ideal in terms of the actual: in order to accomplish a "reflective conversion" of the actual; in order to establish by means of poetry the organic continuity and connection between the two dimensions. The contrasts we have been noting are in fact the elements that must eventually be connected or married; this is the very point and aim of "Faustus and Helen." In Section II of the poem, it is the wanton goddess who is celebrated; here, in the final stanzas of Section I, we move on and upward beyond "Love" to "Beauty" to observe and praise the pure and distant figure ("you who turned away once, Helen"). But finally, Crane wants to suggest that the two divinities are parts of a single being; he wants to present the evidence of experiencing "the two worlds. And at once."

The troubled and bleeding body of the actual world appears to be dying ("The earth may glide diaphanous to death"). The poet—climbing through metaphor, and by means of the poetic "inventions" discovered in the "dust" of the actual and indeed (for Crane) only to be discovered

[12] *The Visionary Company* (New York, 1962), p. 360.

within that fallen sphere—transcends the dust and the blood
to enter the domain of Helen. Here, unlike the crowded
quotidian world with its multitudes and numbers and bloodshot eyes, is a "world which comes to each of us alone"; here
in this white world, having passed from the dark, congested
human city through a series of "white cities" (moments in
the graduation toward ideal beauty), the poet finds a place
beyond time ("hourless days") and change ("continuous").
But just as Helen herself had been described in resonantly
physical detail (breasts, limbs, belly, throat, sides), so her
remote realm and the poet's reverential experience of it are
described in language borrowed from the lower world of
"steel and soil" so ardously transcended—in terms of planes,
axles, and companion ways. Helen's city is, as it were, the
factories of heaven: or it is made to seem so by the art of
Crane's poetry. The effect of that art is, in the poetic sense,
to redeem the fallen world; not, finally, to transcend and
abandon it, but—before "Faustus and Helen" is through—to
find the means of praising it; in one of the oldest and greatest
of theological formulae, not to destroy it but to perfect it.

·VI·

The process continues spiritedly in Section II. Here the
fallen world is explored—not as a domain of tears and death,
but of dance and laughter; if not a world redeemed, at least
a world redeemable. The very act of falling appears as a
necessary adventure; and the presiding goddess is "The siren
of the springs of guilty song." By paying homage to that
charming wanton, the poem learns to smile at the human
and fleshly frailties which she represents and the sense of
guilt is exorcized, the "groans of death" silenced, by song itself. The world is, so to speak, being made ready by poetry
for the poetic grace it will receive in the final section.

This middle portion of the poem is more closely related
to the whole of "Faustus and Helen" than Crane under-

stood, and it develops in a way rather different than he implied. In "General Aims and Theories" of 1925,[13] Crane made much of his intention in "Faustus and Helen" to "embody . . . a contemporary approximation to an ancient human culture or mythology," and to build "a bridge between so-called classic experience" and the "confused cosmos of today, which has no formulated mythology yet for classic poetic reference or for religious exploitation." As examples of these approximations and bridgings and as part of an effort to recapture in modern terms what he called the Greek idea of beauty, Crane said that he "found 'Helen' sitting in a street-car; the Dionysian revels of her court and her seduction were transferred" (in Section II) "to a Metropolitan roof garden with a jazz orchestra" and so on.[14] This sounds as though Crane were fuzzily attempting to borrow Eliot's technique of bringing "classic experience" and mythology to bear upon the confused modern cosmos; but Crane's comments on this occasion shed more darkness than light. Homer's Helen, for example, did not indulge in Dionysian revels, either in Sparta or in Troy; perhaps Crane was thinking vaguely of Shakespeare's Helen in *Troilus and Cressida,* a young woman decidely fond of revelling. Homer and Greek culture generally contribute no more to Section II than Marlowe does to the poem as a whole. Section II announces itself not by Eliotic usages of ancient myth but through the immediate energy and collision of its imagery.

The scene is indeed a metropolitan roof garden, where brass instruments glitter and resound hypnotically ("Brazen

[13] Notes about his theory and practice of poetry prepared by Crane for use by Eugene O'Neill, who at the time was expected to write an introduction to *White Buildings.* The notes were not published until Philip Horton included them as an appendix to his biography.

[14] In the same vein, Crane insisted to Waldo Frank that Section I contained symbolic echoes of Homer and "the rape of Helen by Paris." He may have had in mind the lines about "that eventual flame / You found in final chains, no captive then." I make little of those lines, apart from their strained paradox; and less when I think about Paris and Helen.

hypnotics glitter") and humans dance with gay abandon ("Glee shifts from foot to foot").

> This crashing opéra bouffe,
> Blest excursion! this ricochet
> From roof to roof.

This was the feel and tempo of Crane's own life at one time: "the old bivouacs of New York days," as he recalled them to Munson in January 1923, "when I ricochet-ed 'from roof to roof' without intermission." More largely, it was the way human life itself felt to Crane at this time: a dance, and not a Dance of Death, but a dance of joyful life. He wrote Tate while at work on Section II, "Perhaps it is useless, perhaps it is silly,—but one *does* have joys." As earlier he had testified to the difficulty of expressing any strong personal emotion at all at a time when critical fashion favored the resolutely impersonal, so now he acknowledged the problem of expressing the experience of joy. "The vocabulary of damnations and prostrations has been developed at the expense of these other modes . . . it is hard to dance in proper measure." Crane's dance motif would reach its turbulent climax in the summer of 1926, when, feeling that he was "dancing on dynamite," he composed the portion of *The Bridge* called "The Dance."

Here, in "Faustus and Helen," as he said to Tate, he was aiming mainly at "an idiom for the proper transposition of Jazz into words! Something clean, sparkling, elusive!" The idiom in Section II sparkles and eludes, though it is not what is normally meant by "clean" as applied to poetic language (stripped, uncluttered, pure); and it is jazzy only as language can be jazzy but not as jazz is jazzy. Crane's efforts to contrive verbal analogues of jazz were usually, as here, unsatisfactory. But this is not to say that the swift and bouncing rhythms of Section II, leading as they do into the more assertive movement of the final stanzas, are not in their own way arresting. They serve very well as the musical vehicle of Crane's statement about fallen man.

In an unattractive but poetically justified image at the end of the first stanza, we hear that "nigger cupids scour the stars." The Negro jazz musicians thus function as exciters of love: but of the erotic love proper to *this* world and not of the "white wafer cheek of love" touched in Section I; Cupid, as Crane might surprise us by knowing, was the Roman version of Greek Eros.[15] And as the dance, the stormy music ("snarling hails of melody"), the exuberant horseplay ("Rhythmic ellipses lead into canters") continue through the long night ("Until somewhere a rooster banters")—the poem begins to establish its attitude toward that kind of love and this kind of world. In a frame of mind at once innocent and daring, Crane issues his invitation to join him in yielding to temptation:

> Greet naively—yet intrepidly
> New soothings, new amazements
> That cornets introduce at every turn—
> And you may fall downstairs with me
> With perfect grace and equanimity.

It is an invitation to sin with grace; to fall morally and to fall hard and far (from the roof to the bottom of the stairs) without quite losing one's moral balance, or one's sense of humor. There follows the parallel invitation to take the moral plunge into the dangerous waters of experience, while the more cautious sit at home on dry land, safely law-abiding:

> Or, plaintively scud past shores
> Where, by strange harmonic laws
> All relatives, serene and cool,
> Sit rocked in patent armchairs.[16]

[15] He so appears in *Aeneid I,* which Crane had almost undoubtedly read.

[16] The image of the daring life (poetically daring) as a risking of the open sea is a familiar one. In a letter to James Hessey, in October 1818, Keats remarked, in language which Crane's passage approximates, that: "In Endymion, I leaped headlong into the Sea, and

The relatives (I assume a pun here: both uncles and aunts, those symbols of the super-ego, *and* something opposite to the absolute nature of Crane's thrust into life) are serene and cool; but it is a false kind of coolness, not a coolness beyond heat as in Section I but an absence of heat. The laws they live by look strange from the point of view of the dancing or the plunging life; shortly, in Section III, that rocking-chair existence will appear as an unending "meagre penance." Crane thus announces his attitude toward the life of conventional and self-protective piety. In so doing, he presents his exhilarated version of "the fortunate fall"—that notion so central to the American literary tradition: namely, that what orthodox morality regards as sinful conduct and a re-enactment of the Fall of Man is in fact the necessary and hence the fortunate experience that begets genuine human maturity.[17] And like Henry James Senior, who gave one of the most vigorous accounts of the fortunate fall and who also (like Crane) found eloquent support for his convictions in William Blake, Crane very rapidly dissociates himself from those who, obsessed with man's fallen condition, saw in it only a condition of death:

> While titters hailed the groans of death
> Beneath gyrating awnings I have seen
> The incunabula of the divine grotesque.
> This music has a reassuring way.

This music, the kind Crane is composing and celebrating, is reassuring—by contrast precisely with the other sounds Crane had been hearing, the mournful music of the "poetry

---

thereby have become better acquainted with the Soundings, the quicksands, & the rocks, than if I had stayed upon the green shore, and piped a silly pipe, and took tea & comfortable advice." In Section 46 of "Song of Myself," Whitman urged on his companion with the lines: "Long have you timidly waded holding a plank by the shore, / Now I will you to be a bold swimmer, / To jump off in the midst of the sea. . . ."

[17] I have traced part of this tradition in *The American Adam* (Chicago, 1955).

of damnation" as he had called it, or the ironic music of "humor and the Dance of Death," a definition exactly parallel to the first of the lines just quoted. This life-affirming music is as remote from the death-dance as the smiles of the youthful goddess—in the final stanza—are from the ironic "titters" that Crane unfairly attributed to some of his contemporaries. While the latter, Crane contends, were greeting the death of culture with elegant wit, he himself in the excitement of his dance ("Beneath gyrating awnings") caught the first traces and manifestations ("incunabula") of an unorthodox goddess ("the divine grotesque").

It is this goddess ("still so young"), this delightful temptation to moral danger (this "siren of the springs of guilty song") that is smiled upon and taken to heart in the closing lines of Section II. In accepting her, "we" are accepting our own fallen condition:

> Let us take her on the incandescent wax
> Striated with nuances, nervosities
> That we are heir to: she is still so young,
> We cannot frown upon her as she smiles.

"Striated" means striped or streaked. There is something here of the moral sympathy Crane would direct toward the denizens of "The Wine Menagerie": "poor streaked bodies wreathing up and out";[18] streaked or striated was Crane's way of suggesting moral taintedness, like Eliot's "maculate," spotted. But it is a taintedness that Crane accepts. The siren's guilty song will be played upon the streaked or grooved and ardent human phonograph ("the incandescent wax"—an image related to the later one in "The Tunnel"—"The phonographs of hades in the brain"). It is a song for human life to dance to; it will lighten and alleviate the shadings and anxieties, the frailties we inherit as human beings. As the goddess of our frailties is thus evoked, as in metaphor

[18] Compare also "New soothings, new amazements" in "Faustus and Helen II" with the more fertile line in "The Wine Menagerie"— "New thresholds, new anatomies!"

she wings her way across "the gardened skies," Crane completes the first account of his maturing attitude toward the fallen world.

·VII·

In Section II, the element of guilt in the guilty song is exorcized (as I have said) by the sheer intensity of song itself; as though Crane were elaborating in advance the brief credo—his essential credo about the celebrational nature of life and poetry—he would put forward two years later in "Lachrimae Christi":

> Not penitence
> But song. . . .

In the concluding stanzas of "Faustus and Helen," the song swells into a music as powerful as any in modern poetry. But during much of Section III, the movement is alternately heavy, portentous, and jumpy. The imagination has to work through an acknowledgment of tragedy, a memory of war, an awareness of massive destruction, before it can arrive at the hymn of praise—and praise very "distinctly" of this ravaged world—that it longs to utter. Crane was right to reduce the pace of the final section, as he had originally planned it. "I shall not attempt to make it the paragon of SPEED that I thought of," he informed Munson in August 1922; "I think it needs more sheer weight than such a motive would provide"; and Section III, for all its climactic ecstasy is notably weightier than the preceding sections. Crane said later about the second section that it was "a sensual culmination," and so it was. But in retrospect, that dancing excitement was obviously not a culmination on anything *but* the sensual level. Here, as in *The Bridge,* Crane's imagination refused to jump prematurely to the phase of final rejoicing. Other and much more sombre realities had to be faced before the world of time could be truly and persuasively celebrated; and other connections had to be made.

Death, and death on an enormous scale, was a fact of recent history in 1922; tragedy of an immense scope was a very real event; no poet attempting to write responsibly could evade those matters or content himself with making fun of the death-consciousness they had caused. Crane's personal knowledge of the First World War had been restricted to a short hitch in a Cleveland munition plant; and he was too young, his life had been too provincial, and his education too limited for him to participate in the vast vision of cultural disaster shared by Eliot and others. He could only work with what he knew and what he had. "Faustus and Helen III" is a valiant effort to examine the grounds of Eliot's "philosophic pessimism," and to give expression to the widely different judgment of history and human possibility that Crane nonetheless held.

As Crane attempts to squeeze such broadly ranging considerations into a relatively small poetic space and into his own congenitally tucked-in idiom, the poetry grows exceedingly complex; though the central development is magnificently clear—the irresistible drive of "the imagination . . . beyond despair." "It is so packed with tangential slants, interwoven symbolisms," Crane told Munson, "that I'm not sure whether or not it will [be] understood." He presented the following little chart of the section: "Tragedy, War (the eternal soldier), Résumé, Ecstasy, Final Declaration," and we can usefully take those words as the titles respectively of the first; the second and third; the fourth; the fifth and sixth; and the seventh stanzas. But even with so much guidance, Section III remains challengingly obscure. It merits and it rewards a fairly detailed inspection.

The subject of the opening stanza is—characteristically—not tragedy but the transcendence of tragedy. Death is the central figure: death seated close beside the poet in the darkness, and addressed in three successive images. Death is the "capped arbiter of beauty in this street"—the force (capped like a gunman or a soldier) that determines the fate of beauty *in this street,* in this temporal and mortal world; but that has, by implication, no authority over ideal beauty.

Death is next the representative ("delicate ambassador") of the manifold dead, those cut down by war: who nonetheless return to make their presence felt once more—

> intricate slain numbers that arise
> In whispers. . . .

There is a probable reminiscence here of the seventh of John Donne's "Holy Sonnets":

> arise, arise
> From death, you numberless infinities
> Of soules. . . .

And the probability is strengthened when the grand conclusion of Donne's tenth "Holy Sonnet"—"And death shall be no more; death thou shalt die"—becomes plainly audible behind the third of the apostrophes to death in Crane's poem:

> religious gunman!
> Who faithfully, yourself, will fall too soon.

Donne was talking quite literally about the eternal life, about the defeat of death and the literal ressurrection of the dead that was the promise of Christian doctrine. Crane—and the contrast is a significant contrast of epochs—is expressing his private conviction about psychological and spiritual resilience, and in a way that he would shortly paraphrase for Munson: "After this perfection of death—nothing is possible in motion but a resurrection of some kind." The phrase "in motion" even helps explain the reference in the stanza under discussion to the "motor dawn" that the street is "narrow[ing] darkly into." At this moment of perfect darkness and the sense of death, a resurrection of some kind must of necessity be in motion, a motion symbolized and driven by the dawn. There was (Crane felt) simply nowhere else for the human spirit and for poetry to go.

Death that eternal and hence "religious" killer will "fall," the poem continues,

>   And in other ways than as the wind settles
>   On the sixteen thrifty bridges of the city:
>   Let us unbind our throats of fear and pity.

The death of death (that is, of the death-consciousness) will be no quiet and gradual affair, like the wind settling on a city's bridges; it will be an occasion for triumphant song. Crane told Waldo Frank that "the Fall of Troy, etc." was "also in" this section, and it may be that Troy was one intended referent of the city which has fallen and on whose ruins the dust (wind) slowly settles; not that Troy, so far as I know, was ever said to have sixteen bridges; it sounds more like New York. But the key word here, I fancy, is "thrifty": a word that eventually combines with "meagre" to suggest the worst kind of death that Crane could imagine, that self-withholding lifeless life that is really a death-in-life, and that, in Section III, is radically distinguished from the self-*giving* manner of the "lavish heart" and of the "substance . . . spent beyond repair." The latter is the life of praise, of the song that "our throats" can utter once they are loosed from the tragic emotions that currently clutch at them. The emotions mentioned are, of course, Aristotle's classic pair—pity and fear; emotions which, according to the *Poetics* are first aroused and then healthfully purged out of us by the experience of tragedy. Crane says somewhat the same thing: "Let us unbind our throats of fear and pity"; but his whole attention is on what happens after that, on the death-denying song that follows.

But there is more to be confessed before that song. The next portion is devoted to "War (the eternal soldier)," and it presents a ruthlessly concentrated and imagistically agitated account of a machine-gun attack by a World War I fighter aircraft, from the perspective of the pilot. Phrases stammer like bullets: "corymbulous formations of mechanics," "spouting malice / Plangent over meadows"; and they send us hurriedly to the dictionary, a volume even more indispensable for "Faustus and Helen III" than is usual with

Crane. "Corymbulous," for example, is a rare botanical term meaning "clustering": hence, clustering formations of aircraft. "Corymbulous" also associates with a surprising number of countrified allusions in the later stanzas of Section III: hill, meadows, boughs, blue plateaus, stubble, wine, delve, and thresh; not to mention "mounted cities" and "saddled sky." The number is surprising until we realize that Crane is building a small pattern of pastoral imagery that serves at once to reduce the tragic to the pathetic, and to suggest something alive, glowing, continuing, in contrast with the dark, mechanized world of city streets; a process that would recur more expansively and with a somewhat different emphasis in *The Bridge,* when Crane's pastoral imagination engaged what he there called the "iron age."

The effect is obliquely Virgilian: for in the *Aeneid,* Virgil, good gentleman-farmer that he was, also sought the effect of "violence clothed in pathos" (Crane's phrase for the passage under discussion) by introducing into the bloodiest or most grandiose moments an image drawn from the humble and the rustic life—as when Vulcan, great Lord of Fire, rises and goes to his furnaces in the similitude (Book VIII) of a housewife who must "eke out her slender livelihood" and so rises early to "poke the drowsy embers upon the earth." It is the pastoral context in "Faustus and Helen III" that explains the conversion or shrinkage of the deathdealing fighter-pilot into a frontier cowboy (or perhaps a militant cowboy, an old-time cavalry officer) saddling the sky and mounting it like a horse. The same context justifies, I think, the description at once poetically harsh and humanly touching, of the "torn and empty houses" as resembling "old women with teeth unjubilant"— houses with gaping holes in their walls, staring upward like old peasant women in whose gaping mouths there appears no smile of flashing teeth. "Unjubilant" stands in opposition to the jubilation shortly to come in Section III; just as the phrase "spouting malice," which brilliantly transforms the

wicked rattle of the machine-gun into a vicious outpouring
of human hatred, provides a polar opposite to the outburst
of laughter and praise of man at the poem's end.[19]

The evocation of the then recent First World War is thus
typically constructed by dislocating and realigning the elements under intense rhythmic pressure. But—and this is the
important point—Crane, by means of his particular re-
alignment, has virtually won in advance the poetic and
emotional victory he is aiming at. The floral and pastoral
imagery removes or at least softens a good deal of the
historical horror (i.e., the immediate source of the prevalent death-consciousness); and what remains of that horror
is undercut, poetically and emotionally, by the language
Crane selected. The definition of the war experience is, accordingly, a careful prologue to Crane's statement of his
own attitude to history in the fourth stanza, "Résumé":

> We did not ask for that, but have survived,
> And will persist to speak again before
> All stubble streets that have not curved
> To memory. . . .

There has been a period of ferocious ill-will in human
affairs, and of a force of destruction that nothing, not even
a "hypogeum" (underground or underwater vault: hence
"of wave or rock") could hold out against. We were part
of it; we flew the airplanes and "our flesh remembers."
But we did not desire war nor ourselves declare it: this is
Crane's insistent twenty-four-year-old contention. It was
not an expression of *our* feelings and ambitions (that is, of
Crane's generation and of those like-minded with him).
And so, having survived, we will persist, not in brooding
over the post war waste land, but in uttering from liberated
throats a different song. "Stubble," another country word

[19] The notion of pouring ("spouting") also accounts for the word
"plangent" in the next phrase, "plangent over meadows." "Plangent"
means loud like the sound of waves breaking or pouring onto a
shore.

that means the stumps remaining in the ground after reap-
ing, is a good adjectival noun for bombed streets; and the
qualifying phrase, "that have not curved to memory," after
its primary meaning of "have not disappeared altogether,"
seems to have as its secondary meaning an insinuation about
Eliot's *Waste Land* verdict on the decline of the West. Crane
and his hopeful fellows, the poem at this stage implies, will
speak to those who (in the "Chaplinesque" phrase) "can still
love the world," who can listen because they can believe in
the future; those whom the very real shock of a world war
has not caused to retreat into nostalgia and the belief (as
Crane said with blunt inaccuracy about Eliot) that "happiness and beauty dwell only in memory."

But Crane's title for this part of "Faustus and Helen II"—
"Résumé"—indicates his intention here not only of striking
an attitude toward the present and future but of recapitulat-
ing earlier moments in the poem. The "stubble streets that
have not curved / To memory" remind us perhaps of the
asphalt and the memoranda of Section I; it is time, anyhow,
to remember and re-encounter Helen, as Crane thereupon
does. He will, he goes on, speak to those who have not enlisted on the side of memory—

> or known the ominous lifted arm
> That lowers down the arc of Helen's brow
> To saturate with blessing and dismay.

The syntax of those lines is puzzling. But we may venture
the paraphrase that Crane will address himself to those who,
on the one hand, have not succumbed to nostalgia and yet,
on the other hand, have never experienced nostalgia's anti-
dote, the vision of beauty. The vision has become potent and
ambiguous. In connection with "ominous," "lowers," and
"dismay," Helen's arm seems lifted to strike and she herself
to glower (formerly she blushed and winked); one denies
her only at one's risk, while even to acknowledge her is (as
in Section I) to be at first smitten with dismay at the revealed ugliness of the actual. But her hand is also lifted

in benediction; and in the next two stanzas, the world is increasingly blessed.

This is the poem's moment of "Ecstasy," in Crane's chart, though the résumé also continues in the recollection of imagery and attitudes from Section II. There have been many abstruse speculations about the items that introduce this moment—

> A goose, tobacco and cologne—
> Three winged and gold-shod prophecies of heaven
> The lavish heart shall always have to leaven
> And spread with bells and voices, and atone
> The abating shadows of our conscript dust.

"Three winged," be it noted; not (as the typescript shows) "three-winged," a printer's mistake that has started endless analytic hares. The items have been taken as medieval emblems, though of what only Crane is thought to know; or as debased instances of religious symbolism; or as somehow corresponding to the "druggist, barber and tobacconist" of Section I, though, as a rapid count will show, this leaves either the druggist or the barber in charge of the goose.[20] But there is a hard specificity about the references, and I suspect that the best guess is to see the goose, tobacco, and cologne as Crane's way of getting down to fundamentals. They are the "few herbs and apples" (the derivation, I am reasonably sure, is conscious and direct) that Emerson described himself as hastily snatching in his poem "Days"—a poem that Crane had already echoed in his own "Pastorale."[21] But where Emerson mocked himself for asking

[20] The actual source of the items was a newspaper story, by which Crane was much intrigued, about a Negro being arrested for stealing a goose, some tobacco, and a bottle of cologne from a sort of general store. See "Hart Crane: A Conversation with Samuel Loveman" (pamphlet published by Interim Books, 1964).

[21] Crane's worksheets, as against the final typescript, go far to confirm this possibility. "Days" reads in part:

> To each they [the Days] offer gifts after his will,
> Bread, kingdoms, stars, and sky that holds them all.
> I, in my pleached garden, watched the pomp,

so little of life, Crane is arguing that, enroute to ecstasy, we must take the most commonplace elements that the world has to offer as prophecies of heaven. He is implying, in a way that Emerson would have thoroughly approved, that we must (as Emerson put it in *Nature*) learn to "perceive the miraculous in the common." We must see these commonplace elements as reflectors of perfect beauty ("gold-shod" looks forward to the emblematic "gold hair" of Helen in the next stanza). If the heart is lavish enough—sufficiently "unthrifty"—it will leaven (that is, it will have a transforming influence upon) those earthly items; it will make audible in them bells ringing and voices raised in song. It will

> atone
> The abating shadows of our conscript dust.

These lines are a marked if tightened transfiguration of phrases from Section I:

> this bartered blood . . .
> the body of the world
> Weeps in inventive dust. . . .
> The earth may glide diaphanous to death.

Now the dust of the fallen world is undergoing atonement, and our fading spirits ("abating shadows") are, along with the diaphanous earth, being rescued and redeemed.

They are being rescued and redeemed, of course, by the poetic imagination, once it has consummated its marriage with an envisioned ideal of beauty. The world we know, to say it most flatly, is being saved by poetry: by and in this

---

> Forgot my morning wishes, hastily
> Took a few herbs and apples. . . .

And Crane's early version:

> What did you ask for; what were you refused?
> The privilege of a gift: a goose, tobacco
> And Cologne; or belles [sic] and voices? that you
> sought in vain.

very poem as it has evolved and as it now moves toward its climax. As the phase of "Ecstasy" continues, gathering momentum, it is the imagination that is seen as the source of laughter and the warrant for praise. The mention of Anchises and Erasmus, in the penultimate stanza, may halt us temporarily, if we remember too closely what we know about Anchises and Erasmus; but I think we can hear in those names high-sounding references to every great achievement of which mortal man has been capable *except* the achievement of the imagination and its ally, the lavish heart. (The worksheet bears out this reading; and indeed Crane's earlier version strikes me as superior to his final one.)[22] As against the grand achievements of Anchises and Erasmus, who had restored what had been destroyed (had re-gathered the "blown blood and wine," presumably of shattered Troy and the shattered Catholic and Eucharistic culture), the poetic imagination is summoned by Crane to a comparable but perhaps mightier task—a new kind of re-unification, that of the fragmented elements ("scattered wine") of the contemporary epoch:

> Delve upward for the new and scattered wine,
> O brother-thief of time, that we recall.
> Laugh out the meagre penance of their days
> Who dare not share with us the breath released,

[22] The lavish heart shall win the rape, in sight,
Of ever-virgin Beauty, untouched, untouchable.
It shall see beyond the cautious span
Of mortal wisdom, navel and the womb. See and
relinquish!

In the final version, the navel is associated with Anchises: perhaps with the notion that Anchises was the parent of the new Troy, after the old Troy had been destroyed; while mortal wisdom appears as "Erasmus," perhaps as the representative of a culture-restoring humane knowledge in the wake of the wreckage of the Reformation. I wonder, incidentally, if Crane's phrase "lavish heart" derives from Melville's poem "On the Slain Collegians," where Melville speaks of "All lavish hearts, on whichever side, / Of birth urbane or courage high, / Armed them for the stirring wars."

The substance drilled and spent beyond repair
For golden, or the shadow of gold hair.

Death and the human imagination are fraternal thieves of time, each stealing it away with even more finality than "procrastination" in Young's famous *Night Thoughts* aphorism. In death, time comes to a stop; by the imagination, the entire temporal sphere is transcended. There follows the culminating rejection of the unimaginative life: the life already defined, in Section II, as one of thrift, safety, moralism. That deadly existence, that life of dreary penance, that spirit that does not dare to risk breathlessness ("Know, Olympians, we are breathless" Crane had exclaimed in the preceding section), that fears nothing so much as prodigality of any kind: all this is laughed at; and the poet becomes the prodigal son, willing to seem to waste his spiritual and physical substance in riotous living if he can catch a glimpse even of the shadow of golden hair, of Helen's beauty.

And so the poem arrives at its "Final Declaration":

Distinctly praise the years, whose volatile
Blamed bleeding hands extend and thresh the height
The imagination spans beyond despair,
Outpacing bargain, vocable and prayer.

Music like that almost overpowers analysis; it is one of the finest passages in twentieth-century poetry. But its greatness comes in part from its success in bringing to a supreme climax and conclusion images and elements and attitudes that had made up so much of the stuff of the poem to this moment. What is singled out for praise is just that transitoriness, that culpability and woundedness that Section I had established as characteristic of the temporal world. That blamed and bleeding world, that world bloodied by war and condemned by man, is worthy of praise; for the poetic imagination (as it "Delve[s] upward for the new and scattered wine") sees it extending to the height of the ideal world, continuous with the ideal, beautified and perfected by the ideal. And, so delving upward, the imagination arches beyond despair, and arches too beyond "bargain," beyond the stock-market world where bargains are struck and blood is bartered; even beyond human utterance and beyond prayer. But in the splendor of its vision, it is after all the years that it returns to praise—the irradiated years.

CHAPTER FIVE

The Impenitent Song

REPLYING to Waldo Frank in late February 1923, about Frank's and Munson's evidently perceptive and laudatory comments on "Faustus and Helen," Crane was moved to say:

> I am certain that a number of us at last have some kind of community of interest. And with this communion will come something better than a mere clique. It is a consciousness of something more vital than stylistic questions and "taste," it is vision, and a vision alone that not only America needs, but the whole world. We are not sure where this will lead, but after the complete renunciation symbolized in *The Wasteland* and, though less, in *Ulysses* we have sensed some new vitality.

Thus far had Crane come from the modest visionary act performed in the closing lines of "Chaplinesque"—from the solitary and wistful experience of transfiguration there registered to this exalted notion of a shared poetic vision that, in some as yet unidentified manner, would respond to the needs of America and of the whole world. It was in pursuit of the visionary community so postulated that Crane—who had a sharp sense of the ritualistic punctuation marks in his life—left Cleveland for good around Easter in 1923, within weeks after completing "Faustus and Helen," and settled, with every expectation of permanence, in New York City.

He found there old literary and artistic friends like Gorham Munson, Matthew Josephson, and the Harrison Smiths, and new ones like Waldo Frank and Allen Tate (neither of whom he had met personally until now), Kenneth Burke, Malcolm Cowley, Slater Brown, Eugene O'Neill and Alfred Stieglitz, not to mention writers like cummings and Marianne Moore, whom he encountered on occasion and whose presence could be felt, happily or disturbingly, in the creative, critical, and editorial atmosphere. What he did not find was any kind of genuine community, and hence any kind of nourishing communion. Crane was, in fact, engaged in the same valiant and hopeless quest in which many of his Romantic predecessors had participated—a search for what Coleridge had called "the Clerisy," and Carlyle "an organic Literary Class"; for Emerson's "invisible community." He was searching for an artistic and intellectual elite ("Writing and Teaching Heroes," as Carlyle said) that would not only guard but would transform the elements of the national culture, that would restore beauty and harmony to the contemporary world and thus would, in Whitman's phrase, "put the nation in form." [1] But instead, as the months passed, Crane found pretty much what the others had found: nothing but "factions, gossips, jealousies, recriminations, excoriations." There is no doubt that Crane contributed his share to the tumult, out of his personal violence and exuberance. But he was perhaps more depressed than were his associates by the noisy literary war of nerves and threats which, for him, was a main enemy of that spiritual community he had hoped to belong to. Sometimes, however, Crane felt that the chaos was only the necessary prologue to the birth of that community: for in this period and later, Crane was seized betimes by a conviction about some enormous process of cultural disintegration and reintegration that was in the making during his lifetime. He could express the notion satirically, as in his sardonic report on the destiny of one of the local groups—which, he said, was caught up in "the grand dissolution, birth control, re-swaddling and new synthesizing, grandma-confusion movement." But elsewhere he put the case more quietly, and with a sort of thoughtful urgency.

Soon after his arrival in New York, Crane wrote Alfred

---

[1] On Coleridge and Carlyle, see Raymond Williams, *Culture and Society 1780-1950* (New York, 1958). Emerson's phrase occurs typically in "New England Reformers"; Whitman's in *Democratic Vistas*.

Stieglitz—the brilliantly inventive photographer whom Crane had come to revere as a "great and good man" and a fellow visionary (*"I am your brother always,"* Crane exclaimed to him later)—that "the city is a place of 'brokenness,' of drama." Like the city imaged in "Faustus and Helen," it was a place of partitions and equivocations, a place dedicated to perennial conflict and "twisted by the love of things irreconcilable." But the drama of experience in this fallen world could be exhilarating if the imagination intervened in the right way at the right time. "When a certain development in this intensity is reached," Crane continued to Stieglitz, "a new stage is created, or must be, arbitrarily, or there is a foreshortening, a loss and a premature disintegration of experience." The phrase "or must be" (i.e., created) "arbitrarily" will give pause to certain readers, who might point to it as typical of Crane's bad Romantic habit of trying to force something into being by a sheer exertion of will—rather than contenting himself, as a finite human poet, with a faithful record of the somber and broken actualities of experience, and of his relation to them. On Crane's part, though, it was a statement, put perhaps overbluntly and thus misleadingly, about what he took to be the vast responsibility of art (of the community—nonexistent, as it turned out—of artists) to prod the even vaster historical changes that the current conditions of life made indispensable—a traditional view which Crane always, if not always very clearly, adhered to.

The immediate stimulus for these large, even apocalyptic and somewhat fuzzy prognostications was "a new longish poem under the title of *The Bridge*" which Crane had been "ruminating" even before he finished "Faustus and Helen," and which was to "carr[y] on further the tendencies manifest" in that poem. Crane first mentioned *The Bridge* in a letter to Munson on February 6, 1923; a few days later, he quoted "the first verse" of it to Tate—lines which would be revised into the opening of the "Van Winkle" section. *The Bridge* was to be an account, more far-reaching than

"Faustus and Helen," of the transformation of the fragmented and broken world into the harmonious "world dimensional." The entity to be seen undergoing the miraculous change was nothing less than America itself. With this immense conception, Crane struggled through the spring and summer into the fall of 1923, and managed no more than various unsatisfactory versions (versions both dazzling and dizzying) of what would eventually be "Atlantis."[2] He alternated characteristically between high confidence and despair; but finally he had to set the poem aside, and would not return to it until early 1926. He confessed to his Cleveland friend Charlotte Rychtarik toward the end of September that, although he was "working still on *The Bridge*," he was also "working on some smaller poems that crop out from time to time very naturally."

The major effort and the attending frustrations exhausted him. Crane's energies, so he told his mother, were "about reduced to their minimum"; and in early November, he quit his job with J. Walter Thompson's advertising agency and repaired in near collapse to the country home of Slater Brown and Edward Nagle in Woodstock, New York. It was the first of his recurring and poetically curative pastoral retreats from the broken and the soul-breaking city. When he came back to that city just after the first of the year (1924), he felt himself "a giant in health again," "better than I can ever remember feeling." He brought with him, in finished form, the first of the "smaller poems" with which he would be exclusively occupied for two years to come.

·II·

The lyrics Crane composed between the fall of 1923 and the summer of 1926—they constitute the bulk of *White Buildings*—do not represent any abandonment of his preoc-

[2] These versions were collected by Brom Weber and included as an appendix in his biography. The final version of "Atlantis" was part of the extraordinary poetic yield of July and August 1926.

cupation with personal and large-scale spiritual processes and possibilities. They were written, we might say, in the shadow of the yet unwritten epic, and they sprang from the same beliefs out of which *The Bridge* was first conceived. When in the last month of his life Crane reflected reminiscently in "The Broken Tower":

> And so it was I entered the broken world
> To trace the visionary company of love,

he was referring to almost everything he had written from "Faustus and Helen" onward; poem after poem had explored the shattered world in search of the vision and the love, and the community grounded therein, which might make the world whole. But while some of the poems we shall examine ("Recitative," for example, and "Lachrymae Christi") are rigorously compressed statements of Crane's general view, or of salient aspects of it, each of them is animated as well by a more personal motif, by the poet's response to the vitality he desires and the death he apprehends, to the possible reintegration and the felt division of his individual self. In one perspective, indeed, the subject of a number of these poems, like that of *The Bridge,* is exactly the relation between the divided self and the divided world. It was a relationship which Crane formulated in his own idiom very much the way Emerson had formulated it in *Nature:* "The reason why the world lacks unity, and lies broken and in heaps, is because man is divided from himself." This is certainly the subject of "Recitative," the first of the poems Crane brought back from Woodstock.

Before facing the special difficulties of "Recitative," however, we ought to acknowledge that the lyrics of 1923-1926 contain some of the most notoriously difficult verses of modern times. To some readers, Crane's lyrics have seemed so impenetrable as to arouse a suspicion of fraudulence. One of the best-equipped reviewers of *White Buildings,* Conrad Aiken, concluded, as more than one prominent reader of Crane would conclude, that the poems were simply pretentious fakes. Commenting on this rather mildly (to Allen Tate, in March 1927), and allying himself with his chief source of poetic encouragement, Crane said of Aiken that "He has a perfect right to claim that many of the poems are specious, and call them intellectual fakes, etc. He may quite well believe that he is right on the score. For years, remember, perfectly honest people have seen nothing but insanity in such things as 'The Tiger.'" There is in fact no reason to believe that Crane *aimed* at obscurity; all the evidence supports his remark to Tate that "I have always been working hard for a more perfect lucidity, and it never pleases me to be taken as wilfully obscure or esoteric," and that he "worked for weeks, off and on, of course,—trying to simplify the presentation of the ideas" in "Recitative," the poem he had sent Tate a little earlier.

The difficulties remain. The early readers of *White Buildings* may well be pardoned for failing to understand it, especially since, now, four decades later, it is still possible for perfectly honest critics to come up with radically different interpretations of particular Cranian stanzas or even entire poems. I have no doubt that some of my readings will arouse not only skepticism but consternation among certain of Crane's warmest admirers; I have experienced the same feelings while puzzling through the interpretations of others. But I am sure that when the poems (that is, the post-"Faustus and Helen" poems) are read as a group, as the product of a single large phase of Crane's creative career, many (not all) of their difficulties evaporate. They go far to clarify each other and to reinforce each other. They provide us with the kind of context we always need when we approach a poet as original as Crane, or a poet whose individual talent was, like Crane's, enlisted in a tradition we had partially forgotten. Working with such a context, we begin to notice not only recurring postures and emphases and cadences, but also recurring allusions—to sight and hearing, to the wind, to the color white, to fire, to memory, to tears and laughter—which build into a pattern of symbolism expressive at once of private urgencies and of a decidedly traditional view of experience.

"Recitative" introduces several of the elements just listed. In the fourth stanza, and in freshening lines from which Crane took the title of his first volume, the speaker advises his audience:

> Look steadily—how the wind feasts and spins
> The brain's disk shivered against lust. Then watch
> While darkness, like an ape's face, falls away,
> And gradually white buildings answer day.[3]

We recognize the characteristic act of seeing, or watching: of seeing a characteristic movement not only from darkness to day and from a congested ugliness to a new purity (whiteness), but from the shattered condition to one of restored wholeness. The redeeming agent is the wind: for it is the wind that feasts or celebrates and so makes round and whole again (whereupon the wind "spins" it) the brain's disk that had smashed like glass against the force of animal lust.

Here as so often elsewhere in Crane, the wind is a power analogous to divine grace. Better, it is the power of divine grace as refracted through the Romantic imagination to become the power of poetic inspiration. The wind in "Recitative" is the same mysterious and crucial element which M. H. Abrams, in a notable essay (and adapting a phrase from *The Prelude*), has called "The Correspondent Breeze." This was perhaps the central metaphor in English Romantic poetry; by virtue of it, Professor Abrams wittily remarks, Romantic poetry from Coleridge's "Dejection" ode to Shelley's "Ode to the West Wind" was quite "thoroughly ventilated." [4] Professor Abrams points to the symbolic cor-

---

[3] The comparable reference in "Faustus and Helen," we recall, was to "white *cities*"—"white, through white cities passed on to assume. . . ."

[4] *English Romantic Poets: Modern Essays in Criticism,* edited by M. H. Abrams (Oxford Galaxy paperback, 1960), pp. 37ff.

respondence established by Coleridge and the others between the physical breeze and the motions of the human
spirit—or more complexly, a number of "equations between
breeze, breath, and soul, respiration and inspiration, the re-
animation of nature and the spirit." Far from originating in
Romanticism, of course, and as Professor Abrams reminds
us, those equations can be found in the Old Testament
(Ezekiel 37:9: "Prophesy, son of man, and say to the
wind. . . .") and the New (John 3:7-8: "Ye must be born
again. The wind bloweth where it listeth. . . . so is every
one that is born of the Spirit"), and in patristic writing.
Crane, who was not much of a Bible reader, probably derived his own symbol from Wordsworth—for example, from
the evocation in *The Prelude* of the "visionary power" that
"attends the motions of the viewless winds, / Embodied in
the mystery of words." He was no less probably borrowing
from Shelley's "Ode," where the poet prays to the autumnal
wind to "Make me thy lyre," and to "Be through my lips to
unawakened earth / The trumpet of the prophecy!" Shelley's
allusion to the dead leaves of nature and of his own thoughts
("O wild West wind . . . from whose unseen presence the
leaves dead / Are driven") seems to be echoed in the third
stanza of "Recitative":

> Inquire this much-exacting fragment smile,
> Its drums and darkest blowing leaves ignore.[5]

[5] It is tempting to find Shelley's two lines—

> Scatter, as from an unextinguished hearth,
> Ashes and sparks, my words among mankind—

echoed in Crane's "Praise for an Urn":

> Scatter these well-meant idioms
> Into the smoky spring that fills
> The suburbs.

Some of these echoes are admittedly casual; and when listened to
closely, they often turn out to reverse the *sense,* while retaining the
metaphor, of the original. But Shelley's poetry was more active in
Crane's imagination than Crane's letters suggest.

In any case, the wind for Crane is once again a stimulus to and a symbol of a capacity for active creative vision: a vision which, working through "the mystery of words" and re-quickening what Wordsworth called "the holy life of music and of verse," would rescue the poet and perhaps mankind from the fallen and divided condition.

In most of the poems inspected in this chapter, man's fall is presented as a moral event, something due to aberrant or promiscuous love. It is as though Crane were still shaking off the conventions of Edwardian and modern neoclassical verse; in the more purely visionary lyrics examined in subsequent chapters, the problem is rather psychological and aesthetic, and results not from the immoral but the uncreative life. But the latter motif appears in these earlier poems, too; and what persists is the sense of division. "Recitative," beginning with a reference to Janus, the two-faced God of the Romans, goes on through a series of paired opposites ("at search or rest . . . pain or glee") to speak of something "double" and "cleft," of twin halves, a fragmented smile and a shivered disk. Such duality, Crane explained to Tate, who had evidently indicated a sort of admiring bewilderment, is the first theme of the poem.

"Recitative," he wrote, "*is* complex, exceedingly." But, Crane said, "imagine the poet, say, on a platform speaking it." Hence the title of the work, and the phrase in stanza one about "Reciting pain or glee." "The audience," Crane continued, "is one half of Humanity, Man (in the sense of Blake) and the poet the other. ALSO, the poet sees himself in the audience as in a mirror. ALSO, the audience sees itself, in part, in the poet. Against this paradoxical DUALITY is posed the UNITY, or the conception of it (as you got it) in the last verse. In another sense, the poet is *talking to himself* all the way through the poem." It is at once a helpful and a baffling explanation. But it permits us to identify the mirror references—"the hands that twist this glass," and "I crust a plate of vibrant mercury" (i.e., I make a mirror). And it intimates the three kinds of actual division and potential unity the poem is concerned with: the relation between the poet and his audience, or mankind; the relation between mankind and itself (the divided world); the relation between the poet and his own self. Man "in the sense of Blake" is presumably the figure of Albion who appears fitfully in Blake's poetry until he is given full-scale treatment in the long unfinished prophetic book, *The Four Zoas* and in Blake's final epic, *Jerusalem*.[6] Blake's Albion is Man—"the Universal Man to Whom be glory evermore"; but he is only potentially the latter. As envisioned by Blake, Albion is actually Man as fallen and sundered, and the announced theme of *The Four Zoas* is Albion's "fall into Division and his Resurrection into Unity." "Recitative" manipulates, or tries to manipulate in far too cramped a space and in language too secretive, both the universal and the personal duality; and poses that duality, as Crane argued, against the possibility of a Blakeian recovered unity in the final stanza:

> In alternating bells have you not heard
> All hours clapped dense into a single stride?
> Forgive me for an echo of these things,
> And let us walk through time with equal pride.

It is one of those stirring and genuinely climactic climaxes for which Crane had a supreme talent; few of his stanzas stick more firmly in the memory. This one does so because it is an indissoluble unit. The single instant that contains the whole of time becomes a single "stride" on the long "walk" through the temporal life. More cunningly, it is a unitary and significant pattern of sound. The pattern combines an iambic or "alternating" rhythm which echoes the alternating *ding-dong* of the bells and suggests the notion of duality; and a series of hard single stresses which make audible the notion of unity or singleness ("hours clapped dense" and so on). Echoing the bell-sounds in language, the poet asks forgiveness for another kind of echo—that of Blake in

[6] Both my contention here and my wording reflect an indebtedness to Harold Bloom and especially to his book, *Blake's Apocalypse*.

"Auguries of Innocence," and of Blake's injunction to see
or find "eternity in an hour"; though after the earlier imperative of seeing, Crane here shifts typically to the (for
him) equivalent faculty of hearing. Following Blake, Crane
asks mankind and himself—even while enslaved by time
("Regard the capture here") and while aware of man's divided and animal condition—to look toward the promise
of whiteness, or purification, and to listen for the sound of
wholeness. Both the promise and the sound are supplied by
the creative imagination, working not against or beyond
but altogether within the world of time.

Wedged into the poem are two stanzas—the fifth and
sixth—which deflect the poetic movement and which,
though intrinsically important and studded with remarkable
images, are only tangentially relevant to the main theme.
Paraphrasing bluntly, we may say that Crane reverts in these
stanzas to another major obstacle to creativity—his need for
money, and the dangerous appeal of great wealth. Into an
already congested little poem, Crane intrudes images of the
powerful but deadly worlds of commerce and industry.
Those worlds are represented here, as in *The Bridge,* by the
urban skyscraper, the building (opposite in nature and
hostile to the "white buildings" of poetry) "built floor by
floor on shafts of steel"; and by the tower, which seems to be
entirely constructed of gold. These worlds, these buildings,
stifle poetry and shut the poet off from inspiration. They
"grant" him "no stream"—a remark which Shelley's "Ode"
again helps to decipher, in its reference to the inspiring wind
as a "stream" ("Thou on whose stream. . . . / Loose clouds
like earth's decaying leaves are shed"). And the poet—forced
to work in a business office, as Crane had been, and to earn
his livelihood by attending to hideously boring accounts,
"atrocious sums"—feels suspended in an airless vacuum,
hung up like Absalom, the son of David, who was caught by
his hair and held dangling until his death.[7]

[7] Cf. Crane's citation of dangling Absalom in a letter to Waldo
Frank in June 1926; the letter is discussed in Chapter Eight, below.

Crane was determined to resist and escape this particular danger. The point eventually made in "Recitative" was also made by Crane in a letter to his mother on December 21, 1923, at just the moment when he was laboring over the poem. Explaining why he had quit his job with the advertising firm, Crane insisted that he could be content with very little money, and inveighed against the "bondage" of the business-office life. "One can live very happily on very little, I have found, if the mind and spirit have some definite objective in view. . . . I'm no more fooling myself that the mental bondage and the spiritual bondage of the more remunerative sorts of work is worth the sacrifices inevitably involved." If it turned out that he was simply unequipped to produce poetry of value, he declared himself willing to "tie myself to some smug ambition and 'success' (the common idol that every Tom, Dick and Harry is bowing to everywhere)." But he was convinced about his own powers. So, in "Recitative," after envisaging the greatest imaginable wealth ("the highest towers" whose ribs are made of "wrenched gold"), Crane urges his imagination, along with his gold-worshipping American audience, to "leave the tower," to turn from that false dream of material success.

> The bridge swings over salvage, beyond wharves;
> A wind abides the ensign of your will.

I suspect two puns—on "salvation" and on "whores"—in the first of those two lines: spiritual health, Crane appears to be saying, requires an abandonment of this prostitution of energy, in a reunion or bridging (here the unwritten epic is recalled) of energy and imagination.[8] For creative inspiration, finally, waits faithfully upon any true display ("ensign") of artistic determination, any manifestation (and "ensign," which might unrythmically be read "en-*sign*," picks up punningly from an earlier phrase, "one crucial

---

[8] From Woodstock, Crane wrote Munson that it was going to be a difficult winter, "but I should like to keep away from the city and its scattered prostitutions for awhile."

sign") of that kind of definite objective Crane spoke of to his mother.[9]

Analysis of Crane's poetry ought to be exemplary rather than exhaustive; I shall not linger so long over the achievements and perplexities of individual poems, especially minor ones like "Recitative," in the pages that follow. Not that the reading I have given is really exhaustive: there remain charms unmentioned in "Recitative," and questions unanswered. The lingering, in any case, was due in part to the admission of external evidence; and readers who believe that, as the saying goes, a poem should stand on its own feet will be uneasy with the references to Shelley and the quotations from a private letter. As to that, I confess myself willing to draw upon any scrap of information that may help, or better help confirm, an interpretation; our store of good poetry is not so great that we can afford to lose an addition to it, however small, on grounds of critical purism. But the end in view lies beyond the particular poem. If external evidence is an aid to explaining "Recitative," the latter, thus explained, serves in the reading, say, of "Possessions": the two together shed light on a larger creative effort like "Lachrymae Christi"; and so the process continues until the major poems reveal their shape, their beauty, and their meaning, and the entire body of work by a poet of genius can become our treasured and familiar property.

"Possessions," which was exactly contemporary with

[9] The last line quoted was somewhere in Robert Lowell's mind when he concluded "The Quaker Graveyard at Nantucket" with the words: "The Lord survives the Rainbow of His Will." Mr. Lowell tells me that he was not consciously remembering the Crane poem when he wrote the line, but that "Crane's music" was certainly in his ears at the time. The differences—for example, between Crane's "wind" and Lowell's "Lord"—are no less fascinating that the similarity of the two statements. In "Words for Hart Crane" (*Life Studies*, 1959), Lowell offered a discerning tribute—in the form of extremely cogent comparisons with Whitman, Catullus, and Shelley— to his acknowledged predecessor.

"Recitative," is, if anything, more puzzling yet, and it might be literally unreadable without the example just explored. It is in fact a sequel of sorts to "Recitative." The latter began with the phrase "Regard the capture here"; "Possessions" starts as though at a later and more hopeful stage with "Witness now this trust," an obscure expression of faith in some future rescue of the trapped imagination.[10] For the theme is once again the agonizing threat to creativity of the fleshly impulses. But the treatment of the theme provides even stiffer resistance than before to critical penetration. Crane admitted that "Possessions" presented "an exceptionally difficult problem" in analysis, as against what he insistently felt to be "the real clarity and consistent logic of many of [my] other poems." It could not, he said rather cloudily and ungrammatically, "be technically explained. It must rely (even to a large extent with myself) on its organic impact on the imagination to successfully imply its meaning."[11] A heaviness of tone and a dragging rhythm contribute to that impact: and the more so because the entire atmosphere is transformed at the end in a brief burst of apocalyptic eloquence. In the first stanzas, there are a number of dark sayings (after the initial message of hope) about the rain, loss of direction, the assaults of the flesh, a bolted door; to "black foam" and to "this fixed stone of lust" which the poet then "take[s] up" and "hold[s]. . . . against a disk of light." But the final lines bespeak the staunch conviction that:

> The pure possession, the inclusive cloud
> Whose heart is fire shall come,—the white wind rase
> All but bright stones wherein our smiling plays.

In short, the poem moves characteristically, or rather it peers toward the possibility of sometime moving, from lust to

---

[10] Crane abandoned, or forgot, the point when he placed "Possessions" several items ahead of "Recitative" in the *White Buildings* collection.

[11] In "General Aims and Theories," in Horton, *Hart Crane.*

purity, from darkness to light, from "black foam" to "white wind," from the "fixed stone of lust" to "bright stones wherein our smiling plays."

It also seeks to enact the exchange of one kind of possession for another. The first kind, which is carnal, consists in a blinding submission to the flaming erotic temptations of "the city"—

> I, turning, turning on smoked forking spires,
> The city's stubborn lives, desires.

In contrast to the hellish monotony of that condition, whereby the poet feels himself turned helplessly about by desire like an animal on a spit, there is the second mode of possession—which is creative, and is represented by the pure clean fire within "the inclusive cloud." These two modes are, the poem declares in anguish, rendingly incompatible; and the poet appears as one "tossed on these horns, who bleeding dies." The horns of this particular and private dilemma, Crane had defined for Munson some time before. Speaking of his first new love affair in "two or three years," Crane confessed that "passions of this kind completely derail me from anything creative for days,—and that's the worst of it." The worst of it in "Possessions," too, is that the poet feels "wounded by apprehensions out of speech," and his creative output over the lust-burdened days, amounts to nothing more than

> piteous admissions to be spilt
> Upon the page whose blind sum finally burns
> Record of rage and partial appetites.

One notices the sexual imagery (elsewhere in the poem more overtly homosexual) suggestive of the physical spasm that has prevented the imaginative release.

The sum is the "trembling tabulation" of a thousand sexual misdirections; and it is blind because those episodes have momentarily stopped the exercise of the poetic vision:

through the "black foam" of rain, the poet has "no eyes" for the sky (in Crane's modernistic device, it is the sky that has lost direction and has no eyes for the stone of lust—whatever, by the way, that "stone" is intended to be; perhaps only a symbol of immobilizing heaviness). Yet "Possessions" does move to its concluding glimpse of renovation. The abiding wind of "Recitative," while still the power of poetic vision, has become a force that destroys in order to regenerate. It is associated with the archetypal symbol of purifying fire; and its function is to rase—to destroy—not only the poet's lust but, by implication, the entire city, that "place of 'broken-ness,'" as Crane had called it. This vast mysterious power will obliterate everything *but* "bright stones"—the beautiful effects of the imagination—wherein all true human happi-ness lies. The passage is a handsome one. But just as the metaphors jostle one another throughout "Possessions," so there seems to be an imbalance in the climax. The saving action is too large for its object; and what had been an es-sentially private, even autobiographical, theme gives rise to hints of cosmic transformation—which may have been in-advisably derived from the apocalyptic vision in Blake's "America," where all the hordes of Albion and their "law-built heaven" are consumed by the flames of the great rebel Orc.

The consciousness of "lust" and the sense of moral despair which are features of the two poems just examined were not, in fact, characteristic of Crane, though it has too often been assumed that, given his peculiar habits of carousing, he must have felt that way.

> I am not ready for repentance;
> Nor to match regrets.

This, in the later poem "Legend," is far more recognizable as Crane's usual and poetically more valuable attitude toward the moral dimension of his life. "Legend" was not written until the fall of 1925, almost two years after "Recitative" and "Possessions," and it is evidently a footnote to the "Voyages" sequence and the experience out of which that sequence came. But "Legend" may properly be considered here. With "Voyages," a tremendously passionate and absorbing love affair, far from "derailing" Crane creatively, had engendered the finest imaginative achievement of his career thus far, and Crane knew it. "Legend," which picks up the mirror symbol from "Recitative" and the allusions to smoking, burning, and bleeding from "Possessions," can be seen, in our perspective, as a deliberate rebuttal to the *moral* element of those earlier poems. Better: it is a clarification of moral attitude, a poetic re-thinking of the complex relation between the sexual and the artistic life.

Like most of Crane's lyrics, "Legend" has been interpreted in astonishingly different ways; it seems to lend itself all too readily to grandiose critical predispositions. There is no doubt that it begins on a general note of chaotic movement —both in the external world and in the mirror of the poet's mind:

> As silent as a mirror is believed
> Realities plunge in silence by.

Those coiled-up phrases make a masterful opening. But the occasion for the statement is the continuing experience of physical and emotional love, and Crane turns to that in a tender tone of voice unexpectedly reminiscent of "My Grandmother's Love Letters":

> And tremorous
> In the white falling flakes
> Kisses are,—
> The only worth all granting.

And the poem goes on to a gentle reflection—not on lust or remorse—but on the educational, ultimately the creative, value of such love.

It is to be learned—
This cleaving and this burning,
But only by the one who
Spends out himself again.

We have returned to the spirit of "Faustus and Helen," that is, to Crane's truer spirit. The lesson is clearly not to be learned by the *un*lavish heart, by those who dare not share "The substance drilled and spent beyond repair." ("Spends out" in "Legend" has a more distinctive sexual or orgasmic meaning than "spent" in "Faustus and Helen.") And what is to be learned, through the burning, is—poetry; but only by him who yields constantly to the flame:

Twice and twice
(Again the smoking souvenir,
Bleeding eidolon!) and yet again.
Until the bright logic is won
Unwhispering as a mirror
Is believed.

The "bright logic" now reflected in the poet's mind, as against the irrational plunging realities of the opening lines, is poetry itself: Crane's kind of poetry—poetry that is produced by the interworking "logic of metaphor," as Crane would put it, and especially metaphors involving the imagery of brightness ("bright stones," "white buildings," and so on). "Legend" is a deceptively relaxed example of its subject, for the poem exploits the logic of metaphor to suggest the achievement of it—in the development from the initial silence to the "perfect cry," the ideal song, of the last stanza. The process is particularly notable when the burning and the bleeding—sexual desire and its consequences—become, at the end, the very sources of "harmony."

Then, drop by caustic drop, a perfect cry
Shall string some constant harmony,—
Relentless caper for all those who step
The legend of their youth into the noon.

137

"Caustic" here does not, primarily, mean biting or sarcastic; it has its root sense of burning, and even more its medical sense of a substance that burns away tissues. "Legend," like "Possessions," concludes with the purifying flame: not with the implicit *holo*caust of "Possessions," however, but with a more brilliant imaginative twist whereby the burning and the blood are fused into drops which themselves turn into beads harmoniously strung by the perfect cry.[12]

What Crane had learned was that the real obstacle to creativity was not "lust," but, almost on the contrary, what Blake in the "America" passage cited earlier called "the mildews of despair." It was the reaction to experience of the decayed and distorted Protestant conscience, a bleak piety which reduced all sexual activity to the sin of lust. For a man of Crane's American generation, and for a poet in the age of Eliot, this was a harder lesson to learn than we can now easily remember; and if Crane did learn it, it was mainly through an act of recognition—he had really known it all along. Crane's newly clarified attitude involved no loss of moral seriousness; though, since it sometimes seemed so to his friends, he was not beyond adopting the mask. "I know you think me terrible, and given over entirely to pleasure and sin and folly," he remarked cheerfully to the Richtariks early in 1925. "Certainly I am concerned a great deal with all three of these—and even so, don't get *all* I want." In the poetry, the moral tone is serious enough, but it is serious in a new way—or rather in an older way. Behind Crane's attitude—and perhaps for the sake of flat-footed clarity, I had better say behind his *attitude,* not his conduct—was that of the James family, for whom the word "conscience" was a very bad word indeed, and a sign of lethal egotism. Behind

---

[12] Given the Whitmanian words "souvenir" and "eidolon" in the poem ("eidolon" means image or spiritual manifestation), it may be that the line "shall string some constant harmony" derives from Whitman's reference in "Crossing Brooklyn Ferry" to "glories strung like beads on my smallest sights and hearings." Certainly, "Crossing Brooklyn Ferry" was a poem with which Crane seems to have felt a special affinity.

the Jameses, in a more direct line to Crane, was Blake and his attack upon a range of frozen pieties. It was as one who had learned the danger of moral despair and who had embodied the lesson in song that Crane offered his example to the young: as a "relentless caper"—a playfully serious and morally unrelenting and impenitent model—for those who will in turn move through youthful experience toward maturity. Crane presents his own life as allegory to those who have yet to live theirs.[13]

· I I I ·

The thematic relation between the moral and the creative life was carried to its highest pitch of expression and given its fullest elaboration in "Lachrymae Christi," a poem begun soon after Crane completed "Possessions," though it developed painfully through several stages before its final version in April 1925. But "Lachrymae Christi" is also a poem about large-scale death and rebirth; and as a prelude to it, we may look at the strange short poem "Paraphrase" (evidently of the late summer, 1924). "Paraphrase" also deals with the experience of death, but as something altogether within the poet's individual consciousness.

What is "paraphrased" in the poem is exactly the sensation of physical death: not of dying, but of being dead. "One day," Philip Horton says, "after waking up from a drunken sleep with the impression that he was dead, a few scrawled

[13] Crane's use of the word "legend" probably comes from John Donne's "The Canonization," bits of which ("who's injured by my love?" for example, "We're tapers too," "your eyes / So made such mirrors" and other phrases) hover in the atmosphere of the poem.

> And if unfit for tombes and hearse
> Our legend bee, it will be fit for verse.

Donne, of course, was expressing a kind of devout blasphemy, drawing on the notion of "legend" as the exemplary life of a saint. Crane has a not entirely dissimilar idea in offering his "legend" of an impenitent poetic sinner.

lines of 'Paraphrase' joined the other sheets" (on Crane's desk). The poem is appropriately a cold nightmare of negative images, paradoxically and brilliantly projecting through sensuous allusions the total loss or cessation of sensuous activity:

> how desperate is the light
> That shall not rouse, how faint the crow's cavil
>
> As, when stunned in that antarctic blaze,
> Your head, unrocking to a pulse, already
> Hollowed by air, posts a white paraphrase
> Among bruised roses on the papered wall.

There is the entire experience, including that of writing this poem, of "post[ing] a white paraphrase." (Here, I venture, "white"—following and influenced by "hollowed"—means nothing more than "blank.") Earlier in the poem, there had been the articulated fear of death, somewhat in the manner of Hemingway's short story, "Now I lay Me": the dreadful apprehension that during the night the soul may be snatched from the body. The bedsheets stand guard over "the integers of life," the poet's hands and feet, lest death should come ("skim in") to relax the clenched toes and fold the hands over the body in the traditional way of laying out a dead man in his final rest (his "purposeless repose"). Now there is the thing itself: the fact of death conveyed by a serial denial of life: the light unseen, the captious sounds unheard, the blazing sun that does not warm, the head in which no pulse pounds. The effect is unforgettable; and "Paraphrase" was one of Crane's early favorites.[14]

"Lachrymae Christi" deals with death and resurrection in several areas of reality and, as it were, on several levels. It was the most overtly religious poem Crane had yet written, but it was also, perhaps, the most opaque. The poem is a

[14] He selected it with "Chaplinesque" and "Sunday Morning Apples" to read at a literarily important gathering at the home of Paul Rosenfeld in November 1924. As an encore, Crane read "Faustus and Helen."

struggling meditation that evolves into a prayer: so much is evident, though beyond that one proceeds with caution. It takes hold of the imagination quickly enough, but it manages (to adopt Wallace Stevens's definition of any good poem) to resist the intelligence almost completely. There are oddities of language here remarkable even for Crane (the word "let," for example, used apparently as an adjective meaning "unrestrained," or, given the context, "unbound"). There are obscurities of syntax and reference (the word "its" in the first stanza, I have belatedly realized, must refer not to "sill" but to "machinery"). There are queer puns and internal half-echoes ("venom" and "vermin," "tinder" and "tendoned"). It has seemed to some readers to be a forced concoction of poetic bits and pieces; and indeed, one portion (the tangled parenthesis beginning "Let sphinxes from the ripe / Borage of death") was taken over from another abortive poem. On a first reading, at least, the separate stanzas can sound like discrete and random uprisings of the imagination: an image of some mills in the moonlight; an image of the natural landscape on early spring evenings; apostrophes to a godhead alternately called "Nazarene" and "Dionysus," and seeming to contain elements as well of Orpheus and Saint Sebastian. The blend is undoubtedly imperfect, and the difficulties caused thereby remain insurmountable. The rhythmical movement, too, sounds less assured than usual; it has a broken and a faltering quality, and it does not carry us forward, as elsewhere, through the verbal thickets; nor does the poem flex its rhythmical muscles at the end, as Crane's best poems customarily do—it rather fades away into an uneasy silence. Nevertheless, "Lachrymae Christi" is a fascinating composition that baffles primarily through an excess of insinuated meaning. We must not confuse the pleasure of decoding (which in this case is a great one) with the value of the thing decoded; still, to the persistent and trusting reader, the poem has much of value to offer.

We can work toward its multiple meaning by noticing certain clusters of words and phrases. There is the increas-

ingly familiar reference to "eyes," both human and divine;
and to "smiles"—one "unyielding," one "unmangled." Varieties of "perfidies," "perjuries," and betrayal are mentioned;
and we hear allusions to chanting, "music," chiming,
"whistle" and "song." There is a seasonal pattern, involving
"the year's / First blood," "spring," "compulsion of the
year," and the prayer to the godhead to:

> Lift up in lilac-emerald breath the grail
> Of earth again.

And as to that bizarre godhead, he appears to be himself
burned (at the "charred and riven stake"), and endowed
with the power of burning (he has "tinder eyes" which become "undimming lattices of flame"). These clusters and
patterns have not, as I have said, been sufficiently fused by
Crane's shaping power; there are gaps between them across
which the critical mind has to pass unaided. But we do make
out, I believe, a complex of themes, all quite traditional and,
in the abstract, all harmonious one with another: the recovery of poetic vision, along with the rejection of moral
remorse in favor of a musical celebration of life; the recovery
of the life of nature in the spring of the year; the imagined
death and the prayed-for resurrection of Crane's own brand
of fertility god.

The poem begins with an image remotely comparable to
that in the last stanza of "Chaplinesque": the moon—presumably, as before, the poetic imagination—transforming
ugliness into beauty. In this instance, it is a technological
ugliness of mills and machinery (the unwritten epic again
intrudes) which is dissolved, or rinsed away, till only the
windows remain visible; while the adverb "whitely" hovers
disjointedly nearby, to reinforce the notion of transfiguration; and the machinery's hard or unyielding smile—an
image invoked chiefly to give added stress to its opposite in
the poem's last line—is "sluiced" away by the moonlight
pouring across the window sill. With the mechanical element thus, so to say, imagined out of existence, we are trans-

ported into a pastoral world. It is here, apparently, that the poet has experienced the recovery of creative energy which made the transfiguring act of stanza one possible; but it is a world beset by ambiguity. The fox's teeth are venomous, but the venom is "immaculate" and somehow it restrains or "binds" those teeth. The teeth of nature—"swart thorns"— are no less dangerous; yet they are symptoms of renewed fertility, too, as, in an ingenious image, they flourish or "freshen" upon the very blood they draw. Vast numbers of lilacs on the hillside announce the imminent arrival of spring; but they are perceived as "twanged red perfidies," because (as it may be) their message is premature and hence deceitful.

The poet, too, has been deceitful, or at least unfaithful to his calling. He has permitted himself to utter falsehoods ("perjuries"), and his vision to be "galvanized," as though covered or coated over, metallically; by implication, he has abandoned poetry for riotous living. But in the pastoral environment, as nature revivifies itself in beauty, he feels purified and forgiven, his imaginative power restored, and not only his guilt but the very principle of guilt, the guilt-feeling in general, dissolved by the vigor of song:

> And the nights opening
> Chant pyramids,—
> Anoint with innocence,—recall
> To music and retrieve what perjuries
> Had galvanized the eyes.

> While chime
> Beneath and all around
> Distilling clemencies,—worms'
> Inaudible whistle, tunneling
> Not penitence
> But song. . . .

The language of those hopeful but hesitant lines is entirely connotative, and it is the most radical example we have yet encountered of Crane's use of the "logic of metaphor"—the process Crane would describe as "the so-called illogical impingements of the connotations of words on the consciousness." The passage succeeds only insofar as Crane managed, by contextual and metrical pressure, to shut off the irrelevant implications of words like "pyramids" and "worms," and to bind together the relevant ones.[15] But one can hardly miss the mounting atmosphere begotten by such inter-animating clusters as "anoint, recall, retrieve," "innocence, clemencies, not penitence," and "chant, music, chime, whistle, song": And the climactic lines—"not penitence / But song"—is, as I have several times remarked, Crane's quintessential statement about the dissipation of the Protestant moral sense by the force of poetic celebration. It is in the spirit of Whitman and of that favorite of Crane's among Whitman's poems, "Passage to India":

> Caroling free, singing our songs of God,
> Chanting our chant of pleasant exploration,
> With laugh and many a kiss,
> (Let others deprecate, let others weep for sin,
>   remorse, humiliation,)
> O soul, thou pleasest me, I thee.

And it is a more clear-sighted version of the attitude expressed in "Faustus and Helen II," where the "reassuring" music overcomes "the groans of death," and "the siren of the springs of guilty song" is accepted, and all her smiles.

Crane's song of God begins almost immediately after the announcement of the impenitent song, in the electrifying phrase

Thy Nazarene and tinder eyes.

[15] R. P. Blackmur, in his invaluable essay on Crane ("New Thresholds, New Anatomies!" in *Language as Gesture,* 1952), has a seminal discussion of this aspect of Crane's technique, and its attendant difficulties.

The religious motif in "Lachrymae Christi" involves both tensions (as between Christ and Dionysus, for example) and transformation. There is a development from "the tears of Christ" in the Latin title-phrase to the "unmangled target smile" of the pagan god Dionysus at the end. En route, a subtler shift is registered. The title points to the grieving Christ of the New Testament; but in the line just quoted, that same Nazarene resembles the passionate rebel of Blake's "America." He is, we may say, caught in the very moment of metamorphosis, as his traditionally "tender" eyes are converted, by the substitution of a single letter, into eyes of tinder, eyes that can enflame the human heart—eyes, like the heart of flame in "Possessions" and the "caustic" in "Legend," that can burn away the tissues of corruption and of creative sluggishness. The word "tinder" adds to the meaning of "benzine rinsings" in the poem's opening lines; for benzine, the dictionary tells us, is an inflammable liquid—as liquid as tears, as inflammable as tinder; and we begin to realize the true nature of the power being invoked and the kind of change being experienced.

Toward the end of "Lachrymae Christi," the Nazarene's eyes have become "undimming lattices of flame"—no longer dimmed by tears, no longer a merely potential source of fire. And at the close, the Nazarene gives way to Dionysus, and the flaming lattices melt into the fiery stake where the god of vines and of wine is being consumed. Dionysus had been present implicitly in the lines "as these / Perpetual fountains, vines" (i.e., as *do* these eternal fountains and these vines—they also assert "not penitence, but song"), and even in the title, which is the name of a good Neapolitan wine. Most of all, I suppose, Dionysus is implicated in the entire motif of poetry and of renewal, since he was the deity whose annual death and rebirth was the ritual base of the tragic drama with which he was so closely connected.

Crane emphasizes the relation between the metamorphic divinity and the natural and personal themes by inserting between the first and the second address to the Nazarene a parenthetical passage which touches obliquely *on* those other themes. The passage in question is as viscous as anything Crane ever wrote; I doubt if it would repay an extensive working over. But we sense a drift of meaning—of the power of speech, or poetry, regained out of the very experience of death, or of brooding over it; and as the poet's "tongue" is "cleared," so "betrayed stones slowly speak," a phrase which suggests that Crane may be here picking up, as he would in "The River," the Shakespearian metaphor about the language of nature ("sermons in stones").[16] A closer relation is not merely asserted but established when the divinity is begged to restore life to nature—by restoring life and wholeness to himself. The imperative "lift up," I take it, has as its object not only "the grail of earth" but also "thy face" and "Thy / Unmangled target smile"; while the combination "lift up" and "unmangled" is paralleled by "lean long" and "unstanched"—the latter word being used, unsuccessfully, in its minor meaning of "unextinguished" (hence, "luminous").[17]

"The sable, slendor boughs" suggest, or are intended to

[16] The entire passage was revised from what Crane called his "Blakeian" poem, "At Heaven's Gate"—the title taken from Blake's "Jerusalem," and from the stanza we recall Crane quoting earlier in the article on Stieglitz.

R. P. Blackmur, in the essay cited in note 15 above, has made a well-considered guess about the sentence beginning "Let sphinxes." After noting that it is a direct statement and that "let" is used as an adjective meaning "unrestrained"; and after finding that one of the meanings of "borage" is a "cordial," Blackmur concludes: "One guess is that Crane meant something to the effect that if you meditate enough on death it has the same bracing and warming effect as drinking a cordial, so that the riddle of life (or death) is answered," like the riddle of the sphinx.

[17] "Unstanched" may be an object lesson in the danger of "the logic of metaphor." I think it likely that Crane wanted to jam together in a single word both the idea of "unextinguished" and the usual notion of "unstopped," as of the flowing of blood—so that somehow the god would be, in a burst of connotation, at once wounded and unwounded.

suggest, both the branches from which the tree-god, Dionysus, might be expected to lean, and the cross on which the Nazarene was crucified.[18] In any event, this divinity of many names (many ringing names, we could say: via the pun on "pealing") who undergoes such multiple suffering— Crane's phrasing has him torn apart, burned at the stake, slain by arrows, crucified, and pierced by a spear—is begged to reappear intact. His re-gathered wholeness will be at once a symbolic guarantee and a powerful source of the rebirth of nature and the re-quickening of poetry. Through the intervention of the god, the earth can become sacred, a "grail," an object of poetic worship. Hart Crane was a worshipful poet; a poet who was always in search of some object of genuine reverence, some deity that could be postulated. That search would be given its most eloquent lyrical treatment in "At Melville's Tomb" ("Frosted eyes there were that lifted altars"). But it informs the last portion of "Lachrymae Christi," too, as the recovered poetic vision strains to summon forth the very godhead on which it rested.

[18] For this and other hints about "Lachrymae Christi," I am grateful to Mr. David Clark, whose manuscript on some of Crane's lyrics I had the opportunity of seeing.

CHAPTER SIX

"Voyages"

TAKEN as a whole, "Voyages" is undoubtedly Crane's lyrical masterpiece, a fact which may seem surprising in view of the odd history of its composition. In January and February of 1923, as he was putting the finishing touches to "Faustus and Helen," Crane wrote a poem called "Belle Isle," the last stanzas of which, so he felt, achieved "a kind of revelation," though he was uncertain about the poem as a whole. Several months before, in September 1922, he had written a little rhymeless piece, of which he had no very high opinion, variously called "The Bottom of the Sea Is Cruel" and "Poster." For the time being, there was no connection between these items; but when, in November 1924, Crane found himself "engaged in writing a series" of "sea poems"—to be called "Voyages"—it occurred to him to include the two earlier works as a kind of frame. "The Bottom of the Sea Is Cruel," thus became "Voyages I"; and "Belle Isle" was greatly altered into "Voyages VI." The final revelatory stanza remained virtually intact, but for the rest, only a single image, the useful name of Belle Isle, and scattered individual words, among them such favorites of Crane as "waiting," "white," "river," and "flood," being carried over into the new composition.

These "sea poems" were also, Crane wrote his mother, "love poems," and the immediate inspiration was a love affair with a good-looking young man customarily designated as E. O., a seafaring Northern European temporarily working out of New York, who intermittently shipped to South America "for wages as ship's writer" (in Horton's phrase). The affair evidently began early in the spring of 1924 and continued through the year at something like alternate eight-week periods—E. O. spending eight weeks at sea and then about the same amount of time, or a little less, in the apartment he shared with Crane at 110 Columbia Heights, Brooklyn. It was by all odds the most passionate experience of Crane's life, and it would remain so: "such a dance," he wrote Frank, "as I have never walked and never can walk with another." The fact of his friend's regular and necessary voyaging, combined with the spectacular view of the harbor waters from the lovers' apartment window, led Crane to think of the exalting human affair in terms of the sea. In the completed "Voyages," the sea appears as threat, rival, partner, mimic, enemy, and eventually as a source of vision-ary solace. It was from the outset as though Crane had kept some rendezvous, at once erotic and spiritual, with the sea itself. "I think," he told Frank, "the sea has thrown itself upon me and been answered, at least in part, and I believe I am a little changed—not essentially, but changed and tran-substantiated as anyone is who has asked a question and been answered."

Crane's first creative response to this powerful dialogue with the sea and to the love affair that prompted it was the poem "Sonnet," in April 1924: an unevenly rhymed fifteen-line work that was no more a sonnet in the conventional sense than were the "Sonnets of Apology" of Samuel Green-berg, which, as we shall see, Crane was busy transcribing at just this time. In September of the same year, he wrote and forwarded to Frank what turned out to be an early version of "Voyages IV" but which for the moment was an inde-pendent comment on the progress of his love. It was not until November that Crane conceived of a related *series* of love poems, and that he gathered in "The Bottom of the Sea Is Cruel," and "Belle Isle," rewrote "Sonnet" as the matchless "Voyages III," completed "Voyages IV" and added "II" and "V."

The order of composition of "Voyages"—and it is suf-ficiently typical to warrant rehearsing—was, then: I, versions of VI, III and IV, new versions of each of those, and finally II and V. This raises at once the question whether "Voyages" can be regarded as an integral work: a question that here, as with "Faustus and Helen" and *The Bridge,* bears upon the understanding and evaluation of almost every passage, though that is, perhaps, putting the critical case the wrong way round. When the question about the wholeness and harmony of "Voyages" has been raised at all, the customary answer has been brief and negative. But Gorham Munson thought that "Voyages" was obviously a "suite"—indeed, "the finest love suite composed by any living American," a very sound judgment in my view. A suite it certainly is, in the technical musical sense of a collection of songs on a common theme: or perhaps, cluster of themes—love and death, the sea, time and eternity, song itself, and vision. It is also, I think, a suite in the root meaning of a "sequence." In at least two instances, the individual sections literally, verbally, and syntactically *follow* one another. "I" leads without pause into "II": "The bottom of the sea is cruel. . . . And yet this great wink of eternity" and so on (the sea is dangerous, and yet the sea is after all a glimpse of eternity).[1] "Voyages III" concludes with a singularly lovely line which provides the main clause for the sentence that continues, growing steadily darker, through the first stanza of "IV": "Permit me voyage, love, into your hands. . . . Whose counted smile of hours and days, suppose / I know as spectrum of the sea" etc. But much more significantly, "Voyages" from its beginning to its end unfolds a story—a love story, needless to say—that in its rhythm and content is altogether familiar and expertly conventional.

"Voyages," that is, presents a clear enough and a continuing action, and one that belongs recognizably to an age-old tradition of romance. In it, by convention, the experience of earthly love reaches its peak of excitement

---

[1] A. Alvarez, in his helpful essay on Crane's lyrical poems (*Stewards of Excellence,* New York, 1958; p. 116) dismisses the impression that "II" carries on from the conclusion of "I" as "spurious"—but without giving reasons. One gathers that, since for Mr. Alvarez as for most others, "Voyages" is not a sequence to begin with, it cannot be expected to show *sequiturs* in particular places.

only to be broken off by the departure or death of the
beloved, whereupon the poet-lover finds consolation and a
more permanent kind of gratification in a vision of transcendent beauty or of God or paradise; and in his own
poetic narrative of the entire affair. Petrarch and Sidney
come to mind as notable early practitioners of this genre;
Keats's "Ode on a Grecian Urn" and Whitman's "Out of
the Cradle Endlessly Rocking" are perhaps the later poems
in English with which "Voyages" has most in common.
The Whitman poem especially—from which, in "Cape
Hatteras," Crane would draw an image of Whitman walking the beach near Paumanok and hearing

the wraith
Through surf, its bird note there a long time falling. . . .

—is the significant and light-bearing ancestor of "Voyages."
Crane's sequence, too, was rooted in the joy and pain of
a homosexual love affair and its culmination; and it similarly described, in a series of highly metaphoric projections,
the experience of psychic death leading to the discovery of
the language of vision—that is, to poetry. At times, "Voyages"
almost dissolves this "story" in the sheer flow of its sensuous
imagery; at other times, its suggestive allusions, taken out
of context, seem to carry us into the realm of myth, or into
some boundless domain of splendid un-reason where opposites consort and nameless forces or disembodied pulsations dance out their uninterpretable allegory. But we should
hang on to the traditional, even the archetypal, story in it;
to do so may, at any given moment, seem to reduce the
poem's range, but it is in fact and over all to perceive more
fully the beauty, the poignance, and the power with which
the entire work is endowed.

·I·

"Voyages I" introduces the theme of experience—represented, for Crane as for Herman Melville, by the dangerous

but inviting sea and taking the specific form of a sea-journey which at the same time is and stands for a journey into love. The heart of the poem is in its final stanza, in the poet's would-be address to the "bright, striped urchins" he sees—evidently in a picture or poster of some sort—playing on the beach:

> Fondle your shells and sticks, bleached
> By time and the elements; but there is a line
> You must not cross nor ever trust beyond it
> Spry cordage of your bodies to caresses
> Too lichen-faithful from too wide a breast.
> The bottom of the sea is cruel.

The urchins, as we see, are swiftly transformed by metaphor into ships alerted for departure: their bodies are "spry cordages" or lively ship's rigging. But Crane urges them *not* to put out to sea—not to voyage into a crueler and more encompassing love, but to stay safely on shore or in harbor; to be satisfied with "fondl[ing]" their playthings in innocent affection, and not to submit to caresses from a sea which, in its largeness and power, may dash them against the lichen-covered rocks.

When he first wrote this poem, Crane told Munson that he was not "very enthusiastic" about it; except for its "bold" conclusion, it seemed to him little more than "a kind of poster,—in fact, you might name it 'Poster' if the idea hits you" (it did). But it is one sign of the invigorating whole-ness of the "Voyages" sequence that certain elements in this prologue—elements originally almost purely descriptive—assume in context a much larger suggestiveness. For example:

> And in answer to their treble interjections
> The sun beats lightning on the waves,
> The waves fold thunder on the sand;

also the phrase "bleached by time"; and the image of the boys' fingers "gaily digging and scattering." The erotic dialectic of light and water, the concern with time and timelessness, the constant imagery of hands in the later section of "Voyages" all throw meaning backwards upon such elements.

Later allusions, too, invest what may have been only a peripherally homosexual reference (to "shells and sticks") with less disguised implications; they thus help, retrospectively, to reveal the peculiar danger of the love-voyage which is about to begin. And centrally, of course, there is the image of the sea, the chief figure throughout "Voyages"; and of the individual's relation to the sea, taken as his relation to the menacing temptations of experience generally. In "Voyages I," as Joseph Warren Beach has demonstrated, Crane's image amounts to a fresh statement of a major theme in what was probably Crane's favorite novel, Melville's *Moby-Dick*.[2] Beach points to the close of Chapter 58 in *Moby-Dick* where, after remarking on the "subtleness," "the devilish brilliance and beauty" and "the universal cannibalism of the sea," Melville turns to its opposite, to "this green, gentle and docile earth."

> Do you not find a strange analogy to something in yourself? For as this appalling ocean surrounds the verdant land, so in the soul of man there lies one insular Tahiti, full of peace and joy, but encompassed by all the horrors of the half-known life. God keep thee! Push not off from that isle, thou canst never return.

"Push not off from that isle." So speaks the voice in "Voyages I": "There is a line / You must not cross. . . . The bottom of the sea is cruel."

·II·

But this was only a warning to the uninitiated (Crane called it a " 'stop, look and listen' sign"). It was no more Crane's final exhortation about experience than it had been

[2] *Western Review,* Spring 1956.

Melville's. We recall, in "Faustus and Helen II" the invitation to make the daring plunge into life: "to fall downstairs with me / With perfect grace and equanimity"; or, closer to the symbolism of "Voyages," to "scud past" those "shores" where the trimmers sit in pious safety. Just such bold "shoreless" venturing was commended by Melville; and Beach might have quoted, though he did not, the Melvillian passage that gives the precise parallel for the great shift from "Voyages I" to Voyages II." It occurs in "The Lee Shore" (Chapter 23), when Melville argues that "the wildest winds of heaven and earth conspire to cast [the soul] upon the treacherous, slavish shore"—only to continue:

> *But* as in landlessness alone resides the highest truth, shoreless, indefinite as God—so better is it to perish in that howling infinite than be ingloriously dashed upon the lee, even if it were safety!

The italics are added: for Melville's "but," with the sentence it introduces, has much the same force as the first two words of "Voyages II," recoiling as they do upon the conclusion of the preceding section:

> —*And yet* this great wink of eternity,
>   Of rimless floods, unfettered leewardings,
>   Samite sheeted and processioned where
>   Her undinal vast belly moonward bends,
>   Laughing the wrapt inflections of our love. . . .

"Leewardings" is borrowed straight from *Moby-Dick;* and Crane has succeeded, too, in capturing the Melvillian contrast between the unbounded (shoreless, indefinite, infinite) and the bounded (in Crane, the "wrapt"). So potent indeed was Melville's motif as formulated in "The Lee Shore" and elsewhere, that it plainly affected not only the beginning of "Voyages II" but its ending—where Crane, in strikingly Melvillian language, also urges an unending commitment to "landlessness" since only there can "the highest truth" be sought, even though it be discovered in the moment of calamity, of shipwreck:

> Bequeath us to no earthly shore until
> Is answered in the vortex of our grave
> The seal's wide spindrift gaze toward paradise.

Melville, of course, was speaking about a voyage of thought, of "deep, earnest thinking"; the daring effort of the mind to retain its freedom and to journey through the tempestuous appearance of things to the nature of ultimate reality. Crane was speaking about a (for him) no less daring voyage of love, the effort of flesh, feeling, and imagination to travel to the last reality and meaning of the erotic life. And for Crane, the sea plays a more ambiguous and shifting role. In "Voyages II," it is a still mightier being than in "I," but it is no longer the cruel and destructive lover of the human who submits to it. Instead, as the actual love affair—"*our* love"—gets under way, the sea becomes an imperious rival in love, an absolute and godlike monarch (evidently a queen) whose boundless love and huge embrace of the moon at first make mockery of the limitations of the merely human lovers. The new identification of the sea emerges (to quote again from Crane's theory about "the logic of metaphor") from the "combination and interplay" of the connotations of words as they impinge on our consciousness; and from a rhythmical energy that, as against "Voyages I," seems suddenly supercharged. In "I," however effective its content, the tone was flat and prosaic, and kept at a low key by a number of monosyllabic grammatical binders ("but there is a line / You must not cross nor ever trust beyond it," etc.) that in his later and more highly pressured verse, such as "Voyages II," Crane would do without. The rhythm in "II" is a remarkable mixture of the sense of flowing and that of marching: or better, it suggests a flowing movement that has been stiffened and accentuated into a march—just as the coined word "processioned" visually transforms the rising and breaking waves into disciplined figures marching by in some pageant or parade.

"Processioned," meanwhile, is also one of the important words whose impinging connotation interacts with others to beget the new image of the sea. Along with "samite sheeted" (samite was a medieval silk fabric interwoven with silver and gold), "undinal" (Undine was a water-goddess), "scrolls of silver," and "sceptred terror," it helps make of the sea a godlike ruler of ancient times. What is being stressed about this royal lover in the opening stanza is the absolute nature of her love and the derision she visits, in consequence, upon the finite love-possibilities of man. In one of Crane's most alive and ingenious patterns, the word "wink" leads into another optical image, "rimless," and a portion of the latter word's meaning thence into "unfettered" and "vast" (all words that reinforce as well as add new considerations to the notions of "eternity"); until a primary sense of "wink" returns to evoke and account for the word "laughing":

Laughing the wrapt inflections of our love.[3]

There is an excellent example of Crane's "packed line"— a line that illustrates what Austen Warren meant when, writing about Edward Taylor and linking him with Crane, he remarked: "like greater poets—Donne, Hopkins, and Crane he was impatient of space given to prepositions and articles and other poetic neutralities." [4] The sea's laughter, unimpeded by the customary preposition "at," fairly pours down upon the wrapt nature of the lover's rapture (an arguable pun) and almost drowns it.

But the authority and the arrogance of the sea do not, after all, overpower or disempower (through laughter) the human love. The action in "Voyages" is, as I have suggested, an interlocking double action: the progress of the human

[3] A. Alvarez, *op.cit.,* has traced this pattern in a way that for me was educational.

[4] In *Rage for Order* (Ann Arbor Paperback, 1959), p. 14.

affair as it is dialectically involved with the shifting relation between the poet and the sea. This is Crane's dazzlingly original treatment of an old, essentially a Romantic, convention of love poetry: whereby "nature" (here, chiefly, the sea and the sky) reflects or frustrates, sympathizes with or opposes the movements of human emotion. In "Voyages III," the sea as lover will become the reverent mimic of human sexual behavior; here, in the second stanza of "Voyages II," the two elements—the infinite lover and the finite—grow matched and even. The fearsome sea now holds court as royal magistrate ("sessions"), passes judgment of guilty or not guilty by the expression of her face ("as her demeanors motion well or ill"), and fixes "sentences" that settle the fate of every human enterprise *except* love, that have ultimate power over—

All but the pieties of lovers' hands.[5]

Only lovers are exempt from the "rend[ing]" strength of the sea—not only because, like the sea, they are participants in the experience of love, but also because, in that experience, they also touch something of the divine, the trans-human. Like the wanderers in "The River," they "touch something like a key perhaps."

As the poem's stately flow continues "onward"—impelled by that very adverb at the start of stanza three—the chiming scales ("diapason") of the sea are echoed by the sound of bells from legendary sunken cities like San Salvador;[6] and journeying through the sea-waters, while stars glow like

---

[5] This is Crane's final and typical reworking of a line he originally borrowed from Samuel Greenberg's poem "Man"—"O perfect lay of Deity's crested herb." In Crane's worksheets, "All else than Deity's green crested herb" became: "All else than Deity's steep crested herb," before "Deity's" yielded to the near-rhyme of "pieties" and the full phrase was born. The shift (which was as much one of rhythm as of content) was not quite from the divine to the human, but rather toward shedding a divine aura *over* the human.

[6] Horton, who thus persuasively interprets the reference, says that it was from E. O. that Crane heard about these legends.

crocuses and islands appear as meadows, the lovers partake a little of the sea's eternity and arrive at the full mystery of love, "the dark confessions" latent in the sea's being:

> Adagios of islands, O my Prodigal,
> Complete the dark confessions her veins spell.

Crane said later (in "General Aims and Theories") that the phrase "adagios of islands" referred to "the motion of a boat through islands clustered thickly, the rhythm of the motion etc."; and he felt that it was "a much more direct and creative statement than any more logical employment of words such as 'coasting slowly through the islands.'" Such a phrase, indeed, would have only confused the quality and, as it were, the status of the experience. What is happening is that the voyage metaphor is supplying its own obscure but necessary literal level. Crane and E. O. had never, in fact, coasted together through any cluster of islands; this is simply Crane's figurative rendering of the nature and progress of their relationship—a rendering in which some deliberately faint sense of actual water-journeying is required to add force to the very metaphor from which it derives.

Crane also felt that the word "adagios" "ushered in the whole world of music"—an increasingly important world for "Voyages" as for most of Crane's poetry, but one which had already been ushered in by "diapason" and "bells." The mystery arrived at, in any case, is indicated by the apostrophe to the lover, "O Prodigal." It is the same mystery exposed in "Faustus and Helen"—the paradoxical supremacy of the prodigal life, of "the lavish heart," the utterly yielding and self-giving love. But with this discovery comes a renewed urgency, and the final stanzas are cast in imperatives ("mark . . . hasten . . . hasten") which relax characteristically at the end into a prayer: "Bind us in time. . . . Bequeath us to no earthly shore." Human love is mortal: it exists in time, and time is passing; the relentless passage of time is just what the sea-tides, timeless as they are, continuously measure—"her turning shoulders wind the hours," like a clock. And so:

> hasten while her penniless rich palms
> Pass superscription of bent foam and wave;

hasten while the sea's hands, literally penniless but emotionally rich (the tropical palm tree is of course also intended), pass into the pious hands of lovers the sea's own bounty, the money as it were of its bent foam and wave.[7]

> Hasten, while they are true,—sleep, death, desire,
> Close round one instant in one floating flower.

Those lines have the kind of utter finality—as of some deep and serious emotion perfectly realized in language and cadence—that a lyric poet would be lucky to achieve half a dozen times in his life. The rhythm that hurries briefly and then slows to the solemn tread of "sleep, death, desire," continuing in the soft funereal count of the second line; the countering of imperative and statement; the play, almost the wash, of words against each other; the alliterations and repetitions; even the dimness of syntax and allusion —all gives us poetry in intimate touch with a feeling (about love and death) that is on the far side of logical formulation but that communicates immediately. The entire experience and all its many elements are quietly concentrated in a single entity or image: "one floating flower."

And yet the very beauty of the lines has, I believe, caused a certain misapprehension about "Voyages II" and, by their influence, about a larger range of Crane's poetry. It is true that in the sequence "sleep, death, desire," sleep and death determine the reference of desire—which becomes, exactly,

---

[7] Beach, *op.cit.*, makes the acute guess that for Crane the word "superscription"—which otherwise means simply something written *above*—had the connotation of a coin: from its special use in the Gospel when Jesus says, "Show me a penny. Whose image and superscription hath it? They answered and said, Caesar's." The proximity of "penny" (in "penniless") and the imperial quality of the sea in "Voyages II" do much to confirm the suggestion.

a desire *for* sleep and death; a yearning for oblivion. Crane is indeed saying in some untranslatable way that he and his lover must hasten to enjoy their love while the sea's bounty is still available ("while they"—the bent foam and wave—"are true")—as the setting which gives their love its ultimate and awesome nature. For he knows that, like Keats, he is half in love with easeful death, and perhaps all men are; before death closes sweetly upon them, they must seize the day of love. But, to put it as unequivocally as possible, "Voyages II" is not a *Liebestod;* it is not an expression of the so-called death-wish; it is no evidence of a suicidal impulse. It gives rise, quite on the contrary, to a remarkably firm prayer for life:

> Bind us in time, O Seasons clear, and awe.
> O minstrel galleons of Carib fire,
> Bequeath us to no earthly shore until
> Is answered in the vortex of our grave
> The seal's wide spindrift gaze toward paradise.

To the seasons of the year, Crane thus prays that they may bind the lovers inside this world of time, of which the seasons are the resident powers; and he prays that, so time-bound, the lovers may also see the temporal world as awesome, as a domain to be revered. Such, we can remind ourselves, has been the experience of ardent young lovers generally: to them, in the very ecstasy of their love, the world seems charged with a nearly sacred beauty. But we can also remind ourselves that Crane's prayer to the seasons bespeaks once again his fundamental attitude to life and to poetry, as he had announced it in the grand climax of "Faustus and Helen":

Distinctly praise the years, whose volatile
Blamed bleeding hands extend and thresh the height. . . .

In that same mood, more personally accented, Crane then begs the "minstrel galleons"—the vessels of song on which (always within the metaphor) the lovers make their way rejoicing—not to deposit them on shore until the experience of love has been exhausted. This prayer would be very definitely answered in the conclusion of the "Voyages" sequence—when, in "Voyages VI," the poet passes through a kind of death (symbolized as death at sea), through the grave of his love, to rest his own visionary gaze upon a paradise of timeless beauty, an unearthly shore called Belle Isle. Then the promise of the seal's fixed and spray-swept stare (the image is at once vividly realistic and Melvillian) would be fulfilled; then the floating flower of death would become the "petalled word" of creation.

It occurs to me that the presumptive manner of Crane's actual death in 1932 has been a blinder on the understanding of his poetry. Because he died by his own hand as it seems, and at so relatively young an age, there has been a temptation to find in his writing the constant expression of a suicidal urge, or at least a yearning for nothingness; a profound and dominant desire to be released from this mortal world. But the proudest imperatives of his characteristic poems are directed against the escape from the temporal world and toward the praise of it: "Distinctly praise the years"; "Bind us in time, O Seasons clear, and awe"; "And let us walk through time with equal pride"; to which one can add, virtually, the whole of *The Bridge*. That Crane had a fervent consciousness of death is undeniable; he would scarcely have been a very interesting poet without it. But the force and beauty of lines like those just quoted come directly from his committed *resistance* to that consciousness. If the evidence warranted (and though it is curiously inconclusive, it probably does not), I should be more inclined to reconsider the alleged manner of his death in the light of his poems than the other way round. He spoke for life.

·III·

The life he spoke for, and we cannot insist upon it too often, was life enlarged and illuminated by a divine energy:

or by a human energy raised to a higher power. This is the life realized as the intoxicated fulfillment of love in "Voyages III," where death is mentioned only to be utterly denied. "Voyages III" is the most riotous poem, emotionally, in the whole sequence; its first version, we remember, was Crane's immediate response in April 1924, to the suddenly burgeoning love affair. The poet's sea-journey is now a journey *to* his beloved (the title of the sequence, we remember is "Voyages" in the plural); a movement—toward perfect union—that becomes enormously accelerated. The poetry swirls with gerunds of breath-taking activity, and at a speed too great for normal punctuation. And where, at the start of "Voyages II," the human love saw itself derided by the boundless erotic swellings of the sea, now on the contrary it is magnified beyond measure—since the erotic act of the lovers has become the model imitated by the universe at large.

The whole of "Voyages III" is an elaboration of its strong opening lines:

> Infinite consanguinity it bears—
> This tendered theme of you that light
> Retrieves from sea plains where the sky
> Resigns a breast that every wave enthrones.

The poet's love for his friend is blood-brother to the love discernible between the elements of nature throughout infinity; at once a model for and portion of that love. The sea mounts the sky's proffered breast in a sexual union identical with that of the lovers; or, in keeping with the sea's royal character as established in "II," the sea "enthrones" itself upon the submissive sky. The image is huge and startling; but the convention, sometimes and disapprovingly called the pathetic fallacy—natural elements behaving in sympathetic imitation of human beings—is probably as old as love poetry (especially French and English Romantic poetry) and certainly as common as contemporary popular song, in which breezes continue to woo trees and willows to lean languorously toward water. But perhaps never have the elements engaged in so fierce a mimicry of human sexual combat as in "Voyages III"—

> Light, wrestling there incessantly with light
> Star kissing star through wave on wave unto
> Your body rocking!

All the forms of love—as it were, the various and strenuous embraces of the universe—reach their culmination in the sexual embrace of the beloved. This is the end of the journey: which, through the preceding lines, had been steadily gathering momentum. The poet's approach to the lover had been imaged as a passage along "water lanes," which are "ribboned" because and until the poet "winds" them—winds his way through them, winding them up, till he arrives at the lover's side. He is welcomed by the sea as an equal, a fellow lover and a fellow priest:

> whereto this hour
> The sea lifts, also, reliquary hands.

> And so, admitted through black swollen gates
> That must arrest all distance otherwise,—
> Past whirling pillars and lithe pediments. . . .

The approach of the poet to the sexual encounter is not only a voyage; in the intensity of the experience, it is like a plunge into the very depths of the sea ("through black swollen gates"—through dark and swelling waves). It is also a religious experience. In its gesture of admittance, the sea "lifts reliquary hands"—hands that are or contain sacred relics; that, like the lover's hands in "II," contain or express "pieties." And the poet comes to his lover like a worshipper entering a temple: swept downward through the gates and past pillars and pediments (items one associates with Greek temples and Christian churches), the poet arrives at the steep floor of love.

The bottom of the sea is here anything but cruel; it is the shrine of love. And in it:

death, if shed,
Presumes no carnage, but this single change,—
Upon the steep floor flung from dawn to dawn
The silken skilled transmemberment of song;

Permit me voyage, love, into your hands. . . .

It is another of Crane's great lyrical climaxes; and it marks the moment of climax in the love relationship—a particular or orgasmic climax, which is at the same time, within the sequence, the highest pitch of feeling and intimacy. The language, as it has to be with Crane on such occasions, is almost entirely connotative; but as the words (like all the other elements in this poem) rush toward one another, they create an absolute effect. In the depth of the sea, that is in the depth of an absolute sexual experience, the only death that occurs is not anything like destruction ("carnage"); it is rather an extraordinary physical transformation, lit by an unmitigated joy and felt as song. "Transmemberment" is a handsome homemade word that denies in its prefix the notion of physical *dis*memberment, and in the same prefix indicates a very different kind of metamorphosis —the kind also described in song in Shakespeare's *The Tempest:* "Nothing of him" (of me, of us, Crane would say) "that doth fade / But doth suffer a sea-change / Into something rich and strange." [8] A portion of such richness and strangeness is implied by the word "silken"—as though it were now the humans' love-couch that were "samite sheeted" as formerly the sea's had been.

As a matter of fact, Crane had himself already provided an exact gloss on the passage in his letter of April 21.

I know now that there is such a thing as indestructibility. In the deepest sense, where flesh became transformed

[8] In a boozily excited letter to Slater Brown, in February 1928, Crane spoke of his desire to "wake up at dawn and dip into *The Tempest,* that crown of all the Western World." *The Tempest,* the most visionary of Shakespeare's plays and his supreme handling of the archetypal comic pattern, would obviously have special appeal for Crane.

through intensity of response to counter-response, where sex was beaten out, where a purity of joy was reached that included tears.

Critical language can hardly do better than that; "intensity of response to counter-response" is the precise prose parallel of "flung from dawn to dawn," and "indestructibility" is the whole theme of the lines. But we can notice the oddly effective word "shed." At first it seems to be a queer way of saying "happens"; then, in its meaning of "spilled out like water," invests death with its Elizabethan (and later) sense of orgasm; and finally, assuming from context its more familiar meaning of "gotten rid of," suggests that death has been shaken off through love and song once and for all. It is one of those extra-dynamic words of Crane which impose radical changes on the very element being introduced. And after what used to be called "the little death" has thus put an end to the apprehension of actual death, the poem and the poet relax into that post-erotic peace beyond understanding:

Permit me voyage, love, into your hands. . . .

· I V ·

"Voyages III" represents the peak of the love experience, and the moment when the sense and the sound of song are most powerful. With "IV," a change sets in; and soon the poetic attention will shift from love to loss, and from song to vision. About the early or September version of "IV," Crane told Frank that it was "an 'even so' and 'All hail' to a love that I have known." Despite the past tense, the actual affair with E. O. was by no means over. Crane's friend had been absent for some weeks, and Crane "miss[ed] him terribly," as he wrote his mother; "he is so much more to me than anyone I have ever met." But the great rapture seems to have been over; and "Voyages IV" celebrates and rehearses the love amidst premonitions of its ending.

The case is interesting, however, and constitutes a very telling victory of poetic convention over life. As far as one can gather, it was Crane whose affection began to ebb a little at this time; Crane, and not E. O., whose transport began to diminish. A relationship on the physical level, even one so ecstatic and transforming as this, was simply not adequate for Crane, whose spiritual and creative powers needed profounder sources of satisfaction. Something like that, one judges, is the truth about the actual life. But in the poem, the living conventions of the tradition in which Crane was so consciously working required that it be the lover and not the poet who departs, leaving the poet to seek other and more spiritual consolations. And this, in essence, is the "story" from "Voyages IV" through "VI."

The general sense of "Voyages IV" we make out without undue exertion; but there is in it a notable slackening of poetic muscle. The compact vigor of "III" is dissipated; and the first and third stanzas in particular seem for all their brevity to thicken interminably, piling phrase upon phrase with a loss rather than an accumulation of meaning and intensity. Crane seems here to be poetically grinding his gears, as though he were trying to move the action forward but had not found the way to do so. This may be an internal symptom of his own real feelings; one has the impression, anyhow, that a lack of real feeling has produced— in stanza two, for example—that "succession of labored ingenuities" and that "meaningless violence" that Austin Warren has identified as typical of baroque poetry gone wrong:[9]

> All fragrance irrefragably, and claim
> Madly meeting logically in this hour
> And region that is ours to wreathe again,
> Portending eyes and lips and making told
> The chancel port and portion of our June.

[9] Warren, *op. cit.*

Crane was capable of audacious and often brilliantly significant punning; but the play on "frag" in "fragance" and "irrefragably" and on "port" in "portending," "port," and "portion" is merely tiresome. And Crane probably never contrived a less musical paradox than "Madly meeting logically in this hour"; an opaque statement *about* the logic of metaphor rather than a persuasive example of the same.

For the most part, words bump into one another in the fog of this poem; though some of its phrases—typically, for "Voyages"—receive a kind of clarification and importance from the later sequence: for example, "spectrum of the sea." But occasional meanings do loom up. Stanza one, which, as I have said, toilsomely concludes the sentence that began in "III," also reaffirms the content of its predecessor:

Whose circles bridge, I know, (from palms to the severe
Chilled albatross's white immutability)
No stream of greater love advancing now
Than, singing, this mortality alone
Though clay aflow immortally to you.

Nowhere in the world, in short, from the tropics to the North Pole, is there a love greater than ours—a mortal love that in its very fleshiness ("clay") achieves and celebrates immortality (but how much less splendid it all is than "the silken skilled transmemberment of song," and how reluctant and almost grating the song has become). A later reference to "the incarnate word" has a similar implication, and one Crane had also glossed in the letter to Frank, just before the remark about "indestructibility": "I have seen the Word made Flesh. I mean nothing less." The "chancel port" has a like insinuation of carnal religiosity, and faintly echoes the cathedral imagery in "III."

I take the phrase "lost in fatal tides" and the allusion to resigning "the harbor shoulders" (unless "resign" is a punning sequel to "signature") and to

islands where must lead inviolably
Blue latitudes and levels of your eyes

as a clustering anticipation of the end or death of the love affair. That would be the "even so" aspect of the poem, in Crane's phrase; and the concluding lines offer the "All hail"—

> In this expectant, still exclaim receive
> The secret oar and petals of all love.

Something is obviously wrong with either the grammar or the punctuation of the first of those lines (the worksheets do not help). One can move the words around experimentally; but they are curiously inert and heavy counters. I suppose "still" to be the noun intended, and the comma to be misplaced, and read it: "In this expectant still, exclaim [and] receive," etc. In any event, it is plainly a moment of final celebration, and the gift of the symbols of universal love.

The symbols in question, needless to say, are those of the male genitals, the symbolism being adjusted to the seafaring profession of the departing lover. In context, they are homosexual symbols, which is why they are "secret"— though only secret, and not guilty or remorseful. Homosexual symbolism also hovers inescapably in the imagery of "Voyage III" and infuses "Voyages V"; it is present wherever hands or oars are referred to, and in one perspective it can be seen pervading the whole sequence. This is perhaps the moment to remark that "Voyages," despite its flaws, is not only that rarity in American literature—genuine and personal love poetry; it is also the only truly moving and beautiful poetry of male homosexual love in English with which I am acquainted. It is so because Crane has succeeded in making the passionate love of male for male representative of every kind of human passion: "the secret oar and petals of *all* love." [10]

---

[10] "Voyages," on this ground, probably adds substance to the thesis that Leslie Fiedler has argued in articles and in *Love and Death in the American Novel*—that the most real and intimate relationships in American literature occur between male and male, rather than

· V ·

"Voyages V" is the very instant of farewell:

> Your eyes already in the slant of drifting foam;
> Your breath sealed by the ghosts I do not know.

There is a more than usually distinctive time and setting (or "hour and region" in the language of "Voyages IV"). It it past midnight on a moonlit evening; the lovers are gazing through the open window of their room onto the "bay estuaries." It is a scene they both have loved, for it had been associated with the magical beauty of their union, and the transcendent significance of their love. "That window is where I would most be remembered," Crane had said to Frank; "the ships, the harbor, and the skyline of Manhattan, midnight, morning or evening,—rain, snow or sun, it is everything from mountains to the walls of Jerusalem and Nineveh, and all related and in actual contact with the changelessness of the many waters that surround it." That sense of cosmic (or planetary) totality as represented in a single scene: that actual experience had found expression steadily in the poetry. But now there *has* been a change; though, as I have said, not quite the change that actually occurred:

> moonlight loved
> And changed. . . .

The lover is about to depart; mentally, he has already departed and his eyes are already on the sea-ways ("the slant of drifting foam" that will carry him off), his eyes already busy with other presences that are strangers to the poet.

---

male and female. The latter relation, Mr. Fiedler has argued, usually takes the form of combat, with the female often appearing as a vampirish and lethal force. That notion, too, can be illustrated in Hart Crane's poetry: in the combative couple of "The Wine Menagerie," for instance, and in the second of the "Three Songs" in *The Bridge*.

To the vision of the poet the scene has therefore altered drastically, the process beginning with the first lines of "Voyages V":

> Meticulous, past midnight in clear rime,
> Infrangible and lonely, smooth as though cast
> Together in one merciless white blade—
> The bay estuaries fleck the hard sky limits.

The estuaries, which resemble one another like rhyming words, are a melancholy mirror not of human love and union but of human separation and loneliness. No longer do they engage the sky in mimetic pleasure; they merely fleck its limit (presumably by being spottily reflected in them); and the sky, which once so willingly resigned its breast to the enthroning sea, has now become hard. Nature, as Crane continues to manipulate in his own idiom the long-standing conventional pattern, thus responds imitatively to the moment of division; but at the same time, it seems to have turned against the lovers—to be the very source of the division, a sword that will cut the lovers asunder. It has become a culpable and cruel force, a "tidal wedge."

> What words
> Can strangle this deaf moonlight? For we

> Are overtaken. Now no cry, no sword
> Can fasten or deflect this tidal wedge,
> Slow tyranny of moonlight, moonlight loved
> And changed. . . .

The poet's anguished question is more violent than its literary source in Shakespeare's Twenty-Ninth sonnet: "and trouble deaf heaven with my bootless cries"; for, out of a sense of incomprehensible betrayal, the poet wants not only to trouble but to strangle deaf heaven; but his cry is equally bootless. The moon is unheeding; and where formerly death was wholly denied in a religious ecstasy, now death

has invaded the landscape under a hard sky that is itself
an anti-religious source of cleavage:

> that godless cleft of sky
> Where nothing turns but dead sands flashing.

In one of Crane's most enchanting small passages, a
stanza later, the sea has become piratical:

> No,
> In all the argosy of your bright hair I dreamed
> Nothing so flagless as this piracy.

Crane perhaps remembered at this point his comment on
"Voyages I" when it was still called "The Bottom of the
Sea Is Cruel": that its last line embodied the basic motif
of the poem by resembling "a skull & crossbones insignia."
In "Voyages I," the sea (the scene and symbol of adult
love) has appeared as a piratical power capable of seizing
and wrecking the human ships that put forth upon it. And
this, according to "Voyages V," is what had happened.
"Argosy" means a fleet of ships; and it may have been connected in Crane's mind as in that of many others, though
this is not in fact its etymology, with the mythical ship *Argo*
and hence with the quest-journey of Jason (who figures in
the "Atlantis" section of *The Bridge*). Remembering that
"bright hair" (or, as in "Praise for an Urn" and "Faustus
and Helen," "gold hair") was a regular symbol for Crane
of love and beauty, we can hear him replying to the lover's
grammatically shaky remark ("never to quite understand"):
no, that is so, he does not understand either. Never, during
a love-voyage of almost mythic quality, did he dream of so
unannounced ("flagless") and unprepared for an event as
this scuttling of their love. And yet, forlornly, he begs the
lover to turn back from the window and come to him one
last time, that they may dream together of some far-off
reunion, knowing still it is merely a dream: "Draw in your
head and sleep the long way home."

·VI·

"Voyages VI" is in its own right one of the truly splendid poems in English; and it concludes the "Voyages" sequence with a poetic splendor so appropriate as in effect to provide the subject matter of this final moment. It is a poem of intense visionary straining, sight and blindness are of its essence, and eyes constitute its key reference; and it is a work of the utmost rhetorical magnificence. Vision and poetry: these are what "Voyages VI" is about; vision and poetry as the answer to the death of love and the shattering bewilderment it produced. Out of the vortex of love's grave, the shipwreck of his love, the poet sees and hears the long-awaited answer to "the seal's wide spindrift gaze toward paradise." And the answer ("Voyages VI" consists, structurally, of a prayer and an answer, an "unbetrayable reply") is a glimpse of the paradise of the poet's own aspirations—his creative aspirations; for as he comes to perceive Belle Isle, he also hears issuing from it the "petalled word" of "creation." In Crane's compelling treatment of this greatly traditional movement, the sea is again a decisive agent. The sea that had threatened and laughed at him, that had rivaled, imitated, and turned against him, that had wrecked or drowned him, now exerts its power to rescue and restore the poet.

> Where icy and bright dungeons lift
> Of swimmers their lost morning eyes,
> And ocean rivers, churning, shift
> Green borders under stranger skies. . . .

We have moved, geographically and spiritually, from the warm Caribbean to icy northern waters; as it turns out, from the heat of emotional and physical experience to the cool zone where emotion may be recollected in tranquillity. There may be a literal basis to the symbolic geography. An actual Belle Isle lies north of Newfoundland, off the coast of Labrador and southeast of Cape St. Charles, the place referred to (if any literal reference is intended) in "the cape's wet stone." [11] More valuably for the poem, Belle Isle is situated in the Strait of Belle Isle that leads from the Gulf of St. Lawrence eastward to sea, looking toward morning and the ocean. As "Voyages VI" opens, the poet finds himself in a region and within a complete poetic figure where swimmers struggle through chill ocean rivers toward morning, under skies that are strange to them, and with "eyes" that are "lost." The poet is one of those swimmers, or like them. He too is lost; he does not recognize the new surroundings, the shifting borders; and he has lost his ability to see—that is (again, as it turns out), his capacity to understand the actual world, its excitement and its pain, in the light of an envisioned ideal world. "Voyages VI" begins on the note of desolating incomprehension with which "Voyages V" ended.

It also begins with a tight paradox and an eloquent prayer. The poet is like a drowned and eyeless swimmer; two stanzas later, he is also like a blind sailor on an abandoned ship—he is even that ship itself:

> My eyes pressed black against the prow,
> —Thy derelict and blinded guest.

He had, against all the warnings of "Voyages I" embarked on the dangerous love-journey; he had trusted his "spry cordage," the vessel of his body, to the cruel sea—had, in "Voyages III," descended to the depths of the sea to experience the whole fierce grandeur of human love; but after that grandeur had come the separation and with it the sense of psychic incarceration and of death. And yet it is exactly that imprisoning and destructive sea whose *guest* the poet is, and whose "dungeons" (according to the poem's surprising syn-

[11] In 1919, Crane had written an imagistic work called "North Labrador." But he apparently never visited that region, and may have heard a description of it from E. O: or so Professor Unterecker surmises.

tax) can "lift" the "lost morning eyes" of swimmers like the poet. The sea possesses the power to restore life and light and vision, which is why its icy dungeons are also "bright"; for it is through just such a descent, just such a sea-death, that the adventurous and questing spirit may reach an ultimate perception forever denied to the emotionally landlocked. One must lose one's vision in order to find it. In the poem, the poet knows this; even as Crane knew it to be the inevitable outcome in the poetic tradition he was following; and the voice in "Voyages VI" prays to the ocean rivers that he too may be resurrected and re-enlightened:

> O rivers mingling toward the sky
> And harbor of the phoenix' breast—
> My eyes pressed black against the prow,
> —Thy derelict and blinded guest
>
> Waiting, afire, what name, unspoke,
> I cannot claim: let thy waves rear
> More savage than the death of kings,
> Some splintered garland for the seer.

It is a prayer for an end to the exhaustion of voyaging, a prayer for peaceful rest (later: "unsearchable repose"); for a spiritual haven and a phoenix-like rebirth. It is above all, a prayer for spiritual vision that can once more give rise to poetic utterance. In lines that surge and fall, that pound almost audibly to a turbulent oceanic pulse, the poet urges the sea-waves to "rear" for him an immense poetic theme ("garland"—the conventional symbol of poetic genius and achievement)—a theme even more potent and terrible than the heroic theme of poetry in earlier epochs, the theme of the fall of the mighty ("sad tales of the death of kings," in *Richard II*). For the new subject is the death or fragmentation of poetic vision itself: it is "a splintered garland for the seer" which at the same time, by transposition, is a garland for the splintered seer.

This endlessly reverberating passage contains, among other things, as direct and dramatic a statement as one can find about the nature of the Romantic tradition—one is inclined to say, about the nature of modern poetry, and of a large range of modern literature generally. It bespeaks what is probably the key historic event in that tradition: the emergence of the poet—replacing the king or prince—as the hero of poetry; and of the exacting processes of the creative imagination as the drama that most absorbs the poet's attention. No less in the Romantic tradition (one might compare the moment, for example, with Whitman's "As I Ebb'd with the Ocean of Life,"),[12] the prayer is in great part answered in the very eloquence by which it gets uttered. The sweeping intensity of the poet's address to the waves indicates how far he has recovered his lost powers.

What follows is in a way a recapitulation of what had already happened or at least was already taking place. It is the sea's answer to the ardently waiting poet: the name or word he does not dare to claim—the name of Belle Isle, and the word of creation.

> Beyond siroccos harvesting
> The solstice thunders, crept away,
> Like a cliff swinging or a sail
> Flung into April's inmost day—
>
> Creation's blithe and petalled word
> To the lounged goddess when she rose. . . .

Those sonorous lines are, of course, exceedingly condensed; though they can, once the order of the phrases is straightened out, be made sense of.[13] But they convey a movement of

---

[12] In this poem, one of Whitman's greatest accomplishments, the condition of psychic and creative exhaustion is overcome in the statement of it.

[13] I take "creation's word" to be the subject of "crept away" and the two similes as visual images, first from the vantage point of the water (whence a cliff, as it is passed, can seem itself to be in motion), and second from the vantage point of land (whence the ship dis-

feeling and consciousness—from the sirocco (a hot and blighting wind) to the island, from distractingly oppressive heat to the coolness where insight is possible—which is clear enough, and is thoroughly characteristic. We recall, in "Faustus and Helen I," the shift from the baked asphalt city:

> to somewhere
> Virginal perhaps, less fragmentary, cool;

and we shall encounter a similar transition (or one similarly longed for) in the first of the "Three Songs" in *The Bridge:*

> High, cool,
>   wide from the slowly smoldering fire
> Of lower heavens,—
>   vaporous scars!

It is always a journey from the turgidity of the actual world, and usually from the devouring heat of sexual desire, to the serener beauty of the ideal and to the true source of poetry. This is the journey the poet has virtually completed by the start of "Voyages VI," when he has reached the bright and icy northern waters, and that the sea, by way of answer, now completes for him.

As the voyage and the "Voyages" sequence approach their ending, the language and cadence slow and soften, a profound quiet enters into them. But on Belle Isle, the poet does not forget or repudiate the actual world he has left behind. On the contrary, he finds there the means of understanding it and the terms for describing and rejoicing in it, even as he had in "Faustus and Helen" and as he will—for this would essentially be the theme of Crane's epic—in *The Bridge.* The goddess who rises smiling from her lounge (her "floating dais," Belle Isle itself) is no doubt the goddess of dawn, and the blithe word is *"Fiat Lux."* [14] But, like

---

appears over the horizon). In combination, the two images expand the notion of significant movement—of the passage of consciousness from one place and condition to another.

[14] This was proposed some time ago by Charles C. Walcutt in *The Explicator* Vol. IV, No. 7, May 1946). Mr. Walcutt sees "Voyages

Helen in the earlier poem, she is also the poet's muse and the blithe word is a word *about* creation. Even as she says, "Let there be light!" she also says, "Let there be poetry!" For if the human union has been betrayed and dissolved, poetry will yet emerge from the union between the poet and his goddess; that union is exactly the "dialogue" which her eyes "concede." And in the poetry—that is, of course, in the entire love suite the poet is now enabled to compose— the human world and the human love affair find their identity, their meaning, their justification.

It is, so to speak, a process of poetic transubstantiation: something hinted at in the adjective "petalled" ("Creation's blithe and petalled word") and then made radiantly explicit in the penultimate stanza:

> Still fervid covenant, Belle Isle,
> —Unfolded floating dais before
> Which rainbows twine continual hair—
> Belle Isle, white echo of the oar!

Once again, Crane is redeeming, as it were perfecting, the actual world by the resources of poetry. Crucial elements that, in the earlier sections, served to define the human experience now reappear, purified and made permanent, in the ideal setting; and this is just the creative and spiritual

---

VI" as an elaboration of the Greek myth of Orion, who "was blinded by Oenopian of Chios for having ravished his daughter Merope. Beloved by Eros, goddess of the dawn, Orion made his way to the seaside and recovered sight when the first rays of the rising sun struck his eyes." Many of the elements in that myth do turn up in "Voyages VI." But there is no evidence that Crane knew or was interested in the myth of Orion; and Mr. Walcutt does not make it clear whether what he is really suggesting is a Jungian archetype, a dramatic fable embodied variously and coincidentally in an ancient myth and a modern American poem. My own view is that "Voyages VI" should be read first of all not in the context of classical myth (though the latter may well provide illuminating parallels) but in the context of the "Voyages" sequence of which it is the climax and conclusion; and also of the body of Crane's poetry and letters and a larger body of love poetry and visionary poetry. I remain no less grateful for Mr. Walcutt's particular pointers.

achievement of which the island, like the rainbow in the Old Testament, is a still living covenant, a divine guarantee. In "Voyages IV," the lover's hands had been like a rainbow on the waters ("spectrum of the sea"),[15] and his departure had been symbolized in the abrupt disappearance of his "bright hair." But here, before the island, "rainbows twine continual hair"—*eternal* rainbows braid *eternal* hair. The proffered symbols of physical love had been "the secret oar and petals"; now it is the creative word that is petalled, and Belle Isle is a "white echo" (a pure and transcendent echo) of the phallic oar. And, climactically, "the incarnate word" of "Voyages IV"—the ideal realized carnally, in Crane's phrase "beaten out" in sexual strivings—has become "the imaged Word" which, unlike the lover, never betrays, never forsakes.

> The imaged Word, it is, that holds
> Hushed willows anchored in its glow.
> It is the unbetrayable reply
> Whose accent no farewell can know.

This is the "Word" of poetry—as always, of Crane's kind of poetry; transcendent reality imaged in language, and in a poetic language whose power ("glow") fixes, gives permanence and beauty and settled meaning to, the things of this world. Those things, human and natural, find their true anchorage—according to Crane's quietly surprising figure—not in the sea of the actual but in the steady glow of the ideal.

By the end of "Voyages," there can be little doubt about the nature and content of Crane's so ardently sought after "vision." One has heard it remarked that Crane was occupied with the tactics and intensity of vision, with the excitement

---

[15] Keats once complained that Newton had taken all the poetry out of the rainbow by reducing it to a "prism." In the phrase "spectrum of the sea," Crane may be said to have reversed the process—as in general he was always striving to do—by investing the "spectrum" with poetry. I am grateful to Peter J. Conn for this suggestion.

of pursuing it, rather than with its definable substance. But about "Voyages" there can hardly be any uncertainty. It is a vision of this human life, of the loves we experience, the sufferings we endure, the kinds of deaths we undergo—and of the splendor and beauty of that life when it is viewed under the aspect of eternity and illuminated by the language of poetry.

CHAPTER SEVEN

The Visionary Lyric

I T WAS NOT the illuminated world of "Voyages," but a world quite devoid of significant light that Crane had surveyed in "Emblems of Conduct," a poem written in the summer of 1924, some months before he settled to work on the love suite. "Emblems of Conduct" is a sadly beautiful appraisal of a world no longer animated by a genuine religious or visionary consciousness, and with it we move into a series of lyrics concerned primarily with vision or the lack of it, a series that culminated in "Repose of Rivers," just prior to the composition of the major portions of *The Bridge*.

"Emblems of Conduct" is also one of the attractive curiosities of American literature, for apart from two lines and a couple of phrases, it is simply an artful pastiche of fragments taken from the manuscript poems of a certain Samuel Greenberg. While Crane was staying at Woodstock, just before Christmas 1923, he had been introduced to Greenberg's work by William Murrell Fisher, an art critic and a friend of Crane's host, Slater Brown. The impact was immediate and powerful; but little was known about it until Philip Horton uncovered the facts and presented them via an essay in the *Southern Review* in 1936.[1] It is still unclear how much of Greenberg's voluminous writings Crane managed to read. "Fisher has shown me an amazing amount of material," he wrote Munson, "some of which I am copying." Greenberg, who seems to have composed like lightning, wrote more than six hundred poems during the last bedridden

---

[1] Horton rehearsed the story in his biography of Crane; and in the wake of Horton's revelations, James Laughlin published 22 of Greenberg's poems in 1939. In 1947, Harold Holden and Jack McManis brought out a selection of 135 poems, plus excerpts from Greenberg's longer writings. (*Poems by Samuel Greenberg,* with a preface by Allen Tate; Henry Holt, 1947.)

years of his life; when he died in August 1917, he left seventeen notebooks of poetry, prose, and drawings in Fisher's
care, along with scraps of writing on the backs of menus or
on wrapping paper. According to Horton, Crane took back
with him to New York only a "bundle of five or six notebooks." What is clear, however, is Crane's excitement and
enthusiasm. He described Greenberg as a "Rimbaud in
embryo," and he continued (to Munson): "Did you ever
see some of the hobbling yet really gorgeous attempts that
boy made without an education or time except when he became confined to a cot? . . . No grammar, nor spelling,
and scarcely any form, but a quality that is unspeakably
eerie and the most convincing gusto. One little poem is as
good as any of the consciously-conceived 'Pierrots' of Laforgue."

"Gusto" is not, perhaps, the outstanding attribute of Greenberg's poetry, which while it abounds in exclamations and
is at times charged with dark intensity, is for the most part
sweeter and gentler than Crane's, as though sweetened and
gentled by pain. (Greenberg, a Vienna-born Jew whose impoverished family came to America in 1900, contracted
tuberculosis in 1913 and spent the last four years of his life
in and out of hospitals, suffering, declining, and writing.)
The poetry lacks the kind of dramatic music of which Crane
was increasingly capable; it could be more nakedly and
tenderly personal than Crane's, but it could also—especially
in what Greenberg called his "apology sonnets"—be more
discursive, more given to large and abstract propositions
about the poet, the scholar, mortality, and so on. Those latter
moments reflect the notable influence of Emerson on Greenberg—Emerson's attitudes and phrasing, his blunted, irreg-
ular rhythms, and above all his habit of giving vaguely
allegorical proportions to the materials being dealt with.[2]

[2] Messrs. Holden and McManis (*ibid.*) report that, though Greenberg had read Keats and Shelley, "it was Emerson who confirmed
his mysticism," and they observe that "the titles of many of his poems
are taken from Emerson and Thoreau."

But for all these qualities and for all Greenberg's sensitivity to death and to the wounded life, his is essentially a poetry of joy—and of an explicitly religious joy. This was why Crane, as he became himself ever-more committed to the poetry of non-doctrinal religious celebration, could so much honor Greenberg as against the ironic and self-demeaning "Pierrot" poems of Laforgue which he had admiringly translated only a few years before. "We feel sacredly merry," Greenberg says warmly in "Ballad of Joy"—

> We dance as the innocent summer sun
> In silence and awe—we children of God!

Greenberg was also, like Crane and like the earlier Romantic poets whom both were following, much occupied with the nature of poetry and the status of the poet in an unpoetic age: as in these thought-provoking, Emersonian lines from "The Tempest":

> I live in an age where the age lives alone,
> And lonesome doth it rage
> Where the bard dare not come.

Greenberg's finely chosen word "lonesome" had somewhat the meaning for him that the word "broken" had for Crane; and indeed, one detects in Greenberg's work stray hints of the same large view—of spiritual and cultural fragmentation and mechanization, and of the role of poetry in the ultimate restoration of wholeness and vitality—that Crane had been variously expounding. The poem "East River's Charm," if Crane in fact read it, may have had a belated effect upon *The Bridge;* for Greenberg, too, sees the crowded actualities of the river scene ("where the ferries, tugs and sailboats stirred") dissolved by poetry into a sort of charming pastoral landscape, and in "the stacks of the floating boat" he finds

> the quality ne'er to dissever
> Like the ruffles from the mystified smoke.

In any event, Greenberg's poetry must have appealed to Crane because of its constant and urgent visionary thrust, for example in "Life's Mortality":

> The sparkling visionary light in which we
> Reveal the dream lies as a looking glass
> In our future—

and its daringly, sometimes unknowingly, original method. Greenberg lacked, as he put it, "the knowledge of grammatic truth," but this may only have helped him give such unique and personal expression to his persisting religious quest.

The poem Crane put together as "Emblems of Conduct" draws upon several of Greenberg's so-called "Sonnets of Apology"—so-called because, though they are fourteen lines in length, they vary unconventionally from a three to four and a five stress line, with only occasional and unpatterned rhymes. Horton has traced the compositional process in detail, and we need not go over the whole ground again. But we can notice that Crane's central motif comes from Greenberg's "Immortality," particularly from the reference there to "memories of spiritual gate" (a word Greenberg oddly left in the singular). "Emblems of Conduct," that is, has to do with the reduction to mere historic memory of the once-living reality of the spiritual world. And it is just the force of that melancholy motif that leads Crane to borrow, adapt, and splice as he does.

The matter is sufficiently clear in Crane's first stanza:

> By a peninsula the wanderer sat and sketched
> The uneven valley graves. While the apostle gave
> Alms to the meek the volcano burst
> With sulphur and aureate rocks . . .
> For joy rides in stupendous coverings
> Luring the living into spiritual gates.

That handsomely apocalyptic passage begins as an emendation of some lines from Greenberg's "Conduct":

By a peninsula the painter sat and
Sketched the uneven valley groves.
The apostle gave alms to the
Meek. The volcano burst
In fusive sulphur and hurled
Rocks and ore into the air.

Crane has converted the painter into a wanderer; he has changed "groves" into "graves"; he has lengthened the metrical line and varied the beat; and still more important, he has syntactically related and subordinated the alms-giving apostle to the bursting volcano.[3] The changes were dictated by the thematic intention of Crane's poem, which was *not* the intention of Greenberg's "Conduct," and which gets its first statement in the two lines of stanza one that do not derive from "Conduct." These were: "for joy rides in stupendous coverings," a significant transformation of a line from Greenberg's "The Laureate"—"for joy hides its stupendous coverings"; and "Luring the living into spiritual gates," of which the first half is Crane's own contribution, and the second a pluralizing of the phrase from "Immortality."

Crane's theme is that of a world gone spiritually dead: that has, so to speak, become a spiritual graveyard. To define that deadness, Crane offers an image of its opposite, in a combination and contrast of spiritual meekness and spiritual explosiveness not unlike the alternating tears and consuming flames of the godhead in "Lachrymae Christi." Blake again makes his presence felt: in the impassioned context, the image of joy riding "in stupendous coverings," seems to owe something to the "chariot of fire" that, in *Milton,* Blake

---

[3] I follow the version of Greenberg's poem as edited by Messrs. Holden and McManis. In Horton's version, the last word in the second line of "Conduct" is "graves" (as it would be in Crane's poem); while a comma rather than a period separates "Meek" from "the volcano." I have not had access to the Greenberg manuscripts, but they evidently present extraordinary difficulties for the editor. "We can only hope," say Messrs. Holden and McManis, "that repeated readings of the manuscripts have kept our mistakes at a minimum."

summoned as he started on his grand visionary crusade. The authentic visionary experience, according to "Emblems of Conduct," is a wild eruption of feeling, like a joy ride in some fabulous chariot, through the gates and into the world of spiritual reality. But no such journey is accessible in the actual world; the poet has thus become a "wanderer" in an alien and blighted land, drawing sketches of its graves—that is, writing this poem about its deathliness.

What the actual world consists of—the emblems of *its* conduct—Crane goes on to indicate in lines adapted from both Greenberg's "Perusal" and his "Immortality," but fused into a crisply severe indictment. The emblems of contemporary belief and behavior include radios and the laws of physics, ancient relics and hollow incantations. It is a world submissive to science, mechanical devices, and rationalism; but much worse than that, it is a world in which religious experience is excluded as a living possibility and is regarded as no more than an historical phenomenon, something that belongs to some long-gone age:

> Bowls and cups fill historians with adorations,—
> Dull lips commemorating spiritual gates.

The historicizing of religion has hardly been better expressed than that since Emerson leveled the same charge against the then contemporary Protestantism in his "Address" to the Harvard Divinity School: "Miracles, prophecy, poetry, the ideal life, the holy life, exist as ancient history merely; they are not in the belief, nor in the aspiration of society." For Crane, as well, those who call themselves believers worship historical vestiges rather than a living god; and all appear as a bleak parody of the Magi, coming with gifts to adore the visible Christ.

"Emblems of Conduct" concludes on the note of rest and death and meditative sadness, as though some greatness had departed. The landscape, at the end, is emptied of human content; nothing is left but sea and sky, and dolphins playing:

By that time summer and smoke were past,
Dolphins still played, arching the horizons,
But only to build memories of spiritual gates.

The first two lines are Crane's invention: a peaceful autumnal image (which includes an alliterative phrase picked up for the title of a play by Tennessee Williams) in contrast with the boiling exuberance of stanza one. The living are lured no longer by spirituality. Only in the spectacle of dolphins leaping toward the sky and curving down into the water is there a lingering reflection of man's visionary impulse. They only—like "the seal's wide spindrift gaze toward paradise" in "Voyages II"—remain as an emblem and reminder of a once-active spiritual conduct. Crane is said to have planned to omit "Emblems of Conduct" from *White Buildings,* as being something not really his own.[4] It is fortunate that he was persuaded otherwise; for out of the arresting bits and pieces of Greenberg's poetry, Crane forged a genuinely new creation, a fresh and true utterance of his own imagination and one that gives us a unique opportunity to watch that imagination in process.

·II·

During the months following "Emblems of Conduct," Crane was principally occupied with the "Voyages" sequence and with the love affair with E. O. The sequence was completed in November, and the love affair eventually drifted to its end. For a time Crane busied and exhausted himself in an unsuccessful effort to find a publisher for his first volume of poems: a volume which, at some time after he had employed the phrase in "Recitative," he had determined to call *White Buildings.* By the following spring (1925), Crane was ready for another departure from the city. In

[4] Allen Tate, in his preface to *Poems by Samuel Greenberg.* It was Malcolm Cowley, along with Mr. Tate, who "talked [Crane] into including it"; but even so, Mr. Tate adds, Crane was "not happy about it."

May, he quit the job he had held for a year with Sweet's Catalogue Service (architectural and engineering catalogues), sublet the Brooklyn apartment where he had also lived for a year, and repaired to the nearby countryside, to a farm Slater Brown had newly acquired close to the Connecticut border in Patterson, New York. Here, for a period, he flourished both physically and creatively. "Perfect quiet and rolling hills, almost mountains all around," he wrote his mother (with marked descriptive accuracy) in July; "with apple orchards and lovely groves of trees and rocky glens all about the house." Something of this—the natural beauty, the excellent health, the recovered vitality of spirit—went into the poem "Passage," which he finished early in the summer.

Forwarding a version of "Passage" to Waldo Frank in August, Crane claimed that it was "the most interesting and conjectural thing I have written" (perhaps, as he admitted, because it was "merely the latest"). It is easy to agree with the second of those adjectives. Marianne Moore evidently did so when she returned the poem with a sort of bemused regret from *The Dial,* saying that the editors of that journal "could not but be moved, as you must know, by the rich imagination and sensibility" in the poem, but that its content was "multiform" and that "Passage" showed "a lack of simplicity and cumulative force." There is some justice in the charge of a plurality of subject and focus; but the phrase "lack of simplicity" has an odd edge to it, as though (for example) it should be observed with annoyance that Mallarmé habitually failed to write in English. To make the point more directly, "Passage" is a very complex piece of work indeed. It is at moments too close-packed to be decipherable; its tone is mysteriously ceremonial, like some exotic religious service heard from afar; its dialogue is occult. But the poem can, I believe, carry the submissive reader forward persuasively and meaningfully through a cycle of imaginative experience that was increasingly becoming the fundamental subject of Crane's poetry. Stripped bare, this is a cycle that passes through the sense of vision gained, to vision lost, to vision *about to be* (perhaps) regained.

"Passage" is a ritualistic poem whose ritual quality is announced in opening lines which display at once that fund of imagination to which Miss Moore so rightly alluded:

> Where the cedar leaf divides the sky
> I heard the sea.
> In sapphire arenas of the hills
> I was promised an improved infancy.

Those resounding lines should not be "said" (as one "says" a poem by Robert Frost); they should, obviously, be intoned—especially since sound does the usual work of vision in "Passage," and the key human faculty is hearing rather than seeing. In the sea's voice and later in the speech of the wind, the poet hears the promise of a second birth: the promise, as the poem's title suggests, of a *rite de passage* from one condition to another; a new beginning but better than before. He is, we gather in retrospect, promised the child's direct perception of the spiritual world (in the Wordsworthian manner) combined with the powers of poetic expression developed in adulthood. Then, as against the sound heard on the sapphire heights ("sapphire," for what psychological reason I do not know, had become one of Crane's favorite eulogistic adjectives), there follows a glimpse of the inimical element that had been consigned to the depths:

> Sulking, sanctioning the sun,
> My memory I left in a ravine,—
> Casual louse that tissues the buckwheat. . . .

Amid a little cascade of images, some of them tantalizingly obscure, "memory" appears as something joyless, trifling, and parasitic (a "casual louse"), and sickly (it has a "hidden cough"). Memory may be taken, first of all, as that bad aspect of himself the poet has managed to shed and leave behind as he makes the important "passage"; his personal past, perhaps, his past misconduct and his creative malingering. Remaining that, it also, as the poem proceeds, becomes something more sizable and general. Memory emerges, in fact, as everything that is hostile to hearing and hence to poetry. Of the latter, the true source is, as so often in Crane's visionary lyrics, the inspiring wind:

> Dangerously the summer burned
> (I had joined the entrainments of the wind).

The poet is now the wind's disciple, allowing it to draw or "entrain" him after it; and through an exalted season—the season of "summer and smoke," of the irradiated life that would seem dangerous to the spiritually undaring—he has rejoiced in the vigor of his improved infancy. Signs of that vigor are the strengthened back and the bronzed cheeks of which Crane had spoken in his letter and which here, of course, are signs as well of creative well-being. But even as he listens to the wind's encouraging and beckoning words ("It is not long, it is not long. . . .)—

> the wind
> Died speaking through the ages that you know
> And hug, chimney-sooted heart of man!
> So was I turned about and back, much as your smoke
> Compiles a too well-known biography.

This reversal is the work of memory, which muffles the sound of ideal truth (say, of the "alternating bells" of "Recitative"). And it is very clearly a reversal: within the stiff little action that we make out in the poem, this moment is what classical poetic theory called *peri-pateia*, or turning about. "So was I turned about and back." In the next stanza, the poet, at evening, is back in the ravine where he had abandoned memory when he climbed the hills of vision.

"Passage" does not give us enough for the interpretive generalities we want to make about it. One such generality is the following. Recalling "Emblems of Conduct" and certain other of Crane's writings (including "Faustus and Helen III" and its reference to "all stubble streets that have not curved / To memory"), one is tempted to identify in "Passage" a thematic contrast at once traditional and of continuing importance to Crane. Put most simply, it is the contrast between memory and intuition, as ways of apprehending reality. This is an old argument, and it has given rise to a good many old songs. Crane, if I understand him, is reviving in his own clogged but fascinating idiom the conflict that had enlivened the age of Emerson—the conflict between what Emerson called "the party of memory" and "the party of hope"; between those who, in literature and religion, were committed to the past and the established as the containers of truth, value, and beauty; and those who, like Emerson, believed in "an original relation to the universe," and an immediate perception of beauty or of God.

Crane, a literary descendant of Emerson, was congenitally a member of the party of hope (a notably dwindling party in his lifetime); he had, with some injustice as we recall, named Eliot as the contemporary spokesman for the party of memory and purveyor of the dogma that (in Crane's words) "happiness and beauty dwell only in memory." It is, then, not only his former self that Crane or the poet had sought to escape. It seems also to be an entire cultural attitude, one represented by the "chimney-sooted" (dusty and darkened) "heart of man" which embraces the past and kills off the chance for an original relation with the realm of spirit, content with the familiar and inherited (the "too well-known biography"). And beyond that, perhaps, it is the sheer weight of time and history, of the temporal dimension which—when divorced from or hostile to the timeless—conditions and hampers human aspiration.

In the ravine, the poet engages in an enigmatic exchange with a "thief" who has stolen the poet's "book": who has, we surmise, as agent of the time-burdened world, robbed him momentarily of his poetic powers. (Coleridge's "Dejection: an Ode," with its lament over the failure of his "genial spirits" and of his "shaping spirit of Imagination" hovers behind this stage of "Passage.") Crane's poem here loses all touch with vital experience and recedes into a rather thin and brittle allegory. Into the phrase "smiling an iron coffin," we re-insert the skipped preposition "at," and we find the poet smiling—probably because he is confident about an ultimately happy outcome—at the iron-bound burial of his hopes. He has come back to the ravine to "argue with the laurel"—to argue about the nature of poetry and the sources of creative fertility; I myself take this, fancifully, as a debate about poetry with T. S. Eliot.

In the final stanza, there is the impression of being overwhelmed by all the sands of time that have accumulated since the age of the Ptolemies. Nonetheless, it is to the very drumming of the serpent's tongue ("pure serpent, Time itself," Crane would write a year later) that the poet hears the returning sounds of revelation:

What fountains did I hear? what icy speeches?
Memory, committed to the page, had broke.

Crane ends, characteristically, with questions rather than answers (when his poetry contains answers, they are usually silent ones, as in "At Melville's Tomb"). But it seems evident that the grasp of memory and everything associated with it—memory that is committed to the already written and established, memory escaped from earlier and then yielded to—has been broken; and that hearing, the ability to hear the voice of spirit, is about to be restored. The ceremonial action of "Passage"—its rhythm of gain, loss, and potential recovery—is badly cramped in execution. But it is Crane's honest and accurate account of the continuing rhythm of his own poetic career.

·III·

Almost as though to confirm the prophetic accuracy of "Passage," Crane, after manifesting his renewed visionary and poetic vigor in that bold poem of the summer, promptly descended into the ravine of life during the autumn of 1925, and remained there for the most part until the end of the year. Back in New York City, that is, Crane entered into an unsettled period when his behavior became more and more unpredictable, his temper more inflammatory, his alcoholic bouts more frequent; and his literary output small. His material situation, too, was close to desperate. "For the last six weeks," he wrote his father in early December, and in a tone which mingled deep discouragement with stubborn humor, "I've been tramping the streets and being questioned, smelled, and refused in various offices. . . . My shoes are leaky, and my pockets are empty; I have helped to empty several other pockets, also." But in the course of the fall, Crane managed to complete one of his most consummate lyrics, "The Wine Menagerie"—of which the subject was exactly the condition Crane was now passing through and his determination to emerge from it.

Ironically, for a poem that envisages the dismemberment and decapitation of several males by several females, "The Wine Menagerie" was itself dismembered by Miss Marianne Moore, who cut it, revised it, and decapitated its title—replacing the latter with the mysterious word "Again"—before paying Crane a much needed twenty dollars for publishing the poem in *The Dial*. This seems to have been a unique instance of Crane yielding poetic integrity for a material consideration; and to have done so must have added to the gloom he expressed in his report on the affair to the Rychtariks. Miss Moore, he said, had insisted on "changing it around and cutting it up until you would not even recognize it. . . . What it all means now I can't make out." Nor can the reader, especially since Miss Moore, after deleting the key opening stanzas, chose to keep the one passage—beginning "What is it in this heap the serpent pries"—which really is hard to fathom.

A second irony is that the full version of "The Wine Menagerie," as it appeared eventually in *White Buildings,* communicates rather more rapidly than most of Crane's poems—in its subject and movement, and even in what might be called its plot. The poem is studded with puns that can delight or disconcert, as the case may be. The rhythm is more deliberate than usual, the crescendo and decrescendo slower and more weighty. The mode of discourse is a sort of boozy approximation of direct statement, and by means of it Crane successfully implies the feel and impression of things in a moment of heightened and distorted awareness, rather than the things themselves. Individual words float free, to join and cohere and, thus combined, to send out wave after wave of meaning within the reader's responsive imagination. And at the outset, references to sight, eyes, and vision identify the central motif: in connection with the complex pun of "scansions," they tell us that we have again to do with vision and poetry, and in an uncommonly overt manner.

As contrasted with the remote, ritual action of "Passage," "The Wine Menagerie," as I have said, has a distinct if simple little plot: an actual incident, in a clear setting, with visible characters, and progressing from a meandering meditation to a moment of clear decision—a decision, needless to say, about the exercise of the poet's visionary power and touching upon his creative resolve. The scene is a speak-easy, the time apparently early winter: snow lies on the street outside. The poet, half-drunk and dozing over his wine, observes with paradoxically but quite understandably sharpened senses the place and the people: the fat-bellied bottles on the bar; the onyx wainscoting; a couple on the verge of blows; a small boy who comes in to have a cannister (no doubt his father's) filled with beer; other "crumby" individuals and their shabby "dates." He is, indeed, in what is called in psychology a "hypnagogic state": a state Richard Wilbur has described, in an essay on Edgar Allan Poe and the theme of "the visionary soul," as "a condition of semi-consciousness in which the closed eye beholds a continuous procession of vivid and constantly changing forms." [5] Crane's

[5] "The House of Poe," in *Anniversary Lectures 1959* (a pamphlet published by the Reference Department of the Library of Congress,

poet is inclined to look upon the scene with alcoholically stimulated affection; but he tells himself that this atmosphere—part comical, part animal, part infernal—is anything but one in which poetry can be written. He realizes that he must get up "and walk away," and he departs into the necessary solitude of creative activity.

The thematic note of quickened consciousness is struck at once:

> Invariably when wine redeems the sight,
> Narrowing the mustard scansions of the eyes. . . .

Wine not only improves the sight, it redeems it, and does so "invariably"; later, wine is a source of liberation and will "build freedom up about" the poet; wine (with its faint Eucharistic overtone) here performs the function more often attributed to the wind. And in the narrowing glance, eyes become capable of "mustard scansions." This is a fine and impudent phrase that I can imagine no other modern poet devising. It combines the notion of extreme sharpness, like mustard, with that of scanning, as eyes are said to scan a situation; and then it pulls both notions under the control of scansion, or the art of appraising the meter of a poem. "Mustard scansions of the eyes" is the most tart definition (Crane's punning is infectious) that Crane ever invented for *his* kind of visionary poetry. But it is almost matched a few lines later by the reinforcing allusion to "Glozening

Washington, D.C., 1959). Mr. Wilbur continues: "These forms sometimes have color, and are often abstract in character. Poe regarded the hypnagogic state as the visionary condition *par excellence,* and he considered its rapidly shifting abstract images to be—as he put it— 'glimpses of the spirit's outer world.' These visionary glimpses, Poe says in one of his Marginalia, 'arise in the soul . . . only . . . at those mere points in time when the confines of the waking world blend with those of the world of dreams.' " With Crane in "The Wine Menagerie," we should speak of the confines of sobriety blending with those of drunkenness. Crane's images are much less abstract than Poe's; for all his affinity with Poe, Crane never desired that total transcendence of the material world aspired after by his ancestor.

decanters": decanters—or, more simply, wines—that are aids to interpretation, as one speaks of glossing (more archaically, "glozing") a literary text, and especially a poem. Meanwhile goaded by wine, some force in the poet's mind, here symbolized—in accord with the poem's animal imagery—as a leopard, "asserts a vision in the slumbering gaze." [6] The consumption of much wine has thus suddenly clarified the poet's vision and greatly increased his interpretive and creative powers.

What the poet sees, physically and immediately, is an array of persons caught in various postures of hostility or degradation—couples, mostly, males and females engaged in what Crane regarded as the inevitable and savage battle of the sexes. Centrally, there is a viciously quarreling pair:

> Regard the forceps of the smile that takes her.
> Percussive sweat is spreading to his hair. Mallets,
> Her eyes, unmake an instant of the world.

The man's hard and grasping smile (which in Crane's familiar way will shortly be contrasted with the poet's "receptive smile") and the woman's hammer-like eyes indicate a heterosexual relation reduced to mere percussion: the striking of one body against another. The woman is bent not on uniting but on "unmaking": she would like to beat the other's being into nothingness. Then, however, the couple evidently separates—he to drag his guileful countenance to the window, she to retreat carrying her jealousy with her. Their conduct leads the poet (after an interval of several stanzas) to think of certain classical instances of the slaying of a man by a woman: Holofernes, whose head was cut off by the sternly patriotic maiden Judith; John the Baptist, decapitated at the demand of

[6] Crane could not have known that Thoreau, in his essay "Walking," had described Nature itself in the simile of a leopard: "Here is this vast, savage, howling mother of ours Nature, lying all around, with such beauty, and such affection for her children as the leopard." But Crane's choice of symbol was intuitively correct, and it implied much the same thing.

Salome; Pierrot or Petrushka, in Stravinsky's ballet, slain in turn for daring to pursue his elusive "valentine." All these actual and remembered instances convince the poet that, for his own creative life, he must strenuously avoid an involvement with womankind.[7]

But before that point, the poet's glance had turned to other couples in the speak-easy, with their "poor streaked bodies"—"streaked" like "striated" in "Faustus and Helen II" meaning morally or otherwise tainted—and their unspecified "stigma." The similarity of this phase of "The Wine Menagerie" to Eliot's "Sweeney among the Nightingales" is obvious enough; but it should be mentioned only to emphasize the difference between the two poems. Eliot was skillfully defining a contemporary actuality by juxtaposing its squalor to motifs of classical grandeur and Christian holiness; but Crane is intent precisely on transforming the squalor by an act of vision. The poet is seized with compassion for these soiled or bellicose characters because he has begun to see through them; and doing so, he transfigures them in the very force of his visionary gaze. He is thus able to detect, behind the animal faces in the menagerie-bar and behind the bestial conduct (we recall the "ape's face" in "Recitative") some promise of moral and spiritual beauty:

> Between black tusks the roses shine!

The process of transfiguration had, in fact, begun in stanza two. There it was recorded that "Slow / Applause flows into liquid cynosures"—slowly uttered "yesses," we may say, are evoked by the highly attractive wine bottles; it was about this poem that Horton appropriately quoted William James's statement that "drunkenness expands,

---

[7] Such extreme male apprehension of female destructiveness was no doubt—in Crane's individual case—rooted in a homosexual element, though for critical purposes I am not inclined to stress the fact. The note of creative urgency strikes me as more important. See remarks below on "Indiana," in Chapter Ten, and on "Three Songs" in Chapter Eleven.

unites and says yes"; and that it is "the great exciter of the Yes function in man." The affirmative mood had increased through the jumble of symbolism in stanza four, where, despite much uncertainty of syntax and reference, words like "sapphire" and "carillon" and the image of the arrow speeding heavenwards suggest, by connotation and inter-play, that the poet's vision has begun to penetrate through the junkheap of the actual toward the ideal. The vision achieved is both transfiguring and integrative. The poet sees the bleakly or angrily separated individuals uniting ("their separate wills" are "mint[ed]"); what their eyes had unmade, his eyes recompose. And under his glance, their taint vanishes: in a multiple pun which carries forward the bell-ringing allusion of "carillon" and connects it, unex-pectedly, with the notion of rescinding a bad law (like Prohibition), the poet sees the stigma of these persons being "repeal[ed]." A harsh moral law has been rejected, and harmony and radiance recovered by vision.[8]

In the latter part of "The Wine Menagerie," the poet, his consciousness thus aroused, meditates on his own course of action and listens to anguished admonitions from his poetic conscience. Liberated and strengthened by wine, he determines to seek still further levels of awareness:

> New thresholds, new anatomies! Wine talons
> Build freedom up about me and distill
> This competence—to travel in a tear
> Sparkling alone, within another's will.

R. P. Blackmur has taken the first words of that stanza as his text in a fine analysis of Crane's way with language:

> Some latent, unsuspected part of the cumulus of mean-ing in each word has excited, so to speak, and effected a corresponding part in the others. It is the juxtaposition

---

[8] The concept of poetic vision as affirmative, integrative, and trans-figuring is, of course, Emersonian. See the discussion of Emerson and Crane in Chapter Eight, below.

which is the agent of selection, and it is the combination
of meter and the carried-over influence of the rest of the
poem, plus the as yet undetermined expectations aroused,
which is the agent of emphasis and identification. . . .
The separate meanings of the words fairly rush at each
other; the right ones join and those irrelevant to the
juncture are for the moment—the whole time of the poem
—lost in limbo.[9]

The words, in short, unite even as they are effecting the
union of the human characters observed. "Thresholds"
and "anatomies" are, of course, independently justified as
verbal choices by the earlier images of rooms and of bodies;
but together now, as Blackmur says, they create a fused
impression of freshly opening and expanding possibility—
that is, of perceptual and spiritual and creative possibilities—
beyond anything yet accomplished by the poet in the poem;
he will cross new doorways like the "spiritual gates" the
loss of which Crane had mourned in "Emblems of Conduct."
And the exclamatory phrase leads almost at once to the
similarly expressed purpose of snaring "new purities" and
of inventing "new dominos"—new black-and-white opposites—"of love and bile"; new interpretations of the corruption and purity, the hatred and love, he had been watching
and imagining in the wine-menagerie.

On his journey toward fuller vision, the poet will "travel
in a tear," and he will sparkle alone, submissive to the will
of another. That "other" is of course the wind; and the
reference to it is equivalent to the phrase about joining
"the entrainments of the wind" in "Passage." It may well
be that this version of the recurring motif was derived by
Crane, half forgetfully, from Longfellow's excellent poem
"My Lost Youth," where the burden of the song consists of
the lines:

> "A boy's will is the wind's will,
> And the thoughts of youth are long, long thoughts."

[9] *Language as Gesture* (1952), p. 310.

As to the sparkling tear, Blackmur rightly refers us to some lines of William Blake, as Crane himself would do in his correspondence with Harriet Monroe about "At Melville's Tomb," a few months later. The poet's greatly deepened compassion will have the power attributed by Blake (in "I Saw a Monk of Charlemagne") to "the tear of love"—a power better capable than rebellion or war, according to Blake, of combatting the force of human evil; for—

> the tear is an Intellectual Thing
> And a sigh is the Sword of an Angel King.

The tear and, two lines below, the poet's "receptive smile" will be his weapons for dealing with the murderous and sexually grounded violence and "the forceps smile" earlier encountered. The poet's strength will be not only vision but the charitable vision. He knows what Emerson had known and in *Nature* had declared—that, as to the requirements of the human spirit, "love is as much its demand as perception." Even so, he must travel alone; and at the end, moving in imagination past the ghosts of those destroyed by women, he is about to "fold [his] exile on his back again," and accept the solitude that is essential to his poetic mission.[10]

So, anyhow, he is instructed by the "wit that cries out of me." No doubt this is Crane's adaptation of the "inwit," the moral conscience, whose "agenbite" Stephen Dedalus felt in Joyce's *Ulysses,* a book Crane revered. But if so, it is here very definitely the poetic rather than the moral conscience. "The Wine Menagerie" is as much an impenitent song as the poems examined two chapters above; just as they are to some extent visionary lyrics. The moral "inwit" had been slyly denied in the closely related words "un-

---

[10] The last phrase quoted borrows its metaphor from Stravinsky's "Petrushka" ballet, in which the dancer is a hunchback. The phrase "pivots on a pin" is an image of dancing which, I assume, involves one of the slang words for "leg."

witting" and "remorseless" in the sixth stanza—both, like "relentless" in "Legend," being left-handed ways of saying "impenitent." It is the creative faculty that points to the "frozen billows" of his skill, a phrase that makes additional sense when we remember "Voyages." And it is the same faculty that, by recourse to some arrant colloquial punning on "dates" and "crumbs" that even Joyce might have boggled at, exhorts the poet to leave these surroundings—"and walk away."

·IV·

In the same month (October 1925) that Crane, as far as we know, completed "The Wine Menagerie," he made a start on another poem which, in its final version, would be called "At Melville's Tomb." It was not finished until some time in the winter of 1926, and by that time important changes had occurred in Crane's life. He had in fact abandoned the dates and crumbs of New York City, and for the third time in as many years had made a pastoral pilgrimage into the country. The enterprise, on this occasion, was due chiefly to the generosity of Otto Kahn. In December, and only an astonishingly few days after he applied for it, Crane received from Kahn a grant of two thousand dollars. To a man with leaky shoes and empty pockets, it must have seemed like two million; and Crane moved at once to a farmhouse in Patterson, New York, which Allen and Caroline Gordon Tate had suggested he share with them.

The grant was to make it possible for Crane to devote his whole energy to *The Bridge*—on which, we may recall, Crane for various reasons had been able to do next to nothing for more than two years. As the winter months passed, Crane continued to wrestle with the concluding section, "Atlantis," which was, he wrote Frank in January, "oddly enough emergent first"; and he also began on what he called "the Nina, Santa Maria, Pinta Episode"—later, "Ave Maria," the first numbered section of the epic. It was one of those periodic moments of high confidence, and Crane even dared "congratulate myself a little . . . in having found some liberation from my condensed meta-phorical habit in a form as symphonic (at least so attempted) as this." At the same time, he was reading widely in an assortment of books that might hopefully supply some of the substance of *The Bridge: The Journals of Christopher Columbus,* the histories of William Prescott, Marco Polo; and, in March, "Melville's delightful *White Jacket* as well as a marvelous illustrated book on whaling and whaling ships." [11] It was, apparently, the renewed acquaintance with Melville that stimulated another and perhaps the supreme product of Crane's "condensed metaphorical habit," the extraordinarily beautiful visionary elegy "At Melville's Tomb."

The poem, especially in its third stanza, represents the furthest reach of Crane's visionary imagination in the lyric phase we have been examining:

> Then in the circuit calm of one vast coil,
> Its lashings charmed and malice reconciled,
> Frosted eyes there were that lifted altars;
> And silent answers crept across the stars.

Crane had again realized in language that transfiguration of the "twisted" historical world, with its love of the ir-reconcilable and its "spouting malice," which he had first and more verbosely effected in "Faustus and Helen"; Crane had good reason to place "At Melville's Tomb" immediately after "Faustus and Helen" (and before "Voyages") in *White Buildings.*[12] But the later poem has a deep and steady assurance, felt no less in the settled cadences than in the controlled mobility of the imagery, that testifies to Crane's

[11] Weber (*Letters,* p. 235) has identified this book as *Whale Ships and Whaling* (1925).

[12] Apart from this grouping, I have been unable to make out any significant design in Crane's ordering of the lyrics in *White Build-ings.*

greatly increased command of subject and method. It testifies also to the focusing as well as the expansion of consciousness that resulted from Crane's return to work on *The Bridge*. And it bears valuable witness to the nature of Crane's involvement with Herman Melville.

Between these two writers there is a multiple and profoundly illuminating affinity, one of the compelling continuities in American literature. Both "used words greatly" (to quote Blackmur on Melville again),[13] and never more greatly than when the sea was in question—Melville's "tomb" in Crane's poem is of course the sea itself. Both were driven—Melville with a more pugnacious intellectuality—to expose and define the reality that may lie behind appearances, and that may tragically belie or magnificently redeem those appearances, according to conviction. Both writers, that is, had a kind of metaphysical imagination; or better, an apocalyptic imagination—though Melville's veered toward horror and catastrophe, and Crane's toward the beatific and restorative. Against those all-encompassing visions, each pitted the ineradicable human need for love, especially for male friendship; and both were deeply aware of, and unembarrassed by, the dilemmas of the sexual life. Melville and Crane, too, were alike in the manner and even a good deal of the content of their self-education; and in the vastness of their creative ambition, each resembled the other more than any American literary figure. Both men, finally, addressed these powers and perceptions and visionary searchings to the historical, the actual, and the potential American scene.

Crane first read *Moby-Dick* in 1920, when few of his countrymen had even heard of the book; he was drawn in particular, as it seems, by the closeness of its rhetoric to that of "the dear great Elizabethans." He must have re-read it in the next few years; in the spring of 1926, anyhow, and on the Isle of Pines, he told Frank that he

[13] "The Craft of Herman Melville," in *The Expense of Greatness* (reprinted, 1958, by Peter Smith; Gloucester, Mass.), p. 158.

was reading it for the "third time," and that he "found it more superb than ever. How much that man makes you love him." (After still another reading in 1932, and in a different mood, he called it "a tremendous and tragic work.") We have noticed Crane's skillful borrowings from *Moby-Dick* in "Chaplinesque" and "Voyages." "Repose of Rivers," as we shall see, begins with a kind of pastiche of words and phrases from the same novel. A quotation from one of the poems in *Battle-Pieces,* meanwhile, serves as epigraph to "Cutty Sark" in *The Bridge;* echoes from others ("The College Colonel," for example) are audible in *The Bridge* and "At Melville's Tomb"; and *Battle-Pieces,* Melville's epic assembly of lyric and narrative poems about the American Civil War, is perhaps the major work before *The Bridge* not only to deal on a large scale with the nature and presumptive purpose of America, but, more important, with the great apocalyptic alternatives the country must confront. Beyond this, Crane appears to have read most of Melville's other novels; [14] and he knew some at least of the tales—the giant turtles of Melville's "The Encantadas" are reflected in "Repose of Rivers" and "O Carib Isle!" and the theme of the undelivered message (most notable in "Bartleby") was sounded more than once by Crane.[15]

That theme provides in fact the opening image of "At Melville's Tomb":

> Often beneath the wave, wide from this ledge
> The dice of drowned men's bones he saw bequeath
> An embassy. Their numbers as he watched,
> Beat on the dusty shore and were obscured.

[14] I have quoted the reference to *White Jacket.* Professor Unterecker tells me that among the books Crane had with him on the Isle of Pines in 1926 were *Typee, Omoo* and *Israel Potter,* as well as Raymond Weaver's seminal biography, *Herman Melville, Mariner and Mystic* (1921), a title that could not but appeal to Hart Crane.

[15] I have commented on this shared theme from the opposite, or Melvillian, viewpoint in the introduction to *Herman Melville: a Reader* (Dell Laurel Paperback, 1963). The essay was reprinted in *Trials of the Word* (1965).

Before glancing at Crane's account of that stanza, we should observe several of the characteristic, and revealing, elements it contains. Crane begins here, as he was tending more and more to begin, on the note of a recurring action: *"Often beneath the waves"* (elsewhere, for instance, *"Invariably when wine redeems the sight,"* or *"How many dawns* chill from his rippling rest"). The device works admirably to generalize a concrete experience, to suggest the archetypal while hanging on to the vivid. One is struck, too, by the familiar alternation of the strongly and the faintly marked caesura, something which enriches and sets the pace of the rhythmical movement. And the adverb "wide," one of Crane's favorites, reminds us that Crane frequently achieved a stimulating freshness by avoiding the proper but conventional word and picking instead the word with which it was closely associated *within* some conventional phrase: thus "wide" instead of "far," from the phrase "far and wide."

As to the meaning of the stanza, it was Crane himself who related the "dice"—that is, as he explained, the ground-up bones of drowned sailors—to "certain messages undelivered, mute evidence of certain things, experiences that the dead mariners might have had to deliver." The remark occurred in the much-quoted exchange with Harriet Monroe, who posed a number of questions to Crane about "At Melville's Tomb" before publishing it, along with the correspondence, in the October 1926 issue of *Poetry*. Crane must have been gratified by the opportunity to discourse upon his theory and practice of poetry. One of the consequences of his re-absorption in *The Bridge* was a newly aroused interest in the whole theoretical dimension of his art. It was at this time (specifically, in March 1926) that Crane wrote the long letter to Munson, from which I have quoted in the chapter on "Faustus and Helen," about the relation between "poetry" and "knowledge," wherein he argued that poetry is not a formal expression of abstract knowledge but rather "the concrete *evidence* of the *experience* of . . . knowledge." In remarks that bear immediately upon the Melvillian poem he was then completing, he added as an example of his viewpoint, that as to "the fact of man's relationship to a hypothetical god," poetry did not or should not attempt to articulate the problem "logically"; what it could do was to "give you the real connective experience, the very 'sign manifest,' on which rests the assumption of a godhead." It was in this period, too, that Crane compiled the notes on poetic method—illustrated chiefly from "Faustus and Helen" and "Voyages"—that were published posthumously, by Philip Horton, as "General Aims and Theories."

Harriet Monroe had asked, about the first stanza of "At Melville's Tomb" and in a tone of respectful skepticism, "how *dice* can *bequeath an embassy* (or anything else)." Crane took the occasion to defend again the "logic of metaphor"; and it was here that he defined the process, in language I have several times quoted, as "the so-called illogical impingement of the connotations of words on the consciousness." "Much fine poetry," he was ready to admit, "may be completely rationalistic in its use of symbols." But he made clear his feeling that the best kind of poetry— his kind, though not necessarily his own poems—resulted rather from the "combinations and interplay" of those illogical impingements "in metaphor." The poet's task, one makes Crane out to be saying, is to release the connotative meanings and insinuations of words, sometimes the mere edges and margins of their customary meanings; and to control and intensify these connotations by binding them together—make them work *upon* each other—by means of metaphor, the great binding instrument of the poetic art.

Much depended, needless to say, upon the alert sensitivity of the reader; but Crane expressed his faith in a kind of "short-hand" that existed in the minds of experienced readers of poetry, and that could be trusted "as a reasonable connective agent toward fresh concepts, more inclusive evaluations." The very nature and the future of poetry were at stake, he insisted. "If the poet is to be held completely to the already evolved and exploited sequences of imagery and logic—what fields of added consciousness and increased perceptions (the actual province of poetry, if not lullabyes) can be expected when one has to relatively return to the alphabet every breath or so."

"Fresh concepts, more inclusive evaluations . . . added consciousness and increased perceptions." There is the vital essence of Crane's theory, and an abstract of his practice: what his poems at once deal with and move toward. The prose phrases are, of course, a close parallel to the exclamatory "New thresholds, new anatomies!" in "The Wine Menagerie." Aiming at those things, Crane's poems are persistently *about* them, and about aiming at them; when, with our active cooperation, they succeed, they increase our consciousness of what is involved in the effort to increase our consciousness. Of no poem is this truer than "At Melville's Tomb." The opening stanza in fact, as Crane tried to explain, established the intention: in an image of Melville's constantly heightened awareness that men who have drowned at sea (say, the entire crew, save one, of the *Pequod*) may have arrived through the experience of such catastrophe at "fresh concepts, more inclusive evaluations"— concepts and evaluations which, nonetheless, they are unable to report, and of which their ground-up bones, thrown on the shore, are "the only surviving evidence." Those bones are, as it were, an envoy from the underworld to the land of the living, and, as such, they are a mute statement of the precariousness of human existence: "Dice as a symbol of chance and circumstance," Crane said, "is also implied." Melville, and Crane speaking for him, thus become the new ambassadors of consciousness, the representatives of the enlightened dead.[16]

[16] It is by no means impossible that in writing "At Melville's Tomb," Crane had in mind the last stanza of Melville's poem, in *Battle-Pieces,* "The March into Virginia":

> But some who this blithe mood present,
>   As on in lightsome files they fare,
> Shall die experienced ere three days be spent—
>   Perish, enlightened by the vollied glare.

Harriet Monroe found the second stanza more puzzling yet:

> And wrecks passed without sound of bells,
> The calyx of death's bounty giving back
> A scattered chapter, livid hieroglyph,
> The portent wound in corridors of shells.

"Tell me," she said, "how a calyx (*of death's bounty* or anything else) can give back a *scattered chapter, livid hieroglyph;* and how, if it does, such a *portent* can be *wound in corridors* (of shells or anything else)." Crane replied as follows:

> This calyx refers in a double ironic sense both to a cornucopia and vortex made by a sinking vessel. As soon as the water has closed over a ship this whirlpool sends up broken spars, wreckage, etc., which can be alluded to as a *livid hieroglyph* making a *scattered chapter,* so far as any complete record of the recent ship and her crew is concerned.

As to the line "the portent wound in corridors of shells," it meant, to paraphrase Crane's paraphrase, that the meaningless roaring sound that one hears when one holds a sea-shell to the ear is a portent or symbol of the kind of knowledge to be gained—that is, no distinct knowledge at all—from the spars and wreckage of a sunken ship. We still need a dictionary, however, to tell us, first, that a calyx is the whorl of leaves that forms the outer covering of a flower—hence, by extension *and* by the retroactive ironic effect of "death's bounty," a "cornucopia" or horn of plenty (that is, in the popular slang phrase, "plenty of nothing"); and second, that a minor meaning of "whorl" is convolution —hence, again by extension, a vortex.

One sympathizes with Crane, especially if one has attempted a comparable exegesis of a sizable number of his poems. Crane's attention was focused of necessity (as is the critic's, betimes) upon individual metaphors and even individual words taken in isolation, without regard for the organic development of the poem as a whole. It is from this that there arises the sense, as Miss Monroe said in her reply, of straining, of a rather arid subtlety, of a tortuous effort of mind and will rather than the creative motions of the imagination. But the "livid hieroglyph" and the "scattered chapter" were already implicit in the earlier reference to the obscured and disappearing bones (them-selves, imaginably, scattered and livid), and are no more than an elaboration of it. The first two stanzas are related, moreover, in their characteristic alternation of the faculty of seeing ("he saw . . . he watched") and of hearing ("without sound of bells"—perhaps of the "alternating bells" of "Recitative"). Beyond that, there is the strong and solemn music, a force that binds together the binding metaphors. But much more important than all these considerations is the fact that Crane, in these stanzas, is simply not describing a realistic scene, something containing logically related elements and susceptible to logical discourse either by poet or critic. *He is describing a visionary act.* As in "The Wine Menagerie," he is enacting such an act: the visionary trans-formation of the elements in question (the shore, the bones, the bells, the spars, and wreckage), under the creative glance of a man of genius. This is the way Melville *saw* those elements. And it is precisely the visionary act that reaches its climax in the third stanza—which is, in my judgment, one of the great religious statements of modern poetry:

> Then in the circuit calm of one vast coil,
> Its lashings charmed and malice reconciled,
> Frosted eyes there were that lifted altars;
> And silent answers crept across the stars.

Harriet Monroe found the image of *"frosted eyes lifting altars* difficult to visualise," a criticism about which a long essay could be written. Crane merely said that the line expressed his conviction "that a man, not knowing perhaps a definite god yet being endowed with a reverence for deity

—such a man naturally postulated a deity somehow, and the altar of that deity by the very *action* of the eyes *lifted* in searching" (italics his). This, he could have added, is what he believed Herman Melville to have done, and what he wanted his poetry to do: to postulate, to bring into view by the exercise of vision and language, a divine being, a godhead that might exist at least inside and for the duration of the poem. He could have pointed out that the visionary achievement of stanza three is a consequence of the activity attributed to Melville in the preceding two stanzas: a remarkable conversion of loss into gain. He might have commented on the closely related words "circuit" and "coil," and the sense they combinedly give of the integrative aspect of poetic vision. And he would have been justified in citing the markedly similar Melvillian ending of "Voyages II":

> Bequeath us to no earthly shore until
> Is answered in the vortex of our grave
> The seal's wide spindrift gaze toward paradise.[17]

Death at sea—with all that such an event might symbolize in living human experience, all it had symbolized for Crane in "Voyages"—is, then, the occasion and the source of "added consciousness and increased perceptions." "At Melville's Tomb" ends with the sea-tomb and its most "fabulous" (extraordinary and myth-making) resident. Harriet Monroe argued a little about the suggestion that "compass, quadrant and sextant *contrive* tides" ("they merely record them, I believe"), but she withdrew this objection when Crane answered that this was only a "little bit of 'relativity,'" and that instruments invented to measure some entity have sometimes "so extended the concepts" of it that they might even be said to "have extended the original boundaries of the entity measured." Melville's imagination was, Crane

---

[17] Joseph Warren Beach, in an essay cited earlier (p. 153 above), has pointed to the nearly identical connotations of "frosted eyes" and "spindrift gaze," as of "altars" and "paradise." The lines, as Beach says, are alternate versions of each other.

implied, such an instrument; he did not even bother to say that compasses and quadrants were suitable instruments wherewith to symbolize the genius of that mystical mariner.

Miss Monroe concluded her rebuttal by accusing Crane of a "painfully intellectual search for emotion, for poetic motive. Your poem reeks with brains—it is thought out, worked out, sweated out. And the beauty which it seems entitled to is tortured and lost." So have said many other readers, and so, no doubt, many will continue to say. But it is the exegete who has to think and work and sweat; and it would be a mournful fatality if his brain-stretching were confused with the actual processes of creation. This is a major point which all devotees of modern poetry and readers of modern criticism know perfectly well, but which, somehow, they regularly forget. It strikes me as of sufficient current importance to warrant quoting the sanest formulation of the problem I have read—by Austin Farrer, talking about his analysis of the symbolic poetry of The Book of Revelations.

The author had not with his conscious mind thought out every sense, every interconnection of his imagery. They had worked in his thinking, they had not themselves been thought. If we endeavor to expose them, we shall appear to over-intellectualize the process of his mind, to represent an imaginative birth as a speculative construction. Such a representation not merely misrepresents, it also destroys belief, for no one can believe in the process which is thus represented. No mind, we realize, could *think* with such complexity of thought. Yet, if we do not thus intellectualize, we cannot expound at all; it is a necessary distortion of method, and must be patiently endured by the reader. Let it be said once and for all that the convention of intellectualization is not to be taken literally.[18]

[18] *A Rebirth of Images* (Beacon Paperback, 1963), p. 20.

· V ·

Despite the display of immense poetic power in "At Melville's Tomb," Crane found it impossible to make much headway with *The Bridge* in the weeks that followed. He was tempted to blame his difficulties on the life of hearty rusticality: "A life of perfect virtue, redundant health, etc., doesn't seem in any way to encourage the Muse, after all," he told Munson, reversing an earlier judgment in that matter. ("*Redundant* health," by the way, is a playful phrase worthy of one of Crane's minor poems.) Impatience and the inevitably recurring loss of confidence contributed to an explosive break with the Tates in mid-April. Crane moved out of the Patterson farmhouse, and by May he was down on the Isle of Pines, the place, just off the southwest coast of Cuba, where Crane's grandmother had at one time owned a plantation. In June, he made a trip to the nearby island called the Grand Cayman. When he came back to the Isle of Pines, he felt physically fit ("rather toughened and well") but imaginatively drained. Nonetheless he brought with him two poems, one of them at first, mysteriously, called "The Tampa Schooner," later "Repose of Rivers." [19]

A remarkable aspect of this hauntingly beautiful and, as it were, auto-elegiac poem is that it comprises an eloquent statement about the failure of creativity—at just the moment when Crane was on the verge of the most extraordinary creative period in his life. He told Waldo Frank on June 19, two days after returning from the Grand Cayman, that "at present" he was "writing nothing," and that he could not "build out of an emptied vision"; the latter phrase could serve as alternate title for "Repose of Rivers." It was the next day, in another letter to Frank, that Crane made his most despondent comment about the entire conception of

[19] The second of the two poems, "O Carib Isle!" is discussed in Chapter Thirteen below.

The Bridge: that "the form of my poem rises out of a past that so overwhelms the present with its worth and vision that I'm at a loss to explain my delusion that there exist any real links between that past and a future destiny worthy of it," and so on.[20] (This letter should be precisely dated; it is sometimes quoted as being Crane's ultimate judgment on *The Bridge,* though in fact it was written before the epic was really under way.)

It was not merely his own predicament. Crane, as always, invested the cultural world at large with his personal melancholy and misgivings, just as, during periods of creative satisfaction, that world appeared to stir with new life and immanent beauty. He felt, now, a decline setting in everywhere, and that "it seems demonstrable that Spengler is quite right"; he added a contemptuous reference to "Eliot, Laforgue and others of that kidney . . . whimper[ing] fastidiously" in the cultural sunset. But on the private side, the return to the Isle of Pines had greatly exacerbated his sense of failure. It was Crane's first glimpse of the place since the time, eleven years before, he had come there as an adolescent near the start of a literary career and had experienced certain excited Wordsworthian intimations. Thinking back on that in his moment of despair, and building, after all, out of his allegedly empty vision, Crane wrote a sweetly desolate recapitulation of his poetic career, as it then seemed to him. "Repose of Rivers" has the same kind of significant locus in that career—at its mid-point—that, close to the end of it, "The Broken Tower" would have.

It is the return to the Caribbean that sets off the chain of symbolic reminiscences:

> The willows carried a slow sound,
> A sarabande the wind mowed on the mead.
> I could never remember
> That seething, steady levelling of the marshes
> Till age had brought me to the sea.

[20] See Chapter Eight below.

This is not only a man's reminiscence of his early youth (or to cite the Longfellow poem again, of his "lost youth"); it is also a poet's recollection of the phases of his imaginative life, even, indeed, of his own earlier writings. One is tempted to make a checklist of the poems implicitly invoked, by means of recurring symbols and allusions, in "Repose of Rivers": to name only the most obvious, "Possessions," "Voyages" (especially "Voyages VI," and its "hushed willows"), "Emblems of Conduct" and "Passage." But while willows, the wind, and the sea are familiar items in Crane's symbolic vocabulary, much of the language in the opening stanza just quoted comes from another source—from a passage in the novel, *Moby-Dick,* which Crane had been re-reading and which he cited twice in the first letter (June 19) to mention the new poem. The passage occurs in Chapter Fifty-Eight ("Brit"), and it describes a number of "Right Whales" swimming sluggishly through a sort of sea-meadow of brit, so-called, the herring-spawn on which they fed:

> As morning *mowers,* who side by side slowly and *seethingly* advance their scythes through the long wet grass of *marshy meads;* even so these monsters swam, making a strange, grassy cutting *sound;* and leaving behind them endless swaths of blue upon the yellow *sea.*

The words italicized were evidently extracted by Crane as a single cluster, and, somewhat adjusted, were then used to inform an entirely new metaphoric construct. Given this much, it may also be that Crane's phrase "the black gorge" in stanza three, along with the reference to "the hills," may dimly echo Melville's description, in Chapter Ninety-Six ("The Try-Works") to the "Catskill eagle" that can "dive down into the blackest gorges, and soar out of them again." [21]

[21] The "monsters" of Melville may lie behind the "mammoth turtles" of Crane, though, as I have said, the latter come more probably from "The Encantadas." It might be worth noticing, though here the trail becomes faint, that the words "gulf" and "monsoon," employed by Crane in his lines twenty and twenty-one, turn up in successive sentences in Melville's Chapter Forty-Four ("The Chart").

In any event, the borrowed cluster containing the mowers, the marshy meads, and so on tells us something about Crane's way of reading as well as his way with words: it was not the original metaphor but this particular concatenation of words and sounds that stuck in his imagination. And the crucial change was the replacement of Melville's major element and symbol, the whale, by Crane's major element and symbol, the wind.

This literal Caribbean breeze is, on a symbolic level, the same inspiring and purifying wind whose entrainments Crane had joined in "Passage"; just as, on the same level, it is the same sea which in that earlier poem had promised him "an improved infancy." But the tone here is infinitely melancholy, the rhythm slow and thoughtful. For, recalling how once he had heard the wind and sea—how he had been responsive to creative urgencies—the poet is driven to re-hearse the discouraging pattern of his poetic life. He does so in a series of condensed alternations: between the bright promise and the ugly results ("flags"—like "the ensign" in "Recitative"—and "weeds"); between the felt remembered hell of experience, with its deadly heat, its monstrous shapes and "sulphur dreams," and the "singing willow rim" of the refreshing pond. The latter reference suggests the poetic opportunity confronted and speedily lost:

> The pond I entered once and quickly fled—
> I remember now its singing willow rim.

At this moment of total memory (the memory in which "all things nurse"), he recalls the hideously degrading city he had moved through, with its "scalding unguents" and "smoking darts," like the "smoked forking spires" of the soul-breaking city in "Possessions." "How much I would have bartered"; how much of all this he would have ex-changed for a recovered vision. But he remembers, too, how—once at least, or perhaps periodically and typically— "after the city," inspiration *had* returned: "The monsoon"— a seasonal or periodic wind of the Indian Ocean—"cut across the delta / At gulf gates." He had after all, upon occasion, crossed those spiritual gates, those new thresholds, with the aid of the nourishing wind.

The end of "Repose of Rivers" is thus more effectively ambiguous than even Crane may have realized. In this summer of what felt like "an emptied vision," the poet remembers the sea and the wind, the sapphire and the willows and the steady sound of other summers, other poems, other creative moments:

> There, beyond the dykes,
> I heard wind flaking sapphire, like this summer,
> And willows could not hold more steady sound.

Some portion of Crane's imagination knew better than Crane himself. It is not only that here again Crane had given expression to the feeling of loss, of defeat and self-betrayal, in language so emotionally exact—and in framing images of superb concreteness (one really can hear and see the wind "flaking sapphire")—that the poem represents the opposite of its own overt statement. It is also that somewhere in the poem, especially toward the end, there is the rising hint of some miracle to come. This, as I have said, was in June of 1926. Soon after the middle of July, Crane was "possessed" by a fit of creative activity which it would be hard to match in the history of American poetry. "I feel," he wrote Frank on July 24, "an absolute music in the air again, and some tremendous rondure floating somewhere." On August 3, he felt "as though I were dancing on dynamite." Before the fit subsided, about a month after it began, Crane had written or revised all the main sections of *The Bridge* except "The River" and "Cape Hatteras," and he had composed several of his best independent lyrics. This was Crane's *mensis mirabilis,* what the whole period of the visionary lyric had prepared him for. Nothing quite like it could even be expected to happen to him again.

·II·

THE BRIDGE
A GRACE TO OUR HISTORY

CHAPTER EIGHT

In the Country of the Blind

WHEN CRANE reminded Otto Kahn in September 1927, that Virgil's *Aeneid* "was not written in two years—nor in four," he had been at work on his own epic a little less than two years or a little more than four, depending on how one counts. The poem was first conceived, we remember, in early February 1923; but at that time Crane regarded it as simply carrying further "the tendencies manifest" in the poem he had just completed, "Faustus and Helen," and he predicted that the new work would "probably approximate the same length in lines." Half a year's intermittent devotion to this relatively modest undertaking produced only some scattered idioms that later went into the "Van Winkle" section, and several frustrated versions of "Atlantis"; and the project was temporarily abandoned. Coming back to it at last in the winter of 1926, after a two-year interval, and making as it were a fresh start, Crane labored over "Atlantis" for a few months and then moved on to "Ave Maria"—impelled, now, by a very much larger conception of the poem as a whole. Then there occurred the (for Crane) unparalleled creative period on the Isle of Pines.

"In one month," Crane would say to Kahn, "I was able to do more work [on *The Bridge*] than I had done in three previous years." This, if anything, was an understatement. In addition to putting the important final touches to "Atlantis" and "Ave Maria," Crane, in almost thirty days, wrote "Proem" (or "Dedication" as it was then called), "The Dance," "Cutty Sark," "Three Songs" ("two of three songs have just popped out," he wrote Frank on August 12, and "the last, 'Virginia' . . . may come along any time"), "The Tunnel," and made a start on "The Harbor Dawn" and apparently on "The River."

"I skip from one section to another now like a skygack [sic] [1] or girder-jack," Crane wrote. This exultant report has been offered as part of the testimony when *The Bridge* is being tried for incoherence, though practicing poets, many of whom have known such seeming disorder in their own compositional habits, are unlikely to appear as witnesses in such a case. As a matter of fact, the *Aeneid* itself, according to Suetonius, was put together in somewhat the same way. Virgil did work out a prose version of his narrative; but when it came to converting that version into poetry, Virgil, in the scornful words of Robert Graves, paraphrasing Suetonius, "dodg[ed] from book to book as the fancy took him." He "chose the easiest options first," and it was all of seven years before he had "licked the Second, Fourth and Sixth Book into a fairly presentable shape." [2] The point, in short, is not that Crane moved about from one phase of his poem to another; but that in so short a space of time, and with his epic rhythm (*The Bridge,* I shall argue, has rather a characterizing *rhythm* than a *design*) firmly in mind, he revised or wrote in their entirety ten of the fifteen separable "poems" that make up *The Bridge,* and got some distance into still another. To this considerable extent, *The Bridge* is the issue of a single sustained poetic seizure.

Nine months later, however, and back in Patterson where he had spent a restive and semi-alcoholic fall and winter, Crane announced to his mother that he had done "nothing but insignificant parts" of his long poem "since last July, no *major* work has been done since then." The next month, he felt, "*must* see something accomplished"; and so it did. Crane was essentially a spring and summer poet; like the hero of the *Aeneid,* one is tempted fancifully to say, Crane tended to loiter and misbehave himself during the winter months,

[1] This curious word, which Crane employs in a different spelling in "Cape Hatteras" ("Thine eyes bicarbonated white by speed, O Skygak"), seems to mean a stunt-flyer.

[2] "The Virgil Cult," *Virginia Quarterly Review,* Vol. 38, No. 1 (Winter 1962).

and to remember his calling only with the renewal of the year. By the fourth of July 1927, at any rate, he had finished "Van Winkle" and "The River." In the letter to Kahn on September 12, 1927—the most important document connected with the poem—Crane was able to list and describe the entire contents, except for "Quaker Hill," in their proper or final order, though two of the sections listed, "Indiana" and "Cape Hatteras," were yet to be composed.

There followed another two-year stretch in which virtually nothing was done or added, and during which *The Bridge* was for long months never even mentioned. It was not until some time in 1929 that the work again aroused Crane's creative energy: and then mainly because he had the promise of its publication by Harry and Caresse Crosby, whom he had met in Paris in the early winter. He remarked to a friend on May 1 that he had not "so far completed so much as one additional section to *The Bridge*," but that "it's coming out this fall in Paris, regardless." Under the new impetus, in August, he introduced what he called the "gloss notes," those marginal directives that were ill-advisedly strewn through the first two parts of *The Bridge*. By September, he had finished the crucial and critically much-undervalued "Cape Hatteras" and was on into "Quaker Hill" and "Indiana." It was a mild poetic fit but a real one: "I know what to plan on fairly well when I get into one of these fevers of work," he wrote Caresse Crosby. On the day after Christmas, having concluded "Indiana" and "Quaker Hill"— "in a rage of disappointment," according to Philip Horton— he sent the latter to Caresse Crosby with the flat statement that "[this] ends my writing on *The Bridge*." Like certain other major poets, it seems, Crane was experiencing a state of black reaction after so enormous an effort; and, measuring the achievement against the ambition, he may even have been in a mood to destroy his great work. But in fact the poem was published in Paris by the Black Sun Press in February 1930; and in New York by Livewright, in April.

Almost exactly seven years had thus passed, in and out of

the creative vineyard, since Crane first ruminated his "new longish poem." The bulk of it was written between July 1926 and July 1927; nevertheless, the facts just recited force upon us—more seriously than with "Faustus and Helen" and "Voyages"—a question about wholeness and harmony, about the poem's formal success or failure. No one was more aware of this than Crane. In the September 1927 letter to Otto Kahn, he alluded to the vast amount of energy he had had to expend before "my instincts assured me that I had assembled my materials in proper order for a final welding into their natural form." Each individual section of the poem, Crane said, had presented its own unique *and* two-fold problem: "not alone in relation to the materials embodied within its separate confines, but also in relation to the other parts, *in series,* of the major design of the poem." This, though heavily expressed, is clear enough, and I shall eventually contend for Crane's success in just the terms laid down.

But the general question bristles with difficulties, some of them semantic, others springing from critical expectations based on traditional notions of form, of symmetry, of pattern and momentum. I have thought it wiser to discuss the question retrospectively, after exploring the poem phase by phase. We may, however, try to determine in advance the *genre* of the poem. "I am really writing an epic," Crane insisted in the letter I have been quoting; and it was at this point that he mentioned the *Aeneid* as a major paradigm for his undertaking. "I feel justified," he added, "in comparing the historic and cultural scope of *The Bridge* to this great work." There was some real basis to the claim; and yet nothing could, finally, be more misleading.

·II·

The ground of the comparison was, of course, the subject and purpose of the two poems. Crane felt at times, or at least he tried to feel, that his subject really was the greatness of his contemporary America, an objectively and historically realized greatness, just as Virgil's subject was the achieved greatness of his contemporary Rome. Crane knew that his subject *matter* was rather internal than external, that it consisted rather in psychological and spiritual attitudes than in military and political actions. But there were moments when his reason deluded his imagination into believing that he was at work upon a traditional millennial epic, the purpose of which—like that of the *Aeneid*—was to celebrate the recent conversion of an age of iron discord into an age of golden harmony. And this accomplishment was to be made manifest, as it had been in the *Aeneid*, by re-enacting in the present the noble deeds (again, for Crane, spiritual and visionary deeds) of a legendary past. During the *mensis mirabilis*, Crane told Waldo Frank how "extremely exciting" it was for him "to handle the beautiful skeins of this myth of America— to realize suddenly, as I seem to, how much of the past is living under only slightly altered forms, even in machinery and such-like." A year later, he was still able to say to Kahn that, as to the historical content of his poem, he was aiming primarily at "an assimilation of this experience, a more organic panorama, showing the continuous and living evidence of the past in the inmost vital substance of the present."

It is not clear how much of the *Aeneid* Crane had read; the citation of it may have been no more than a shrewd rhetorical tactic, given the literary atmosphere of the decade; but one gets a strong impression that Crane had definitely read *in* the first four books, and possibly beyond them. He was an astute reader of poetry, and he must have been struck by the near perfection of the classic design unfolding in the poem, by its image of an extraordinary and ultimately knowable order existing in external fact in the poem's universe. He would have been quick to observe—and this would have seemed exemplary for his own purpose—that the large analogies and connectives which give classic shape to the *Aeneid* work not only horizontally (back and forth across historical time), but vertically too (up and down a scale of heroic and divine being). Not only does the poem's contemporary hero, Augustus, emulate the feats of earlier conquerors and pacifiers, and especially the feats of Aeneas. Augustus is also a purely human being who repeats the actions of a semi-divine figure (Aeneas was the son of a goddess); and those actions in turn repeat the characteristic actions of the gods themselves, especially of Apollo and Saturn.

Let me offer an illustration, whether or not Crane, in his reading, ever arrived at it. In Book VIII, on the fabulous shield designed and decorated by Vulcan, Aeneas sees the picture of Caesar Augustus, aeons in the future, entering "the walls of Rome in triumphal procession" and visiting the temple of Apollo, after his victory at Actium.

Caesar, enthroned in the marble-white temple of dazzling
   Apollo,
Inspects the gifts from the nations and hangs them up on
   the splendid
Portals: subject tribes pass by in a long procession—
A diversity of tongues, of national dress and equipment.
Here Vulcan had represented the Nomads, the flowing
   robes of
Africans, here the Leleges, Carians, Gelonian bowman.[3]

Caesar Augustus is magnified in the image, because he is represented as doing—on the level of human political ritual—what, elsewhere, Aeneas, Apollo, and Saturn are said, in various but comparable ways, to be doing. Apollo, in an extensive simile in Book IV, is shown performing an annual ceremony of unification: every year, Virgil reports,

Apollo leaves Lycia, his winter palace,
And Xanthus river to visit Delos, his mother's home,
And renew the dances, while round his altars Cretans and
                                        Dryopes
And the tattered Agathyrsi are raising a polyglot din.

[3] Translated by C. Day Lewis, in the Anchor paperback edition (1954) of the *Aeneid*.

The image of Apollo is, in turn, prescriptive of what the divinely descended Aeneas must do. He must, that is, abandon the winter palace in Carthage, where he is disobediently lingering at that very moment; he must journey to the maternal home of the Trojan race—which, as he discovers, is the land of Italy; and he must there restore the ceremonies of his displaced people, while around him will sound the polyglot din—if not of Apollo's Cretans and Dryopes, or of Caesar's Africans and Leleges—at least of Latins and Arcadians and Trojans. Doing this, Aeneas will also follow the example of another god, Saturn, who (it is narrated in Book VII), at some time in the remote past, had come down from Olympus into barbaric Arcadia and

> made a united nation of this intractable folk
> Scattered among the hills, gave laws to them. . . .
> His reign was the period called in legend the Golden Age.

It is the mission of Aeneas, emulating Saturn, to create out of war and violence an age of gold for his time; and it will be the mission of Caesar Augustus, emulating both Aeneas and Saturn, to bring back peace, harmony, and greatness to the Roman people after the wars that had beset Virgil's generation.

Crane must have sensed, as we do, that Virgil was doubtful about the contemporary accomplishment, and almost mournfully skeptical about the entire historical process, the Augustan revolution, to which he had been invited to address his initially lyrical talents. Crane must have noticed that it was more often darkness rather than light, and death rather than rebirth—the death of the city and the suicide of Dido in the early Books, later the visit to the underworld, the suicide of Amata, the slaying of Turnus—which summoned forth Virgil's highest descriptive powers. But this would only have added to the immense value and appeal of Virgil's poem and made the more admirable Virgil's tenacity in carrying his epic enterprise to its appointed end. For *The Bridge* was also the epic effort of an initially lyrical poet; a suicide is glimpsed within the first twenty lines; and its starting point is a city caught in the very heart of darkness, in the dead of winter, in the age of iron:

> The City's fiery parcels all undone,
> Already snow submerges an iron year.

The Bridge begins with this complexly desolate image of multiple submergence: of human possibilities buried deep beneath an urban, a commerical, and a technological civilization; where the brightly lit windows of office buildings reveal, to the poetic vision, the essential business of the culture—by being *seen as* glowing parcels or packages, bought and wrapped up by day, then undone or unwrapped as the lights go out and the windows darken.

It was Crane's ambition—or so it occasionally seemed to him—to trace the reversal of all this, to show a Virgilian conversion of iron into gold, winter into spring, darkness into light. It was to show those hostile elements overcome by an actual nobility of spirit and largeness of vision in America, where the present age could be discovered re-enacting on the level of spirit the great accomplishments of Christopher Columbus. For Columbus was to be the Aeneas of Crane's American *Aeneid;* and its Caesar Augustus, its contemporary hero, would be none other than the country's communal soul, which, ennobled by faith, would make evident its attunement to divinity. All in all, the Virgilian comparison could not but have been exceedingly tempting; and indeed, American literary history is strewn with the wreckage of earlier writers, from Joel Barlow and his *Columbiad* onward, who had fallen prey to the same temptation and had sought to adopt to the American circumstances the example of the Roman triumph. If *The Bridge* did not join that debris, it was because Crane's imagination was too honest. He had in fact abandoned the Latin model before *The Bridge* was fully under way, and later references to it simply belie what his imagination had long known and what his creative vision had already built for him.

Crane's key statement on this phase of the evolution of *The Bridge* is a letter to Waldo Frank on June 20, 1926, and it is one of the most eloquent statements in English on a fundamental Romantic dilemma—that is, the tormentingly problematical relation between a subjective vision and an external, historical reality. For two months, Crane began, he had been "confronted with a ghostliness that is new." He went on:

> The validity of a work of art is situated in contemporary reality to the extent that the artist must honestly anticipate the realization of his vision in "action" (as an actively operating principle of communal works and faith), and I don't mean by this that his procedure requires any bona fide evidences directly and personally signalled, nor even any physical signs and portents. The darkness is part of his business. It has always been taken for granted, however, that his intuitions were salutary and that his vision either sowed or epitomized "experience" (in the Blakeian sense).

If a poet, in other words, is to express a vision of contemporary spiritual heroism, for example, he must honestly feel that such heroism can be externally validated; not that it must shine in every facet of the life described, but that in intuiting a certain greatness the poet is responding to something that is really there at work, however faintly, amid the fallen world—and that can, with the poet's assistance, be made to realize itself more completely.

What had happened was that Crane had lost his faith in the barest potentiality of the grandeur he was emotionally eager to postulate. "Intellectually judged," he continued, "the whole theme and project" of *The Bridge* "seems more and more absurd." He had believed himself in possession of "authentic materials" that were "worthy of the most supreme efforts I could muster."

> These "materials" were valid to me to the extent that I presumed them to be (articulate or not) at least organic

and active factors in the experience and perceptions of our common race, time, and belief. . . . [But] however great their subjective significance to me is concerned—these forms, materials, dynamics are simply non-existent in the world. I may amuse and delight and flatter myself as much as I please—but I am only evading a recognition and playing Don Quixote in an immorally conscious way.

The form of my poem rises out of a past that so over-whelms the present with its worth and vision that I'm at a loss to explain my delusion that there exist any real links between the past and a future destiny worthy of it. The "destiny" is long since completed, perhaps the little last section of my poem is a hangover echo of it—but it hangs suspended somewhere in ether like an Absalom by his hair. The bridge as a symbol today has no significance beyond an economical approach to shorter hours, quicker lunches, behaviorism and toothpicks.

It would be Quixotic and irresponsible, Crane was thus sombrely concluding, to continue with a poem whose visionary content did not correspond in any way or on any level to any aspect, real or potential, of the existing condition of things in the American world. While his major symbol, the bridge, might represent for *him* several kinds of ideal union, to the American mind at large it signified only a faster path to a faster dollar. And the present age, far from continuing and re-animating the great visions of the past, was a dismal degradation of the past; America's spiritual destiny lay buried in the vanished age of Whitman.

If Crane had persisted in this mood, and in the view of the relation between poetic vision and historical reality that it rested upon, he might have written a poem like *The Waste Land;* and indeed certain moments in *The Bridge*—especially the section called "Three Songs," in which three contemporary female figures represent three burlesques and debasements of the shadowy female divinity discovered in the mythic past of "The Dance"—look at first glance to be in the Eliot manner, though in fact they are not. But it is much more probable that Crane would not have written any long poem at all.

The difference between the despair Crane voiced in late June 1926, and the soaring confidence he expressed a mere thirty days later (when he felt "an absolute music in the air again") is not due to a recovery of faith in the spiritual potential of America, though Crane would sometimes seem to say so. It was due to an almost incredible recovery of poetic energy, *and* to an immensely strengthened conviction about the role and power of such energy. The basic fact is that in late June, Crane could hardly write a line of poetry he felt to be worth saving; while, as I have said, between the later part of July and the end of August he wrote or revised or completed three-fourths of his entire epic, as well as a few fine independent lyrics. And the implication of that fact was this: that if America had failed him, his poetic resources had not; and the latter might even in the long course of time work to the redemption of the former. Abandoning the classical model, with its assumptions about history and reality and the mimetic aim of poetry, Crane reverted by splendid instinct to one of the traditional Romantic strategies. *The Bridge* began to take on the shape of what M. H. Abrams, talking about the age of Wordsworth, has so usefully defined as an "apocalypse of imagination."

The poets discussed by Professor Abrams in his brilliant essay [4] entertained even higher hopes for their contemporary world than Crane would do about his, and they passed through a similar process of radical disillusionment and renewal of hope on different terms. The revolutions in France and (though less so) in America seemed to them at first to be the world-transforming cataclysms foretold in the biblical Book of Revelations, and their minds were seized by the intoxicated belief that the Kingdom of God on Earth, the New Jerusalem, was literally about to be established once

[4] "English Romanticism: the Spirit of the Age," in *Romanticism Reconsidered* (English Institute Essays, 1963).

and for all. But their hopes were bitterly betrayed; the millennium of social justice gave way—in France—to an epoch of blood-lust and tyranny. Remarkably enough, as Professor Abrams tells us, the apocalyptic spirit of the English Romantic writers was not quenched by this; but it underwent of necessity a profound alteration. Wordsworth, for example, retained his "millennial hope in revolution," and continued to express that hope "in a fusion of biblical and classical imagery." "But," Professor Abrams continues,

> the hope has been shifted from the history of mankind to the mind of a single individual, from militant external action to an imaginative act; and the marriage between the Lamb and the New Jerusalem has been converted into a marriage between subject and object, mind and nature, which creates a new world out of the old world of sense.

So it was with Blake in *Jerusalem* and Shelley in *Prometheus Unbound,* both efforts, in Professor Abrams' words, "to reconstitute the grounds of hope"—by turning away from historical actuality to formulate within the poems a new relation between consciousness and reality. That relationship, valid in and for the poem as the issue of the creative imagination, might somehow and some day extend its validity beyond the poem, by inseminating the consciousness of others. The new poetic intention, in any event, was perfectly articulated by Shelley at the close of *Prometheus Unbound:* it was

> to hope till Hope creates

From its own wreck the thing it contemplates.

Almost every word I have been quoting can be applied without much modification to Hart Crane and *The Bridge;* though Crane's drastic cultural loneliness—as an American Romantic in a neoclassical age—prevented his rational mind from always or wholly grasping just what it was his imagination was up to, and from any sustaining sense of the total

propriety as well as the splendid ancestry of his poetic purpose. But in his elegy on Melville, Crane had already described the visionary act of poetry in lines that perhaps
deliberately echo those of Shelley: that is, the creation out of
the wreckage ("and wrecks passed without sound of bells")
of the thing contemplated, the visionary creation of the very
godhead itself:

> Frosted eyes there were that lifted altars
> And silent answers crept across the stars.

Something like this, on a vastly larger scale, became the true
epic purpose of *The Bridge*. To put it as flatly as possible,
the emergent subject of *The Bridge* was not the actual or
even the latent greatness of an actual and contemporary
America. Its subject was hope, and its content a journey
toward hope: a hope reconstituted on the ground of the
imagination in action; while the thing hoped for was the
creation in *poetry* of a new world—forged out of the old
and fallen world, which had failed him, by the very vigor
of the poet's own transfiguring vision.

·III·

"Vision" is the key word and the key element in *The
Bridge,* the poem's beginning and its end. As early as March
1923, in a letter containing one of the first references to *The
Bridge,* Crane had written Gorham Munson that "The modern artist needs gigantic assimilative capacities, emotion,—
and the greatest of *all—vision.*" Vision and the assimilative
capacity were in fact, for Crane as for his Romantic predecessors, one and the same thing. But if the modern artist
needed such vision, and in very large measure, it was because the world in which he wrote so abysmally lacked it.
The real challenge to writing an epic of modern America
was not only its dismal, disorderly vulgarity, a vulgarity
symbolized for Crane by "quicker lunches, behaviorism and
toothpicks." It was what William Morris (in a phrase Crane

presumably did not know) called the *"eyeless* vulgarity" of modern civilization.[5] Twentieth-century America suffered above all from a failure of vision. The country whose greatness Crane had wanted to celebrate had become the country of the blind, and in doing so had lost all connection between its time-enclosed world of everyday experience and the world of timeless beauty. The situation Crane's American epic confronts and seeks to redeem is presented in its opening lines: when the sea gull's wings—so often seen at dawn, a spectacle beautiful in itself and a symbol of the perfect harmony of great opposites—gradually

>   with inviolate curve, forsake our eyes
> As apparitional as sails that cross
> Some page of figures to be filed away;
> —Till elevators drop us from our day.

That last line contains much of importance, and virtually provides the motive for the quest-journey soon to be undertaken in *The Bridge*. It also, and not quite by the way, bears a striking resemblance, in its structure and cadence, to the final line of Eliot's "Prufrock": "Till human voices wake us and we drown." The resemblance is striking because in the two lines Eliot and Crane are manipulating a comparable paradox to notably different effect. For Eliot, his aging spokesman drowns not "in the chambers of the sea," in his dream of romantic love and youth renewed, but in the dry world of human voices to which he is rudely awakened; and the poem offers an instance of pathetic romantic folly. For Crane, the elevators that literally carry us up to the dull business office, to the first chores of the actual morning (and the original version of this line was: "—And elevators heave us to our day"):[6] these same elevators also "drop us," they

[5] Quoted from Morris's *How I Became a Socialist* in Raymond Williams's *Culture and Society* (1958), pp. 160-61. Italics added.

[6] In December 1929, Crane proposed the change to Caresse Crosby. Mrs. Crosby voted for the original, and the line so appears in the Paris edition. The second and more familiar version was introduced into the New York edition.

wrench us away from our true "day," our morning vision of the pivoting sea gull. We drop upward every morning into blindness, as Prufrock awakens into death by drowning. But Crane's poem at this point is offering an instance not of folly but of genuine spiritual disaster, and a human situation the poet must bend all his energy to alleviate.

It is a situation which Crane endlessly returns to in *The Bridge*. The same image of vision possessed and vision lost— of the appearance and disappearance of the envisioned object—recurs in every section, on almost every page of the poem; and the struggle to recover the vanished emblem of beauty (a sea gull, the shoreline of the new world, a dream-companion, a mother's smile, a mountain meadow) is constantly taken up anew. Every phase of experience in *The Bridge* passes the poet through the cycle of gain and loss; every phase provides him with its special synecdoche for the whole of experience. Structurally, in this regard, *The Bridge* might be described as a pattern of synecdoches, a series of rehearsals of the characteristic event in Crane's imaginative world. But the lines just quoted from "Proem" point to one of the major sources of interference to vision. The spectacle of beauty and harmony which forsakes our eyes each morning, which fades into a mere apparition—like the daydream of sails and far sea-journies a man might have while working over the accounts in a broker's office (one recalls the moment in "Faustus and Helen I," when, amid the materialistic congestion of Wall Street, the mind "is brushed by sparrow wings")—this spectacle is not lost completely "till elevators drop us from our day." Elevators are, of course, the first instance in *The Bridge* of that "encroachment of machinery on humanity" of which Crane spoke in an early letter to Otto Kahn. They are the first manifestation in the poem of a literal American age of iron.

Three-quarters of a century earlier, Henry David Thoreau had pitted himself valiantly against that very encroachment. "I will not," Thoreau had said, speaking of the cattle-train making its noisy way across his Concord landscape and by means of it speaking of the entire threat posed by the new technology, "—I will not have my eyes put out and my ears spoiled by its smoke and steam and hissing." But in Crane's view, the eyes and the ears—those interchangcable instru- ments of vision—had been quite put out and spoiled for the modern American and even, temporarily, for the poet, and precisely by the smoke and the steam and the hissing of the age of iron. We must not, however, exaggerate or misrepre- sent the role of "the machine" in *The Bridge*. In "The River," Crane seemingly attributes to the machine the terri- ble cleavage between a myth-possessing past and an eyeless present ("iron, iron—always the iron dealt cleavage"), and in "Cape Hatteras," he sees modern man reduced to a pure identification with the airplane he flies ("Man hears himself an engine in a cloud"). But money is always as intrusive as machinery in Crane's poem. And in any case, Crane was as much concerned with certain dire qualities of spirit (blind- ness, hatred, greed) as with the actual machine-produced and machine-producing things with which those qualities terribly collaborated.

Crane had in mind what Carlyle had in mind when, in 1829, exactly a century before Crane finished *The Bridge*, Carlyle had defined his own era as "the Age of Machinery, in every outward and inward sense of that word." "Not the external and physical alone is now managed by machinery," Carlyle contended, in language that, itself echoing Blake and Coleridge, would echo down through D. H. Lawrence to Hart Crane and so many others, "but the internal and spiritual also." "Men are grown mechanical in head and in heart, as well as in hand," Carlyle wrote. "Mechanism has now struck its roots down into man's most intimate, primary sources of conviction," and even "religion" had become "for the most part, a prudential feeling grounded on mere cal- culation." Like Carlyle, and like the earlier Romantics, Crane was most concerned about the cold demonism of the heart, the dark Satanic mills of the human spirit—qualities that led to and were in turn intensified by the increasingly technological culture. For all its uniqueness of idiom, *The Bridge* thus confronts the most familiar and traditional of the problems confronted by the literary imagination since the Augustan age; and it is the most traditional of poems.

·IV·

Crane's poetic response to the problem was itself squarely in the Romantic tradition; but though he drew much from the great English phase thereof, he belonged even more intimately to the American strain—of which Emerson, if not the initiator, was the chief head and fount.[7] Crane would, for example, have saluted almost every word of Emerson's argument, in the essay called "Art," that it is the very instinct of artistic genius "to find beauty and holiness in new and necessary facts, in the field and road-side, in the shop and mill"; and that, "proceeding from a religious heart," artistic genius must and will "raise to divine use the railroad, the insurance office, the joint stock-company." Crane's religious heart had, for years, been sublimating that insurance office, stock market, and mill in poems like "Faustus and Helen" and "Lachrymae Christi," and it would continue to do so on a larger scale in *The Bridge*. Crane shared similarly (if unknowingly) in one of Emerson's fundamental ambitions, as expressed in an early and only recently published lecture on "The Humanity of Science": the ambition, namely, "to unite severe science with a poetic vision";[8] this is the gist of his own essay of 1929, "Modern Poetry."

[7] In a paper read at the English Institute in 1965, Professor Charles Davis contended persuasively that Bryant and Poe anticipated Emerson in several major motifs—especially that of "The Inward Journey." Crane was, of course, much involved with Poe; but it is also hard to believe, though the evidence is incomplete, that he did not know and make use of several of Bryant's poems: for example, "The Fountain" (with its image of the serpent and the eagle) and "The Hurricane."

[8] *The Early Lectures of Ralph Waldo Emerson: Volume II* (1964), p. 36.

Crane was as exercised as his American predecessors had been by the threat posed by technology; but his essential attitude, hard pressed as it may have been, was a brand of Emersonianism. He felt, like Emerson, that technology was, after all, not really hostile to poetry, if only because nothing was hostile to poetry, or at least nothing was immune to it. In his important exploration of this entire theme in nineteenth-century American literature, Leo Marx has observed how little Emerson, in marked contrast to some of his contemporaries, allowed himself to be openly disturbed by the new technology; and Professor Marx suggests aptly that for Emerson the industrial revolution could be taken as "a railway journey in the direction of nature." [9] It was literally such a journey, since the railroad could carry the young American away from the urbanized East to "the nervous, rocky West"—these words are Emerson's—which was "intruding a new and continental element into the national mind"; and it was metaphorically and more significantly so, as providing a set of "new and necessary facts" in and through which the enlightened perception could discern a new range of beauty and holiness. Thus would Hart Crane in "The River" pursue *his* imaginative railway journey toward the West, till the express train, dancing across the American heartlands, changes into the great river which escorts the poet into the world of myth.

But Crane's affinity with Emerson goes far beyond a shared reaction to the encroachment of machinery; the two writers held in common a general view of the relation between the imagination and reality, of which the reaction to the machine was only one crucial consequence. This affinity, which is immense, is the more remarkable, since, though Crane read and invoked several of Emerson's poems, he seems to have read few if any of those essays by Emerson in which the general view is articulated. Emerson reached him indirectly, for the most part, one assumes, by way of

[9] *The Machine in the Garden* (1964), p. 238.

Whitman; but he reached him in depth, and in a way that reminds us how deviously literary traditions perpetuate themselves, especially in this country. Indeed, to establish a body of ideas that may serve as the intellectual groundwork of *The Bridge,* we can do no better than to rehearse some of Emerson's major attitudes and convictions.

Emerson also believed his America to be the country of the blind. His word for the illness of his age was not "mechanism": it was (in a letter to Margaret Fuller) "ophthalmia"—a deficiency of vision, and of the kind of vision that might raise the mechanical to a divine use. Man had become "near-sighted," Emerson said in his talk to the Harvard Divinity School, "and can only attend to what addresses his senses." One consequence was a disastrous shrinkage in man's stature: "Now man is ashamed of himself; he skulks and sneaks through the world, to be tolerated, to be pitied." (Emerson would, with rough poetic power, draw the same portrait of man blinded, debased, and ashamed in his poem "The Sphynx.") Both the diagnosis and the cure were formulated at the climax of *Nature,* in lines uncommonly trenchant even for Emerson:

> The problem of restoring to the world original and eternal beauty is solved by the redemption of the soul. The ruin or the blank that we see when we look at nature, is in our own eye. The axis of vision is not coincident with the axis of things, and so they appear not transparent but opaque.

There is Emerson's own version of the "apocalypse of imagination," the great imaginative act by which the human spirit will again be married to the nature of things: but a spirit reunited with itself, and a nature become transparent and susceptible to vision.

We can collect the chief attributes of human vision, according to Emerson, from various passages in *Nature*— that epochal little book of 1834 which Carlyle, upon receipt of it, roundly declared to be a "true Apocalypse," and which Emerson, forwarding it to his British friend, more modestly described as "only a naming of topics." It is a naming, in particular, of the phases of the visionary act. That act is, to begin with, integrative—as, in Coleridge's influential word, it had been "esemplastic," and later, for Crane, it would issue from a "gigantic assimilative capacity." At the outset of *Nature,* Emerson speaks of "the integrity of impression made by manifold natural objects" (his immediate example being the landscape which, though "indubitably made up of some twenty or thirty farms," strikes the true perceiver as unified)—the impression, that is, made upon the person "whose eyes can integrate all the parts," in fact, upon the poet. Related to the compositional power and ultimately more valuable is the power of transfiguration. "The eye," Emerson wrote in his journal, "possesses the faculty of rounding and integrating the most disagreeable parts into a pleasing whole." [10] In *Nature,* he elaborated on that notion time and again until, in the exalted conclusion of the book, he surveyed the transfiguration of the whole world which a fully restored human vision would some day accomplish: "So fast will all disagreeable appearances, swine, spiders, snakes, pests, madhouses, prisons, enemies, vanish; they are temporary and shall no more be seen."

I am obliged to pause here over an engrossing question. Readers of John Keats will perhaps seem to hear, in the Emersonian remarks just quoted, an echo of the famous "Negative Capability" letter Keats wrote his brothers George and Tom in December 1817, and especially of the key sentence: "The excellency of every Art is its intensity, capable of making all disagreeables evaporate, from their being in close relationship with Beauty & Truth." I am not really interested in specific influences, but in illuminating affinities, with the aim of identifying Crane and *The Bridge* by identifying the traditional and Romantic cast of Crane's

[10] For notice of this and similar journal entries, I am indebted to Sherman Paul's excellent book, *Emerson's Angle of Vision* (1952).

mind and imagination. But it can be pointed out that, though Emerson, writing in the early 1830's, could hardly have read a letter written by Keats a decade and a half before, Crane, in the 1920's, most certainly could have. It might be argued that Crane's closeness to Emerson rests in part upon his responsiveness to Keats, which would say something further about the mysterious nature of literary continuities. Crane could only have assented to another proposition, offered by Keats via a quotation in a letter of about the same time, that the imaginations of poets *"consecrate what'er they look upon";* but in doing so, he would also be reaffirming his descent from Emerson, whom we have just heard saying much the same thing.[11] It was probably, as I shall suggest in the next chapter, in Crane's conception of the poem, the poetic construct, as "power in repose" that he was most nearly Keatsian and least Emersonian.

Part of the transfiguring power, to return to Emerson and *Nature,* was the ability to perceive the extraordinary in the near at hand—or, as he put it in *Nature,* to perceive the miraculous in the common.

> The invariable mark of wisdom is to see the miraculous in the common. What is a day? What is a year? What is summer? What is a woman? What is a child? What is sleep? To our blindness, these things seem unaffecting. . . . But when the fact is seen under the light of an idea . . . we behold the real higher law.

Crane had sought to reach and make evident in verse that mode of perception from his earliest lyrics. The closing lines of "Chaplinesque" may again be recalled, and now as providing a tiny paradigm of Emerson's theory of visionary transfiguration and miraculous perception:

> but we have seen
> The moon in lonely alleys make
> A grail of laughter of an empty ash can. . . .

[11] See W. J. Bate, *John Keats* (1964), pp. 232-63.

And *The Bridge* is a sustained effort—not only to integrate and assimilate the congested and often appalling manifold of the contemporary scene—but to transform it by an act of imagination: working, however, on materials almost heartbreakingly less tractable than the summer and sleep, the day and the year referred to with such bland confidence by Emerson.

But Crane held decisively, as *The Bridge* makes clear, with Emerson's belief that the visionary act is and has to be an act, on the part of the observer, of *self*-integration and self-transformation. In the journal entry which Emerson revised into the "transparent eyeball" passage in *Nature,* he contended that in the act of vision "the mind integrates itself again. The attention which has been distracted into parts, is reunited, reinsphered." For it is only the redeemed soul, Emerson insisted in *Nature,* that can restore original and eternal beauty to the world it contemplates. This explains the dramatic purpose of "Powhatan's Daughter" in *The Bridge,* and of its imaginative journey which is also an inward journey: a search not only for a mythic apprehension of nature and history, but a search for the poet's full identity, his reunited self. Even after that self is found, another and darker inward journey awaits the poet in "The Tunnel," the needful encounter with another phase of himself in the guise of Edgar Allan Poe.

The effect of the reintegrated self upon the world it envisions is radically creative; something new comes into being—according both to Emerson and to Crane. In *Nature,* Emerson regularly asserts his conviction that nature (everything that is not spirit) is not "rooted and fast" but "fluid . . . ductile and flexible," that "spirit alters, molds, makes it. The immobility or bruteness of nature," said Emerson, "is the absence of spirit; to pure spirit, it is fluid, it is volatile, it is obedient." *The Bridge* attempts a poetic demonstration or application of that principle, though, as it must always be added, with the imagination struggling with a "nature" far less rapidly obedient than Emerson had assumed. But it was Crane's purpose, as it was Emerson's and that of the English Romantics to create "a new world out of the old world of sense," to borrow again the phrase of Professor Abrams. What is actually created, of course, is a work of art, a poem; and the world the poet composes exists first of all within and for the duration of the poem. But (to repeat) it obtains a wider existence insofar as it has its proper inseminating effect upon the consciousness of readers. The products of the poetic imagination, Emerson declared in "The Poet," have

> a certain power of emancipation and exhilaration for all men. . . . We are like persons who come out of a cave or cellar into the open air. This is the effect on us of tropes, fables, oracles and all poetic forms. Poets are thus liberating gods. Men have really got a new sense, and found within their world another world, or nest of worlds; for the metamorphosis once seen, we divine that it does not stop. . . . Therefore we love the poet, the inventor, who in any form, whether in an ode or in an action or in looks and behavior, has yielded us a new thought. He unlocks our chains and admits us to a new scene.

The poet is a liberating god who "unlocks our chains and admits us to a new scene." The apocalypse of imagination could not be more happily defined; and it is onto just such a new scene that Crane and his poem admit us when we arrive at "the yellow chestnut glade" in the section called "The Dance," and Crane's apocalyptic vision reaches its climax.

But if the visionary act, for Emerson and Crane, is integrative and self-integrative, transfiguring, creative, and emancipating, it is also unending. "We divine," Emerson remarks, "that it does not stop." Emerson's very important essay "Circles" is dedicated to this idea: namely, that as "there is no end in nature," so there can be no end to the activity of the imagination as it works upon nature. In Emerson's figure, "around every circle another can be drawn." Another circle, in fact, must always be drawn by the really venturesome spirit. "The extent to which this generation of circles, wheel without wheel, will go," wrote Emerson, "depends upon the force or truth of the individual soul." The undaring soul will pause at the first boundary; *but*—

> if the soul is quick and strong it bursts over that boundary on all sides and expands another orbit on the great deep, which also runs up into a high wave, with attempt again to stop and to bind. But the heart refuses to be imprisoned.

This is close to the meaning of Crane's spirtually intoxicated Christopher Columbus, in "Ave Maria": when, himself invoking the circle image ("This disposition that thy night relates / From Moon to Saturn in one sapphire wheel"), Columbus pronounces his own unceasing quest for knowledge and his own determination to "expand another orbit on the great deep," and another yet beyond that—

> still one shore beyond desire!
> The sea's green crying towers a-sway, Beyond

And this is why *The Bridge* concludes not with an exclamation of achievement, not with a statement of finality, but with a question: "Is it Cathay?" For—and this is something Crane knew much more deeply and painfully than Emerson —vision is never final, nor can it ever be sustained. It breaks each morning; and when recovered, it must press ever forward toward new thresholds, new anatomies.

·V·

The lines just quoted from "Ave Maria" are, of course, a direct echo not of Emerson but of the closing lines of Walt Whitman's poem, "Passage to India":

> O my brave soul!
> O farther farther sail!
> O daring joy, but safe! are they not all the seas of God?
> O farther, farther, farther sail!

From the moment in 1923 when Crane began to meditate a "new longish poem" to be called *The Bridge,* he felt himself, as he told Munson, "directly connected with Whitman." There seems no doubt that the most seminal of Whitman's poems for *The Bridge* as a whole and for many particular moments in it was "Passage to India"; and it is even likely that the "vast rondure" Crane felt "floating somewhere," at the outset of the *mensis mirabilis,* was among other things the cosmic roundedness celebrated by Whitman in the same poem: "Thou rondure of the world at last accomplished." There is, to be sure, a great deal more of Whitman in *The Bridge* than "Passage to India"; in the "Cape Hatteras" section alone, ten or twelve of Whitman's poems are quoted or audibly borrowed from (including "Song of Myself," "Crossing Brooklyn Ferry," "The Wound Healer," and "Whoever You Are Holding Me New in Hand"). But all this suggests, correctly, that the very large Whitman aspect of *The Bridge* resides primarily in the poetical texture and may best be exposed in the course of analysis. Here we may limit ourselves to more theoretical considerations—in general, to the observation that the whole of *The Bridge* was composed in the spirit of Whitman's essay of 1871, *Democratic Vistas.*

This was an essay Crane expressly admired, both for its savage indictment of American "materialism" and "industrialism" (as Crane once wrote Allen Tate, trying to explain why he, Crane, was so enamored of Whitman); and for its staunch belief that only poetry could rescue the country from the spiritual blindness and moral degradation that resulted from the elements indicted. It was a huge burden which Whitman laid upon the poetic imagination in *Democratic Vistas:*

> It must still be reiterated, as . . . the deep lesson of history and time, that all else in the contribution of a nation or age, through its politics, materials, heroic personalities, military *eclat,* etc., remains crude, and defers, in any close and thorough-going estimate, until vitalized by

national, original archetypes in literature. They only put the nation in form, finally tell anything, prove, complete anything—perpetuate anything.

This doctrine, which contains notable Emersonian ingredients, appears yet more ceremoniously in "Passage to India," written about the same time: [12]

After the seas are all cross'd, (as they seem already
                     cross'd,)
After the great captains and engineers have accomplished
                     their work,
After the noble inventors, after the scientists, the
                     chemist, the geologist,
                     the enthnologist,
Finally shall come the poet worthy that name,
The true son of God shall come singing his songs.

By those same songs, in the words of the poem and the spirit of the essay, "all these separations and gaps shall be taken up and hook'd and linked together"; and "Nature and man shall be disjoin'd and diffused no more."

It was to this concept of the mission of poetry, and implicitly defining his own epic, that Crane was referring in his remarks on "Modern Poetry," when he argued that despite Whitman's "faults as a technician and his clumsy and indiscriminate enthusiasm," he, "better than any other, was able to coordinate those forces in America which seem most intractable, fusing them in a universal vision which takes on additional significance as time goes on. . . . His bequest," Crane concluded, "is still to be realized in all its implications." Crane took it as a main part of the task he was assuming in *The Bridge* to realize some, at least, of the implications of that visionary legacy. Doing so, he invoked a national original archetype of his own: the bridge itself; hoping thereby to assist a little at putting the nation in

[12] The poem was written in 1868, the year in which Whitman also wrote the first portions of the essay.

form—at giving to an industrialized nation a spiritual form, a shape of grace. Doing so, he also took as the symbol of his poetic intention the legendary place, Cathay, which all ancient passages toward India had sought for.

> To you, too, Juan Perez, whose counsel fear
> And greed adjourned,—I bring you back Cathay!

So speaks Crane's visionary mariner, Columbus, in "Ave Maria." "Cathay," Crane told Waldo Frank, "is an attitude of spirit . . . throughout" the poem. To bring back Cathay, to renew that attitude of spirit by the resources of poetry, would be to liberate the American consciousness in the age of iron. It would be to lead modern American man onto a new scene, into what Emerson, in *Nature,* called man's true dominion: that dominion, in Emerson's words, which man "shall enter without more wonder than the blind man feels who is gradually restored to sight."

CHAPTER NINE

"Proem" and "Ave Maria": The Post-Christian Idiom

THE BRIDGE begins—in "Proem" and, by a significant juxtaposition, in its companion piece "Ave Maria"—with a prayer; but a prayer less of a traditionally Christian than of an Emersonian variety. "Is not prayer," Emerson asked rhetorically in *Nature,* "also a study of truth—a sally of the soul into the unfound infinite?" *The Bridge* is written out of a belief like that; and not only its many explicit prayers but its many voyages and journies may be taken as just such sallies of Crane's poetic soul toward new visions of truth. In "Proem," the primary object of the poet's prayer is, of course, Brooklyn Bridge, which is besought as a mediator between two realms of being: the bridge, that is, as it appears in the poet's transfiguring view of it. So observed, the bridge becomes (or is begged to become) the answer to a certain spiritual condition brought about by a certain recurring experience. The first example of the latter is in the poem's first stanza:

> How many dawns, chill from his rippling rest
> The seagull's wings shall dip and pivot him,
> Shedding white rings of tumult, building high
> Over the chained bay waters Liberty—

until, in lines already glossed, the wings fade from sight and the actual world of business offices, filing cabinets, and elevators close in around us.

The gull is real enough: as real, for instance, as the sprayswept seal gazing toward paradise in "Voyages II"; and anyone who walks the broad raised wooden pathway across Brooklyn Bridge can watch the sea gulls dipping and pivoting and, perhaps, soaring seaward to the Statue of Liberty at the far end of the bay. The gull's movement is made palpable in precise rhythms of the opening stanza, in the charcteristic rhythmic motion (reminiscent, in this and other ways, of the opening stanza of "At Melville's Tomb"); in the alternation between distinctive pause and unimpeded flight. But Crane's words, those agencies of his vision, transform the gull into one of the poem's major symbols: a symbol of purity ("white," Crane's charismatic color) and harmony ("rings"), and of graceful motion-in-repose, with which is associated the idea of sound-in-silence and freedom-in-restraint. It is all of this—the gull and all it is made to represent—that regularly and tantalizingly "forsake[s] our eyes," and so as to make the poet "think of cinemas," of movie-houses everywhere, places to which multitudes of people constantly go to stare at the screen, in the dumb and constantly disappointed hope of some ultimate and permanent revelation:

> Never disclosed, but hastened to again,
> Foretold to other eyes on the same screen.

This, I suspect, is Crane's subtle emendation of Whitman's assertion in "Crossing Brooklyn Ferry" that other eyes *will* be granted the same apocalypse as the poet, the same sustaining vision of the harbor scene ("Others will watch the run of the flood-tide, / Others will see the shipping of Manhattan north and west, and the heights of Brooklyn to the south and east"). Here the vision is foretold to other eyes, but it remains a question whether it will ever in fact be disclosed to them.

What the poet confronts, in any case, is a calamitous loss of vision: a fall (or "drop") from "the world dimensional," as he had called it in "Faustus and Helen I," a world of purity and harmony, into the blinded world of "things irreconcilable." He shares in and he speaks for and out of the fallen condition of the contemporary world; and he will have to make a far journey of consciousness and prayer— like Satan in the Book of Job, and in the sentence Crane

247

oddly took as the epigraph for his poem, he will have to go (imaginatively, in this case) to and fro in the earth and walk up and down in it—before he can recover the vision in the light of which that world may stand redeemed.[1]

Brooklyn Bridge, meanwhile, looms into view—"And Thee, across the harbor, silver-paced" ("across" in the sense of curving across, or arching over). The bridge comes into view not, *qua* bridge, as the supreme and persisting object of appeal; but as a kind of promise of possible eventual success for the poetic quest—as a sublime particular instance of the general possibilty. For it is seen as, and it is made by metaphor into, a complex mediator between everything connoted by the sea gull and everything connoted by the elevator. Like the elevator, it is a typical product of the iron or technological age; but like the sea gull, it has its own inviolate curve of motion, and it manifests a miraculous beauty of mobile repose and disciplined freedom:

> silver-paced
> As though the sun took step of thee, yet left
> Some motion ever unspent in thy stride,—
> Implicitly thy freedom staying thee!

So potent is the sense of the bridge's organic vitality that usual contrasts get reversed, and nature seems for the moment to adjust itself to art: that natural measure of time, the sun, synchronizes its movement with the pace of the bridge.

I used the phrase "to art" (in the last sentence), because not only is Brooklyn Bridge, quite literally as well as in this poem, a work of art. It is *this* work of art. The bridge

---

[1] No more than this, I think, is implied by Crane's epigraph. It seems to have a merely verbal (rather than contextual) relevance, like that other phrase from the Book of Job which Melville invoked in the epilogue to *Moby-Dick*: "I only am escaped alone to tell thee." I do not find in it—as does Alan Trachtenberg (*Brooklyn Bridge: Fact and Symbol,* 1964)—an acknowledgment of evil, or satanism, as central to human experience: mainly because I do not find a consciousness of evil very notable in *The Bridge* generally.

is the poem, or perhaps we should more safely say it is *like* the poem being written about it, the poem called by that name. Crane's Romantic habit of implying multiple equations, all of them at last equated with poetry itself, can be bewildering; but the point needs to be made. As described in "Proem," the bridge is not merely an ideal of mediation; it is also an ideal of the poetic construct as such, what Crane hoped his long poem might approximate. It is an ideal of "power in repose," as Crane formulated it in a letter to Frank (August 1926), speaking about "Powhatan's Daughter." This was also John Keats's ideal of poetry, or one of his ideals: in the formula contained in an early work, "Sleep and Poetry," the great poetic creation was described as—

> the supreme of power;
> 'Tis might half slumbering on its own right arm.

(Those lines, by the way, provide a main clue to the puzzling address to God in "Ave Maria": "O Thou who sleepest on thyself.") For Crane, the qualities of freedom-in-restraint and motion-in-rest, attributed to the bridge, blend with the quality of force-within-form as the defining attribute of poetry: imaginative energy controlled by all the formal elements employed, by meter, rhyme, stanzaic structures, and by the larger rhythmic sweeps of consciousness that give the epic such "design" as it possesses. It might be added here that, though Brooklyn Bridge as an actuality disappears from the poem for long periods, the ideal it represents never fades from the poet's imagination; that ideal, on the contrary, is being progressively realized as the poem realizes itself. Crane does not, as he has been charged with doing, lose hold of his central subject in the course of *The Bridge*.

As "Proem" goes forward, the ideal—in the unexpected fifth stanza—is set against its opposite, when some unrestrained lunatic ("bedlamite") dashes out of some hole or other, sways momentarily on the bridge's parapet, a scream implicit in his wildly billowing shirt, and then (presumably) plunges to his death, the horror accompanied by the silent derision of others who callously drive on by. The headlong rush, the noisy confusion, the self-destruction, and the heartlessness suggested by that packed dramatic image all serve to emphasize the contrasting qualities of the bridge: its free restraint, its stately formal movement; later, its potential celestial music, its promise of renewed life, its message of compassion.

Nature thereupon becomes almost aggressively mechanized in the brilliant figure of stanza six, where the noonday sun is seen edging its way down the side of a building on Wall Street (that domain of commerce, that symbol for Crane of the broken world), like a combination acetylene torch and buzz saw:

> Down Wall, from girder into street noon leaks,
> A rip-tooth of the sky's acetylene. . . .

Mention of noon reminds us that the entire day leaks away in "Proem," from dawn through the passage of the morning, to noon and into the afternoon, and on to the starlit evening and the midnight darkness. To some extent, "Proem" in this regard offers a synecdoche of the entire poem; for in a distant perspective, the whole poetic adventure can be seen following the round of the day, from "Harbor Dawn" to the moment of "midnight on the piers," late in "The Tunnel." In a closer perspective, however, we discover that daily round recurring at regular intervals, each adding another version in small of the larger experience. Similarly, there is the hint of the seasonal cycle in "Proem," from the summery atmosphere of the middle stanzas to the dead of the year at the end:

> Already snow submerges an iron year;

and the visionary journey will continue, for example from the "virgin May" of "The Dance" on through the season denoted in the section called "National Winter Garden." But similarly, also, that cycle recurs at various stages in the

epic, a key aspect not only of its general but of its characteristic movement.

The visionary act by which the poet—raising his voice in
this moment of darkness and winter and iron—seeks to
accomplish his work of conversion is, thus, not only strenuous
and painful; it must, in the nature of things, be repetitive.
It is a constantly renewed effort to *see* the contemporary
world and contemporary man differently, the Emersonian
effort to restore "original and eternal beauty" to the world
by bringing the axis of vision into harmony with the axis of
things—for example, and to begin with, by seeing Brooklyn
Bridge, that thing of steel and wire, as a mediator between
the actual and the ideal. The later stanzas of "Proem" suggest
the fuller force of the visionary effort by seeing the bridge
rather as a path between those realms—what various religious
traditions have called "the way." For the significance with
which Crane's poetry invests the bridge is, finally, a religious
significance, and bears upon man's relation to divinity.

The freedom bespoken by bridge and gull is not, accordingly, the social and political freedom symbolized by the
Statue of Liberty. Something of the rhetoric and feeling of
the lines by Emma Lazarus placed inside the statue's pedestal
("Give me your tired, your poor, / Your huddled masses
yearning to breathe free, / The wretched refuse of your
teeming shore") lingers in Crane's phrasing: "vibrant reprieve and pardon . . . prayer of pariah . . . unto us lowliest." But the political aspect of the Romantic tradition and
Democratic Vistas is reflected very dimly, if at all, in *The
Bridge*. The revolution Crane was aiming at was a revolution
of consciousness, like that he ascribed to Whitman in "Modern Poetry," where he identified Whitman as "a revolutionist
beyond the strict meaning of Coleridge's definition of genius"—because, in the remark quoted, Whitman had fused
America's most intractable forces "into a universal vision."
The act of emancipation Crane hoped for was not that of a
statesman-hero (say, of a Lincoln), but rather that of Emer-

son's "liberating god": that is, of the poet, the figure who "unlocks our chains," our imprisoned perceptions, "and admits us to a new scene." And in "Proem" and the poem that unfolds from it, the new scene onto which the bridge—as thing, as symbol, as promise, as path—is to lead the modern consciousness is the ground of a genuinely religious revelation.

In the last stanzas of "Proem," the language rises to a religious intensity. The bridge is said to offer some distant reward ("guerdon" is Crane's aptly archaic word) [2] in some obscure "heaven." Its network of steel rope seems, to the poet's ear, fairly to sing the absolution for our sins, a rescue from our fallen condition (*"vibrant* reprieve and pardon"); for it has become at once a harp, an altar, a choir—and more than that:

> O harp and altar, of the fury fused,
> (How could mere toil align thy choiring strings!)
> Terrific threshold of the prophet's pledge,
> Prayer of pariah, and the lover's cry. . . .

Thus observing the bridge's "fearful symmetry" (and the Blakeian echo is here stronger than usual), the poet's vision is accomplishing what Crane had attributed to Melville in "At Melville's Tomb." It is "lifting" an altar; in Crane's note about the Melville poem, it is "postulating a deity somehow, and the altar of that deity by the very *action* of the eyes *lifted* in searching." The steel ropes have become an instrument, before or above that altar, playing a hymn to the deity invoked. (This, incidentally, is what one feels must have been the intention of the Roeblings, father and son, in designing the remarkable pattern of perfectly aligned vertical and

---

[2] Cf. Milton's use of the word, in *Lycidas* (line 73), in the sense of "recompense."

> But the fair guerdon [i.e., fame] when we hope to find,
> And think to burst out into sudden blaze,
> Comes the blind Fury with the abhorréd shears
> And slits the thin-spun life.

diagonal wire riggings. With or without Crane's poem in mind, the pattern does indeed seem very like a harp—and at times almost sounds like one.) And the bridge is multiply invoked: as the fulfillment of some age-old prophecy, the awe-inspiring gateway (a "new threshold") into the spiritual world; as the answer to the prayer of the spiritual outcast, and to the cry of the lover, of one who, in the phrase in "Chaplinesque," can "still love the world."

What Crane is doing in these stanzas is to bombard the reader's imagination with words and phrases whose connotations, as they interact and combine in metaphor, will accumulate into some immense if yet unspecified religious experience. The experience gathers additional effect in the enchanting ninth stanza, when the bridge becomes a path to eternity:

> Again the traffic lights that skim thy swift
> Unfractioned idiom, immaculate sigh of stars,
> Beading thy path—condense eternity:
> And we have seen night lifted in thine arms.

The lines correspond handsomely—as to content, figurative language, and the distribution of stress—to the reverberating lines of "Recitative":

> In alternating bells have you not heard
> All hours clapped dense into one single stride?

Both passages announce the Blakeian and Cranian apprehension of eternity, "condensed" and "clapped dense," in a moment of time. In "Proem," that apprehension is yet more radically "created" than in the earlier poem: for example, by the expertly visual image of the traffic lights which not only dot and punctuate the bridge's unbroken expanse but (like the sea gull) *skim* across it. The lights seem to "bead" the bridge's "path," as though they were occasions of prayer, like the beads counted upon the rosary by a Christian believer praying to his own intercessor between humanity and divinity, the Blessed Virgin Mary. Romantic and Christian religious allusions further intermingle when the bridge—as an exemplar of redemptive poetry—is described as an "unfractioned idiom," a harmonious and harmonizing utterance that can at once elicit and make audible the sound of heaven, the "immaculate sigh" of the stars. And this "Marian" cluster, upon which I shall comment a little later, reaches its climax in an extraordinary line, wherein another matchless visual image—the bridge, by its shape and its lights, seeming to push the darkness upward and away—is exploited to suggest (in context) the figure of the Madonna holding up the Child-savior. "And we have seen night lifted in thine arms."

"Proem" concludes with the poet's prayer for a mediation of his own devising:

> O Sleepless as the river under thee,
> Vaulting the sea, the prairie's dreaming sod,
> Unto us lowliest sometime sweep, descend
> And of the curveship lend a myth to God.

Here Crane sets the grammatical and emotional "mood" of *The Bridge,* as he embarks on his large-scale prayer, his soul's "sally . . . into the unfound infinite," with crowded references to some of the elements he will encounter on the journey: the river, the sea, the American hinterland. He prays to the bridge, sleepless while the earth sleeps at midnight, that it will (faintly, like the grace-bearing dove of Christianity) descend to mankind in mankind's lowliest, most utterly fallen and blinded, condition: "And of the curveship lend a myth to God." It is almost a critical betrayal to dismantle the word "curveship," so many of the ingredients of "Proem" has it fused and with such finality; but it secretes too ingenious a pun not to remark upon it. The "curve" in the coined word relates the bridge's arching curve to the inviolate curve by which the sea gull, at dawn, had forsaken our eyes; and it thus suggests that the lost morning vision may—by means of the bridge and of what the bridge has been made to represent—yet be recovered. The second syllable recalls the sails that had similarly been glimpsed and had vanished; while it also adds dignity to the object addressed (as who should say "your lordship"; or, closer to Crane's verbally playful purpose, "your worship"). But Crane perhaps knew that the word "ship" is equivalent to the word "nave" in religious architecture—from the Latin word *navis*.[3] The nave is the central passage or path across which the believer moves to come into God's presence at the altar; by its etymology, it is therefore both the way and vessel which carries the believer along the way.

So, in any case, it will be with the curveship of the bridge. The bridge, by Crane's imaginative vigor, has been transformed into a church, an altar, a shrine of worship; into the path the worshipper must traverse to arrive at the godhead; into the vessel which will transport him there. It is all these things by virtue of the "myth" which it has been seen to embody, and which it can lend or make accessible to the lowliest of men, as the shaped force that will mediate between man and God. As a single symbolic object, the bridge is not, of course, a myth in the familiar sense of a *story*— say, about the life, death and rebirth of some god. It is a myth in the alternate but no less valid and traditional sense of *revelation*: a revelation in the form of what Whitman called a national and original literary archetype. The story, such as it is, consists in the poet's journeying effort to arrive at such a revelation, and by means of it to see all of contemporary America, and its intractable forces, as the bridge had been seen in "Proem."[4]

[3] He may also have known that the German word for the "nave" of a church is in fact *schiff*. "Worship," by the way, does come from a combination of "worth" and "ship"; and I have no doubt, myself, that Crane was intuiting all the possibilities of the suffix.

[4] The distinction between myth as history or sacred tale and myth as revelation (Christian, Platonic, or otherwise), and the application of that distinction to *The Bridge*, are being elaborated in a forthcoming study by Helge Normann Nilsen, a young Norwegian student. Mr. Nilsen points out that critics who accept the first definition tend to regard *The Bridge* as a failure (with no story-structure in it), while those who accept the second find the poem to be a success.

·II·

With "Ave Maria," the setting shifts with seeming abrupt-ness from contemporary New York on a winter's night to mid-Atlantic in the early winter of 1493. We pass from the figure of the poet waiting, alone, on the piers beneath the great bridge to the figure of Christopher Columbus stand-ing, alone, on the deck of the *Santa Maria,* returning to Spain after the first voyage to the New World—the "Indian emperies" and "the Chan's great continent," as Crane puts it and as Columbus believed it to be. "This Columbus is REAL," Crane wrote Waldo Frank in the first days of his *mensis mirabilis,* almost beside himself with excitement; and the Columbus of "Ave Maria" is indeed drawn to a real ex-tent from historical sources, chiefly Columbus's so-called *Journal* and Prescott's *History of Ferdinand and Isabella,* both of which, we recall, Crane had been reading earlier in 1926 when he began work on this section. But the language and feeling of the section, and the quality of the experience being undergone, are in good part Whitmanian and derive especially from "Passage to India"; while the heroic mariner's posture is Cranian—and an analogue for that of the poet: standing alone, peering out across vast distances, journeying in imagination between two separated worlds, hoping to join the envisioned splendor of the one to the known actuality of the other, and always fearful of disaster. "Ave Maria," as I have said, is a companion piece to "Proem," the second half of *The Bridge*'s twofold invocation. It offers another version in small of the poetic adventure which is about to start—a version and also a model, thereof, as of his-tory transfigured.

The transition from "Proem" to "Ave Maria" is, in fact, managed smoothly enough. The metaphor of the bridge as rosary in "Proem"—with the traffic lights as its beads—is a main source of continuity; for "Ave Maria" is what one says, ten times, at the heart of the prayer-cycle and while counting the beads. There was also the suggestion, aided in context

by the juxtaposition of "beading" and "immaculate," of the
Madonna holding up the Child. (I assume that Crane, like
many others, thought that the phrase "immaculate conception" referred to the conception of Christ rather than of
Mary.) The bridge, as intercessor between man and God in
Crane's new dispensation, has thus been verbally associated
and, by the quiet push of metaphor, leads naturally back to
the intercessor in the old. The Virgin Mary was, moreover,
the special protector of mariners and of special importance,
historically, to Columbus; she is properly invoked at this
stage by the American poet who, as a modern spiritual
voyager, is the emulative heir of the discoverer of his country (in just the way Caesar Augustus was the emulative heir
of Aeneas, the hero who established *his*).

There, is finally, the quotation from Seneca's *Medea* at
the head of the section: *"Venient annis, saecula seris,"* and
so on. Crane has been belabored for using this passage, on
the grounds that it is pretentiously irrelevant and that, anyhow, Crane probably misunderstood the Latin lines. But the
passage is entirely relevant to Crane's theme; and if Crane's
acquaintance with foreign languages was not—as Henry
James said about Whitman's—deplorable, it is critically
dangerous to dismiss his use of them out of hand. The lines
in question are the conclusion of a choral chant in *Medea,*
a chant which has been reminiscing about the quest-voyage
of the Argonauts and the heroism of Jason, a figure who
flickers briefly in the "Atlantis" section of *The Bridge.* The
chorus has sung of a time when land was divided from land;
of the great enterprise by which the Argonauts conquered
the sea and "made the land one"; of the vengeful resistance
offered *by* the sea (in language that challenges Crane's own
splendid and turbulent sea-imagery in "Ave Maria"); of
the pacification of the sea and the creation of new cities.
Now, in the five-line passage actually quoted, the chorus
looks beyond the present "to an age in the far-off years when
Ocean shall unloose the bonds of things, when the whole
broad earth shall be revealed, when Tethys [Jason's helms-

man] shall disclose new worlds, and Thule shall no longer be the limit of the lands." The choral song as a whole offers another mythic analogue and paradigm, somewhat in the Virgilian manner, for the quest-journey of Crane's Columbus and the theme of the division and the union of the lands; and via Columbus, it offers another analogue for the entire poetic endeavor in *The Bridge*. Similarly, the lines selected for quotation—with their sense of the eventual revelation of new worlds and the stretch of vision beyond "ultima Thule" (a Baltic island anciently regarded as the northernmost point of the earth)—are almost equivalent to the conclusion of "Ave Maria":

> still one shore beyond desire!
> The sea's green crying towers a-sway, Beyond. . . .

"Ave Maria" divides, as so many of Crane's poems divide, into a meditation and a prayer: a meditative account of the voyage to and, thus far, from the New World, addressed primarily to absent human friends; and a prayer, or canticle of praise, addressed to the God with whom the Virgin Mary had interceded. Speaking to the two friends who, in their turn, had interceded for him with the human Queen, the "two faithful partisans of his quest," as Crane says in a gloss note,[5] Columbus begs them to witness "the word I bring." That word—which identifies what Columbus has "seen" and what "no perjured breath / Of clown nor sage can riddle or gainsay"—is the word "Cathay." "I bring you back Cathay."And with this crucial statement, we approach a definition of the central action of *The Bridge*. Action in the literary sense, as Francis Fergusson has been reminding us, is the working-out of some motive or purpose, and it can

---

[5] Luis de San Angel, collector of ecclesiastical revenues in Spain, really did "rein" Columbus's "suit" into the royal court and into the "great heart" of Isabella, riding in (on a donkey, Crane observed in the worksheet) to plead the case of Columbus's proposed search for the country of the great Khan. Juan Perez, the Queen's confessor, was no less helpful in allaying the emotions of fear and greed among other competitive parties.

in any given case best be formulated initially by means of an infinitive of purpose. The action of *The Bridge,* then, is: "to bring you back Cathay." For Crane, in the remark quoted earlier, Cathay was "an attitude of spirit, rather than material conquest throughout." It is indeed and throughout the poem an attitude of spirit *as against* material conquest; and the key purpose both for Columbus in his imagined age and the poet-seeker of Hart Crane's actual age was to restore a spiritual attitude which a blind devotion to material conquest (in "Cape Hatteras," for example, the physical conquest of space) had suppressed or threatened to suppress.

As "Ave Maria" continues, Columbus remembers the first almost unbearably thrilling view of the new continent at dawn: when—

<blockquote>
faith, not fear,
Nigh surged me witless. . . . Hearing the surf near—
I, wonder-breathing, kept the watch,—saw
The first palm chevron the first lighted hill.
</blockquote>

That inverted-v-shaped tree is the long-awaited sign of the "truth"—of the real existence of the continent and of a westward approach to it—belief in which, back in Genoa, had made Columbus an exile. By analogy, it is also the redemptive vision of beauty for believing which the poet, too, had become an outcast (a "pariah") in the streets of the modern city. Columbus recalls and silently tells his friends how, when dawn gradually "clear[ed] that dim frontier," some natives came to the shore crying: "The Great White Birds!" The exclamation (invented, I believe, by Crane) tightens the analogy by bringing the sea gull of "Proem" and his "white rings of tumult" back into the poem and by relating the spectacle of the gull, with its symbolic connotations, to the historic vision of the New World. But, as in "Proem," that extraordinary experience, that first-light vision, is being meditated as the evening dusk begins to fall, and at a moment of very grave danger from the churning seas. "It is morning there," Columbus says; but—

Here waves climb into dusk on gleaming mail;
Invisible valves of the sea,—locks, tendons
Crested and creeping, troughing corridors
That fall back yawning to another plunge.
Slowly the sun's red caravel drops light
Once more behind us. . . .

("Observe the water-swell rhythm that persists until the Palos reference," Crane told Frank with justifiable pride. At a moment like this, one wants to paraphrase Keats's saying about Shakespeare: "Which poem of Crane's do you like best? I mean, in which is the sea most prominent?" In the passage just quoted, the metrical variation alone would be worth several pages of analysis.) So the sun vanishes like a small ship—"caravel"—disappearing in the distance, as the two caravels, the *Pinta* and the *Nina,* had in fact already been lost in the "troughing corridors" of the ocean. So light is lost, or "drops"; and all will be lost—the word, the demonstrated truth, will never be brought back into the fallen world—should *this* "keel one instant yield!"

Crane's energetic description of the violent storm the *Santa Maria* had to pass through off the Azores (the natives said later that it was the most frightful tempest they had ever seen) is mostly taken from Columbus's *Journal,* especially from the entries beginning on February 14, 1493. There one can read of the "record" of the voyage written down by Columbus and sent "floating in a casque"; [6] of the stripping down of the sails ("under bare poles scudding"); of the be-

[6] A certain to-do has been made of Crane's spelling of the word "casque." In the worksheet it appears as "cask" ("some testament committed in a cask"); but in the published text, it was changed to "casque," which seems not to be an acceptable spelling for the word as meaning "small barrel." "Casque," which means a small Spanish helmet, can itself be spelled "cask." Crane, who spelled as accurately as the next poet, was probably attempting—in this case unsuccessfully and even pointlessly—a Joycian pun which would fuse the Admiral's helmet (as a symbol of authority) and the little barrel in which he dispatched his all-important record. The cask, by the way and however spelled, was never in historical fact recovered.

wilderment and terror which led the crew to the verge of mutiny; of the loss of sleep ("shadow cuts sleep from the heart"—in the shadow of assorted dangers, Columbus did not sleep for more than seventy-two hours); of the eventual calming of the storm, as Columbus believed, by the intercession of the Virgin Mary (who, in Crane's words, "dissuades the abyss"); of the first signs of approaching land and safety—an herb, a stray branch, some weeds.

Before that, Crane's Columbus had appealed to the Virgin in a prayerful parenthesis:

> (O Madre María, still
> One ship of these thou grantest safe returning;
> Assure us through thy mantle's ageless blue!)

The Virgin's compassionate answer had been "some inmost sob, half-heard" which dissolves the demonic derision ("whelming laughter") also half-heard from the sea-sources of terror and destruction; and which calms the "tempest-lash" and (in an effective pun) the "surfeitings." The *Santa Maria* sails out of the stormy darkness into the sunlit blue of an ocean whose waves seem to dance in endless harmony with the onward-carrying winds. It is a moment of sudden and intense visionary confidence: a vision granted to human eyes that during the time of danger had been "Starved wide on blackened tides," much as, in "Voyages VI," the eyes of the sea-threatened poet-lover had been

> pressed black against the prow,—
> Thy derelict and blinded guest.

It is, in "Ave Maria," a vision of perfect and rounded totality: the horizon, the visible world, has become—

> This turning rondure whole, this crescent ring
> Sun-cusped and zoned with modulated fire
> Like pearls that whisper through the Doge's hands.

The word "rondure" no doubt echoes Whitman's use of it—"Thou rondure of the world at last accomplish'd"—in

"Passage to India"; and perhaps Whitman's own invocation of Columbus in that poem ought to be quoted here, for if it is not very taking, poetically, it serves to enlarge our sense of the Columbus of "Ave Maria," and, via the constant analogy, of Crane's sense of his poetic self:

Gigantic, visionary, thyself a visionary,
With majestic limbs and pious beaming eyes,
Spreading around with every look of thine a golden world,
Enhuing it with gorgeous hues. . . .
(History's type of courage, action, faith.)

For both Whitman and Crane, Columbus was "history's type" exactly because he was (in their view) the creative source of the golden world; it was his pious and visionary "look" that made the world golden and gave it its gorgeous colorings. So it is with the envisioned "rondure" in "Ave Maria"; but on this, Emerson can supply a more effective commentary. In "Circles," Emerson begins by declaring:

> The eye is the first circle; the horizon which it forms is the second; and throughout nature this primary figure is repeated without end. It is the highest emblem in the cipher of the world.

The eye perceives—or rather, more actively, it shapes ("it forms")—the horizon as a perfect circle; and gradually, in this broadening perception, the human eye comes to see the natural "rondure" as an emblem of God. For Crane's Columbus, too, the eyes on board the ship do not simply observe, they compose, they "accrete and enclose" a rondure which is in perpetual motion, a *turning* rondure (in Emerson's fine phrase, a "flying perfect").

This circling and dazzling visible cosmos will shortly be the transparent source of a poetic vision of a whirling, dancing, circling godhead. But in the interval, Columbus announces his awareness of the element which might block that vision. The word "ring"—"this crested ring"—which started as a synonym for "rondure," leads out of another of its meanings through "pearls" to Columbus's anxiety about King Ferdinand's delirious greed for jewels, for material acquisition rather than an enkindled attitude of spirit:

> —Yet no delirium of jewels, O Fernando!
> Take of that eastern shore, this western sea,
> Yet yield thy God's, thy Virgin's charity!

It is an injunction not to asceticism but to moderation: to a right ordering of the gods. Nonetheless, as the worksheets show, Crane did associate Ferdinand with a primary desire for material wealth, and contrasted him with Isabella's primary devotion to Christ and Columbus's principal drive toward knowledge—that "seething wheat / Of Knowledge" later mentioned in "Ave Maria": not rational knowledge, of course, but a pursuing vision of divine *and* natural perfection.[7] The solemn warning follows:

> —Rush down the plenitude, and you shall see
> Isaiah counting famine on this lee!

This is the obverse of the prophet's "pledge" in "Proem": if you (Fernando-humanity-contemporary America) hurry to devour the plentiful material riches of the new world, you will be faced by a spiritual famine like that prophesied by Isaiah.[8] In the process of heedless getting and spending, you will starve the visionary impulse and shall see nothing but ruin.

[7] In a scribbled note, Crane categorized his three main characters thus:

> Columbus will—knowledge
> Isabella's will—Christ
> Fernando's will—gold.

Below that, there appear these lines and changes:

> —And they who mutinied against her Christ
> Who gave the jewels (for whom she offered jewels)
> went with his lust for gold, alas!
> Fernando, thou!

[8] Crane may have had in mind the parable in Isaiah V. about laying waste the vineyard.

The long, impassioned prayer which concludes "Ave Maria" was described by Crane, in the letter to Frank, as "the great *Te Deum.*" It does invoke the phrase which opens the canticle in the Order for Daily Morning Prayer: *"Te Deum laudamus"*—"we praise thee, oh God"; and it does approximate greatness, in language that strives as by its own propulsion to go beyond language, as vision goes beyond vision. It is another sally of Crane's poetic spirit into the unfound infinite, and a mightier and more exultant one than the sally recorded in "Proem."

The first two stanzas of the prayer, despite their curious punctuation, are really a single unit: a single cry of appeal and of praise to a cruel, an omnipotent, a loving, and an unfathomable God. Analogies again breed analogies. In the opening lines—

> O Thou who sleepest on Thyself, apart [,]
> Like ocean athwart lanes of death and birth—

God is made to resemble not only the ocean sleeping on its own sea-paths, but the bridge itself, as defined in "Proem." He shares the bridge's ideal nature of power-in-repose ("implicitly thy freedom staying thee"), and in a way that is verbally closer to Keats's image of "the supreme of power" as "might half slumbering on its own right arm." By virtue of that similarity, the God addressed also resembles a great poem and the poetic ideal of force held in restraint. He is a God, as well, who mysteriously and severely tests man's ability to work out the divine plan for mankind:

> [who] dost search
> Cruelly with love thy parable of man,—
> Inquisitor! [9]

[9] The image of God as Inquisitor had been employed by Emily Dickinson, a poet Crane had read at least as early as 1925 (to judge from a letter to Waldo Frank in July of that year) and whom he was coming to revere. Emily Dickinson's poem "The heart asks pleasure first" ends with the heart asking "of its Inquisitor / The liberty to die." The correct version, unavailable to Crane, is "the *privilege to die.*"

Of this God, who so enigmatically contains and withholds
the truth of man's origins and his destiny—

incognizable Word
Of Eden and the enchained Sepulchre—

of this incalculable and soundless being, this wordless Word,
Columbus beseeches a spoken word of promise:

Utter to loneliness the sail is true.

Let they voice assure me in my solitude that my journey is
in the direction of truth. And to the God who (in the next
stanza) is the agent of final destruction and final salvation,
who, in a splendid image, disputes authority with the mast
of the journeying ship, grappling with it, visiting the ship
with consuming fire—

[who] arguing the mast
Subscribest holocaust of ships—

and yet whose fiery visit may also be the strange fire known
as the corposant, electrical charges which light up the night
and which made it possible for the *Santa Maria* to voyage on
through the darkness to the New World: to this fearsome
and protective deity Columbus-Crane cries:

Te Deum laudamus, for thy teeming span! [10]

God is praised not only for the world-spanning ocean, but
for the whole rounded world itself. This is the world as seen
by what Columbus has called God's "primal scan"; but it is
also the cosmic rondure *within which and through which
God becomes perceptible to the poetic vision.* This teeming
temporal world—this "amplitude that time explores"—increasingly, as the poem surges to its climax, yields glimpses
and echoes of the godhead:

[10] Columbus described the corposant seen off Teneriffe as one of
the marvels by which "God had shown that His Hand was upon
[me] and with [me]." Hence Crane's phrase "Thou Hand of Fire."
Crane must also have had in mind the episode of the corposant—
"holy body," also known as "St. Elmos's fire"—in Chapter One
Hundred and Nineteen of *Moby-Dick*.

> This disposition that thy night relates
> From Moon to Saturn in one sapphire wheel:
> The orbic wake of thy once whirling feet,
> Elohim, still I hear thy sounding heel!

Here and in the concluding stanza that follows—

> White toil of heaven's cordons, mustering
> In holy rings all sails charged to the far
> Hushed gleaming fields and pendant seething wheat
> Of knowledge—

Crane is drawing upon almost his entire vocabulary of praise, to articulate the most intense religious and visionary faith. The words and phrases themselves join and dance together, ecstatically, even as they announce the ecstatic perception of the dancing God. For in the gleaming wheel made by the visible planets, Columbus sees a trace of the whirling deity and hears the sound of His feet. And so, planets and stars, ever-more transparent emblems of God, form celestial circles ("heaven's cordons") gathering within their "holy rings" (recall "white rings of tumult" in "Proem") *all* ships, all seekers after divine revelation, and draw them onwards till the very face and head of God are seen at last by the mortal eye: "round thy brows unhooded now—The kindled crown!"

The very meridians (circles which pass through the celestial poles and zeniths at any place on earth) participate in the dance and the dance-imagery by revealing God's purpose through their own wild circlings:

> acceded of the poles
> And biassed by full sails, meridians reel
> Thy purpose.

But God's purpose is not to be grasped once and for all; it must be pursued in an endlessly renewed quest. Revelation whets the appetite for revelation, and gives rise to new ones.

>   still one shore beyond desire!
>   The sea's green crying towers a-sway, Beyond
>   And kingdoms
>   naked in the
>   trembling heart—
>   Te deum laudamus
>   O Thou Hand of Fire

The first two lines of that queerly punctuated passage have been glossed earlier, and by reference particularly to Emerson's remarks in the essay "Circles" which so plainly underlies "Ave Maria"—Emerson's account of the courageous soul seeking always to "expand another orbit on the great deep," and of its "generation of circles, wheel without wheel." After the word "Beyond," Crane subdues the exclamatory tone by breaking the final lines into five separate phrases; but the poet's heart, I take it, trembles not with fear but with an excitement that shakes the core of being, as vision discerns still further shores and kingdoms become nakedly visible. And God is praised once more for his "Hand of Fire": the divine hand which could "subscribe holocaust of ships," but which had also "sen[t] greetings by the corposant." Columbus, in his journal, expressed the firm conviction that the corposant off Teneriffe had shown "that His Hand was upon [me]."[11] Neither Columbus in "Ave Maria" nor the poet at this stage of *The Bridge* has any doubt whatever that God's fiery hand will light the voyager's way to new worlds of revelation.

·III·

Among modern poems in English, *The Bridge* is the religious poem par excellence; and Hart Crane is the most religious of modern poets. But the pervasive religious character of *The Bridge* is of a kind that escapes easy definition. Some readers, indeed, find it hard to acknowledge the reli-

[11] See p. 265, fn. 10 above.

gious element at all; or, if acknowledged, to take it very seriously. There has even been a tendency to regard it as a matter of occasional rant, a sort of intermittent stamping of the poetic feet (in "Ave Maria" and "Atlantis," for example)—a noisy, discordant somewhat, willful and perverse, that drowns out the beauty of sound in the equally occasional but, as it is claimed, more "successful" poetic fragments. We must, as I said much earlier, make several distinctions before we can usefully and meaningfully employ the word "religious" to categorize Crane's epic.

To begin with—and it is a big point at which to begin—the religion voiced in *The Bridge* is not, or does not readily appear to be, the Christian religion. It is not, whatever else it may be, the mode of Christianity we know to be deeply at work, with a dark and terrible power, in most modern Christian religious poetry: the poetry of Eliot, sometimes of Allen Tate and Robert Lowell (or the fiction of François Mauriac, of Bernanos, of Graham Greene). The characteristic idiom in that body of writing tends to stress human finitude, sinfulness, and spiritual incapacity; the unredeemable ugliness of the actual world; and the always undeserved and, what is more, unseekable and utterly mysterious and trans-rational activity of divine grace. If these are what we are to accept as genuine expressions of the Christian religious attitude, then Crane's idiom in *The Bridge* is certainly not Christian and maybe (by the usual implication) not even religious. But if we bring our sympathetic dispositions to bear upon *The Bridge,* we discover that it contains a surprising mixture of the post-Christian idiom and something unexpectedly and no doubt unknowingly traditional. *The Bridge,* I shall suggest, enacts and traces the disappearance of a once authentic Christian idiom as something no longer accessible. Having done so, however, it does not abandon the religious possibility as such; it is not post-Christian in the currently fashionable sense of post-*religious,* of having lost all consciousness of or interest in the noumenal world. Crane's poem goes on to generate a new religious idiom which can serve a new religious purpose—but a purpose based on a very old conviction.

The Christian vocabulary is drawn upon frequently enough in *The Bridge*. A single stanza of "Proem," as we have seen, contains several mutually affecting insinuations about the Virgin Mary, a prayer to whom provides the title for the next section. In "Ave Maria," the appeal to the Virgin is followed by a monitory glimpse of the Old Testament prophet Isaiah, and this in turn by a canticle in praise of God. Within Crane's greatly modified "Te Deum," we encounter the name of Elohim, one of the Hebrew words for God used by the authors of the early books of the Old Testament as an alternative to Yahweh. (Crane seems to have invoked the name Elohim purely for its tonal value; theologically speaking, the name and figure of Yahweh would probably have been more appropriate.) [12] In later phases of *The Bridge* we meet with "Easters of speeding light" and "seraphic grace" (both in "Cape Hatteras"), and hear ambiguous salutations to Eve, Magdalene, and Mary (in "Three Songs"); the example of Lazarus, beneficiary of the most memorable of the New Testament miracles, is invoked (in "The Tunnel"). Elsewhere, vocables like "the Word" and "the Cross" are evasively pronounced; and the poem is not lacking in hosannas and choirs, altars and naves.

But those random Christian ingredients do not appear in pure form, nor are they evenly distributed throughout *The Bridge*. Elohim, for example, is caught up in a whirling and decidedly un-Biblical dance, a sort of Dionysian revelry. And the references tend—as genuine Christian references, rather than sources of floating metaphor—to be concentrated in the earliest sections of *The Bridge*. They can be observed first mingling with and then yielding to more primitive

---

[12] "Elohistic narrative," Father John Becker informs me, "is more sober and precise than Jahwistic." It "more sharply distinguishes between God and man," it is "more morally exacting" and "reflects a deeper sense of sin"—all characteristics which would be at odds with Crane's religious attitude.

religious allusions and entities. This important process is neatly condensed when, in "The Dance," the Virgin Mary implicit and explicit in "Proem" and "Ave Maria" is punningly metamorphosed (by deleting a single letter) into "virgin May," a seasonable symbol for the earth-goddess Pocahontas. The Christian God of Columbus's "Te Deum," already poetically invested with pagan associations, similarly gives way entirely to "the old gods of the rain," who lie beneath Iron Mountain in "The River"—"the first *and* last gods" (italics added) as Crane goes on to call them in "The Dance." Then, however, somewhere between "The Dance" and "Cutty Sark"—as we leave the smoky mythic glades of the former and re-enter the godless chaos and South Street saloons of the latter—the primitive religion which had temporarily assumed control of the poem itself disappears.

The religious development of *The Bridge* is beset with difficulty—both for the poet and the reader—and I do not wish to claim for it any greater coherence than the situation allowed. The situation was that of a modern American poet gifted with or tormented by an overpowering religious impulse, confronted by a cultural world which (so he felt) denied him either the terms or the substance of religious expression: a world, that is, which either seemed lacking in any vital religious impulse at all, or which formulated its religious sentiment in a way wholly alien to Crane's sensibility. Crane's cultural loneliness, in this regard and others, was extreme; and it would be a matter for critical anguish, did not one remember the obstinate ebullience with which he continued on his poetic business. He marched, in Thoreau's phrase, to the music which *he* heard—"an absolute music," as he told Waldo Frank; and he listened to it for at least sufficiently long stretches. The nature of that music of the absolute, that religious consciousness, is what we want to consider, now and in subsequent chapters. A few summary glances at the religious element, or the rejection of it, in the writing of some of Crane's most distinguished contemporaries can give us a modest but much needed context for discussion.

It was during the gestation period of *The Bridge* that the religious issue approached its first real crisis in the world of American letters. For three centuries before that time, American writing had manifested a more steadfast religious impulse than perhaps any other national literature contemporary with it; though, from the nineteenth-century beginnings of a native literature onward, it had admittedly been a perplexed and wayward impulse, at odds with the sectarian Protestant forms imbedded in society and institutions—forms against which, the religious impulse of our best writers was in revolt. American literature, in short, had always been emphatically religious in motive, but for many decades before 1920 it had almost never been unequivocally Christian in expression. Retroactive attempts to Christianize the work of Thoreau, for example, or even of Hawthorne, have normally met with defeat and have done obscure disservice to the cause both of religious and of literary understanding. Nonetheless—with the presumptive exception of Melville, poised as he was between the fierce imperatives of belief and non-belief—American writers during the past century were not inclined to bring into doubt the very existence of a deity. They tended rather to transfer the religious question from the domain of theology to that of the creative imagination, and to establish it there amid fresh tensions, by means of new languages and dramas. It was not until after the First World War that there occurred in this country what had occurred some time earlier (as it seems) in Europe: a definite shrinkage of belief in any kind of god at all. The feeling, as it spread, engendered a stricter or more desperate humanism on the one hand; and on the other, a peculiarly sombre and beleaguered religious consciousness. We can mention a few such responses, without in the slightest intending to do more than minimal justice to the writers examined.

For Wallace Stevens, who (with Edmund Wilson) is the most resplendent and intellectually courageous of atheists in modern American letters, the death of the Christian God—and "the death of one god is the death of all," Stevens has said [13]—was a colossal event which made possible something more significant yet. It made possible the true birth of *man:* or perhaps better, the birth of the true man, "the central man" as Stevens called him, the essential human being. It gave rise to a truer poetry, a poetry which would no longer offer "aesthetic projections" of divinity, the way Stevens believed poetry had so often done in the past; it would be a poetry which would deal forthrightly with man and reality. And the gods were incontestably dead and gone. "To see the gods dispelled in mid-air and dissolve like clouds," Stevens remarked reminiscently in 1951, "is one of the great human experiences. It is not as if they had gone over the horizon to disappear for a time; nor as if they had been overcome by other gods of greater power and profounder knowledge. *It is simply that they came to nothing*" (italics added). What had been so belatedly discovered, in short, was not that god was dead, but that god had never been alive; it had all been an aesthetic delusion. The event did leave one, Stevens admitted with a certain irony, "feeling dispossessed and alone" for a while, "like children without parents." But the realization came soon enough that "there was always in every man the increasingly human self, which . . . became constantly more and more all there was." Now human beings could "turn to a fundamental glory of their own and from that create a style of bearing themselves in reality. They [could] create a new style of a new bearing in a new reality." The creation of that style was, of course, the responsibility of poetry in action.

In his early poem, "Sunday Morning," replying to the troubled young woman who, while assenting to the dis-

---

[13] "Two or Three Ideas," in *Opus Posthumous* (1957); the quotations immediately following are from the same essay.

appearance of Christian belief, still felt "the need of some imperishable bliss," Stevens proposed several paradoxical sources for such bliss—perishable sources of the imperishable. There were the evanescent beauties of nature, beautiful exactly in their evanescence (for, the poet declares, "death is the mother of beauty"). There were the quail that "whistle about us their spontaneous cries," "sweet berries" that "ripen in the wilderness," assorted "comforts of the sun" which shines down on us now from a closer and a "friendlier sky"—friendlier because no longer the alleged realm of distant and indifferent gods. There was also the "enduring love" of human beings for each other: the enduring value of the mortal love of inescapably mortal men, men who are imagined chanting

> Their boisterous devotion to the sun,
> Not as a god, but as a god might be;

and who

> shall know well the heavenly fellowship
> Of men who perish and of summer morn.

Those natural comforts and that human fellowship retained their attraction for Stevens over the years, as essential elements in the endless dialectal play between the poetic imagination and the "new reality." But for the later (and it is now generally felt, the greater) Stevens, it was the play itself—it was the imaginative act—that became the supreme resource of godless humanity. The artistic creations of men took the place of the belief of men in gods; they performed the exact same function that religious belief had once performed, but they could do so more directly, more honestly, and with far more validity. Stevens returned to this theme again and again in his *Adagia* (proverbs and reflections, notebook jottings, included in *Opus Posthumous*), and always with the utmost resolution:

> After one has abandoned a belief in god, poetry is
> that essence which takes its place as life's redemption.

. . . The relation of art to life is of the first importance especially in a skeptical age since, in the absence of a belief in God, the mind turns to its own creations and examines them, not alone from the aesthetic point of view, but for what they reveal, for what they validate and invalidate, for the support that they give. . . . Poetry is a means of redemption. . . . God is the symbol for something that can as well take other forms, as, for example, the form of high poetry.

Stevens's notion of poetry as redemptive—as containing as much revelation as man needs to distinguish fundamental truth from fundamental falsehood, as providing firmer support and profounder consolation than religious belief ever had done: all this sounds familiarly Romantic; and the essay from which I have quoted includes a sturdy defense of the Romantic imagination. Within that tradition, Stevens should, obviously, be related rather to the thoroughgoing humanism of Keats than to the transcendent visions of Shelley. Quite unlike Hart Crane in his own time, accordingly, Stevens was almost systematically opposed to the "lifting" of "altars" by the visionary imagination; and far from desiring to create a new godhead, a new object of worship, by means of poetry, he wanted rather to "decreate" divinity, especially the Christian divinity.[14] This is the very burden, for example, of the poem "Chocorua to its Neighbor" in *Transport to Summer* (1947), where the mountain, gifted with speech, reflects upon "the prodigious shadow" of Jesus Christ and cuts it down to purely human size:

[14] Stevens adapted the word "decreation" from Simone Weil's religious use of it for his own exclusively humanistic purposes. In "The Relation between Poetry and Painting" (1951; *The Necessary Angel,* pp. 174-75), Stevens referred to Simone Weil's discussion of "what she calls decreation"; and goes on—as though paraphrasing Mlle. Weil—to say: "Modern reality is a reality of decreation, in which our revelations are not the revelations of belief, but the precious portents of our own powers." Quoting Stevens in turn (*The Continuity of American Poetry;* 1961, p. 412n), Roy Harvey Pearce comments astutely upon the crucial shift in the meaning of the key term as it passes from Simone Weil to Stevens.

Now I, Chocorua, speak of this shadow as
A human thing. It is an eminence,
But of nothing. . . .

Not father, but bare brother, megalfrere,
Or by whatever boorish name a man
Might call the common self, interior fons,
And fond, the total man of flubbal glub. . . .

Having thus dispensed with Christianity by reducing
Jesus Christ to "whatever boorish name a man / Might call
the common self," to the stature of an ordinary man among
ordinary men, Stevens did not thereafter, like certain other
Romantics, seek to disclose another or newer kind of religious experience. The whole aim of Stevens's knowing and
invulnerably atheistic humanism was to speak humanly of
human things, because, as he said in the same poem,

To speak humanly from the height or from the depth
Of human things, that is acutest speech.

Given full expression in "the form of high poetry," that
acutest speech enlarges into humanity's "Supreme Fiction,"
a fiction immeasurably superior to—and more valuable and
enduring than—the fictions men had for so long created
for themselves about the nonexistent gods. Stevens's poetry
in the last rich years of his life shows every twist and turn
of which the imagination is capable in its engagement with
reality; criticism will not soon, if ever, be done with its
compelling variety and novelty. But whatever its other
allegiances and aspirations, that remarkable body of poetry
is never for an instant unfaithful to its altogether human
and secular vision.

For Wallace Stevens, then, poetry was not exactly a substitute for religion. It was, rather, a total replacement of
religion—and not quite in Matthew Arnold's meaning either
(that is, of poetry as supplying emotions equivalent to those
supplied by religious belief), but a replacement of religion
in the way that truth replaces illusion. Among Stevens's

and Crane's contemporaries, it was Ernest Hemingway who most memorably dramatized the modern effort to find a substitute for religion within the human sphere: to find on the level of human activity something, as it were, "like" a religious experience, something—some action or some person—that might be invested with a religious feeling of sorts. On the part both of Hemingway and of his characters, the attempt turned out, perhaps inevitably, to be a tragic one.

Hemingway too—not unlike the poet in "Sunday Morning," though without that poet's air of sad serenity—turned to the comforts of nature and to human love, as sources of consolation. But the consolation sought for, in the perilous world of Hemingway's fiction, was of an almost desperately prayerful nature. Trout-fishing and duck-hunting, for instance, with all the meticulous strategies involved, became elevated into religious exercises—ritual actions which seem like urgent silent prayers, counterspells to ward off the encroachment of malign forces. They were, hopefully and for the time of their duration, "momentary stays against confusion," to adapt Frost's definition of any good poem; and against something more terrifying than mere confusion. But in *A Farewell to Arms,* which is on balance Hemingway's best novel, the young lovers, Frederick Henry and Catharine Barkley, tragically aspire to much more than that.

The love of man for woman, in the book, is subtly and most deceptively juxtaposed to the love of man for God. The language describing the Swiss countryside, where the love affair reaches its fullest satisfaction, ambiguously echoes the language describing the Italian Abruzzi, the novel's symbol of the home country of true Christian believers. A briefly seen character, the aging Count Treffi, tells Henry that "You are in love. Do not forget that is a religious feeling." So it is: in the sense expressed by Catharine Barkley when she insists to her lover with quiet passion: "You're my religion. You're all I've got." Robert Penn Warren, who has analyzed this aspect of *A Farewell to*

Arms with the greatest critical tact, accurately defines the love of Henry and Catharine as an attempt "to find a substitute for universal meaning in the limited meaning of the personal relationship." [15] It is just the discovery of the inexorable limitation of the purely human and personal that constitutes Henry's tragic perception, in the denouement. Catharine's death in the hospital delivery room, far from being a freakish accident, is the very sign and reminder of human limitation—that is, of human mortality. And Hemingway, who in one of the book's most famous passages had dissociated himself from the old moral and religious vocabulary, puts the tragic case in the modern American baseball idiom: "You never had time to learn. They threw you in and told you the rules and the first time they caught you off base they killed you."

If this hardly rises to the choral rhetoric of Greek tragedy, the insight is distinctly classical and represents one of the extremely few examples of genuine and traditional tragic understanding in twentieth-century American literature. It is based on a traditional recognition—arrived at elsewhere in Hemingway's time only by Dreiser and Faulkner—of the identity of the destructive element. For it is "they"— not the Austrian or Italian armed forces, but the powers that invisibly be, the gods themselves—who resist and strike down any human being who seeks ultimate or religious satisfaction in exclusively human terms; who dares to attribute to a human encounter the quality of an experience of divinity. "Stay around and they would kill you." That, for Frederick Henry, is the final statement of the human condition, and of man's tragic fallacy.

We can round out this little dialectic by passing on from the atheistic humanist and the seeker after religious substitutes to consider one or two aspects of an authentic believer. T. S. Eliot is the most conspicuously Christian of

[15] Introduction to Scribners Modern Standard Authors edition of *A Farewell to Arms* (New York, 1949).

English-language poets in this century, and probably the most conspicuously Christian writer in the last century and a half of American literature. A literary generation that grew up in his fabulous shadow needs to be reminded of his uniqueness in this respect. The Christian element in Eliot's writing is unique in other respects, among them the fascinating and hesitant manner in which he moved toward it—from the humanistic irony of his Laforguian phase, through the cross-cultural forays of *The Waste Land* and the brilliantly shifting play of spiritual awareness in *Ash Wednesday* to the remarkable formulation, in "The Journey of the Magi," of the heavyhearted, the well-nigh intolerable, condition of the (at last) fully committed Christian in a non-Christian world.

This gradual and painful development is the continuing subject of Eliot's major work, and we may cut into it at the moment, in the closing portion of *Ash Wednesday*, when Eliot is on the verge of final conversion—of a total acceptance of Christianity and its definition (or Eliot's view of its definition) of spiritual health. Eliot is the exemplary modern poet of the experience of religious conversion. No other poet has written so handsomely about it or with greater psychological acuteness: about the real agony of conversion, the immense reluctance of the soul to pass or to be dragged across the threshold of belief—the wavering, the weighing of alternatives, the rebellion, the sudden resurgent impulse to fall back into the natural state:

Wavering between the profit and the loss
In this brief transit where the dreams cross

This dreamcrossed twilight between birth and dying
(Bless me father) though I do not wish to wish these things
From the wide window towards the granite shore
The white sails still fly seaward, seaward flying
Unbroken wings

And the lost heart stiffens and rejoices
In the lost lilac and the lost sea voices. . . .

That vision from the wide window of the white sails and the gull's unbroken wings takes us back to the "inviolate curve" of the sea gull's wings and the "apparitional sails" glimpsed from the office window overlooking the river, in "Proem"; and nearly all the difference between Eliot and Crane is implicit in the two passages. For Crane, the images invoked represent the very creation and object of true redemptive vision: the observed harmony of opposites, of worlds, of orders of existence and orders of consciousness. For Eliot, the flying white sails and the unbroken wings are the ultimately dangerous temptation. They are the most insidiously false of the false dreams by which the "weak spirit" is beset in the moment of potential conversion, at the final crossroad of truth and falsehood. They are the consequences not of vision but of spiritual blindness, a visitation from the ivory gates whence only false dreams issue:

> And the blind eye creates
> The empty forms between the ivory gates.

The poet does not want to long for these things; but his spirit, despite himself, expresses a last spurt of defiant desire —desire for those natural beauties which his spirit *must* reject, if it is to be eligible for the purifying and saving grace of God. Elements which Stevens, in "Sunday Morning," had named as sources of assuagement in a godless world are seen by Eliot as typical objects of wrong-hearted longing:

> And the weak spirit quickens to rebel
> For the bent golden-rod and the lost sea smell
> Quickens to recover
> The cry of quail and the whirling plover. . . .

The extreme pathos of the religious requirement is almost perfectly conveyed by the wistful beauty of Eliot's verbal music—the nostalgic appeals to the treacherous senses, to sight, to sound, and to smell, the cadences that linger and harden. But that natural world must not only be rejected. It must be destroyed within the consciousness of the penitent. For all Eliot's devotion to Dante, the poet of Thomism, and to Jacques Maritain, the most distinguished of modern Thomistic philosophers, Eliot's essential attitude has never been Thomistic in kind. It has never rested upon the conviction, as formulated by St. Thomas, that grace perfects nature rather than destroys it. Eliot, like most of his Christianizing contemporaries, has followed in the line of Pascal, and of Pascal's insistence (which Eliot emphasized and praised in an essay on the French writer) on a radical *dis*continuity—even on antagonism—between the orders of being, between nature and grace.

I have used the word "penitent" as a synonym for "believer"; for if *Ash Wednesday* like *The Bridge* is cast in the form of a long and richly varied prayer, the prayer in Eliot's case is not at all—as it is for Crane—a sally of the soul into the unfound infinite. It is on the contrary the slow and anguished appeal of one who confesses his sinful weakness and who beseeches strength, absolution, and blessing. "Bless me father." *Ash Wednesday* is in part Eliot's own "Ave Maria," and indeed Eliot draws directly from the traditional prayers to Our Lady. The first section closes with the familiar: "Pray for us sinners now and at the hour of our death / Pray for us now and at the hour of our death"; and the next section counts off the paradoxical attributes of the Virgin in a manner carefully derived from the rosary prayer-cycle:

> Lady of Silences
> Calm and distressed
> Torn and most whole
> Rose of Memory
> Rose of forgetfulness
> Exhausted and lifegiving
> Worried reposeful

and so on. Here as elsewhere, Eliot is not only attesting to the (for him) truth-invoking power of the Christian vocabulary; he is focusing that vocabulary on what (again for him) is the essence of the genuinely religious consciousness. It is above all the consciousness of human nature as fundamentally sinful; as fatally shut off from the divine nature when left to its own devices; as in dire and perpetual need of an intercessor; helpless to seek and utterly damned without God's inexplicable gift of grace.

Eliot carried into his exceedingly persuasive (because exceedingly profound and beautiful) poetry the dictum of T. E. Hulme that "dogmas like that of Original Sin . . . are the closest expression of the categories of the religious attitude." Largely because of Eliot and his writings, that has been an enormously influential statement in modern culture; though it is time, I think, to remember that there are other and arguably closer expressions of the religious attitude than the dogma about Original Sin (which, as it has normally but not always been elaborated, is a curiously man-centered and earth-bound doctrine). A doctrine of incarnation—*the* incarnation or *some* incarnation—might, I venture, more directly express a religious attitude, and would represent, as it were, a more theocentric way of thinking. But Eliot's congenital motivation is indicated in the answer of Celia Copplestone in *The Cocktail Party,* when Harcourt-Reilly, the psychiatric mystifier, asks her about "the second symptom" of her spiritual dis-ease. "It sounds ridiculous," she says, "but the only word for it / That I can find, is a sense of sin."

Belief thus begins to stir with the first awareness of personal sinfulness, and after conversion, the figure of the believer is primarily the figure of the penitent. Eliot is at once a traditional and a very searching observer of the spiritual life when he notices that the consciousness of sin tends to deepen rather than to diminish after the experience of conversion. "I have had a vastly greater sense of my own wickedness, and the badness of my heart," says Jonathan

Edwards, a cultural ancestor of Eliot, "than ever I had before my conversion." For now the soul can measure itself against perfect goodness, and survey the huge abyss of being that lies between. On its religious pilgrimage, therefore, the sinful spirit must at each step be forbidden, must forbid itself, to rejoice in earthly things, in the human reality and the natural pleasures on this side of the abyss. It is only the lost heart, the stubborn heart determined on its damnation, that stiffens and rejoices. The sinner must pray that he may learn to despise the earthly and cleave only to the heavenly, to dismiss the former and care only for the latter; and that he may learn almost literally to keep quiet and sit still:

> Teach us to care and not to care.
> Teach us to sit still.

·IV·

Against that background, we can hazard a few obvious but perhaps useful remarks about the religious aspect of Hart Crane and *The Bridge*. Like Stevens, Crane believed that poetry was redemptive of human life, that it was the major modern source of revelation; but unlike Stevens, Crane felt that poetry was not an absolute replacement of a belief in God, but rather a visionary force capable of creating, of bringing into view, new objects of religious belief. Crane too wanted to speak of human things, but he wanted to speak of them at once humanly *and* transcendentally; he wanted, for example, to speak of Brooklyn Bridge as a bridge, as an altar, as the very site and symbol of a godhead. Like Hemingway, Crane sought religious values in human actions and temporal actualities; but where Hemingway and his characters made the grand tragic mistake of seeking religious substitutes in the natural world, Crane saw the divine *within* that world, energizing and illuminating it. Crane had a religious consciousness no less active than that of Eliot, and like Eliot he prayed for a mediator between the orders of being. But Crane's religious imagination was only sparsely and, as it were, initially Christian—at least, in the usual modern meaning of Christian. It was unburdened by the sense of sin as *the* defining element of human nature. And (what is almost the same thing) it was one of Crane's staunchest and most Emersonian convictions that the orders of being—of man and God, the temporal and the timeless, the actual and the ideal—though calamitously dislocated within the modern consciousness, could again become continuous and contiguous one with another: exactly by being so envisioned in poetry. Thus did Crane, in his modern Romantic manner and by his Romantic strategy, approximate dimly and unknowingly the great theme of St. Thomas—that nature is perfected by grace rather than opposed, rejected, destroyed, and utterly transcended; thus did he combine the post-Christian with an old conviction.

It should be added, of course, that for Crane as much as for the other three writers, not only was the religious issue paramount; the attempt to deal with it imaginatively and honestly was the severest and sometimes the most discouraging challenge the modern artist had to face. Crane did not proceed out of any easy affability of spirit. It was a constant struggle against demons, and against the treachery of the creative gift. This will be evident enough as we press our way through the heart of Crane's major poem. What we shall discover—if I may offer a little *précis* in advance— is something like the following.

In "Proem" and "Ave Maria," Crane juxtaposes a new religious vision, one accessible to the twentieth century, with the old religious vision of the fifteenth century and the age of Columbus. The new vision is associated with a remarkable product of the machine age, but it is also touched with hang-over metaphors from the Christian epoch. The old vision is addressed in part to the Virgin Mary, but in turn it begins to dissolve in figurative language expressive of a new mode of consciousness. These two poems and visions, thus juxtaposed, indicate what we may call the religious situation, in Crane's view of it: something old, something new, something borrowed, and a general stage of urgency and anticipation. After this Cranian version of the opposition and continuity, made famous by Henry Adams, of the Virgin and the Dynamo, the poem and the poet depart on their religious quest.

In the long section called "Powhatan's Daughter," the poem is, so to speak, burrowing through and beneath the Christian dispensation toward what, for Crane, was a more fundamental and primary religious sensibility. In "The River," we are told of country folk who "confess no rosary or clue," but who "count . . . the river's minute by the far brook's year." These are un-self-conscious participants in a sort of religion of nature: beings who find answers to such ultimate questions as they may ask not by means of traditional Christian practices (like confession or the counting of beads), but by observing the processes of nature, the flow of waters, the round of the seasons. Doing so, Crane goes on to say in "The River," they "touch something like a key perhaps." In "The Dance," moving onto the smoky ground of a new revelation, Crane indicates what it is those vagrant rustics possess a key *to,* if they did but know. It is a world governed by a mythic apprehension of reality, of nature, of experience—a world in which these things are seen and responded to as elements in a grand and recurring mythic drama. It is the remote and marvel-ridden age of the old rain gods—those gods who now, in the modern period, lie buried beneath iron (that is, technological) mountains of forgetfulness, of blunted awareness. For "The Dance," after leading us onto that mythic scene, acknowledges the death of the old gods. The historic slaughter of the American Indians ("Across what bivouacs of thine angered slain") becomes, in Crane's handling of it, a trope for the willful destruction or suppression by the modern mind of the mythic and hence of the religious imagination.

The Bridge is, in short, a poem fully cognizant of the enormous cultural event known as the death of God; and it seeks with all its energy to discover and disclose the real nature of that death, finding it not simply in the waning power of Christianity but in the loss of the religious consciousness itself. But *The Bridge* is unique in being the only large-scale work of literature in its generation which, in the light of that event, is finally concerned not with the death of God but with the birth of God. *The Bridge,* as a poem, is a thing of words; and the religious phenomenon that occurs in it is to some extent a matter of names. Edmund Wilson, in a statement I have had occasion to quote elsewhere, has remarked briskly that "The word *God* is now archaic and it ought to be dropped by those who do not need it for moral support." As though recognizing in advance the historical justness of the contention, Crane does indeed let the word "God" drop out of his poem for a very long stretch. It appears often enough, and in varying forms, in the first half of *The Bridge;* but it is virtually unheard in the second half, from "Cutty Sark" onward— until it surges back into the rhetoric with which "Atlantis" opens: "As though a god were issue of the strings."

The phrase condenses much. It is, at the last, as though a new god were the very creation of what Crane, in "Proem," had called the bridge's "choiring strings"—those elements, in actuality the steel ropes of the actual bridge, which had been metamorphosed by poetry into the strings of a harp and the voices of a choir. The god, this is to say, is the issue of poetry and the poetic vision. For after invoking and then dropping the word "God" and the names of God, Crane, as the second half of his epic moved toward its own climax, had begun to invoke the word "poet" and the various names of poets: Herman Melville, Walt Whitman, Emily Dickinson, Edgar Allan Poe, William Blake. These are not themselves gods, of course. They are rather avatars of the figure saluted by Whitman in "Passage to India": "the poet worthy that name, / The true son of god" who shall come singing

285

his songs of harmony and redemption. They are instances of the archetypal mastersinger destined to restore the religious consciousness to modern man, to requicken the sense of divinity hovering within the actual—when the actual is envisioned poetically. They are phases of the authentic modern hero—phases of himself, as Crane no doubt dared to hope: the hero who will do for his time what Columbus had been seen doing for his—bring back Cathay, a true wonder-working attitude of spirit, into the contemporary world.

CHAPTER TEN

"Powhatan's Daughter"

THE SECOND numbered section of *The Bridge,* containing five separable poems and called "Powhatan's Daughter" (i.e., Pocahontas), is exactly what Crane, during the great month, was determined that it must be: "that basic center and antecedent of all motion," as he wrote Frank; "—'power in repose.'" It is indeed the very heart and center of the epic movement, that toward which and away from which all the action flows. It is in particular the source both of the movement and of the meaning of the sections that follow it—though this is not to imply (I shall later argue the point) that "Powhatan's Daughter" or any individual part of it should be taken as *the* middle of *The Bridge* in the Aristotelian sense of middle.[1] "Powhatan's Daughter" also provides what most readers have judged to be the richest moments (the last eight stanzas of "The River") and the dreariest moment ("Indiana") of the entire poem, though such judgments have usually been made out of context, whereby each individual part is evaluated as "a separate canvas," which Crane agreed each was, but is not, as Crane also insisted, taken "in relation to the other parts, *in series,* of the major design" of *The Bridge.* All in all, "Powhatan's Daughter" is an astonishing achievement, one realized in a constant rise and decline, a gathering and loosening of intensity, a sort of poetic hastening and loitering; and in language and rhythms that articulate this shifting interior activity across an immense vista of history, myth, and the personal life.

It begins with Crane's most obsessive theme: a vision, even a presence, experienced and then lost. It goes on to a multiple imaginative quest-journey, westward in space

[1] See p. 320, below; and the final section of Chapter Twelve.

and backward in time, to the poet's childhood and the nation's pre-history, in search of that lost vision with which the poet is convinced he has a rendezvous. The journey picks up momentum as it proceeds down the Mississippi— "which you will notice," Crane told a correspondent, "is described as a great River of Time"—to the open sea and the domain of the timeless. In "The Dance," the poem arrives at last on what Crane called "the pure mythical and smoky soil"; it enters an apocalyptic setting where, amid a series of vast, blurred metamorphoses, the myth-infested Indian world enacts its final ritual. It is here that the poet—identifying so completely with the sacrificial rite that he feels the very arrows in his own flesh—re-covers the vision of spiritual nobility and undespoilable physical beauty, a vision of life enhanced by myth, which will make up his transfiguring image of contemporary America. The section ends somewhere on "the long trail back"—back to the East, to the city, and the contemporary world, with the poet beginning to assume his role as the heir of and the missionary from the vanished race.

The American Indian, it is clear, provides the major symbol of this section; and Pocahontas, the daughter of Chief Powhatan, is of course the primary figure. A little later, I shall comment upon the peculiar "status" of the Indian in Crane's poem—his mode and place of poetic existence, as it were—and upon the cogency and propriety of Crane's choice of Pocahontas. But there remains something a bit mystifying about the epigraph to "Powhatan's Daughter," and its glimpse of the Indian Princess as "a well-featured but wanton yong girle . . . of the age of eleven or twelve years" who used to make the Indian boys do cart wheels in the market place, while she followed after them "and wheele[d] so herself, naked as she was, all the fort over." Crane took the passage neither from the book in which it first appeared, William Strachey's *History of Travaile into Virginia Britannica* (about 1615), nor from the book which quoted at some length from Strachey,

William Carlos Williams' *In The American Grain* (1925), but from a review of the Williams book, in *transition,* by Kay Boyle.[2] This exhibitionistic maiden from Virginia, in any case, scarcely seems to resemble the earth-goddess encountered in the Adirondacks during the Appalachian spring of "The Dance"—the goddess who "is virgin to the last of men."

She may, however, be fairly close to the historical Pocahontas. The usually reliable Strachey reinforces the account given by the far from reliable Captain John Smith, who in his *General Historie* (1624) remembers with assumed vexation how the Princess and her women came "naked out of the woods . . . singing and dauncing with most excellent ill varietie, oft falling into their infernall passions" and "torment[ing] him . . . with crowding, pressing and hanging about him, most tediously crying, Love you not me?"[3] Such an erotically teasing nymph is rather like the striptease dancer named Magdalene in "Three Songs"; and Magdalene is herself a parody and debasement, detail by detail, of the Pocahontas envisioned in "The Dance." My guess is that Crane intended, by starting with a picture of the historical Pocahontas as a naked young wanton, to point forward to his poetic conversion of unwashed fact into beautiful archetype—Strachey's "Pocahuntus" into his own

[2] Crane apparently did read *In The American Grain,* though it is not clear when he did so; and he is said to have acknowledged his debt to it and to Williams' early poem "The Wanderer" for part of the "argument" and of the imagery in *The Bridge.* The acknowledgment was made, it is believed, in a letter to Williams (date uncertain) which was accidentally destroyed by Dr. Williams' maid. See John Unterecker, "The Architecture of *The Bridge,*" *Wisconsin Studies in Contemporary Literature,* Vol. 3, No. 2, Spring-Summer 1962. See also below, p. 359.

[3] Quoted by Philip Young in his delightful and invaluable essay, "The Mother of Us All: Pocahantas Reconsidered," *Kenyon Review,* Vol. xxiv, No. 3, Summer 1962.

The spelling of the Indian Princess's name provides a problem. To avoid confusion, I have decided to follow Crane's spelling— Pocahontas—especially since most of my references are to Crane's rather than to the historical figure.

veiled "Pocahontas whose brown lap was virgin May."
Neither fleshly beauty nor the wheeling motion are lost in
that conversion, which, in the manner characteristic of *The
Bridge,* affects a reconciliation of opposites and a reminder
of continuities.

· I I ·

The title and content of "Harbor Dawn" take us back
to the opening lines of "Proem," while, conversely, the
perspective has faded forward, the gloss note tells us, "400
years and more" from the end of Columbus's late-fifteenth-
century *Te Deum*. Set against the double invocation of the
first two sections, on a morning in the American 1920's,
the poetic adventure begins: the search for something like
a Columbian vision, the available legacy of a legendary past,
wherein the contemporary world may be seen imbued with
grace as the bridge was seen to be in "Proem."

We are back overlooking the East River, and we witness
again the chill gulls at dawn and eventually the early
morning sun: "The sun, released—aloft with cold gulls
hither"; though this particular winter dawn is enshrouded
in fog and thinly blanketed by snow, the same snow,
presumably, which had submerged the "iron year" at the
midnight of "Proem." As before, a vision of beauty—here,
a dream of blissful union—fades out when "day claims our
eyes," and (later) "The window goes blond slowly": the
blondness of the physical morning light, by an easy pun,
bringing with it the spiritual blindness of the awakened
poet, dragged slowly back from dream-filled sleep into the
actual world. The process in "The Harbor Dawn" is one
of mist clearing into blindness.

Sounds are even more important here than sights; and
at least once, Crane hooks together the auditory and the
visual in one of his most original and precise images: when
the muffled noises from the harbor are transmuted into
shrouded signals, "gongs in white surplices"; the phrase

summons up appropriately vague religious associations—the bell rung during the Eucharistic service, the flowing white surplice of the priest.[4] The poem washes back and forth with the current of sound—in drifting stanzas of differing length, with occasional gentle rhymes as sounds from below the poet's room intrude, die away, intrude again; and as the poet is partly roused, dozes again, and is once more awakened by the clamor. There is the hoot of foghorns, and the more grinding sound of lumbering trucks and throbbing winch-engines; there is the harsh voice of a drunken stevedore yelling "Alley-oop!" There is, in short, the deafening and blinding daily encroachment on the human consciousness of the machine and of graceless disorder. But this recedes momentarily and merges with restful music: "distant chiming buoys" and "sirens" metamorphosed from shrill mechanical whistles into mythical females who "sing to us."[5] The cool "feathery fold" of the sky "suspends. . . . / This wavering slumber" (it is, evidently, a good wintry morning for sleep). And the poet returns, for one final embrace of the mysterious and enchanting, the "blessed," figure by his side.

We identify her, on this first encounter, through the qualities the poet curiously attributes to her: "singing arms"; eyes that "drink the dawn"; a forest that "shudders in

[4] Crane's knowledge of liturgy was no doubt limited, but his creative intuition as always was sound. In the Anglican service, at least, the bell is usually rung by the priest at the moment when the wafers and wine are being transubstantiated into the body and blood of Christ—a supernatural process akin to Crane's process of poetic transfiguration.

[5] L. S. Denbo, in *Hart Crane's Sanskrit Charge,* draws attention to Crane's differing account of the harbor sounds in letters of November 1924, and February 1925. "There was a wonderful fog for about 18 hours last week," Crane wrote in the first. "All night long there were distant tinklings, buoy bells and siren warnings from the river craft. It was like wakening into a dream-land in the early dawn." But in the second, he spoke irritably of "the bedlam of bells, grunts, whistles, screams and groans of all the river and the harbor buoys, which have kept up an incessant grinding program as noisome as the midnight passing into new year."

[her] hair"; flesh that "our feet have moved upon." These
are of course ingredients in a dream-image, and as such
exempt from any logic except the logic of metaphor. What
the poet addresses in urgently murmuring italics is a female
figure who shiftingly is or becomes the American earth
and landscape: the earth that drinks the morning dew; a
land of lakes and forests and trembling trees; the very
ground we walk upon. It is, conversely, that earth and
landscape condensed by dream into a magically beautiful
female. It is that immortal entity later to be named Pocahontas and to be designated (in "The Dance") as "the
torrent and the singing tree," whose sibilant hair is the
llano grass ruffled by the wind, and whose "eternal flesh"
(in "Cape Hatteras") is "our native clay" with its "depth
of red." Her eyes, in "The Harbor Dawn," are "wide" and
"undoubtful," by contrast with the blindness and uncertainty
elsewhere insinuated in the poem, and by contrast too with
the several single eyes, glittering and sightless, of the in-
animate monsters on the other side of the harbor—the
"bright window-eyes" of the "Cyclopean towers across
Manhattan waters." It is, by submitting in erotic reverence
to the reality of the American earth that the poet can, so
he hopes, find his own eyes opened and his doubts removed.

But the dream dissolves; the fog clears. The poet wakes
into the modern, eastern, urban day; and simultaneously,
a star in the remote pastoral west disappears as though into
sleep:

> The fog leans one last moment on the sill.
> Under the mistletoe of dreams, a star—
> As though to join us at some distant hill—
> Turns in the waking west and goes to sleep.

In search of that star and that union of visionary love
("mistletoe of dreams": a phrase barely rescued by context
from tinkling sentimentality), and to keep his appointment
with his vanished and only dimly known beloved, the poet
sets forth.

·III·

"Van Winkle" is relatively prosaic and conversational; its rhythms are pedestrian, its rhymes sparse; and as always, when Crane's imagination was (here quite deliberately) being held somewhat in check, it depends a good deal upon sheer verbal play: puns on such proper names as Far Rockaway, Golden Gate, Sleepy Hollow, and the *New York Times*. This first groping phase of the poet's journey is framed by lines which suggest a paradigm of his undertaking in the long leap of the transcontinental highway:

> Macadam, gun-grey as the tunny's belt,
> Leaps from Far Rockaway to Golden Gate.

The names of the Long Island village and the San Francisco bridge are lucky for Crane's purpose, which is itself, of course, one of bridging the great divided elements, and of rocking away, so to speak, from the iron world to the far threshold (the "spiritual gates") of golden Cathay. One would like to believe that Crane knew the etymology of "tunny" (in America, more usually "tuna"), from the Greek word for "leap"; it would ensure the connection between the metaphoric tunny and the "eyeless fish" in "the River" who "curvet"—that is, who leap curvingly, like the highway and the tunny—over a "sunken fountain." Those cross-country miles, in any case, unwind in the poet's brain to the sound, and like the sound, of the unending tune of a nearby hurdy-gurdy. And as they do, the poet's memory winds back into his own childhood.

The poet is en route to the subway, as we might not have known (except for a single slight reference to "car-change" in "Van Winkle"), had not Crane explained as much to Otto Kahn in the September 1927 letter. "The walk to the subway," he wrote, "arouses reminiscences of childhood, also the 'childhood' of the continental conquest, viz., the conquistadores, Priscilla, Capt. John Smith, etc." Those continental elements, in fact, enter the poem exactly by means

293

of the personal memory: the poet's (literally Hart Crane's) recollection of the history books, folklore, stories, and poems he had read in school. The principle at work—and it continues to work through the next two parts of "Powhatan's Daughter"—is Romantic and traditional; as formulated by Emerson, it is the principle that "the whole of history is in one man, it is all to be explained from individual experience," and that there is "a relation between the hours of our life and the centuries of time." [6] In *The Bridge,* a relation is discovered between the hours of the poet's life and the centuries of American history and pre-history; without such a relationship, both Crane and Emerson believed, history is an undecipherable chaos, and the historical present is meaningless.

Out of the random name-dropping, as though summoned by the sound, there emerges a bemused guide to that history, Rip Van Winkle, who is also and somewhat gratituously made to inhabit Washington Irving's other famous tale, *The Legend of Sleepy Hollow.* He is like the poet, he is a part of the poet; and he finally merges with the poet. Rip Van Winkle, too, has just awakened, like the poet in "The Harbor Dawn," from a long dream in which he had visited a realm of legend; and his mind wobbles between the contemporary actuality and the half-remembered dream—neither properly "here" nor "there." Crane indicates the split by splitting the name: as Rip, he is absorbed by his vision and oblivious to the world of practical affairs; as Van Winkle, he is caught up in the dusty demands of the immediate life:

> *And Rip forgot the office hours,*
> *and he forgot the pay;*
> *Van Winkle sweeps a tenement*
> *way down on Avenue A.*

Just as the poet stakes everything upon the recoverable reality of the morning vision experienced and lost, so Rip Van Winkle (in a second nursery-rhyme stanza) insists upon

[6] *The Early Lectures,* II, 15.

the validity of his pastoral image—an image of pastoral beauty preceding and still underlying the urban spectacle:

> *He woke, and swore he'd seen Broadway*
> *a Catskill daisy chain in May.*

Another "exile in [the] streets," Rip joins and fuses with the poet on the quest for the dream-scene of the mountain meadow: where, indeed, the poet and the poem will arrive at last in "The Dance."

But the chief reminiscences in "Van Winkle" are personal ones, and they are seedings of what become major symbols and participate in the epic's generalized pattern of meaning. The poet remembers the paper monoplanes he and his schoolmates used to launch, and the family of garter snakes they used to stone: items which will be associated with the large abstractions (too large and too abstract, in my opinion) of space and time. The latter, the reference to the garter snake, is the more subtle and interesting:

> Recall—recall
>
> the rapid tongues
> That flittered from under the ash heap day
> After day whenever your stick discovered
> Some sunning inch of unsuspecting fibre—
> It flashed back at your thrust, as clean as fire.

The image is strikingly visual and unambiguous; but retrospectively, we realize its suggestiveness. Everything later associated with rapid tongues and serpents, with the sun and flashing brilliance, with the cleansing and purifying fire: all this spiritual splendor lies buried and unsuspected "under the ash heap day" (Crane's artful division of the phrase "day after day" permits us to isolate the first "day")— under the contemporary world which, in its unredeemed form, seemed to Crane, as it had to Scott Fitzgerald, to be a valley of ashes. With the mature poet's help, that splendor will recoil upon the modern effort to destroy or suppress it by stone and iron.

More personal yet and more disturbing are memories of his parents: of a whipping the poet's father once administered with a branch stripped from a lilac tree; of an *"unconscious* smile" his mother *"almost* brought me *once* from church" (italics added)—

> It flickered through the snow screen, blindly
> It forsook her at the doorway, it was gone
> Before I had left the window. It
> Did not return with the kiss in the hall.

Familiar references cluster in this autobiographical passage: the flickering image of the desired object; the smile forsaking both the poet's and his mother's eyes; the ensuing blindness. The paternal whipping was no doubt a source of continuing resentment; but in *The Bridge* it is "the lost mother"—rather than, as more normally in the epic tradition, "the lost father"—whom the poet needs, longs for, and journies far in search of. (There is a good deal, one gathers, to Allen Tate's expressed belief that in his actual life Crane sought—and according to Mr. Tate, desperately failed to find—in his friends, in his homosexual adventures, in his very relation to the world, a replacement for the parental and, in his later years, especially for the maternal love which had been denied him.) [7] In "Powhatan's Daughter," the poet does realize a sufficient assuagement for his mother's unsmiling lovelessness in the smiles and the tears of Pocahontas, and in the poetry that elicits them both.

· I V ·

"Van Winkle" concludes with the poet and (in Crane's phrase) his guardian angel boarding a subway, equipped only with scattered memories of earlier times in the personal and the national life ("Have you got your *'Times'*—?"). [8] In

---

[7] See below, p. 386.

[8] In the Paris edition, this line read simply: "Have you got your paper—?"

"The River," the transporting vehicle on the quest-journey is transformed, as in a waking dream, from that typical urban conveyance, the subway, into a transcontinental express train—that century-old representative of the age of technology—and then into the great river, that timeless achetype of the flow of time itself. Amid the first sputtering lines of "The River," the twentieth century, epitomized by a train of that name, whizzes off westward (accompanied by Horace Greeley's best-known advice) into "the telegraphic night" and in a fury of sight and sound—

> whistling down the tracks
> a headlight rushing with the sound—

through the preposterous jumble of the contemporary American epoch.

It is a jumble of advertising and Broadway entertainment, where commerce alternates on the same level of importance with the Holy Ghost, and Wall Street competes in value with the Virgin Birth. Crane felt that here, as in "Faustus and Helen II," his rhythms had approximated those of jazz; but apart from a fuzzy initial echo of that jaunty ballad "The Darktown Strutters Ball" ("I'll be down to get you in a taxi, honey"—"Stick your patent name on a signboard / brother"), there is rather an unpatterned jumpiness, with an occasional rhythmic thump that, as someone has suggested, is closer to the jazz rhythms of Paul Whiteman than to the New Orleans tempos Crane evidently aspired to.[9] And even those echoes give way to more pertinent and sardonic borrowings from Shakespeare's most memorable pastoral romance:

> WITHOUT STONES OR
> WIRES OR EVEN RUNning brooks connecting ears
> and no more sermons windows flashing roar
> breathtaking—as you like it . . . eh?

[9] James Dickey, in a letter to the author.

In the urban world of money and the machine, there are no more sermons, no more revelations of God; there are, especially, no sermons to be listened to in the stones and running brooks of nature; human beings are no longer united ("connect[ed]") by a shared vision; and this is the way the denizens of that world prefer it—they are sure they have everything anyhow. But this first portion of "The River" goes on to reverse the motif that had recurred so often in *The Bridge* up to this point. It is not, here, the white sea gull or the vision of the New World or the presence of a shadowy beloved or the spectacle of the Catskills in May or a mother's smile that forsakes our attentive eyes. It is the twentieth century that now vanishes from view, carrying with it (in Crane's gloss note) "the dins and slogans of the year," the noisy chaos and the false formulations of the temporal life:

> So the 20th Century—so
> whizzed the Limited—roared by and left
> three men, still hungry on the tracks, ploddingly
> watching the tail lights wizen and converge, slip-
> ping gimleted and neatly out of sight.[10]

Thus, in Crane's expansive metaphor, the express train has fulfilled the paradoxical function prophesied by Emerson: it has carried the human spirit westward into the heart of nature, in an earnest of its eventual accommodation both to nature and spirit. And the phrases culled ironically from *As You Like It* lead in fact into the domain of the pastoral and toward the mythic.

The opening of "The River" is not, poetically speaking,

[10] This same device—of juxtaposing glamorous transcontinental movement, along with financial and technological power, with the figure of the hungry vagrant—was exploited by John Dos Passos in the final pages of *U.S.A.* (1936), for a rather different artistic purpose. Devoted as Dos Passos was to Whitman, it was the democratic and egalitarian rather than the visionary Whitman that he sought to recover.

very beguiling: a commotion of language striving to reflect a commotion in culture. But its staccato quality, its free and nervous verse, its lack of rhyme and of capital letters at the start of lines—this willful patternlessness is part of the developing pattern in what is probably the most handsomely composed of the "separate canvases" that make up *The Bridge*. After the lines just quoted, the poem gathers itself into a series of slow, stretched-out stanzas with increasingly regular iambic pentameters and increasingly audible rhymes: until it settles into a steady flow of quatrains and the high formality of alternating rhymes to conclude, as the river reaches the sea, in a four-line unit with a *single* rhyme:

Poised wholly on its dream, a mustard glow
Tortured with history, its one will—flow!
—The Passion spreads in wide tongues, choked and slow,
Meeting the Gulf, hosannas silently below.

The pattern of sound is very definitely an echo of the sense; for the journey being enacted is precisely a movement away from chaos through a kind of loose order to the experience of significant design and on to a glimpse of perfect union.

But Crane's language asks us to think not only of a movement *away from* the world of trains and telegraph wires, but also of a probing *beneath* that world. The poet travels in search of a reality that is at once spatially and temporally remote from the city (far in the west and the historic past) and also buried under the here-and-now of the modern actuality. As the train disappears in the night, the poem shifts attention to "The last bear, shot drinking in the Dakotas" who "Loped *under* wires that span the mountain stream," and then to "some men" who "go ruminating through" the Middle West *"Under* a world of whistles, wires and steam" (italics added). It must be remembered that in the crucial perspective the poet never departs from his metropolitan environment, and that the many-faceted journey from "Van Winkle" through "The Dance" is also a many-faceted metaphor of his attempt to recover in vision what, in "Cape Hatteras," he calls:

> Those continental folded aeons, surcharged
> With sweetness *below* derricks, chimneys, tunnels

(italics added). It is a movement of consciousness toward something that is, after all, still available at this place, in this time.

But, as I remarked in the previous chapter, the poem is also burrowing beneath a contemporary Christianity—which, as the opening of "The River" implies, had become hopelessly entangled with, hopelessly compromised by, Wall Street and the commercial culture—seeking a more fundamental and enduring religious revelation. The three homeless and hungry men who watch the train's tail lights disappear are a stage toward that revelation. They represent the race of ignorant wanderers who are, all unknowingly, closer to the divine than ever the city-folk can be; pastoral Charlie Chaplins, so to say, new Cranian instances of the lowest of the low who can yet point the way toward the great transformation scene. "Blind baggage" though they be (unenlightened human lumps carried about in freight cars), "Blind fists of nothing, humpty-dumpty clods," they nevertheless "touch something like a key perhaps." "Something like" and "perhaps" must be stressed, for these vagrants have no more brains than a bird ("Strange bird-wit") and no more vision than a colt ("one who had a colt's eyes"). But they are, at least, perfectly indifferent to the spurious unions and the false dreams contrived by telephone and telegraph, to the deceptive possibility of "communicating" across long distances—

> Keen instruments, strung to a vast precision
> Bind town to town and dream to ticking dream.

They are indifferent to the devices of traditional Christianity. Instead they

count
—Though they'll confess no rosary nor clue—
The river's minute by the far brook's year. . . .

Time's rendings, time's blendings they construe
As final reckoning of fire and snow.

Saying no "Ave Maria's," they hear, if faintly, the sermons
in the running brooks; and like instinctive grammarians,
they "construe" the divisions and unifications of experience
as reflections of the phenomena of nature. Beyond them lies
the true possibility: in the language of "Cape Hatteras," the
possibility of "conjugat[ing] infinity"—of reading the very
shape of the godhead in the visible heavens.

The poet—again, literally Crane himself—had known such
characters; as a child, he used to see them behind his father's
cannery works (in Warren, Ohio). He remembers them as

wifeless or runaway
Hobo-trekkers that forever search
An empire wilderness of freight and rails.

They were "the ancient men," but they were also incorrigibly
childlike; and in Crane's Emersonian belief, it is just because
of their perpetual childhood that they could dimly intuit the
female body in the natural landscape:

—They know a body under the wide rain;
Youngsters with eyes like fjords, old reprobates
With racetrack jargon,—dotting immensity
They lurk across her, knowing her yonder breast
Snow-silvered, sumac-stained or smoky blue—
Is past the valley-sleepers, south or west.
—As I have trod the rumorous midnights, too.

The poet too, as this stirring passage continues, has heard the
sounds and rumors of the earth-goddess. Dreaming at his
desk in the city, near "the lamp's thin flame," he has heard
"Trains sounding the long blizzard out," speeding from
winter into spring and "into distances I knew were hers."

301

What he hears, in particular, are the voices of Indian children in the far wind-swept distance announcing the remote Indian epoch: which, typically, is clutched at and swiftly disappears:

> Papooses crying on the wind's long mane
> Screamed redskin dynasties that fled the brain,
> —Dead echoes!

Before the poet's consciousness can re-enter that mythic world, he must be capable of a certain kind of perception: the perception of all time and space—or at least all American time and space, American history, and the American landscape—as condensed in a single divine female body. He has on occasion achieved this remarkable and quite untranslatable vision:

> But I knew her body there,
> Time like a serpent down her shoulder, dark,
> And space, an eaglet's wing, laid on her hair.

(I remain uneasy with those symbols and that image.) But those were rare and tantalizing glimpses. The poet has miles still to go; he has not yet journied beyond the world of time, nor seen fully beyond the enormous actuality of the iron age—of that mechanistic culture which has buried the mythic apprehension. He is aware of the old mythology, but he knows that the modern world has been drastically cut off from it:

> Under the Ozarks, domed by Iron Mountain,
> The old gods of the rain lie wrapped in pools
> Where eyeless fish curvet a sunken fountain. . . .

The rain gods, who are not dead but sleeping, are nourished only by "eyeless fish" (Crane never misses an opportunity to stress the theme of blindness) who leap to pilfer grains of corn from resentful crows. This is the gods' only recompense for the destruction of their forests and the "rendings" of "iron":

their timber torn
By iron, iron—always the iron dealt cleavage!

The chief representative of that iron, the express train, now glides back into view. But in the poet's vision, as though strengthened by meditation on the slumbering divinities, the train begins to change its nature: and the continuities it had sundered begin to re-establish themselves. The train emerges "from tunnel into field," into the natural world. Like a giant human, it "strides the dew" and "Straddles the hill"; its rapidly revolving wheels seem now rather to dance than to crush, and they remind us inevitably of the "sapphire wheel" of the planets in "Ave Maria," through which Columbus discerned the circling dance of God. Surely some splendid revelation is at hand; and the "Pullman breakfasters" are urged, at this propitious moment, to

lean from the window, if the train slows down,
As though you touched hands with some ancient clown,

and to "hum *Deep River*" with the hungry ancient men on the tracks. Doing so, the urbanites might also touch the key those wanderers touch, and know the meaning of the deep onward flow of the Mississippi.

The citation of *Deep River* is the final turning-point of the poem, and to the sound of it the express train is transformed into the river and the journey assumes its true direction. The haunting Negro spiritual provides the allusion to "Jordan's brow" two stanzas later, and it is the "liquid theme" heard in the swelling voices of the "floating niggers" two stanzas beyond that.[11] The theme is death and the after-

[11] These phrases are virtually all that remain in *The Bridge* of Crane's original notion (as described to Otto Kahn) of an entire section dealing with a Negro porter on an express train, who was to be seen and heard making up the beds and singing of his sweetheart and his namesake John Brown. That unrealized Negro, as the descendant of slaves, might well have been another and thematically valuable representative of the "lowliest," the slaves of

life: or rather, the longed-for passage from this earthly existence to the blessed land ("the biding place" referred to still
later in "The River") which is man's proper home. It is the
musical accompaniment of the poem's passage, which now
begins, down the Mississippi to the sea: a passage, in the
poetic rendering of it, which is also a movement out of
time—not from earth to paradise, but from the actual to
the mythic. The river itself is soundless: "You will not hear
it as the sea . . ."; those many who have drowned in it
merely "drift in stillness"; its "wide tongues" are "choked,"
and when it reaches the gulf, it "hosannas silently below."
Yet it flows steadily and smoothly to the interior music of
the old spiritual.

Like Brooklyn Bridge and like the God of "Ave Maria,"
the river is many things; and nothing in the entire poem is
more impressive than Crane's poetic realization of its symbolic multiplicity. We must once again hold on hard to the
logic of metaphor if we are to perceive its distinctive and
fused natures (and not, almost literally in the present case,
be swept out to sea by the beauty and momentum of the
verse). The river, first of all, is emphatically the actual
Mississippi, from Cairo, Illinois, to the Gulf of Mexico—its
musky smell on a summer evening, its heavy majestic flow:

> Damp tonnage and alluvial march of days—
> Nights turbid, vascular with silted shale
> And roots surrendered down of moraine clays:
> The Mississippi drinks the farthest dale.

The crowding polysyllables, the lack of breathing space, the
strong and out-of-the-way language (turbid: muddy; mo-
raine: debris)—these are poetic equivalents of the thickly
burdened river-in-motion. But the river's "alluvial march"
is also a march of days and of nights. It is, in the modern
cliché, the march of time; the river is the almost militant

---

time, to whom the bridge is begged to "lend a myth." But Crane's
imagination—perhaps unfortunately—was never hospitable to, or
easy with, material of this social and political order.

onward flow (like the sea in "Voyages II" it is "processioned") of time the devourer, time the leveler. In the
river, many men drown; in the dimension of time, all men
die—not only the wandering hobos, but the Pullman breakfasters and those who occupy the seats of authority—"For
you, too feed the River timelessly." All become "Grimed
tributaries to an ancient flow."

And yet the river—always, be it remembered, in the poet's
articulation of it—also provides a way out of time and beyond death. Along with the onward flow of time, there is
simultaneously a backward flow of the imagination. "I'm
trying in this part of the poem," Crane explained in a letter
of July 4, 1927, "to chart the pioneer experience of our fore-
fathers—and to tell the story backwards. . . . The reader
is gradually led back in time to the pure savage world"—
the world observed in the next section, "The Dance." His
vagrants are again the connective agency: as wanderers and
seekers in the present day, they are, in an excellent phrase,
"born pioneers in time's despite," and one is reminded of
"Louisiana, long ago." [12] They do not themselves discover
any new frontiers; but they win much for the poem by taking us back in these allusions to the frontier days and the
true pioneers. So the poem passes "over De Soto's bones"
and surges backward to the boundaries of time and history.

As it does so, the river assumes the more complex role of
time striving to escape from time—seeking to liberate itself
from its own temporal burden. In the climax, it "flows

[12] Those last words are part of Crane's affectionate tribute to Mrs.
T. W. Simpson—"Aunt Sally," as Crane called her—who had been
Crane's housekeeper during the miraculous days on the Isle of Pines.

"—And when my Aunt Sally Simpson smiled," he drawled—
"It was almost Louisiana, long ago."

"You'll find your name in it," Crane wrote, sending Mrs. Simpson
a copy of "The River." "I kind of wanted you in this section of
the book. . . . For you are my idea of the salt of all pioneers, and
our little talks about New Orleans, etc., led me to think of you
with the smile of Louisiana."

305

within itself, heaps itself free." Many images cluster and converge in this and the other concluding lines of "The River," and many associations loom in the reader's imagination. The river, coiling within itself, is like a serpent—like *the* serpent which, in "The Dance," Crane identifies as "Time itself," and relates to Maquokeeta; earlier it has been described as "sliding prone," serpent-like, and it reveals "a jungle grace." It resembles the rain gods: it is "Like one whose eyes were buried long ago"; it has its own "timeless eatage," and it too has been asleep—upon reaching the Gulf, "The River lifts itself from its long bed." And as the river flows within itself and heaps itself free, it associates with the God of Columbus's *Te Deum*—"O Thou who sleepest on Thyself"—and hence with the sea to whom that God had been compared. In the burst of similitudes to which *The Bridge* periodically gives rise, the river is like the bridge in its free restraint and like that supreme entity which the bridge resembles: the great poem.

The point to be made is this: all these hints and allusions, these echoes and similarities, are not only part of a process of identification. They are also part of a process of poetic expansion and elevation. We are concerned not simply with what the river *is* or has been made to become verbally. We are concerned with the area, the mode of reality, the spiritual atmosphere, so to speak, into which Crane's extraordinary resources and his interacting connotations have transported us. Within the climactic metaphor of "The River," we have arrived at the open sea:

> . . . Ahead
> No embrace opens but the stinging sea.

Within the larger context of *The Bridge,* we have been swept out of time into the time-conquering world of myth, a world characterized in the next section by Pocahontas and Maquokeeta. "I also unlatch the door to the pure Indian world which opens out in The Dance section," Crane remarked, adding in words any critic must devoutly echo, "it has been

a very complicated thing to do." It is the more complex because we have reached the edges of something larger yet:
a world for which the "pure Indian world" is itself only a
major symbol; a world in which the transfigured bridge,
the sea, the Christian-pagan God of "Ave Maria," the rain
gods, the serpent of time, the river, the Indian royalty, and
great poetry all have their shared, their separate and fused,
their timeless being.

· V ·

In "The Dance," the long-sought-after vision is at last
experienced, and in an almost violent shift of setting. The
poem moves onto an entirely new scene—as indeed it must,
for new insights require crossing new thresholds, and the
supreme visionary act requires (by the very nature of art)
its own supreme location: the apocalyptic ground of the
journey's climax. But before reaching that ground, Crane
re-enacts once more, and now by reference to his key symbolic figures, the little drama of appearance and disappearance. This occupies the first four stanzas of "The Dance,"
and it begins with questions:

> The swift red flesh, a winter king—
> Who squired the glacier woman down the sky?
> . . .
>
> And in the autumn drouth, whose burnished hands
> With mineral wariness found out the stone
> Where prayers, forgotten, streamed the mesa sands?

Questions, which have been sparing and mostly rhetorical
up to now, are the proper mode of discourse at this crucial
moment. "The Dance" records the temporary climax of the
prayer which informs *The Bridge*—the climax of the poetic
soul's "sally . . . into the unfound infinite." And Crane's
questions, like those of Keats in "Ode on a Grecian Urn"
("What men or gods are these? What maidens loth?") and
in "The Fall of Hyperion," are the kind of speculations and

307

uncertainties that crowd the consciousness when, as W. J. Bate has observed, the poet extends knowledge "into the forest and 'untrodden regions' of the mind and of the unknown generally"; and as he does so, "the number of points at which we touch the unknown increases, and with it the number of questions." [13]

For the time being, the answers to these opening questions remain tentative and hazy. For what the poet has first to stress is exactly the temporal and psychological distance between the modern consciousness and the mythic view of reality. The latter held sway in an epoch when man's environment was looked upon as charged with magic and astir with divinity: when the annual passing of winter into spring, for example, was taken as the escorting across the heavens of a "glacier woman" by a "winter king." By this manner of perceiving things, the phenomena of nature around the seasons—the wild horses galloping through the canyons in spring, the spouting of streams, the growth and death of wheat in summer and fall—all were interpreted as the cyclical activities of a single immanent earth-goddess:

> *She* ran the neighing canyons all the spring;
> *She* spouted arms; *she* rose with maize—to die

(italics added). In such an epoch, the discovery of much-needed water during the annual drought was regarded as the rain god's answer to long since forgotten prayers; and as the consequence of the tribal chief's magical knowledge wherewith (like Moses smiting the rock at Horeb) he is able to release from the desert stone enough water to inundate the sands. The figure inquired after—a god in stanza one, a priest in stanza two—has "swift red flesh" and "burnished hands." He is an Indian; and in Crane's treatment of him, he is the embodiment of the mythic apprehension of experi-

---

[13] *John Keats,* pp. 512, 588. See also Geoffrey Hartman's discussion of "surmise" in Wordsworth's poetry and of "the enlarged role of surmise in Romantic poetry" generally, as against the age of Milton (*Wordsworth's Poetry 1787-1814* [New Haven, 1964], pp. 9ff.).

ence. But even as the poet invokes him, he withdraws, fades
into semi-darkness, separated from "us" in our modern world
by the broad abyss of time and a sundering of consciousness—
across which, however, he still sends messages of hope:

> He holds the twilight's dim, perpetual throne.

> Mythical brows we saw retiring—loth,
> Disturbed and destined, into denser green.
> Greeting they sped us, on the arrow's oath:
> Now lie incorrigibly what years between. . . .

Not quite incorrigibly: for the poet, in the very idiom
of the initial stanzas, is pursuing his immense effort to
summon that mythic vision (those "mythic brows") back
into effective being—to make it, in fact, his own. He is already able to envisage the natural spring landscape as the
divine female, though as a phenomenon in the past:

> There was a bed of leaves and broken play;
> There was a veil upon you, Pocahontas, bride—
> O Princess whose brown lap was virgin May;
> And bridal flanks and eyes hid tawny pride.

And in subsequent stanzas, the poet makes his way back to
the presence of Pocahontas precisely through his heightened
capacity to see as the Indian saw (at least within the confines
of this poem), to perceive the elements of nature as the
physical attributes of the Princess. On his final, brief journey—the metaphoric direction of which is now *upward*: an
ascent to the heights of vision—the poet sees the shining
hair of Pocahontas in the crescent moon; he sees her feet in
the mingling streams of a waterfall ("Feet nozzled wat'ry
webs of upper flows") and her "inaccessible smile" in a
mountain ledge in the Adirondacks. As always, hearing
keeps pace with seeing; the poet, steadily repossessing himself of the old or "Indian" way of responding to reality, has
learned to interpret the *sounds* of nature ("I learned to catch
the trout's moon whisper"). And when the crescent moon

declines, he sees it replaced by a single star "Cupped in the larches of the mountain pass," until it bleeds "immortally . . . into the dawn." He has reached that western hill where, in "The Harbor Dawn," union was promised with the sleeping star; and his arrival is coincident with, it is the same as, his recovery of the visionary power.

The account of this little journey includes personal memories of Crane's boyhood excursions, when he used to go canoeing "below the mill race" and to take "the portage climb." To get back to the eternal youth of America, he revisits his own youth, as he had in "The River." But as the poet ascends the mountain and gains the ledge, actuality melts once more into a dream vision, and, dream-like, he fairly flies to the scene of the great ceremony:

> Over how many bluffs, tarns, streams I sped!
> —And knew myself within some boding shade:—
> Grey tepees tufting the blue knolls ahead,
> Smoke swirling through the yellow chestnut glade. . . .

"Here," Crane told Otto Kahn, "one is on the pure mythical and smoky soil at last"; and to signalize the fact, Crane effects a striking change of momentum. A stanza that begins with a headlong rush slows and lingers in the last two lines: each of which contains six clear stresses, with an extra stress as it were on the word "grey" (to emphasize it, amid the rapid play of color) and upon "smoke," the identifying symbol of this section.

Slowed almost to a stop, the poem pauses while the poet peers and listens, watching the growing cloud of smoke, hearing the swelling sound of dancing feet—until he experiences a sense of radical release:

> its rhythm drew,
> —Siphoned the black pool from the heart's hot root!

and he enters the forest glade to witness and to participate in the ritual dance. The glade, as I have said, is the scene of an apocalypse—the new ground, which the poet has led us onto, of an ultimate revelation. The latter takes the form of a sort of ultimate dance: the fulfillment not only of the circling dance of God Columbus had perceived in the planetary wheel, but also, one feels, the fulfillment of all the dances that had animated Crane's poetry from "The Bridge of Estador" onward. With an intense if hazy urgency of language, the Indian Prince Maquokeeta is seen undergoing sacrificial death; he is being consumed at the stake (like the divinity in "Lachrymae Christi"), while, within the flames, he continues to dance exultantly. And not only do the other Indians stamp and dance about the pyre, the very trees of the forest move, reverently, in Orphic measure:

> A birch kneels. All her whistling fingers fly.
> The oak grove circles in a crash of leaves.

As in other moments of comparable intensity of vision, all the elements of reality—the divine, the human, and the natural—seem to move in intoxicated concert; while language strives to beget the sublime ferocity it is describing:

> And every tendon scurries toward the twangs
> Of lightning deltaed down your saber hair.

(Such language will, hopefully, echo in the reader's ear until at least the "Cape Hatteras" section, where it will be reinvoked to a crucially different purpose.) Exclamations and imperatives, insistent pleas and prayers fill the poetic air:

> Dance, Maquokeeta! snake that lives before,
> That casts his pelt, and lives beyond! Sprout, horn!
> Spark, tooth! Medicine-man, relent, restore—
> Lie to us,—dance us back the tribal morn!

It is the poet who is that medicine man; and it is he who is in the act of restoring the lost morning vision, in a dance of "tribal" metaphors. The lie besought is not some willed illusion, some confessed evasion of the true nature of things; rather, it is the "sacred lie"—*le mensonge sacré*—which in the *symboliste* and modern Romantic tradition (recall

Stevens's "supreme fiction") is the highest truth the imagination can aspire to.

What is happening is that the poet—seeing and hearing in the most concentrated manner ("I saw . . . I heard . . . I saw")—becomes altogether identified with the sacrificial princely figure.

> Spears and assemblies: black drums thrusting on—
> O yelling battlements,—I, too, was liege
> To rainbows currying each pulsant bone:
> Surpassed the circumstance, danced out the siege!

> And buzzard-circleted, screamed from the stake;
> I could not pick the arrows from my side.

It is an act of extreme empathy, like Whitman's association with the harried, wounded, and symbolic Negro slave: "I am the man, I suffer'd, I was there." It is also an act of self-encounter. More, it is an act wherein the self is re-united; the poet has rejoined his own visionary capabilities. "The reason why the world lacks unity, and lies broken and in heaps," we have heard Emerson saying, "is because man is disunited with himself." Here in "The Dance" the journey ends (temporarily, at least) in a meeting and a marriage of the essential aspects of the poet's consciousness—his "Reason" and his "Understanding," as Emerson would have called them. A vision of the *world* as whole and harmonious will, hopefully, follow.

In the letter to Otto Kahn, Crane sought to explain his relation to the Indian figures represented in "The Dance." "I also become identified with the Indian and his world," he said; and this "is the only method possible of ever really possessing the Indian and his world as a cultural factor. I think I really succeed in getting under the skin of this glorious and dying animal, in terms of expression, in symbols, which he himself would comprehend." Those symbols no doubt include the eagle of space ("swooping in eagle feathers down your back") and the serpent of time ("snake that lives before" and so on). But Crane is not, of course, possessing the Indian and his world "as a cultural factor," and historical familiarity with the actual American Indian will only divert the reader's understanding. Crane is, quite legitimately, deploying a phenomenon of American cultural history as an element in a purely poetic and visionary structure. In the guise of bridging the distance between the modern American world and the old Indian world, Crane is in fact re-uniting the modern consciousness (that is, *his* modern consciousness) with the mythic sensibility. The latter is simply postulated, for the sake of the poem, as a quality of the Indian age; and whether it really was or was not is beside the point.

As to Maquokeeta, consequently, one may well be reminded of the exchange between Cleopatra and Dolabella in *Antony and Cleopatra:* when the captive queen, after praising the dead Antony in the most extravagant terms, asks, "Think you there was, or might be, such a man / As this I dream'd of?"—and Dolabella answers with kind practicality: "Gentle madam, no." But if Crane were so answered, he might have echoed Cleopatra's spirited rejoinder: "You lie, up to the hearing of the gods." Crane could have argued—not that his Indian world was an historical fact—but that, insofar as Whitman and Melville, as Emerson and Poe and Emily Dickinson had actually lived and written and entertained persuasive visions, there had in very fact been a period in American history when the human situation was seen as informed by miracle and terror, when the natural landscape was regarded as hospitable to divinity, and human experience took the constant shape of significant ritual. To all this, it should be added and remembered that, in Crane's generation and especially in the 1920's, popular culture (films, songs, anecdotes) invested the American Indian with many of the qualities postulated by Crane. It should be added, too, that Pocahontas —to whose symbolic being we and the poem will shortly return—was almost as central to popular culture as to Crane's poem. Pocahontas was indeed a sort of cliché of popular culture; and it was one of Crane's achievements in *The Bridge* to detect the potent basis of that cliché—the sense, let us say, of extraordinary fleshly female beauty, at once alien and intimate—and to draw from it fresh and ennobled meaning.[14] It would, finally, be after reading Whitman that, in "Cape Hatteras," the poet experiences again "that deep wonderment" about

> our native clay
> Whose depth of red, eternal flesh of Pocahontas. . . .
> Is veined by all that time has really pledged us.

The death of Maquokeeta is at the same time his absorption into the Indian cosmos, and the promised end of that cosmos itself:

> And saw thee dive to kiss that destiny
> Like one white meteor, sacrosant and blent
> At last with all that's consummate and free
> There, where the first and last gods keep thy tent.

Maquokeeta "persists," Crane wrote, "only as kind of 'eye' in the sky," a notion darkly set forth in the twenty-first stanza:

> Thewed of the levin, thunder-shod and lean,
> Lo, through what infinite seasons thou dost gaze—
> Across what bivouacs of thine angered slain,
> And see'st thy bride immortal in the maize!

Muscled (thewed) by the lightning (levin) and clothed in the thunder which had been released by the apocalyptic death-dance, Maquokeeta stares out—from an epoch or realm where such dances were characteristic occurrences— across the ensuing centuries and the destruction of his people. But it is the poet who has acquired the visionary power to see an immortal bride in the growing things of nature. "Though other calendars now stack the sky"—though we live now in an age of skyscrapers and smokestacks—it is still

[14] See the essay by Philip Young (n. 3 above).

possible, or once again possible, to see the world in a transfiguring vision.

Like certain other heroes of the American mythopoeic imagination—Ishmael in *Moby-Dick,* for example, and Isaac McCaslin in *The Bear*—the poet can say to us: "I only am returned alone to tell thee." What he has to tell us is the burden of the remainder of *The Bridge,* but the message begins at once in the final stanzas of "The Dance." Several major events are here taking place, and we must as it were try to see *through* one to the other if we are to grasp it all. To start with, spring returns to the earth; the natural world is born anew. This is the perennial outcome of the perennial fertility rite of antiquity and legend, whereby the sacrificial death of the god or tribal chief or of the scapegoat is the source of life's renewal. In the Indian epoch postulated in "The Dance," the death of the princely demigod restores vitality to his world; and the passage from winter into spring is envisioned with perfect clarity as the awakening and liberation of Pocahontas—the spring thaws are the conversion of the goddess's wordless winter dream into song:

> High unto Labrador the sun strikes free
> Her speechless dream of snow, and stirred again,
> She is the torrent and the singing tree;
> And she is virgin to the last of men.

(Again, one hears in those last lovely lines a faint stress on the word "she.") Almost the entire American landscape takes the form of the divine body quickening into new life:

> West, west and south! winds over Cumberland
> And winds across the llano grass resume
> Her hair's warm sibilance. Her breasts are fanned
> O stream by slope and vineyard—into bloom!

But the spring season thus described returns simultaneously into the poem—into *The Bridge,* after the long journey that began on a winter morning when the divine beloved disappeared; and it is a promise of revitalization and spiritual emancipation in the poet's own *contemporary* world. Uniting himself with the Indian god, the poet becomes the "liberating god" of Emerson's essay; and if Maquokeeta's lonely persistence is (somehow) the gift of Pocahontas, the freedom of the modern consciousness may eventually be the "largesse" of the poet; for it is his imagination which perceives and articulates the regained fertility in the stanzas quoted.

The questions that follow, therefore, have a different tonality from those with which "The Dance" began. They are cast in the present tense—

> And when the caribou slant down for salt
> Do arrows thirst and leap?

They are questions that assert, questions that observe and affirm with wonder and awe the union of all the cloven elements: the Indian and the modern age, the old divinity and the natural world ("And are her perfect brows to thine?"), time and space:

> Now is the strong prayer folded in thine arms,
> The serpent with the eagle in the boughs.

The poet and the Indian prince, long separated by the incorrigible years, are fused in a dance that carries them out of the Indian epoch and past the frontier farms ("*We* danced, O Brave, we danced beyond their farms") and on into the timelessly enduring, the permanent here-and-now. The poet's strong prayer has been answered; he has found his myth to God; the union is complete.

·VI·

"Indiana," the tail-piece of "Powhatan's Daughter," is not, as has sometimes been said, the worst poem ever written by a great poet. Whitman was guilty of coarser blunders, and Keats, on certain early occasions, was hardly less inept. But it is a flat, almost an inert, piece of work. The language struggles wearily with puns on "Indian" and "gold"; and the metrical pattern (five-stress, four-stress, five-stress, three-stress) is something Tennyson could have managed brilliantly, but it was not Crane's natural style. Nor is it the genre of poetry suited to Crane: a thin narrative mode—not the dream-narrative, bursting with symbolism, of "The Dance," but a sort of life-on-the-old-farm story, with individual characters bearing names like Jim and Larry. Crane was probably right in feeling that his structure needed a transitional phase between the climax of this phase and the start of the next phase of his epic—between the mystical intoxication of "The Dance" and its apocalyptic rendezvous, and the exploration of the fallen modern epoch that begins in "Cutty Sark." No doubt it seemed sensible to continue his journey metaphor by focusing on "the long trail back" —from West to East, from past to present. But one could have hoped for a better transitional poetic piece than this, especially since the implications of the experience recorded in "The Dance" can *only* reveal themselves retrospectively as the vision acquired attempts to operate in the eastern present.

The poem is spoken by a frontier woman, evidently the widow of an Indiana farmer who, with his family, had joined the goldrush of 1859, had died in the course of it, and had been buried "far / Back on the gold trail." Connections are made, rather slackly, with earlier portions of *The Bridge:* in addition to the title-name, "Indiana," we learn that the woman's dreams have been rent by "bison thunder"; her "folks" and her husband's "came out of Arrowhead"; and the object of their westward trek, "a dream called Eldorado," can stand as a minor and frontiersman's version of the Cathay of Columbus and the forest glade of the poet. But the main connection aimed at is what Crane, in an explanatory note, called "the transference of the role of Pocahontas to the pioneer white." In "Indiana," this takes place when the woman, looking out of her eastbound covered wagon, sees "a homeless squaw" traveling sadly in the opposite direction. The white woman holds up her first-born child, and the squaw's eyes—till then "sharp with pain"—light up with love; she nods and smiles back over her shoulder as she disappears.

This is not without meaning, though it reflects a kind of tired vagueness. Here, in any case, when the representative visionary figure vanishes, vision itself is not lost: continuity is affirmed via the figure of the white woman. She is an example of the maternal love denied the poet in "Van Winkle"; and she also has the gift of seeing the divine and the beautiful glowing within the actual—in the one stanza in the poem quite worthy of Crane, she recalls how:

> The pebbles sang, the firecat slunk away
>   And glistening through the sluggard freshets came
> In golden syllables loosed from the clay
>   His gleaming name.

This is the sermon she is able to hear in the stones or pebbles: a sermon about the name of God. But her capacity is about to be transferred to her son, Larry, who in turn is about to take to the sea:

> I'm standing still, I'm old, I'm half of stone,
>   Oh, hold me in those eyes' engaging blue;
> There's where the stubborn years gleam and atone!—
>   Where gold is true! [15]

The son is of course the poet, heir of the pioneer explorers and through them of Pocahontas and Maquokeeta; his will be the vision announced (in this unhappy stanza) which will redeem the modern commercial world and atone for its dedication to false gold and false values generally. One could elaborate on other suggestions provided by "Indiana"

---

[15] John Hollander has remarked in conversation that the voice in these lines can be heard as whining and self-pitying: the repellent voice of a grasping mother who sees her mother's boy about to leave her. "Indiana," we remember, was written in 1929, a year after the final break with Grace Crane, and only a few months after the miserable quarrel between Hart Crane and his mother over the legacy from Mrs. Hart.

—the poet-son as a voyager, for example; but to do so would be to misrepresent the poem, or rather to do the poem's work for it. "Indiana" is after all not much more than an array of notations and hints about some mode of transference, of succession and continuity—not very coherent, if looked at too closely, but perhaps sufficient (Crane must have hoped) to carry the reader and the poem into its new major stage.

CHAPTER ELEVEN

The Road to Quaker Hill

THE BRIDGE has, so to speak, a shifting middle. Depending upon perspective, it could be argued that the second half of the poem begins with "Indiana," [1] or, as Crane seems to have believed, with "Cape Hatteras," or with "Cutty Sark." But these arguments are misleading, for *The Bridge* does not really have a "second half." It does not respond to usual notions of symmetrical design; and what we observe is not a single point which is unmistakably midway in the poetic action, but rather a series of moments at which the action takes a series of new but analogous directions. The first of these to consider here is "Cutty Sark," where the poem drops completely into the dark of the contemporary world and visibility grows instantly difficult and must be strained for. An immediate sign of the new condition is a half-blind and sleepy creature —a tall and drunken sailor encountered by the poet in a South Street saloon, on the Manhattan side of Brooklyn Bridge. This real and symbolic figure (the wreck, perhaps, of the visionary seagoing Larry of "Indiana") is also the first of a number of *parodic* characters scattered significantly through the later portions of the poem. For parody is almost the inevitable method of those portions, since now, after "The Dance," the poet has something by reference to which the contemporary actuality appears as parodic and debased.

The sailor is one who "keep[s] weakeyed watches" and "sometimes snoozes"; like the sleep-bemused Rip Van Winkle, he does not quite know where he is, or what time it is: "that / damned white Arctic killed my time." The experience of the sea has not liberated and prepared him; it has ruined him. He is almost literally a fish out of water: "that spiracle!" he gasps, alluding to the so-called "blow-

[1] This is the opinion of L. S. Denbo, *Hart Crane's Sanskrit Charge.*

320

hole" or spout-vent of the whale; "my lungs— / No—I can't live on land—!" He represents in general the lost and wandering modern being, cut off from the past and from the sources of perception—bewildered, blinded, and suffocated by the urban chaos. His mind may reach vaguely for a better reality:

> I saw the frontiers gleaming of his mind;
> or are there frontiers?

But typically he lurches out into the street and is nearly destroyed by the machine, nearly run down by a passing truck.

As to the poet, however, the liquor consumed has fortified his visionary power, as wine had redeemed the sight in "The Wine Menagerie." He begins to hear musical intimations of the ideal city, the drowned Atlantis, rising from the depths of the sea; and as he walks back across the bridge to his Brooklyn home, he enjoys a rum-inspired vision of the gallant old clipper-ships of the previous century. The words of the song being played on the pianola, "Stamboul Nights," fade woozily into another song; "dreams" become "drums" and then "drown" (as though in a sloweddown illustration of Crane's characteristic poetic technique); "weave" turns into "wreathe" and "Stamboul Rose" gives way to the exclamatory "ATLANTIS ROSE" (rose, that is, from the "galleries of watergutted lava," and associated via the latter word with Pompeii). Amid the squalor of the dark saloon, in short, the poet becomes aware of the loftier possibility, and remembers his mission: which is, to "start some white machine that sings." The phrase condenses the whole purpose of *The Bridge* and defines the action, or poetic motive, as effectively as the statement of Columbus in "Ave Maria": "I bring you back Cathay."

For the entire intention is, of course, to see and hear the age of the machine purified and made musically beautiful, as in the choiring strings of the bridge itself. Later, on that bridge, the poet sees below him not the tugboats and warships and cargo vessels of the actual harbor, but the English and American clipper-ships of a vanished epoch. "Music still haunts their names," Crane said to Otto Kahn; and he lapses pleasurably into a Homeric Catalogue: *"Thermopylae, Black Prince, Flying Cloud," "Rainbow, Leander"* and *"Nimbus," "Taeping"* and *"Ariel"*—names which, needless to say, have additional historical and contextual connotations. "Where can you be?" he asks, in closing. For their world, like that of the Indian rain gods, is divided from the modern world by the invasion of iron. Those "old and *oaken"* navies (italics added) have, in one of the phrases quoted from Melville's *Battle-Pieces* in the poem's epigraph, been replaced by ships of iron. In Melville's words from the same poem:

> The rivets clinch the iron clads,
> Man learns a deadlier lore.

"Cutty Sark" is a light and clever poem, rather than a beautiful or imaginatively energetic one. The rhythms are nerveless and the language fuzzy—as no doubt befits the setting, and the spiritual slackness and the casualness of human relations which are being observed (the sailor, after leaving abruptly, "forgot to look at you / or left you several blocks away"). But it is crowded with verbal hints and continuities, a sort of verbal stock-taking. There are hinted references to the tragically disastrous quest-journey of Melville's Ahab ("Murmurs of Leviathan he spoke") and to the more mysterious catastrophe of Poe's Gordon Pym ("that damned white Arctic"). An echo of "Proem" ("the dawn / was putting the Statue of Liberty out") leads to more numerous echoes of "The Dance": "dance," "drums," and "lava"; names like Black Prince and Flying Cloud; a glimpse of the splendid female savage, the spring-blooming Princess Pocahontas—when the British clippers are envisioned, surprisingly, as "savage sea-girls / that bloomed in the spring." There is an anticipation of "Three Songs" in the emphasized word "shine," and the allusion to the ship *Leander*—"last trip a tragedy." One discovers without undue effort what Crane is aiming at; but the aim discerned appeals more, perhaps, to the mind than to the imagination, especially when Crane's cross references get muddled incongruously with Gilbert and Sullivan.

He is, obviously, once again remarking the fateful division of worlds—the present and the past, the actual and the mythic, the temporal and the timeless. But he is also suggesting ways of re-unifying them. In the latter part of "Cutty Sark," there is a movement parallel to that of "The River": like "The River," Crane told Kahn, "Cutty Sark" also "starts in the present and 'progresses backwards,'" and the purpose as before is to manipulate vanished beauties of the historic past in order to reach beyond and outside of time. He must, as earlier, resort to questions and surmises:

> where can you be
> *Nimbus?* and you rivals two—
>
> a long tack keeping—
>
> > *Taeping?*
> > *Ariel?* [2]

But the poet is equipped now with the resources he journied so far to acquire. He is equipped, above all, with an idiom, a vocabulary, a pattern of verbal allusion. By means of it, the new effort of liberation may go forward; and the poetic mood, though wondering and nostalgic, is not without its modicum of cheerfulness.

· I I ·

"Cape Hatteras" is the massive pivot of the long phase of *The Bridge* here being examined, and it is one of the most

---

[2] The *Taeping* and the *Ariel* were "rivals two" in the great tea race of 1866 from Foochow to London. *Ariel* won by a margin of ten minutes, after a voyage of ninety-nine days. For this information, I am grateful to Mr. Jack Kligerman, a student of Professor Walter Sutton at Syracuse University.

remarkable English-language poems of the century. It is not without flaws. There are some sickly rhymes and an occasional awkwardness, even vulgarity, of phrasing; it seems too long drawn out—not in itself, but by comparison with the other important sections. But it remains, I think, a masterpiece: a meditation of almost incredibly protracted imaginative vigor, some 250 lines, most of them composed of weighty and resonant words wedged close together, with heavy syllables multiplying, and pentameters often stretching into hexameters. ("The line-lengths are longer than in any other section," Crane wrote Caresse Crosby at the end of August 1929, when the poem was nearly finished,"—so long, in fact, that to preserve them unbroken across the page I think we ought to change our plan regarding page size.") Rhetorically, much of "Cape Hatteras" is poetic rant of a supreme and traditional kind, the fierce and joyous rant of a poet who, however sombre his subject may sometimes be, is exercizing to the utmost his talent for sonorous declamation and his love of it.

Properly appreciated, "Cape Hatteras" should put an end to the theory that Crane's creative powers were declining in the period when (desperately, it is sometimes alleged) he sought to bring *The Bridge* to its completion. They were not declining—they were changing, maturing, expanding. "Cape Hatteras" is poetry of a somewhat different order from that of "The River" and "The Dance," though its difference does not lessen but rather increases its *fitness* in the overall poetic scheme. On the one hand, that is to say, "Cape Hatteras" is a closer accommodation than any other section in *The Bridge* of the traditional linear and progressive English epic style with the special impulses of the modern Romantic imagination. It suggests what Crane might have done with the epic poem about Mexican history and legend he once ruminated. On the other hand, its peculiar profundity and beauty, the excellent and steady sense that it makes, derive from its place in the epic design. Out of context, indeed, "Cape Hatteras" is almost indecipherable and invites the woeful misreadings it has received; it has been the special victim of the incorrigible tendency of Crane's critics (there are honorable exceptions) to read the individual parts of *The Bridge* as though each had to prove itself to be a totally self-sufficient whole. In context, however, "Cape Hatteras" turns out to be not only a longer but in some respects a larger effort than "The River" and "The Dance," and to be, if anything, more coherent than either—though its coherence depends at every step upon our quickened memory of the texture and movement of those superb poems.

Departing from the prodigious paradigm of the opening lines—vast fragments of nature slowly sinking and convulsively rising (like the "worlds that glow and sink" in "The Tunnel")—"Cape Hatteras" consists of a nearly seamless series of sinkings and risings, with substance and meaning accumulating solidly throughout. As always in *The Bridge,* it is the poetic vision of perfect beauty that alternates with the appearance of the fallen world. More precisely, it is a redemptive vision associated with Walt Whitman and inspired by a reading of (and innumerable citations from) his poetry that alternates with the observed belligerent hell, the apocalyptic horror of contemporary America. And the aim—again as always in *The Bridge,* but now with a heightened sense of promise due to the enabling presence of Whitman—is to marry the alternating elements and thus to harvest the hell. There are four main alternating phases (smaller ones can also be made out) in "Cape Hatteras," and I shall treat each of these in separate sections.

The globe-circling imagery of "Cutty Sark" ("Bright skysails ticketing the Line, wink round the Horn / to Frisco, Melbourne. . . .") leads, at the start, to a glimpse of that future moment prophesied by Whitman, in the stanza in "Passage to India" from which Crane borrowed his epigraph, when, all voyaging completed, the human soul is ready to confront and embrace divinity:

Reckoning ahead O soul, when thou, the time achiev'd,
The seas all cross'd, weather'd the capes, the voyage done,
Surrounded, copest, frontest God, yieldest,

the aim attain'd,

As fill'd with friendship, love complete, the Elder Brother

found

The Younger melts in fondness in his arms.

(Except for the last line, which in its metrical drive sounds more like Crane than Whitman, this stanza like most of "Passage to India" is impossible to read aloud; it must surely have been the visionary content rather than the poetic quality that drew Crane to this tiredly turgid work.) The same notion is repeated in the opening of "Cape Hatteras," where recollections of world travel—the "grey citadels" seen and the "ancient names" heard, gypsies in Marseilles and priests in Bombay—give way to a vision of divine beauty. The journeying poet returns to his own homeland and his own hearth, there to read Whitman and via Whitman to perceive once more the mythic beauty of his native earth eternally available beneath the features of the iron age:

> Or to read you, Walt,—knowing us in thrall
>
> To that deep wonderment, our native clay
> Whose depth of red, eternal flesh of Pocahontas—
> Those continental folded aeons, surcharged
> With sweetness below derricks, chimneys, tunnels—
> Is veined by all that time has really pledged us.

Such a vision, according to the bleak law of experience painfully adhered to in *The Bridge,* is never more than momentary, and even as he enjoys it, Crane foresees its immediate disappearance:

> time clears
> Our lenses, lifts a focus, resurrects
> A periscope to glimpse what joys or pain
> Our eyes can share or answer—then deflects
> Us, shunting to a labyrinth submersed
> Where each sees only his dim past reversed.

This is the customary duplicity of the world of time in *The Bridge*. But in "Cape Hatteras" the vision-destroying element insisted upon is modern man's insensate desire to conquer physical space, and the cosmic warfare it has led to. The visible heavens, the poet continues, are a "star-glistered salver of infinity," and they can indeed be traversed; but they can be "subjugated never"; the lust for subjugating the sky only propels man into the "blind crucible of endless space." But the contemporary epoch *is* the day of the tyrannical airplane: "the eagle dominates our days," and "we know the strident rule / Of wings imperious." [3] Space, as a calamitously false object of love and desire, is deftly associated with other such falsities; and its beckoning smile (like the mother's in "Van Winkle") vanishes to leave man blind and wretched:

> Space, instantaneous,
> Flickers a moment, consumes us in its smile:
> A flash over the horizon—shifting gears—
> And we have laughter, or more sudden tears.

(That last line, as moving and well-balanced as any Crane ever wrote, ranges beyond context to formulate a characteristic play of emotion in the world, as Crane, like the rest of us, experienced it: "And we have laughter, or more sudden tears.") There follows Crane's extremely penetrating and beautifully shaped and worded analysis of human motivation in the scientific era:

> Dream cancels dream in this new world of fact
> From which we wake into the dream of act;
> Seeing himself an atom in a shroud—
> Man hears himself an engine in a cloud!

In a culture worshipful primarily of scientific fact, the old dreams of human dignity and noble accomplishment are

---

[3] Though some good guesses have been made—by Denbo and others—about the references to Adam and Hesperus in this stanza, I confess myself still baffled by them, and feel obscurely guilty to be so.

repudiated, and man sees himself as a figure of absolute insignificance, destined only for the grave; by recompense, as a revenge against reality, man has recourse to sheer blind action and imagines himself as a pure machine hurtling through space.

If the couplets just quoted sound a little like Alexander Pope in a mild frenzy, the next stanza shifts—in the pattern of alternation—toward the easier rhythms of Walt Whitman, who is now invoked as the exemplary poetic seer and as an abiding guarantee of the visionary possibility. Crane begins by quoting the title, which is also the first line, of Whitman's "Recorders Ages Hence," he himself being the most devoted of those recorders. But he goes on to cite or hint at Whitman's "Starting from Paumanok" and "Out of the Cradle Endlessly Rocking":

Walt, tell me, Walt Whitman, if infinity
Be still the same as when you walked the beach
Near Paumanok—your lone patrol—and heard the wraith
Through surf, its bird note there a long time falling. . . .

In the course of "Cape Hatteras," and in addition to the poems mentioned and "Passage to India," Crane makes effective use of many other Whitman poems, among them: "Song of Myself," "Crossing Brooklyn Ferry," "Years of the Modern," "Song of the Open Road," "Vigil Strange I Kept on the Field One Night," and, in the last lines, "Whoever You Are Holding Me Now in Hand." If Crane felt "directly connected with Whitman" in 1923, when he was first contemplating *The Bridge,* he had very nearly identified himself with Whitman in 1929, when he was finishing the poem. Rarely has a modern poem been so nourished and permeated by the actual writings of another poet: to an end and a degree altogether different from Eliot's expert cultural pilferings. Crane is not only paying tribute to Whitman and making use of him. He is embracing Whitman in much the same way the "Younger [Brother]," the human soul, melted in fondness into the arms of the Elder Brother, God, in "Passage to India." For Whitman is at once the historical author of *Leaves of Grass,* and the paradigm poet, *the* poet as such whose other avatars in the second half of *The Bridge* have the names of Melville, Emily Dickinson, Blake, and Poe. He is, to make the point again, "the true son of God" of "Passage to India," the being who, after all seas are crossed and the engineers have done their work, "shall come singing his songs."

The God of traditional theology, as I said in an earlier chapter, is succeeded in the latter part of *The Bridge* by the visionary poet, and his name gives way to the names of poets. In "Indiana," it was God's "gleaming name" that could be seen in "golden syllables loosed from the clay"; but now it is the eyes of Whitman the poet which

> Gleam from the great stones of each prison crypt
> Of canyoned traffic . . . Confronting the Exchange,
> Surviving in a world of stocks.[4]

In consort with Whitman's "syllables of faith," the modern poet can at least strive to free the spirit from that urban congestion, to redeem in poetic vision the stock-market culture Crane had explored and transcended in "Faustus and Helen I." In the "empire wilderness of freight and rails," as Crane had defined contemporary actuality in "The River," within the "labyrinth" where time has driven us, Whitman is at once the true son of God and a second and greater Columbus, leading man toward the true empire which is of the spirit:

Not this our empire yet, but labyrinth
Wherein your eyes, like the Great Navigator's without ship,
Gleam from the great stones. . . .

---

[4] "Cape Hatteras" is occasionally prophetic in more limited ways than the vast overall vision it pursues. Who has not experienced, raging, the "prison crypt / Of canyoned traffic," in metropolitan jam-ups worse than anything Crane could have imagined?

The poet, the twentieth-century Columbus of the imagination, must emulate that transfiguring, myth-affirming gaze of Whitman, must possess himself of those "Sea eyes and tidal, undenying, bright with myth!"—and become again the liberating god.

Beginning with the line "The nasal whine of power whips a new universe," the poem turns again to contemplate the ferocious obstacle which poetry must try to cope with. Man's ear is deafened (Crane's regular alternative way of saying that man's eye is blinded) by the tremendous noise of the machine—by the modern dynamo which has replaced the virgin Pocahontas as the object of reverence; and the world, elsewhere imaged as a huge stock market, is now depicted as a "gigantic power house." The lines articulating all this are unmatched in their kind and deserve to be quoted (and bravely chanted) in full:

The nasal whine of power whips a new universe. . . .
Where spouting pillars spoor the evening sky,
Under the looming stacks of the gigantic power house
Stars prick the eyes with sharp ammoniac proverbs,
New verities, new inklings in the velvet hummed
Of dynamos, where hearing's leash is strummed . . .
Power's script,—wound, bobbin-bound, refined—
Is stropped to the slap of belts on booming spools, spurred
Into the bulging bouillon, harnessed jelly of the stars.
Towards what? The forked crash of split thunder parts
Our hearing momentwise; but fast in whirling armatures

and so on, to the dizzying climax.

In the usual indictment of "Cape Hatteras" as some sort of poetic disaster, it has been said that the style is an exhausted and unconscious parody of Crane's best style (in the way a tired or aging writer often does unwittingly parody his own characteristic idiom and rhythm); and this passage is pointed to as the most conspicuous example thereof. But the passage

is, of course *a very deliberate and conscious self-parody,* and
as such it is brilliantly successful. It is a general parody of
Crane's persistent thrust toward "added consciousness and
increased perceptions," as he put it in the letter to Harriet
Monroe. The poetic version of that thrust—for example, the
phrases "new thresholds, new anatomies!. . . . new purities. . . . new dominoes of love and bile" in "The Wine
Menagerie"—is parodied here in the ironic ebullience of
"new verities, new inklings," and later "new reaches. . . .
new latitudes" which are arrived at in the "new realm of
fact," the "new universe" of mechanical power. But it is also
a particular and careful parody of earlier moments in *The
Bridge*—of the intoxicated *Te Deum* of Columbus, and the
turbulent vision of "The Dance." Amid the deafening roar
of the gigantic powerhouse, the eyes are stung to blindness,
and the spirit is overwhelmed by power: not power-in-repose, Crane's poetic and cultural ideal, but power unrestrained; and the unrestraint is manifested in the din of
language, the reeling alliterations, the preposterous imagery.
The new verities are catastrophic falsehoods, the new inklings are hunches about hell. "The long moan of a dance is
in the sky" once more, but it is a scream rather than a moan;
and it is not Indian braves nor circling planets, but things
mechanical—pistons and ball bearings—which, amid a very
different thunder and lightning, perform the grotesque
parody of the ritual dance:

> axle-bound, confined
> In coiled precision, bunched in mutual glee
> The bearings glint,—O murmurless and shined
> In oilrinsed circles of blind ecstasy!

Almost every word in those astonishing lines is bent to
Crane's parodic purpose, to a systematic reversal of the
salient feature of the ideal: freedom with control, song and
joyfulness, endless circling, ecstatic vision. If the essential
imagery in "The Dance" is apocalyptic in Northrop Frye's

constricted use of the word (the imagery of the new heaven and earth), then the imagery here is what Frye calls demonic; and like all demonic imagery, including that in the Book of Revelations, it is by nature a reversal and parody of the apocalyptic. Indeed, as the poem proceeds, it answers its question, "Towards what?"—*where* is this explosive power heading—by saying: straight into hell. The opposite possibility is punningly remembered in the next stanza, where the Wright brothers are seen making their first flight "from Kill Devils Hill at Kitty Hawk"; a truly heroic enterprise, and at the same time, for these "windwrestlers," a great creative act:

> Stars scribble on our eyes the frosty sagas,
> The gleaming cantos of unvanquished space. . . .
> What ciphers risen from prophetic script.

But the opportunity to reach "new [spiritual] latitudes," to decipher the meaning of the universe and to record its poetry,

> soon give[s] place
> To what fierce schedules, rife of doom apace!

The fierce schedules are the strategies of war—the planned annihilation and doom toward which the machine of the heroic brothers was all too quickly diverted. So it was that the Homeric dream gave way to the experience of hell:

> While Iliads glimmer through eyes raised in pride
> Hell's belt springs wider into heaven's plumed side.

The dogs of war are loosed ("War's fiery kennel"); and the aerial combat now described is composed of warfare across the ages, an expression of man's never-ending destructive impulse.[5] Medieval tournaments and Indian scalping parties intermingle with the colliding aircraft, in lines that carry forward the devastating parody of "The Dance":

---

[5] "War in General" was Crane's title for this part of "Cape Hatteras" in the worksheets.

332

This tournament of space, the threshed and chiselled height,
Is baited by marauding circles, bludgeon flail
Of rancorous grenades whose screaming petals carve us
Wounds that we wrap with theorems sharp as hail!

Worse, almost, than the hatred and the killing is the hypocrisy—presumably on the part of governments—which de-
fends it all as a noble necessity: "War's fiery kennel" is
"masked in downy offings"; the slaughter is provided with
sharp theoretical justification. (The almost uncanny, far-
ranging, and continuous prophetic quality of "Cape
Hatteras" need hardly be stressed.)

A couple of stanzas later, Crane reminds Man-the-aviator
once more' that his soaring instrument could have been used
for the best of purposes:

> Remember, Falcon-Ace,
> Thou hast there in thy wrist a Sanskrit charge
> To conjugate infinity's dim marge—
> Anew . . . !

This, as L. S. Denbo first made clear, is the key summary
statement. Man could have attempted to *con*jugate infinity:
to read the "prophetic script" earlier referred to; he could,
by further exploration of the skies, have sought like Columbus to perceive the divine shape in the physical universe, to
read the ideal in the actual. He can still attempt this; but
what he has done so far is to try to *sub*jugate infinity, by an
arrogant and wholly physical invasion of space. Instead of
achieving a vision of truth, he has become blinded by sheer
speed of motion ("Thine eyes bicarbonated white by speed,
O Skygak"); he is, so to speak, blind drunk with the space-
conquering power of the machine: "thy stilly eyes partake / What alcohol of space." The result is catastrophe: the
twisting, spiraling plunge of the "lead-perforated fuselage,"
the plane shot down and crashing on the Cape, in an extensive verbal and typographical stunting that for once (with
Crane) works effectively:

333

Giddily spiralled

                 gauntlets, upturned, unlooping
In guerilla sleights, trapped in combustion gyr-
Ing, dance the curdled depth

                     down whizzing
Zodiacs, dashed

           (now nearing fast the Cape!)

                 down gravitation's

                    vortex into crashed
. . . dispersion . . . into mashed and shapeless debris. . . .
By Hatteras bunched the beached heap of high bravery!

This new and hideous dance of death will leave the corpses
of humanity piled as high as the "bivouacs of thine angered
slain" foreseen by Maquokeeta.

   Three asterisks now indicate a pause, and a much-needed
one if the reader is to catch his breath before the long final
turn of "Cape Hatteras." Then Whitman re-enters the poem
for the third time, and with him comes a vision beyond
hatred and beyond death (both personal and national,
physical and spiritual), a vision of life and love renewed.
The structure of "Cape Hatteras," at this stage, somewhat
resembles that of "Faustus and Helen III," where the recalled
experience of world war and of aircraft "spouting malice"
gives way to the distinctive praise of "the years"; and Whitman has something of the symbolic role of Helen in the
earlier work. It is in part the Whitman of the Civil War
poetry, Whitman the wound-dresser, that is appropriately
invoked: Whitman whose verses bestir in the poet the
memory of the Civil War and of all wars in which America
has been tragically engaged:

   memories of vigils, bloody, by that Cape,—
Ghoul-mound of man's perversity at balk
And fraternal massacre! Thou, pallid there as chalk,
Hast kept of wounds, O Mourner, all that sum
That then from Appomattox stretched to Somme!

(One winces, admittedly, at that last rhyme, indeed at both rhymes in the passage.) But it is also Whitman entire, the poet whose salute to the grass contained the visionary message of spiritual rebirth and fraternal love—who

> dost wield the rebound seed!
> The competent loam, the probable grass. . . .
>
> O, upward from the dead
> Thou bringest tally, and a pact, new bound
> Of living brotherhood!

Crane has specifically in mind here "Song of Myself," and, among others, the lines in section 38:

Corpses rise, gashes heal, fastenings roll from me.

I troop forth replenish'd with supreme power,
> one of an average
> unending procession.

This is the Whitman, the poet goes on to say, who "has beat a song" beyond the historical fact, beyond (and the adverb has the same force it had at the close of "Ave Maria") the furthest sallies of aircraft or the flights of birds: "beyond. . . . the flight of ravens. . . . past condor zones. . . . past where the albatross has offered up / His last wing-pulse. . . . there and beyond!" It is a song that makes visible the heights the imagination is capable of; and so, the poet can say, "Ascensions of *thee* hover in me now" (italics added).

With Whitman, the spring season also returns to the poem, as it periodically must and does: this time in a very accurate personal reminiscence which is also another transfiguration of the natural scene—

> Cowslip and shad-blow, flaked like tethered foam
> Around bared teeth of stallions, bloomed that spring
> When first I read thy lines.

335

Inspired by Whitman, the poet goes back in memory to—and recreates in imagination—the landscape of "The Dance," the domain not only of mythic beauty but of significant utterance. "White banks of moonlight" whisper to him; "oak-vizored palisades" are "speechful"; and the thunder—which emanated from the powerhouse and destroyed his hearing—has regained an Indian eloquence which "Set[s] trumpets breathing in each clump and grass tuft." Whitman, who has thus made possible this renewed consciousness of physical nature as imbued with religious meaning, is, in lines following, capable as well of transforming our consciousness of the other, the hostile forces confronted in "Cape Hatteras." The poet addresses him as "Our Meistersinger," who did exactly what the poet is determined to do—"set breath in steel"; and he blends Whitman with Elohim and his "sounding heel" in "Ave Maria" as the true source and exemplar of mythic union:

> And it was thou who on the boldest heel
> Stood up and flung the span on even wing
> Of that great Bridge, our Myth, whereof I sing!

(The oddly limp and passive quality of those would-be climactic lines is due, I think, to the uncharacteristic number of neutral words and phrases, of mere verbal fillers.)

The span flung by Whitman is above all the communicated love that binds men to each other and humanity to God:

> *Panis angelicus!* Eyes tranquil with the blaze
> Of love's own diametric gaze. . . .

This fine image of visionary love encircling and hence drawing all men together derives from Whitman's assurance in "Song of Myself" that "the kelson of the creation is love," and from the vision at the close of that poem:

Do you not see O my brothers and sisters?
It is not chaos or death—it is form, union, plan—it is
eternal life—it is Happiness.

Such is the persuasive disclosure attributed to Whitman in "Cape Hatteras":

> O, something green,
> Beyond all sesames of science was thy choice
> Wherewith to bind us throbbing with one voice,
> New integers of Roman, Viking, Celt—
> Thou, Vedic Caesar, to the greensward knelt!

There is man's true empire: the empire of universal harmony which displaces the "empire wilderness," the limited thresholds onto which the doors of science had opened ("sesames of science" is a phrase of delightfully broad and repeated applicability); and it is the creation in poetry of a Sanskrit conqueror who triumphed exactly by conjugating the infinite, and who brought into being—or at least who showed how to bring into being—an empire greater than the Roman achievement of the historical Caesar.

The spiritual bridge built by Whitman, the poet continues, with exclamations mounting, was a "span of consciousness"; and within it, the crashed airplanes are seen as miraculously restored; and the machine is anointed with grace—it is, as Emerson had predicted, "raised to holiness":

> Toward endless terminals, Easters of speeding light—
> Vast engines outward veering with seraphic grace. . . .
>   thy vision is reclaimed!
> What heritage thou'st signalled to our hands!

As part of that heritage, the rainbow—that "still fervid covenant" of "Voyages," that promise of life redeemed—is observed above the "ghoul-mound" of the Cape. And holding Whitman's hand in his own, the poet is "Afoot again, and onward without halt," moving with inextinguishable hope to the nourishing memory of still further lines from "Song of Myself":

> Myself moving forward then and now and forever. . . .
> I skirt sierras, my palms cover continents,
> I am afoot with my vision.

·III·

If "Three Songs" were removed from *The Bridge,* the reader would observe a smooth and logical development from the end of "Cape Hatteras" to the beginning of "Quaker Hill." The reclaimed vision of Whitman in the former would serve to heighten one's awareness of the bovine blindness described in the latter—the complacent ignorance of those who are immune to the slightest significance in the seasonal change; who, in the symbolism of *The Bridge,* have no inkling whatever of Pocahontas. But *The Bridge* does not progress like that—it does not have that particular *kind* of momentum. And in any case, before arriving at his harsh appraisal of the "Promised Land" in "Quaker Hill," Crane wanted to explore another aspect of the Pocahontas theme, an aspect that had come into prominence in the later phases of "Cape Hatteras": the theme of love. In "Three Songs," it is not so much Whitman's "sea eyes . . . bright with myth" that the poet focuses, but his

> eyes tranquil with the blaze
> Of love's own diametric gaze.

In three images, arranged in artful sequence, the generalized love motif gradually narrows to the relation between man and woman, to heterosexual love in the contemporary world —or rather to the crudeness and failure of heterosexual love, as those qualities are articulated in a series of images which are, mostly, debasements and parodies of the imagery associated with the Indian earth goddess.

This is an appropriate moment to reflect a little on the course of the love motif in *The Bridge,* and upon Crane's habit—and his primary structural principle—of synecdoche. We have heard Emerson, speaking of man's need to satisfy "all the demands of the spirit," remark in *Nature* that "love is as much its demand as perception." *The Bridge* bears witness to an identical belief. But while the theme of perception is omnipresent and consistent, the theme of love seems to slide quickly in and out of the poem, and to be manifested in widely differing ways. There are the human lovers whose cry is heard in "Proem," and there is the love of God, of the Virgin Mary, and of visionary knowledge in "Ave Maria." There is the maternal love that fails in "Van Winkle," and the maternal love that remains constant in "Indiana" (and that will recur in the figure of the "Wop washerwoman" in "The Tunnel"). There is the relation between man and man that vaguely dissolves in "Cutty Sark," and the pledge of "Living brotherhood" in "Cape Hatteras." [6] There is the love of Prince for Princess in "The Dance," and of the poet for a stockbroker's secretary in "Virginia." There are betrayals of love and fulfillments of love, just as there are true and false objects of love and desire.

But the principle at work amid this seeming random is a simple one, though of such importance that one is tempted to place it in italics. It is the principle of synecdoche: that is, for Crane any mode of love is an instance of every mode of love; betrayal in any mode of love is a betrayal of every mode of love; and all the varieties of love foregather in man's love of reality itself. "In the uttermost meaning of the words," Emerson said in the passage quoted from above, "thought is devout, and devotion is thought." This exceedingly profound and traditional insight was shared

[6] Male homosexual love is no doubt included somewhere in the pattern, but I do not believe it should be insisted upon. Abstracting a human impulse from various of Crane's poems, one can easily enough explain the impulse, as in a case history, by reference to homosexuality; but this would rarely deepen one's understanding of the poem itself. Such a method, as I said earlier (in Chapter Seven) would yield particularly obvious results with "The Wine Menagerie" —a real-life sense of woman as lethal, as wanting in fact to cut one's head off, is patently homosexual in origin. But this is not what the *poem* is about. There, as here in "Three Songs," the attitude to women is related primarily to anxieties about the poetic calling, and the poet's visionary resources.

by Crane. He could, accordingly, interchange at will, as the object of what Emerson called man's "holiest affections," a mother, a goddess, a mistress, a bride—or a friend or all of humanity or Walt Whitman or the natural landscape or the modern world.

"Three Songs" expresses the poet's intensifying effort to find in some actual human female form the representative of his divine beloved. The spirit's demand for love here takes a certain precedence over the demand for perception, though the latter is not neglected, nor can these virtually twin needs of the spirit be separated. But it is the true object of holiest *affections,* rather than of vision, which in "Three Songs" follows the familiar cyclical pattern of *The Bridge:* which eludes and then foresakes the poet's grasp, and then seems, perhaps, to be on the verge of returning. A first impression of "Three Songs" may well be that it consists of three initially unrelated poems, written at sundry times and places and brought together only for this occasion. But it should be remembered that they were all written during the great month and, apparently, in the order of their published appearance. They were clearly intended to be exactly what they are: an emotional version of the large design of the entire epic. And though the poet is confronted only by degradations of his "cosmic" love, "Three Songs" is nonetheless the statement of a person who, for all the ugliness and the lovelessness experienced, can still love the world (in the phrase from "Chaplinesque"), and, so loving it, can attempt to transform it by his devotion.

The epigraph, from Marlowe's unfinished "Hero and Leander," draws attention to the legendary youth who, in order to unite himself with the maid Hero, swam the Hellespont nightly from Sestos to Abydos—until, one stormy night, on his way back to Sestos, he drowned. Leander's last trip, as the poet had said jauntily in "Cutty Sark," was a tragedy. Stretching things a little, one can see a certain relevance of the Leander story to at least the first of the

"Three Songs." Here, returning—presumably from the land of myth and the domain of his loved one—across some unidentified body of water, the poet and all of male humanity are metaphorically "drowned," in the last line of "Southern Cross." There is also no doubt a kind of Eliotic irony in juxtaposing the figure of Hero with the human females dimly encountered in the sequence.

What the poet seeks, in any event, is indicated in the first stanza of "Southern Cross," which is, so to speak, the prologue or "Proem" to "Three Songs." He wants to be related to some as yet nameless woman, not as ghost to ghost but as man to woman; and at the same time, he wants to be related to her as the constellation Southern Cross, high in the heavens, is related to the night:

> I wanted you, nameless Woman of the South,
> Not wraith, but utterly—as still more alone
> The Southern Cross takes night
> And lifts her girdles from her, one by one. . . .

He wants to be rejoined with that presence which vanished with the harbor dawn, but to be joined with her within the temporal world: in a manner at once wholly human and physical, but also comparable to what might be called celestial love-making; in an eroticism that transcends the fires of lust:

> High, cool,
>   wide from the slowly smoldering fire
> Of lower heavens,—
>   vaporous scars!

To shift the reference, he seeks Pocahontas in a human female who will *be* human and yet will simultaneously be to him as Pocahontas, the goddess immanent in the land, has been to him: who will be incarnate and yet unfallen. This ambition, be it added, is much simpler and more familiar than critical paraphrase of it can suggest.

In "Three Songs," the ambition is, moreover, familiarly

frustrated. The original or divine name of the nameless woman is Pocahontas; her human names—in what Northrop Frye might call her displaced human forms—are potentially several, but actually none. No one of the names invoked, questioningly, answers to the poet's needs. The first of the three false avatars, Eve, is indeed the very type of fallen female humanity:

> O simian Venus, homeless Eve,
> Unwedded, stumbling gardenless to grieve.

"Simian"—upon which the word "simmering" later puns —suggests the animal nature of this debasement of the love goddess; more important, Eve, in contrast to the bride Pocahontas, is "unwedded"—and evidently unweddable. The contrast thickens in the penultimate stanza, where the "warm sibilance" and "keen crescent" of the hair of Pocahontas, as the poet remembers them from "The Dance," are replaced by the Medusa-like "stinging coil" of Eve's "rehearsed hair," which the sea-water has "combed . . . with black / Insolence" through the night. As against the pure Pocahontas, the inhabitant of nature, Eve is artificial ("rehearsed"), lust-driven ("simmering"), and promiscuous (she is "docile, alas, from many arms").

It is the fading memory of the Indian Princess that wounds and torments the poet. "I wanted you," he says again; and continues—

> It is blood to remember; it is fire
> To stammer back . . . It is
> God—your namelessness.

This telegraphic passage might be translated thus: it is wounding to remember *you,* Pocahontas, and to discover only *you,* Eve; for you, Pocahontas are the divinity that I now seek to recover in human guise, but your absence is indicated by my inability to assign your name to any actual woman. In the wake of the ship on which, for purposes of this poem, the poet is journeying, he discerns not the divine or apocalyptic image but only the demonic; and instead of seeing the goddess's smile, he hears the laughter of devils:

> And this long wake of phosphor,
> iridescent
> Furrow of all our travel—trailed derision!
> Eyes crumble at its kiss. Its long-drawn spell
> Incites a yell. Slid on that backward vision
> The mind is churned to spittle, whispering hell.

Vision collapses (and so perhaps, for the moment, does poetic control, which should have suppressed that yell of horror), as love is betrayed. Similarly, at dawn, the constellation disintegrates and "Light drown[s] the lithic trillions of your spawn." This enigmatic line implies, I suppose, the general effect of woman upon man, which is not unlike the effect described in "The Wine Menagerie." Male humanity (all the countless sons or "spawn" of Eve) is spiritually paralyzed, turned to stone by woman's Medusa-like nature, and it characteristically drowns in the light of the actual day. Eliot's "Prufrock" is again being remembered: "Till human voices"—and they are the voices of women— "wake us and we drown."

With the strip-tease dancer of "National Winter Garden," we arrive at the second false avatar, and at the furthest debasement of the feminine ideal. This experience in a burlesque theater is, in fact, almost literally a word-by-word burlesque of the poetic experience of Pocahontas. The poem is all compact of verbal play—beginning with the title which, in addition to being the name of a famous New York strip-tease theatre, tells us that we and the entire national scene and culture are again envisaged as buried in the depths of winter; while the Garden of Eden from which Eve was ejected ("stumbling gardenless to grieve")—the American dream and promise, so to say—has become a scene of cheapest vulgarity. The parodic element permeates "National Winter Garden" more completely than any other of these later sections of *The Bridge,* so much so that a detailed gloss would only emphasize the obvious. In the first stanza alone the dancer's "outspoken buttocks" (a posterior candidly inviting assault) are a parody of the "singing arms," the singing tree, heard and seen in the body of Pocahontas; the "distant cloud" of "The Dance" is reflected sardonically in the messy confusion of a "cloudy clinch" and a "flagrant, sweating cinch" (literally a saddle-belt; here presumably a g-string). The Princess's eyes which once "hid tawny pride" have yielded to the grabby glances of the audience's "bandy eyes" (eyes set unattractively far apart); and while "there was a veil upon you, Pocahontas, bride," this contemporary and actual dancer is stripping naked—there are "no extra mufflings here."

Thereafter, the drums, the music, the thunder and lightning of the Indian dance are replaced by "fireworks," "a tom-tom scrimmage," and "a somewhere violin"; a meaningless uproar which is the "cheapest echo of them all." The white purity of Pocahontas, with her "speechless dream of snow," is abandoned by Magdalene in favor of ruby and emerald sprays upon her body; she neither smiles nor grieves; and, seeking something like the beautiful hair of Pocahontas, the poet merely glimpses the sandstone grey of the dancer's pubis ("A caught slide shows her sandstone grey between"—i.e., her legs). And so it goes: a dance of bouncing teats and grinding hips at the uttermost extreme from the exalted ceremonial circling of the Indian dance (not to mention the planetary dance of "Ave Maria"); and "silly snake rings"—"turquoise fakes"—are all that remain of the image of time as a serpent or of the serpentine river that led to the world of myth.

While the poet waits for the nameless woman to come to him ("Always you wait for someone else though, always"), what confronts his eyes in the actuality is only a blonde, dancing obscenely in a smoke-filled theater. As *this* dance reaches its orgasmic climax, his strongest temptation is to flee the entire realm of the flesh:

We wait that writhing pool, her pearls collapsed,
—All but her belly buried in the floor;
And the lewd trounce of a final muted beat!
We flee her spasm through a fleshless door.

Though the visual image there is accurate indeed (as anyone knows, who has seen the particular kind of sex-dance
Crane evidently has in mind), the language is also effecting
a passionate reduction of all heterosexual love-making to
something overwhelmingly repellent—from which the poet
wants to flee across the threshold of spirit. "Yet," the final
stanza begins: nevertheless, and despite the disgust and even
the terror—

> to the empty trapeze of your flesh,
> O Magdalene, each comes back to die alone.
> Then you, the burlesque of our lust—and faith,
> Lug us back lifeward—bone by infant bone.

The essential sense of that otherwise cryptic stanza is conveyed in the progression from "die" to "lifeward," and it involves, I assume, a typical Cranian paradox. It is exactly the
spirit's demand for love that requires every man to return
to the flesh—though he can only die alone there: in the
Elizabethan sense of the orgasm as the "little death," in the
Romantic sense of the death of consciousness, and in the
more hopeful sense of the "death" that was "shed" in "Voyages III." Woman as a purely sexual creature may be no
more than a burlesque of the ideal woman, as lust is a burlesque of faith; still, the sexual life must be entered into if the
lost beloved is to be found again. The lover must return to
the flesh just as the poet must return to the urban and the
actual; for the death submitted to—and this principle, too,
works analogously throughout *The Bridge*—is the only path
to the life desired. So it *is,* after all, Magdalene who brings
us back to life: who gives us life, almost as though we were
her children ("infant"). Reaching through fleshly love, the
poet has intimations of maternal love; for every form is the
promise of every other.

The final two lines of "National Winter Garden" are the familiar turn in the characteristic cycle "Three Songs" passes through. It is the moment when the descending movement—toward blindness, lust, chaos—changes into a movement of ascent; and in "Virginia," eyes are appropriately turned upwards, while through the mood of playfulness and light irony, one hears the sound of a slender hope. Mary, the young stenographer of "Virginia," who works in a brokerage office in the Woolworth building ("high wheat tower . . . nickle-dime tower"), is certainly a far cry from that human Pocahontas the poet wants and waits for; but she is, as it were, a tease of a quite different kind of Magdalene. She is virgin not by nature but for prudent financial reasons:

> O rain at seven,
> Pay-check at eleven—
> Keep smiling the boss away.

She fends off her predatory boss with smiles, keeps her job, collects her pay, and waits, one imagines, for a better offer. But the verbal associations with Pocahontas are not, in this case, undiluted parody.

The pun on chastity in the poem's title and the implicit reference there to the Indian Princess (Virginia was, of course, the home of the historical Pocahontas), a glimpse of blue eyes, a scarlet scarf (which is a veil of sorts), golden hair: these do not, in context, suggest another unequivocal debasement of the ideal figure. Mary provokes the poet's wry smile, for one thing, because she is the exasperating obverse of both the Eve and Magdalene types—*she* is what the actual world has to offer the man who seeks not so much physiological but spiritual virginity. In her high tower and in her refusal "to let her hair down," in the slang phrase, she represents a mock version of the qualities observed and sought after in the introductory stanza of "Three Songs":

> High, cool,
>   wide from the slowly smoldering fire
> Of lower heavens. . . .

346

But high up, far away and cool-natured though she be, Mary may yet—so the poem's tonality, its *playful* play, permits us to think—let down her golden hair to her lover, like that other princess in the fairy tale, and smile upon him.

We have moved, too, from the autumnal atmosphere of "Southern Cross" and the winter season implicit in the second song to the spring season—the season of Pocahontas. At this moment of what might be called the poem's seasonal synecdoche, there is even a hint of some future reunion with the princely bridegroom:

> And Spring in Prince Street
> Where green figs gleam
> By oyster shells!

It is noon on a day in May, a time of daffodils, violets, and "Peonies with pony manes"; and if it is by no means the richly burgeoning season of "The Dance" and "Cape Hatteras," it seems to be at least a faint re-claimable promise thereof. The poet knows that, in a culture where the stock market has replaced the church, he should most properly address the strategically inaccessible object of his desire as "Cathedral Mary." But his song—in its combination of nursery rhyme and Tin Pan Alley—[7] does not entirely conceal a stir of hope: hope that the nameless woman, perhaps virginal like Mary and sexual like Magdalene, may sometime be found again.

· I V ·

We must not expect, however, that Crane will move on immediately from that meager spring and minimal optimism to a vision of the full satisfaction of spiritual needs. His structural method, as well as his emotional and imaginative honesty, forbade so easy a development. There are other

---

[7] I believe there was a popular tune in the twenties, which Crane is said to have liked, with a title or first line that went: "What are you doing on Saturday, Mary?"

cycles to pass through, other areas to explore and facts to face, before the poet is ready to sing his hymn to the bridge in "Atlantis." In "Quaker Hill," the scene shifts from New York to an upstate summer resort (just outside Pawling, in actual fact, and not far from Patterson); and epic attention shifts from intimations of spring in "Virginia" to the moneyed class of Americans who can scarcely tell one season from another:

> They keep that docile edict of the Spring
> That blends March with August Antarctic skies.

These persons—"the Czars of golf," Crane calls them in a phrase which anticipates F. D. Roosevelt's "economic royalists"—are fatally bereft of the visionary capacity which perceives the life span of divinity in the round of the seasons:

> the rich halo that they do not trouble
> Even to cast upon the seasons fleeting
> Though they should thin and die on last year's stubble.

In spring grass and winter snow, they see nothing *but* grass and snow; and after taking account of them, the poet himself, by the poem's end, experiences a descent of the spirit in the descent of autumn leaves.

The love motif, which here blends nicely with the theme of vision, has similarly shifted—from the longing for heterosexual union to reflections on the problem of friendship:

> We, who with pledges taste the bright annoy
> Of friendship's acid wine. . . .

Crane, as usual, exploits the actuality. Quaker Hill had, from the late eighteenth century onward, been the site of a Quaker Meeting House, where the "Friends" regularly foregathered; it was, indeed, a distinct and homogeneous colony, a recognizable community, and for a while it even had its own post office. From all this, Crane derives words, phrases, and motifs which supply much of the substance of the poem. The Quaker doctrine of brotherly love provides the occasion for meditating questions about the amount of trust one can really place in mankind ("our store of faith in other men"), about the possibility of a true "meeting" between humans, about people becoming "friends," and even about a postman; and these lead to the overriding question about the human community in which the poet so ardently longs to participate: "Where are my kinsmen and the patriarch race?" They are not to be found, at any rate, on Quaker Hill, which is now simply the scene of fat complacency. To assert his potential for love—love of man, love of reality—the poet must again come down to the lowliest aspects of life, and he must exercise his most primary perceptions:

> So, must we from the hawk's far stemming view,
> Must we descend as worm's eye to construe
> Our love of all we touch.

"Quaker Hill" was the last section of *The Bridge* to be conceived by Crane (it was the only section not even mentioned in his letter of September 1927, to Otto Kahn); and it was the last completed. On the day after Christmas 1929, Crane wrote Caresse Crosby: "I am hastily enclosing the final version of 'Quaker Hill,' which ends my writing on *The Bridge*. You can now go ahead and finish it all." He told Caresse Crosby that it was not as long a poem as expected; he had several more verses "roughly, in notes," [8] but

---

[8] To judge from the worksheets, Crane at one time planned to temper his indictment of America in "Quaker Hill" with a defense of the country against a cynical contempt attributed to Europe:

> This gift of credulous reception, American
> Invitation to abusive retrogression—say—
> When Yankees die there's just as good a sunset,
> Though Yankees say it, as on Mandalay.
> I've seen that playful, generous heart gone filched
> While all of Europe laughed and spied
> In the old way, and kept the cynical straight path. . . .

Strictly in keeping with his Romantic American ancestry, Crane had a deep-rooted suspicion of Europe and resented its attitude toward America—feelings which his recent experience in England and France had done little to lessen.

he felt that "the present condensation is preferable. 'Quaker Hill' is not, after all, one of the major sections of the poem: It is rather by way of an 'accent mark' that it is valuable at all." "Quaker Hill" is rather long drawn out and slow moving for an "accent mark." But it is a sufficiently meaningful and poetically useful survey of one phase of American society and of the poet's—Crane's or any poet's—relation to it; of the blind loveless vulgarity which, in the 1920's seemed to Crane to be the dreary outcome of the American dream of a Promised Land; and it is a touching statement, too, of the poet's determined effort to exert upon this condition the redemptive forces of love and vision. It is a somewhat depressing piece of writing, however, and one suffers empathically with the temporarily tiring poet. Apart from the lively malice of the first stanza and the forlorn sweetness of the last two stanzas, plus an occasional stately line, it tends to drag. The punning is excessive and heavy; the rhymes are arbitrary (one hardly knows whether Crane used "uncoy" because he needed a rhyme with the no less awkwardly coined noun "annoy," or vice versa); and we have the impression that at times Crane is simply pushing words around on the page. The critical mind is not spurred to devise meanings for all these fumbling phrases.

Nonetheless, what is clear and effective in "Quaker Hill" is the sense of death. The theme is introduced in the second of the poem's two epigraphs, which is from one of Emily Dickinson's earliest poems about death—as felt encroaching, here, with the departure of summer:

> The gentian weaves her fringes,
> The maple's loom is red.

("My departing blossom / Obviate parade," the poem continues; later: "Summer, sister, seraph, / Let us go with thee!") It is the death sense that gives "Quaker Hill" its contributory meaning and, by a familiar paradox, its poetic vitality. The death apprehended is that of a former dream: in this case, the dream of America as an ideal community founded on mutual love and on a shared vision of spiritual possibility. To the poet, the windows of a palatial hotel called Mizzentop—which had been abandoned in the late 1920's and so was itself metaphorically dead—seem to gaze backward toward that dream:

> Long tiers of windows staring out toward former
> Faces. . . .
>   like eyes that still uphold some dream. . . .

But, now, gazing out himself from a vantage point where one used to have a vast encompassing view of the landscape, the poet finds only death staring back at him from all points of the compass:

> High from the central cupola, they say
> One's glance could cross the borders of three states;
> But I have seen death's stare in slow survey
> From four horizons that no one relates.

Neither the physical nor the spiritual horizons are "related"— are bound together by the integrative and shared vision—any longer. The Promised Land is now promising only to real estate agents and bootleggers; and the community of love has degenerated into "Hollywood's new love-nest pageant." The noble heritage of the past ("the ancient deal") is forgotten and has become the food for the wood louse (who eats "the ancient deal / Table"). "Where are my kinsmen and the patriarch race?"

The poet's kinsmen are all dead and gone: they are the "Dead rangers" and "scalped Yankees" mentioned in the following stanza; and the vanished patriarch race is represented by "slain Iroquois," who stand for all the "angered slain," the lost dynasties of the Indian race which in turn stand for the mythic consciousness. To that race, the poet must turn—as he has once already turned—for guidance. But he must also acknowledge and accept the actual condition of things, which includes a deep cleavage between present and past: the poet has to "Shoulder the curse of sundered parentage," as a terrible truth, with a consequent personal responsibility, he cannot avoid. (Denbo is surely right in saying that, though "Crane is undobutedly thinking of his own parents" in that much-quoted line, the main reference is to a larger and more generalized sundering, of a sort acknowledged in "The River.") He must realize that the only "word" awaiting him in the contemporary world is not the white promise of life renewed or renewable, that the postman will bring him only "birthright by blackmail," an "arrant page" (page of writing, page as messenger-boy) "That unfolds a new destiny to fill." What is left for the poet is nothing more than his own creative abilities, his own transfiguring vision and love; and to achieve the latter, he must, in the lines quoted above, descend "as worm's eye to construe / Our love of all we touch."

Such a love is "construed" in a song rising out of the depths of pain, and in the words of a poet who has tasted love turning to ashes on his tongue:

> Yes, while the heart is wrung,
> Arise—yes, take this sheaf of dust upon your tongue!
> In one last angelus lift throbbing throat. . . .

The poet will accept the dusty deathiness which is part of his inherited curse. But like the mournful and lovely "triple-noted" little melody of the whippoorwill (a melody which rises sharply only to slide sadly downward), his song will express the suffering heart in so sweet a manner as to "save" us, to rescue the heart from terror and shield love from despair. This, he says, is the same "stilly note / Of pain that Emily, that Isadora knew," and that both, by implication, transmuted into an assuaging beauty of poetry and dance. Emily Dickinson, at least in the poem quoted, did so by drawing upon the resources of a highly individual religious faith. Isadora Duncan—who, in the first of the two epigraphs, declares that "no ideals have ever been fully successful on this earth"—attempted to do so, as Crane remembered, by adapting to dance patterns the poetry of Walt Whitman.[9] Crane was following both examples: invoking Whitman and the tradition he represented in composing a song of thoroughly personal religious ardor, which might preserve and perpetuate love even "when love foresees the end," even as the last leaves of autumn—

break off,

descend—

descend.

[9] On December 12, 1922, Crane wrote Gorham Munson about his "excitement at seeing Isadora Duncan dance on Sunday night" in Cleveland. The audience had responded to the "glorious" performance by "silence and some maddening cat-calls." Crane continued: "I felt like rushing to the stage, but I was stimulated almost beyond the power to walk straight. When it was all over she came to the fore-stage again in the little red dress that had so shocked Boston, as she stated, and among other things told the people to go home and take from the bookshelf the works of Walt Whitman, and turn to the section called 'Calamus.' Ninety-nine percent of them had never heard of Whitman, of course, but that was part of the beauty of her gesture."

CHAPTER TWELVE

"The Tunnel" and "Atlantis": The Rhythm of *The Bridge*

THE SUBWAY RIDE in "The Tunnel," from mid-Manhattan under the East River to the Brooklyn side of the bridge, is the most desperate of Hart Crane's journies. Departing from the final words of "Quaker Hill," it is of course a "descent"—a plunge, almost, down into the land of the dead. For the world which had been variously perceived as a huge stock market and a gigantic powerhouse appears, in this more rending inspection, as the scene of death-in-life; and the death which had hovered in "Cutty Sark" and had become violent in "Cape Hatteras" and pervasive in "Quaker Hill" now emerges as very nearly the absolute condition of the modern scene. This section may be regarded as a traditional epic phase, corresponding to the visit to the underworld in the eleventh book of *The Odyssey,* the sixth book of the *Aeneid,* and the *Inferno;* and as Denbo has pointed out, the subway is "an ideal image" for Crane's purpose, since it makes possible so close a parallel "between the literal action of the hero and the symbolic implications of a Dantean journey."

To this we should add the symbolic implications of an *inward* adventure; for the journey remains Romantic and Cranian, and it consists of a descent of consciousness leading to another self-encounter, but one opposite in nature to that of "The Dance." Indeed, the experience in general here is opposite to that of "The Dance." The death-land traversed is characterized by the total, if temporary, defeat of the instruments of vision. Eyes and ears fail utterly in this unseeing world of meaningless noise: "Blank windows gargle signals through the roar." And in a metaphor which realizes perfectly the final degradation of love, the quenching of its fires by the ineffable vulgarity of the modern spirit, love is "A burnt match skating in a urinal." Worst of all, the poet arrives at a moment of greatest doubt about his own visionary and poetic capacities, his entire creative achievement.

Although the specter of Edgar Allan Poe is encountered during the journey, and some phrases from Poe are thereby elicited, the resident poet of "The Tunnel" is William Blake. For the poem's epigraph, Crane took two lines from Blake's "Morning," the whole of which should, however, be kept in mind:

> To find the Western path,
> Right thro' the Gates of Wrath
> I urge my way;
> Sweet Mercy leads me on
> With soft repentant moan:
> I see the break of day.

> The war of swords and spears,
> Melted by dewy tears,
> Exhales on high;
> The Sun is freed from fears,
> And with soft grateful tears
> Ascends the sky.

(In Blake's symbolic geography, as a footnote in Crane's presumptive edition explains, "Pity" inhabits the Western part of the world, with "Reason," "Desire," and "Wrath" assigned respectively to the North, the South, and the East. "The Western Path" which Blake and Crane are following is thus the way of compassionate love.) Blake's most famous single phrase is invoked at the start of the subway ride: "Out of the Square, the Circle burning bright." More important, the passage on Poe draws rhetorically from the great hymn in Blake's *Milton*. The lines:

And did those feet in ancient time
    Walk upon England's mountains green. . . .
And did the Countenance Divine
    Shine forth upon our clouded hills?
And was Jerusalem builded here
    Among these dark Satanic mills?

—these find as it were their demonic counterpart in Crane's questioning lines:

    —And did their riding eyes right through your side,
    And did their eyes like unwashed platters ride?

Blake's presence is indispensable. It supplies a crucial counterforce to the ghastly image of Poe, and beyond that to all the modes of death confronted; via a different and perhaps more subtle poetic strategy, it acts the way Whitman and his poetry acted in "Cape Hatteras"—as a redemptive resource, and as a promise that the "dark Satanic mills" of the contemporary American industrialized world will give way to the New Jerusalem, or in Crane's case to the newly risen Atlantis. The epigraph, one therefore feels, is more than an apt quotation from an old master. It is an invocation of sorts, a prayer for spiritual and creative strength: the immense strength the poet knows he must have if he really is to shoulder the curse of his broken culture, to explore to the depth its deathly condition, and to transcend that condition at last by re-enacting the terrible experience in verse.

As this extraordinarily well-modulated poem gets under way, the situation is this. The autumnal season of "Quaker Hill" has given way to winter; the fact is not stressed, but it is at least a chill evening, cold enough to make the poet slap his arms against his chest in a manner resembling a creature of the snow country ("you find yourself / Preparing penguin flexions of the arms"). The spiritual atmosphere is no less wintry. There is death in the air: the death of innocence and of the hope of heaven that has typified the human drama everywhere the poet has been exploring it, in all "the thousand theatres" of city life. To descend, now, into the subway is to go down to the heart of that ubiquitous death, to experience the contemporary world fully and unevasively as a kind of frozen hell. No wonder the poet hesitates and "can't . . . quite make up [his] mind to ride."

Nor can he draw upon the traditional comfort and spiritual power of the Christian religion: or so I read the somewhat baffling lines—

> let you—also
> walking down—exclaim
> to twelve upward leaving
> a subscription praise
> for what time slays.

The lines are not so much baffling in themselves—the reference, I suppose, is to the religion represented by the twelve apostles, which the poet can praise and even subscribe to for what it once was and accomplished, but the vigor of which has been destroyed by historical change. But the passage strikes me as oddly out of place at this stage of the overall poetic enterprise. The poet, anyhow, urges himself on into the darkness, knowing that however harrowing the trip may be, the subway nonetheless "yawns the quickest promise home"; the way to a recovered vitality leads, as always, through the experience of death. He makes himself as small as possible to burrow through the mob emerging from the subway ("Be minimum, then, to swim the hiving swarms")—he shrinks, that is, into his smallest and most concentrated spiritual being to survive the ordeal. At the entrance to the subway, on the brink of the dreadful adventure, he almost turns back in panic:

> boxed alone a second, eyes take fright
> —Quite unprepared rush naked back to light.

But he braces himself, sustained perhaps by the Blake from whom he has just quoted and by the visionary company in general. He goes through the turnstile and boards the train; and he is instantly in hell.

It is a hell featured, as it has been elsewhere in literature, by endless bleak repetition, by a sterile circling of incident, expression, and sound (another demonic opposite to the great dance imagery earlier in *The Bridge*):

> In the car
> the overtone of motion
> underground, the monotone
> of motion is the sound
> of other faces, also underground.

Voices, echoing hollowly, utter random nothingness, phrases disjoined from sense:

> potatoes
> to dig in the field—travlin the town—too. . . .

Or they bespeak the contemptuous dismissal of love and of simple human generosity: the greed and coarseness of woman:

> 'fandaddle daddy don't ask for change. . . .
>   if
> you don't like my gate why did you
> swing on it, why *didja*
> swing on it—'

and the heartlessness of man:

> 'after
> the show she cried a little afterwards but. . . .'

The poem is here cutting far beneath parody (the parody, for example, in "Magdalene") toward the almost purely sombre. For these wearily circling phrases are the freezing reiterations of the very death of love: repetitions that go round and round in the poet's mind announcing that death, as he passes through the actual tunnel and the tunnel of his own consciousness:

> The phonographs of hades in the brain
> Are tunnels that re-wind themselves, and love
> A burnt match skating in a urinal.

Crane exploits a part of that beautifully and complexly rendered metaphor—namely, the tormented mind as a subway system—in the hallucinatory vision he now entertains of Edgar Allan Poe. It is Poe who is slowly identified by a severed head swinging from the strap inside the car, while his body "smokes" on the tracks, far behind:

> In back forks of the chasms of the brain,—
> Puffs from a riven stump far out behind
> In interborough fissures of the mind. . . .

Poe is greeted, first, by a series of Keatsian questions (like those addressed to the "winter king" in "The Dance"), as the poet peers through the gloom and the horror: "Whose head is swinging from the swollen strap? / Whose body smokes . . . ?" and then: "why do I often meet your visage here?" The poet does so for two closely related reasons. For one thing, Poe always comes forcibly to mind "here," that is, when the world expresses itself to the poet as an inferno, because Poe is the major American example of the Romantic poet harried and destroyed by his own loveless society. Or so he seemed to Crane, who found corroboration for this view of Poe (as he told Waldo Frank in November 1926) in William Carlos Williams' *In The American Grain*.[1]

---

[1] The book, Crane said, "is an achievement that I'd be proud of. A most important and *sincere* book. I'm very enthusiastic—I put off reading it, you know, until I felt my own way cleared beyond chance of confusions incident to reading a book so intimate to my theme. I was so interested to note that he puts Poe and his 'character' in the same position as I had *symbolized* for him in 'The Tunnel.'" Crane is referring to the last pages of Williams' essay on Poe, where, quoting the same phrase of Poe's that Crane would use, Williams wrote: "It is especially in the poetry where 'death looked gigantically down' that the horror of the formless resistance which opposed, maddened, destroyed him has forced its character into the air, the wind, the blessed galleries of paradise, above a morose, dead world, peopled by shadows and silence, and despair—It is the

Poe's visionary genius (his "eyes like agate lanterns") is contrasted with the blind, hate-filled destructiveness of his contemporaries, in the inversions of Blake I have mentioned:

> —And did their riding eyes right through your side,
> And did their eyes like unwashed platters ride?
> And Death, aloft—gigantically down
> Probing through you—toward me, O evermore!

The first of those lines distantly and appropriately relates the martyred poet to the crucified Christ with a spear in his side; it heightens the suggestion that the American world brutally destroys its only potential redeemer. Crane then brings Poe's own language to bear: not only the exclamation "evermore!", an echo of the recurring lament in "The Raven," but the entire line "And Death aloft—gigantically down. . . ." This derives from Poe's "The City in the Sea," which, as it describes the very home and kingdom of death—

> Lo! Death has reared himself a throne
> In a strange city lying alone
> Far down within the dim West—

is continuously pertinent to the experience in "The Tunnel." Poe's death-city is lit by "No rays from the holy Heaven," but only by "light from out the lurid sea," an infernal light which streams up walls and turrets—

> While from a proud tower in the town
> Death looks gigantically down.

By adopting the latter phrase, the poet in "The Tunnel" associates himself profoundly with the ruined figure of Poe (death comes "Probing through you—toward me"), to the point of recognizing in that figure a phase or a dreadful po-

---

compelling force of his isolation." Williams also spoke of Poe's imagery as arising from "the desperate situation of his mind," and stressed above all Poe's intense but unanswered need for love: "Had he lived in a world where love throve, his poems might have grown differently."

tential of his own being; in somewhat the way, perhaps, that Spencer Brydon encounters the specter of the horrifying potential of himself in Henry James's "The Jolly Corner." It is a desperate moment indeed; and there is therefore a special urgency to the question which next arises:

> And when they dragged your retching flesh,
> Your trembling hands that night through Baltimore—
> That last night on the ballot rounds, did you
> Shaking, did you deny the ticket, Poe?

The question is whether Poe—drunk, exhausted, humiliated though he was—managed to withstand the efforts of the Baltimore hoodlums who (according to historical report) tried to make Poe cast a number of illegal ballots for their "ticket" of political candidates. If so, if Poe succeeded in hanging on to some fundamental integrity, then by implication the poet, Poe's alter ego, may find the internal resources to *deny* the false destructive values the world would force upon him in his own sometimes shattered condition.

As the journey continues, the poet's fellow passengers seem more and more to be the walking dead, and their destination the grave:

> For Gravesend Manor change at Chambers Street.
> The platform hurries along to a dead stop.

> The intent escalator lifts a serenade
> Stilly
> Of shoes, umbrellas, each eye attending its shoe. . . .

That image of the procession of the dead, and particularly the final phrase, comes (forgetfully, I suspect) from *The Waste Land,* and a passage where Eliot is in turn borrowing from Dante's *Inferno:*

> A crowd flowed over London Bridge, so many,
> I had not thought death had undone so many.
> Sighs, short and infrequent, were exhaled,
> And each man fixed his eyes before his feet.

The literal train, at this stage, rounds a curve and enters the tunnel proper, for the journey under the river; and, nudged verbally by the adjective "demented," it is also metamorphosed into an escorting demon:

> Daemon, demurring and eventful yawn!
> Whose hideous laughter is a bellows mirth.

It is the same demonic laughter that Columbus had heard in the menacing waves, and the poet in the "trailed derision" of the ship's wake in "Eve."

In the two stanzas where the subway takes the form of a "Daemon," Crane artfully—almost too artfully, for the effect is nearly buried in a crowded complexity of language—juxtaposes two radically contrasting images having to do first, with literal and second with metaphorical children. On the one hand, an immigrant Italian cleaning woman, her hair covered against dust by a handkerchief, appears as a humble example of maternal devotion; while, because of her assigned birthplace, she is a faint reminder of Columbus and hence of the divine mother, the *Madre Maria,* through whose intercession the "whelming laughter" was silenced:

> And does the Daemon take you home, also,
> Wop washerwoman, with the bandaged hair?. . . .
>
> O Genoese, do you bring mother eyes and hands
> Back home to children and to golden hair?

This instance of mother love, like that in "Indiana," is a promise of every mode of love, and of the beauty regularly symbolized for Crane in "golden hair"; it stands as an inextinguishable possibility *against* the image of love as a burnt match in a urinal, and it is another of Crane's recurring images of those lowliest ones who carry within themselves the seeds of our redemption. On the other hand, there follows the suggestion that the subway—the demonism of a machinery, of America's "dark Satanic mills," used for ends other than those of the spirit—will simply destroy the longed for rebirth, as someone might throttle a newborn child. In a series of what might be called "baby images," the subway's roar is likened to the hideous laughter attendant upon "the muffled slaughter of a day in birth"; metaphorically, it vaccinates "the brinking dawn / With antennae toward worlds that glow and sink"; it spoon-feeds the age (here the figure gets badly congested) with all the potentially splendid knowledge of science—only to kill it. Within this thick metaphor, the figurative child seems, alternately, to be barely born (in references to navels and umbilical cords) and to be several weeks or even several months old; but pediatric exactitude is probably not to be asked for of this poet. The essential contrast, the apocalyptic alternatives as it were, is clear enough: the world will love, or the world will die.

Crane returns to the feeling that he too, like Poe, is a ravaged victim of this world, that he has been ground down, indeed squashed flat, by the wheels of the age of iron, by the technological consciousness: "O caught like pennies beneath soot and steam." Much worse than this (for he will not, after all, shift the guilt), he has to confront what now seems to him his own disastrous failure as a poet. For all his passionate desire to create a song which will restore beauty to the contemporary reality, he feels he has betrayed his mission—has failed to keep the creative rendezvous; and that, far from being a voice of vision, he is no more than a noisy bundle of nerves—

> shrill ganglia
> Impassioned with some song we fail to keep.

(Crane's harshest critic never contrived a more severe or better-worded indictment of his poetry, and especially of *The Bridge*.) This, carrying forward from the encounter with Poe and intensifying that experience, is truly the moment of greatest crisis: a moment familiar enough in the Romantic tradition, one arrived at by all the English Romantic poets sooner or later, and in America by Whitman: for example in "As I Ebb'd with the Ocean of Life," where

Whitman felt that all his creative efforts were no better than driftwood and debris, which he too darkly inspected to the sound of laughter. This is not merely the sense of death: but the death of that one talent whereby death may be overcome. And yet, for the poet in "The Tunnel" as for the others, the image of spiritual and creative regeneration, and of a renewal of love, does persist. He can still imagine a personal resurrection as miraculous as that of Lazarus, and still hear the sound somewhere of what, in "Voyages VI," he had called "the unbetrayable reply"—the visionary promise of enduring life, the Word of final explanation which will be imaged in the actual words of his poem:

> And yet, like Lazarus, to feel the slope,
> The sod and billow breaking,—lifting ground,
> —A sound of waters bending astride the sky
> Increasing with some Word that will not die . . . !

The Word is the word of perfect love, perfectly and enduringly realized in poetry. And out of his agonized feeling of defeat and death, the poet is able to pronounce his most passionate word of love and praise: "Kiss of our agony thou gatherest."

That phrase, spoken first while the poet is still passing through the tunnel, is repeated some lines later, after he has reached the Brooklyn side and has left the subway to stand beneath the piers of the bridge, seeking to "read" the darkness, to find the meaning in it—"thumbing the midnight," as one might thumb the pages of a mysterious but all-important book. He has made his way through the Gates of Wrath; and he can say again, though now in a somewhat different tone of voice:

> Kiss of our agony Thou gatherest,
> O Hand of Fire
> gatherest—

The repetition of the cry of Columbus ("O Thou Hand of Fire") is altogether suitable, for the poet has journied through his own terrible tempest and has survived—and by means exactly of his own poetic energy. He is able—like the poet in Auden's elegy on Yeats—to rejoice, to offer up a kiss of love to the contemporary world despite all the horrors that beset it and him; and like that same poet, he is able to "make a vineyard of the curse," and so gives thanks to the God—his poetic inspiration—which allows him to do so. Crane's poet has made a vineyard of the curse of a sundered culture: and exactly by writing a splendid poem about it.

It should be remembered that, for all the death experienced in "The Tunnel," the poem was written at a time of extraordinary creative fertility, the happiest period in Crane's life. Just as the worst of all deaths, for Crane, was the death of his talent, so the enactment of death in powerful poetry was the truest triumph over death. And just as the gloom in "Quaker Hill" was largely, when all is said and done, a creative gloom, a despondency at least as much about his poetic abilities as about contemporary America, so the excitement that arises out of the agony at the end of "The Tunnel" is an excitement about creativity. Nor could it be otherwise for a poet who believed, as deeply as Whitman and Shelley and Blake had believed, that the poet really was the true son of God, and that only the poetic imagination could transfigure ugliness into beauty, hatred into love, death into life. That imagination had passed the terrible test in "The Tunnel," and the exaltation of "Atlantis" is justified.[2]

· I I ·

"Atlantis" is Crane's supreme apocalypse of imagination, the revelation of universal radiance and harmony, of a world

[2] It should also be remembered that, while Crane began work on *The Bridge* by attacking the final section, "Atlantis," and while "Atlantis" was the first part to arrive at something like its completed shape, nonetheless it was not really finished until the summer of 1926, and Crane even tinkered with it after that. The point is, that "Atlantis" was in fact as well as in spirit a culmination of most of what had gone before. See, for example, his use of language drawn from "The Dance," as mentioned on pp. 366 and 370 below.

transfigured; a revelation begotten and (for the brief duration of the poem) sustained by the sheer power of poetic vision. Like portions of "The Dance" and "Cape Hatteras," and like the *Te Deum* of Columbus, it is poetic rant of an extravagant order; and it rather asks to be read—and read aloud—than to be chipped at by critical analysis. The latter, for a particular reason to be mentioned, will never fare very well with "Atlantis." But for anyone who has followed *The Bridge* with sufficient sympathy and understanding, its final section offers few problems of interpretation (though one could, as always, go into considerable detail about the vigorous ingenuity of some of the phrases). I shall restrict my commentary to a few basic and no doubt obvious points.

The poem consists of twelve eight-line stanzas, some of them rhymeless but most showing occasional rhymes and half-rhymes; and, driven by a beautifully controlled imagination, the stanzas, as they march by our consciousness, exemplify Crane's poetic ideal of power in repose—for though intense ecstasy and intense anxiety intermingle in the verses, and though the language seems at times about to explode, the final effect is one of stateliness and of measured grandeur. "Atlantis" is, moreover, a hymn: that is, a sung prayer; the last and most highly wrought of the poetic soul's sallies into the infinite—toward that

> Everpresence, beyond time,
> Like spears ensanguined of one tolling star
> That bleeds infinity

addressed in the final stanza. And here, as earlier, all of nature, perhaps all of reality, is caught up in the act of prayer: even the waves of the sea (in stanza seven) appear, like the birch grove in "The Dance," to be "kneeling" as they take part in the devout song.

We begin, of course, where we began in "Proem," confronting Brooklyn Bridge directly; and the bridge is being steadily and absolutely invested with the qualities of greatest poetry, or in keeping with the chief metaphor of "Atlantis," of greatest music. But as against the darkness and the winter with which "Proem" concluded, we are here in a night of "shuttling moonlight" which will soon (in stanza six) give way "to cycloramic crest / Of deepest day"; and to judge from the references to "the vernal strophe," "the lark's return," and the "whitest flower. . . . Anemone," we are at the very instant when winter yields to spring. (Crane probably chose the anemone, in part, to go with the word "Answerer." But he was always delicately precise in his floral allusions; and the so-called "wood anemone," which Crane has in mind in stanza eleven, was well chosen—it is a small, exquisite, pure white flower, that appears between early April and late May.) "Atlantis" is a multiple and interacting thrust of language and spirit toward morning and spring, and toward the "Everpresence" and the redemption of history and the temporal world.

In the early stanzas, the poetic thrust takes the form of an ascent: an upward movement as emphatic as possible, in contrast with the downward spiral that began in "Quaker Hill" and continued to the lowest depths of "The Tunnel." The poet's gaze rises literally and physically, following the vertical suspenders of the bridge till (in stanza three) it reaches "the twin monoliths," the two granite towers that loom at the center of the bridge. This is the peak of actual perception, "the loft of vision"; but at the same time, the poet's spiritual vision has been ascending, transfiguring the bridge at every step—seeing "the bound cable strands" as a "flight of strings," hearing "Sibylline voices flicker[ing]" in the stirring of the wires. And under the enormous pressure of imagination, as the elements envisioned are converted like lightning into immense symbols, the long curve of the bridge appears as "One arc synoptic" which unites all the tides beneath it; while those tides, in turn, represent all the phases of history bound together by vision.

The spiritual and visionary aim is, in fact, double. It is to perceive the union (hence as it were the acceptable truth) of history, of past, present, and future; *and* to do so, by seeing through the temporal to the timeless. This the poet now exultantly feels he can do. In stanza four, his eyes take flight like the sea gull in "Proem"—"Sheerly the eyes, like seagulls stung with rime." And in their hovering flight, the eyes observe "tomorrow" fading into "yesteryear"; and they are able to

> link
> What cipher-script of time no traveller reads
> But who, through smoking pyres of love and death,
> Searches the timeless laugh of mythic spears.

The poet is himself that traveler; for he is the one who, in "The Dance," had visited the domain of mythic spears and witnessed the smoking pyres of love and death. More confidently than ever, he now draws upon that experience and the imagery in which it was articulated to read and understand the language of time. In the following stanza, he is even able to penetrate the "aeons" of "silence" which have buried the cities and heroes of legend: to hear echoes of Tyre and Troy, and of Jason who, in a perhaps appropriate archaism, is heard "hesting" or commanding a "shout," his crew's roar of defiance apparently against Æolus, the god of the winds, whose blasts are wrecking the *Argo* in the Sicilian straits.[3]

To discover the meaning of history, is simultaneously, to translate it:

> O Choir, translating time
> Into what multitudinous Verb the suns
> And synergy of waters ever fuse, recast
> In myriad syllables. . . .

It is in a sense to depart from time ("We left the haven hanging in the night"), to journey to its furthest boundary

---

[3] According to one item in the legend of Jason and the Argonauts, the ship was struck by a fierce North Wind which drove them all the way to the interior of Libya. I do not know Crane's source (if any) for the allusion in "Atlantis"; but he seems to be revising the legend so as to suggest an actual shipwreck, thus associating the *Argo* with the destroyed cities.

("here at time's end"—as in "The River"), and to go beyond
it:

> Sight, sound and flesh Thou leadest from time's realm
> As love strikes clear direction for the helm.

It is to arrive at a vision of eternal being, of the "Everpresence, beyond time." But this tremendous process does
not in any way involve a rejection of the temporal and the
actual, any more than the very similar processes in "Faustus
and Helen" and "Voyages" had done. What is happening,
as usual, is a visionary wedding of the timeless and the
temporal, the ideal and the actual. And by this achievement,
the iron age is seen as infused with radiance, indeed with
wisdom; and the winter of the spirit passes into spring.
Of all this, and in one of the most beautifully packed and
endlessly ponderable figures Crane ever contrived, Brooklyn
Bridge is at once the supreme instance and the utterly
dependable guarantee:

> O Thou steeled Cognizance whose leap commits
> The agile precincts of the lark's return.

To gauge the force, one might almost say the mood, of
those lines (indeed, of the whole of "Atlantis"), one might
set them against the awed, bemused, and ironic response
of Henry Adams to the dynamo he had spent days observing
at the Great Exposition of 1900: "To Adams, the dynamo
became a symbol of infinity. . . . he began to feel the forty-
foot dynamo as a moral force, much as the early Christians
felt the Cross. . . . Before the end, one began to pray for
it." [4]

The chief difficulty of "Atlantis" lies not in any obscurity
of reference, especially since most of the allusions repeat

[4] *The Education of Henry Adams* (Modern Library Edition),
p. 380. It is noteworthy that, in the extraordinary paragraph from
which I have quoted, Adams exploits the archetypal image of the
whirling wheel ("this huge wheel, revolving . . . at some vertigi-
nous speed") to realize his image of the dynamo as a kind of new
divinity.

or summarize earlier moments in *The Bridge*. The almost overpowering difficulty is rather that this is a work of total synthesis, one which at every point is trying—and successfully, I believe—to say everything at once, not only to suggest but verbally to enact a pervasive universal harmony whereby every aspect of reality is linked with everything else. The typical words employed are "link," "fuse," "yoking," "bind," "stitch," "complighted," and "conclamant"; and the typical phrases are "one arc synoptic" and "leap and converge." "Atlantis" is thus bound to defeat criticism, whose main instrument is exactly analysis. Any statement about the visionary reconciliation of time and eternity, of the ultimate victory over death therein accomplished (the "fell unshadow" of the bridge is "death's utter wound"), or of the now unimpeded movement toward spring and morning: such a statement simply cannot, without falling into hopeless confusion, also acknowledge the other two major elements everywhere present, active, and invoked in the poem—that is, poetry or song, and the bridge itself. We have arrived once more, and for the last time, at that burst of similitudes we encountered, for example, in "Ave Maria" and "The River"; only here they have very nearly become absolute equations. The bridge and the poem are really, now, one and the same thing, just as they are always the source of vision *and* the universal harmony envisioned.

When Crane, in language further absorbed from the imagery of "The Dance," writes:

> From gulfs unfolding, terrible of drums,
> Tall Vision-of-the-Voyage, tensely spare—
> Bridge, lifting night to cycloramic crest
> Of deepest day—

it is at once the bridge which is transforming darkness into light, as to some extent it had done in "Proem"; and also the bridge as itself transfigured by poetry; and also the poetry itself. "Tall Vision-of-the-Voyage" is an excellent epithet for the bridge, which quite realistically can be said to *look like* a journey over the waters; but the whole of Crane's long poem is—it contains and expresses—the vision of a voyage. If the bridge can be described, synaesthetically, as a "swift peal of secular light," the poem aspires precisely to that quality—to a revelation of perfect beauty to the outer and the inner ear and eye. In the kind of paradox which is essential for Crane's purpose, it is in its secularity that the bridge is an opening onto the sacred; and that self-same sentence could be repeated with the word "poem" substituted for "bridge." When, speaking about the mysterious and lovely sounds emanating from the bridge, Crane says that it is "as though a god were issue of the strings," he is of course speaking about his poem: the final aim of which is the musical creation of a godhead. But only in the final stanza of "Atlantis" and of *The Bridge* are these two elements at last formally equated: "One Song, One Bridge of Fire"—and by verbal association, One God, or "Hand of Fire." The formula is unavoidable: the song is the bridge is the godhead.

The phrases just quoted lead to the question:

> Is it Cathay?
> Now pity steeps the grass and rainbows ring
> The serpent with the eagle in the leaves . . . ?

and to the poem's concluding line: "Whispers antiphonal in azure swing." Once again, as in the poem on Melville, after poetic vision has "lifted" the godhead, silent (or almost silent) answers creep across the skies. The question lingers: "Is it Cathay?" Has the poet done what, in the guise of Columbus, he promised to do—has he "brought [us] back Cathay"? Before venturing an answer, we can notice a curiosity in the place-naming of this final section. One would expect the section to be called "Cathay"; and in fact the Atlantis of the title is only referred to once: "Atlantis— hold thy floating singer late!" The legendary city first described by Plato in the *Timaeus*, the land sent to the depths of the ocean by the sea-god in punishment for its sins of pride and lust but which might some day rise again into view, restored and redeemed: this was obviously useful for Crane's mythic design and his apocalyptic enterprise; and he had, we remember, alluded to Atlantis hazily in "Cutty Sark" (along with a remote hint about it in the borrowing from Poe's "City of the Sea" in "The Tunnel"). Allan Trachtenberg has shown that for voyagers in the age of Columbus, Cathay and Atlantis were nearly equal attractions and were even a little confused with each other.[5] Crane may or may not have known as much (he probably did). But the principle of naming at work in "Atlantis" is the same as that in "Lachrymae Christi": "Names peeling from thine eyes." The object of the great quest can and indeed should be assigned a variety of names, no one of which points to its full nature, and any one of which if chosen as *the* proper name would slightly falsify by relating the end in view too closely to one particular legend or historical epoch or religious tradition. It can thus be called Cathay or Atlantis, or by the name of any vanished city: Tyre or Troy, for example, or the Pompeii dimly suggested by the "water-gutted lava" of "Cutty Sark."

But whatever its name, we know what this country is. It is the country of vision. It is this world as seen with compassionate love and transfiguring vision: with the "soft grateful tears" of Blake's "Morning." It is the cities and the fields of America seen like this:

> With white escarpments swinging into light,
> Sustained in tears the cities are endowed
> And justified conclamant with ripe fields
> Revolving through their harvests in sweet torment.

It is the land of music: of that music bespoken in the Platonic epigraph, which is "the knowledge of that which relates to love in harmony and system." It is the domain of love, and above it gleams the rainbow of the covenant:

[5] *Brooklyn Bridge: Fact and Symbol* (New York, 1964), pp. 161-65.

"Now pity steeps the grass and rainbows ring / The serpent. . . ."

Or rather—and to this crucial modification we must always return—it is the continuing and passionate urge toward all that. For "Atlantis," Crane's hymn of praise to the creative imagination, arises from the knowledge that vision is precarious at best, and that it is never final. It scarcely endures beyond the moment of its utterance; one must always struggle to recover it and then to go beyond it. This is a radical truth, and one has only to stare out at the world for half a minute to be convinced of it. The visionary imagination at its farthest thrust works only in questions and surmises—to which the answers are silence or tantalizing whispers. But the vision lasts at least as long as the questions, and it is sustained by their intensity; while it lasts, the questions sound like their own answers.

·III·

Much has been written about Crane's quest for an "absolute vision," or, in a somewhat more communicative phrase, for a "vision of the absolute." To this bothersome critical theme I shall return in the next chapter, especially when considering "Royal Palm" and "The Broken Tower" (poems of 1926 and 1932 respectively). But my discussion of "Atlantis" is intended to suggest that if we need a label for Crane's ultimate visionary ambition, we might better speak of a vision of "totality" rather than of the "absolute." (Exactly the same could be said of Whitman—for example, in "Crossing Brooklyn Ferry.") Such language always verges on the fuzzily pontifical; but the distinction is not, I believe, a trifling one. What we witness in "Atlantis" is the end of a long integrative process whereby several bursts of similitudes have led to the perception of multiple equations—and then almost, but not quite, to an envisioned one-ness of all modes and phases of being. The latter, if ever arrived at (and Crane knew it was just beyond the poet's reach), would be so different from a vision of the absolute as to be nearly its opposite. It would, that is, be opposite to the misleadingly called "Platonic vision" Crane is sometimes said to have aimed at.[6] What Crane did aim at in *The Bridge* is what he always aimed at: to see "the two worlds. And at once." In "Atlantis," as to a much more modest degree in "Faustus and Helen" and "Voyages," Crane sought to body forth a vision in which countless aspects of this world, themselves united by the poet's esemplastic eye, were seen in union with the "Everpresence," the irradiating power of the simultaneously perceived world of ideal beauty and love and harmony. Not the absolute pure, to make the plain point once more, but the absolute inextricably wedded to the actual, seen and known by means of the actual even as it serves to transform the actual: this was Crane's regular purpose and *his* brand of totality.

These reflections bring us to some final remarks about the totality of *The Bridge* itself—about Crane's epic poem as a whole. I do not scruple here or elsewhere to refer to *The Bridge* as an epic, or alternatively as simply a long poem. The question of genre need not, in fact, seriously delay us: not because the question lacks fascination, but because it has been more or less satisfactorily settled by a range of recent commentary on Anglo-American Romantic poetry, and particularly on the large-scale works that have come out of it, from Blake's *Jerusalem* and Wordsworth's *The Prelude* onward. It is in part a matter of imaginative extension. *The Bridge* has the makings at least of a traditional epic abundance: moving as it does through an array of geographical places and physical settings, of historical epochs (however fleetingly touched upon) and momentous events both real and legendary, of wide varieties of ex-

---

[6] See below, pp. 413ff. What seems to be meant by "Platonic vision" —as invoked, for instance, by Marius Bewley in the passage below referred to—is rather a *Neo*-Platonic vision: an unmediated, unveiled, uncontaminated glimpse of pure transcendent reality. Plato, in the central dialogues, is closer to the method and, as it were, to the constantly double vision of Hart Crane.

perience—and, keeping pace with these other elements and determining their selection and coloration, of every mode of consciousness. But all this grows out of the personal reminiscences and the private urgencies of an individual man and poet; so that the poem can be accurately described as a "personal epic": to borrow the phrase that Harry Levin (himself borrowing from Stephen Dedalus's discourse on lyric, epic and dramatic in *A Portrait of the Artist*) applied to Joyce's *Ulysses;* and, closer to home, that William Carlos Williams applied to his own massive endeavor, *Paterson.* Robert Frost put the case most succinctly when he observed about some much younger American poets that he hoped one or two of them would live long enough to write an epic, since "a good epic would grace our history. Landor has set an example in prolonging the lyric out of all bounds." [7] The specific allusion to Landor is baffling; but the formula is perfect. Crane, in *The Bridge,* extended his own kind of lyric beyond all bounds, and, doing so, he bestowed upon our history—or our consciousness thereof—that gift of transfiguration of which poetry is capable and which, by analogy, seems a form of grace.

Identified in this fashion, *The Bridge* belongs clearly enough to the now well-established tradition of the modern and Romantic epic. Roy Harvey Pearce, in a ground-breaking essay, has explored the American phase of this tradition, and has assembled the chief features of the exceedingly ambitious long poem which does not, in the classical manner, memorialize a hero and a noble accomplishment of olden times, but which creates a heroic figure appropriate to the present and days to come. [8] Poetry of this order, as Whitman —whose "Song of Myself" remains the supreme example of the American Romantic epic—insisted in the preface to the 1855 *Leaves of Grass,* is by definition "creative," and it

---

[7] Introduction to *New Poets of England and America* (New York, 1957), eds. Donald Hall, Robert Pack, and Louis Simpson.

[8] "Towards an American Epic," in *The Continuity of American Poetry* (Princeton, 1961).

has "vistas." The heroic figure thus brought into view is not a warrior or a faith-driven pilgrim or even an individuated human being, any more than the context is a lucidly evolving narrative. The hero is essentially the poetic imagination itself, vaguely personified, and the context is a welter of contemporary actuality. It is perhaps tempting to call any prolonged work based upon the interplay of those two elements (whether of the Hart Crane or Wallace Stevens or W. C. Williams variety) a "tertiary epic," to distinguish it from the secondary or Virgilian mode, with which, as I argued much earlier, it can have certain deceptive initial affinities.[9] But as I also argued, such a designation only takes us into a nest of perplexities. As a way of avoiding these somewhat stale semantic controversies, the phrase of Professor Abrams—"apocalypse of imagination"—is probably the most useful for suggesting the nature and intention of a poem like *The Bridge*.

The real problem raised by *The Bridge* today is, however, less that of its genre than that of its structure: of such form as it seems to be striving to realize, of the method of its organization, and the source of its momentum. Here again, I have not scrupled to refer to the individual parts of *The Bridge* alternately as "sections" and as "poems." For the formal problem is not inherent in Crane's poem, but in our critical vocabulary. We still lack the terms to indicate what, on the formal side, *The Bridge* is quite successfully doing; and bringing to bear upon it terms that do not fit, we have blamed the poem rather than the terms. Looked at in an Aristotelian perspective, *The Bridge* is undoubtedly so flawed as to be the poetic failure (magnificent or otherwise) it has so monotonously been declared to be. The best response to those charges is the one that arch-Romantic D. H. Lawrence made to a severe critic of his fiction: "What you call faults, I call characteristics." But it is just those character-

[9] I am thinking of the terms "primary" (Homeric and oral) and "secondary" (Virgilian and written) epics, as used by C. M. Bowra in *From Virgil to Milton* (New York, 1948).

istics one finds it difficult, not to grasp, but to describe; and as I attempt, in closing, to do so, I shall inevitably be circling and spiraling over the same observed phenomena, as though in critical emulation of the poetic procedure of *The Bridge.*

Kenneth Burke, who has the most powerful speculative critical mind of our time (in the most expansive meaning of the word "critical"), comes nearest to helping us out. *The Bridge,* for example, does not show and never intends to show what Burke (in *Counter-Statement*) calls "conventional form": form which draws attention to itself, form for its own sake—form, in the Aristotelian sense, as the fundamental cause or source of the poem's very existence. An immediate sign of the absence, from *The Bridge,* of conventional form is this: that nothing in the poetic conception dictates the exact order or the exact number of its parts. In the later portions of the poem, sections could be shuffled a little; and one or two of them could have been deleted from the published text without the reader feeling any sharp sense of loss. More obviously, several sections could have been added. Among Crane's worksheets, in fact, there is a prosy piece called "Lenses," which according to Crane's notation was to appear "directly preceding Tunnel," as section "VII or VIII"; and on the back of the "Harbor Dawn" worksheet, Crane listed the final contents of *The Bridge,* but implied by two squiggly lines between "Quaker Hill" and "The Tunnel" that he still contemplated inserting a couple of poems there.[10]

Still proceeding negatively, with Burke's help, we may remark that although *The Bridge* has a fairly distinctive beginning and a fairly distinctive end, it has no *distinctive* middle. But these honorable old terms are unsatisfactory as regards *The Bridge.* Crane's poem not only has more than one beginning, it has more than one kind of beginning: the invocation of the bridge and the anticipatory survey of

[10] This listing is undated; it may date from as late as 1929, and almost certainly much later than the "Harbor Dawn" passages on the other side of the sheet.

"Proem," the invocation of the mixed divinities of "Ave Maria," the start of the poetic journey in "Harbor Dawn." And its ending is no more decisive than Crane's visionary convictions made possible. For what *The Bridge* does reveal throughout is not a classical symmetry but an ebb and flow of consciousness and perception and emotion: a recurring rhythmic movement, as I have said, rather than a carefully wrought design wherein each moment, each development, has its singular and unalterable place. *The Bridge* is by no means unique in this respect, though in its time it was unmodish. Other arts have, more recently, been animated by a similar non-classical creative idea: the idea of "a stream of energy rising and falling with areas of concentration and areas of expansion," as it has been expressed in a remarkable statement about modern architecture which is rich in implications for the architecture of *The Bridge*.[11] But while

[11] Mrs. Ralph S. Brown, Jr., in a letter of 1965, having to do with architectural planning for the Bennington College campus—a project for which Mrs. Brown was chairman of the Trustees' Committee. I have Mrs. Brown's kind permission to quote from this long and fascinating letter (it runs to five thousand words), which will some day, I hope, be printed in full.

Mrs. Brown speaks of "some of the new ideas that are beginning to stir" in the field of architecture, and what she has to say about the desirable shape of the Bennington campus is almost startlingly close to what I have tried, more cumbersomely, to say about the asymmetrical fluidity of *The Bridge*.

There are many possibilities to be explored. For example, why not think in terms of a continuous whole, something that would be neither one big building nor forty small ones, but both— something supple and wandering—partly indoors and partly outdoors, a weaving of rooms and courts and walks—jumping a space here to form an island, flinging out a wing there, two stories somewhere and one story somewhere else . . . all this not exactly one building, not exactly many, not exactly a building at all, simply a stream of energy rising and falling with areas of concentration and areas of expansion, each piece capable of having its own architectural identity . . . able to push its way up through the roof or out through the walls or down into the ground if it wants to, and yet all these separate identities able to speak to one another, each division, even each subject able to be

the visionary effort as such may be understood to be unending, the visionary *poem* does reach its genuine if precarious conclusion. This particular exercise of imagination does exhaust itself, and no further excursion would be artistically appropriate beyond the last lingering questions of "Atlantis," however many might have been added along the way. Here Romantic fiction can supply some useful analogies—Melville's *The Confidence Man,* for example, and Lawrence's *Women in Love,* in both of which the overall adventure could have been thickened or reduced by a number of episodes, but in neither of which (despite their artfully ambiguous endings) could any subsequent scene have been tacked on without artistic damage. So it is with the to-and-froward poetic journey of *The Bridge.*

Between the poem's wave-like start and its elusive finish, there occurs the long movement of consciousness away from the mechanical and urban and toward a mythic interpretation of nature and human experience; followed by the serial exploration of various centers and corners of contemporary life, carried out by reference to the vision and especially to the visionary language acquired in "The Dance." To this extent, *The Bridge* can be said to have two unequal halves, logically enough related. But even that relationship will seem deceptively clear, and the sense of it will lead only to critical frustration, until we recognize the manner and method of the poem's progression. For the latter is, of

itself and yet able to open out in many directions. A structure like this doesn't need to have any particular beginning or end— certainly no monumental center; it can be expanded almost indefinitely, and at almost any point; its interior spaces can be reassigned in almost any way as points of pressure shift.

One presumptive difference between campus architecture, as here envisioned, and a modern Romantic epic poem is that the latter should have an at least apparent end (that beyond which nothing is aesthetically imaginable). Apart from that, the above remarks— after the proper substitutions are made ("poem" and "poems" for "building" and "buildings" and so on)—are uncannily relevant to *The Bridge.*

course, not at all straightforward and linear (a journey out, a journey back, and so on), but is rather a succession of poetic twists and spirals and diversions. One of the creative principles at work is what Burke (in *The Grammar of Motives*) postulates as the "act-scene ratio," according to which any significant new act in the evolving art-work—in this case, a new act of consciousness—requires a new scene or setting to make evident the full scope of its significance. Hence, in *The Bridge,* as the poet's consciousness darkens and brightens, narrows and enlarges, we observe the shift from the poet's room at dawn to a walk to the subway, to the Mississippi, and then a smoky glade in the Adirondacks; and after that, to a dimly lit South Street saloon, Cape Hatteras, a resort for the rich, a steamer, a burlesque theater, a street in Manhattan, the tunnel under the East River, the bridge in starlight. And in almost every setting, the essential experience of vision lost and vision gained repeats itself.

It is indeed "repetitive form," in Burke's terminology, rather than "conventional form" that characterizes *The Bridge.* The various parts, though in many ways disparate, cohere—they "speak to one another" and "open out" into each other, to borrow again from the architectural letter mentioned above—because the same kind of experience is being continuously passed through, and the poetic diction is constantly echoing and repeating and parodying itself. Each version of the central experience, as we have had so many occasions to say, is a synecdoche; each stands for all the others, and taken together they accumulate into that same central experience the poem as a whole is enacting. The form, in other words, is not some special arrangement of these repetitions; it is that felt rhythm of life which the repetitions themselves gradually force upon our reader's imagination: the rhythm, as always, of vision briefly enjoyed, vision lost, vision recovered.

This is, manifestly, not to say that *The Bridge* is a static poem, but rather to suggest the species of progression that can be made out in it. It is what Burke calls "qualitative progression"—not the progression from event to event, as in a skillfully contrived narrative (say, by Henry James) or a well-made play; but the progressive realization of the true nature of things. The realization—and this is more evident in the later than in the earlier sections of *The Bridge,* particularly in "Cape Hatteras," "Three Songs," and "The Tunnel"—is invariably twofold. It is, first, to disclose the actual degradation, the spiritual blindness, the absence of love, and the atmosphere of death in contemporary America: disclosures effected in good part by verbal parody in the sections just named. But then, in each situation, it is to show that world, or some aspect of it, suddenly if momentarily transfigured. In "Atlantis," needless to say, the act of transfiguration reaches its climax, as the grand visionary language of "Proem," "Ave Maria," and "The Dance" come back, unmodified, into play.

It is by reflecting on that method of progressive realization that we come at last to detect the source of the poem's momentum. For some one thing is steadily happening in *The Bridge;* something is not only being disclosed and revealed, but some positive activity is pushing ahead. If *The Bridge* does not, certainly, contain a clear narrative sequence, neither is it a haphazard meandering of the Quixotic or picaresque imagination. What gives the poem its momentum, I suggest, is an *unflagging process of permeation.* Alvin Kernan, in *The Plot of Satire* (1965) has demonstrated brilliantly that great satire—Pope's *Dunciad* is his paradigm—has a very definite and powerful plot, but not a plot of Aristotelian design with a logically distinguishable beginning, middle, and end. It is a matter, instead, of some overwhelming characteristic gradually and thoroughly permeating some large given entity—a society, a culture: the progressive conquest of English life, for example, by the quality of brutal stupidity. When the process is seen to be complete and the human condition has become altogether brutalized and stupefied, chaos is come again ("Lo!

thy dread empire CHAOS is restored"), and the work of art has run its course.

Though the quality and the end in view are radically different, something of the same thing happens, is persistently happening, in *The Bridge*. The plot of *The Bridge* is the gradual permeation of an entire culture by the power of poetic vision—by that ever-pursuing, periodically defeated but always self-renewing visionary imagination which, as I have said, is the true hero of the Romantic epic. When this heroic force has invaded and uncovered and transformed as much of the culture as it knows, beauty and harmony have come again; it gives voice to its ultimate hymn of praise, and the poem is done. Great satire, Kernan implies, is almost by definition apocalyptic, and throbs with comical and scornful premonitions of the end of the world. Great visionary poetry—and *The Bridge* is the most compelling example in our century—is no less apocalyptic, but in its own kind. The pulsations of *The Bridge* intimate a world not ending but a world reborn, or about to be reborn, out of the enormous creative struggle of the imagination.

·III·

KEY WEST AND OTHERS

CHAPTER THIRTEEN

Thresholds Old and New

WHITE BUILDINGS was published in December 1926, and over the next months it received speedier and more widespread consideration than (or so one feels in the usual perspective of literary history) it would receive today, forty years later. The responses, however, were about the same as those Crane's poetry has elicited ever since: on the one hand, along with the ambiguously celebrational introduction to the volume by Allen Tate, there was the warm and discerning praise of men like Yvor Winters and Waldo Frank, who identified Crane as one of the most original and accomplished American poets of his time; on the other hand, there were charges of pretentiousness, willful obscurity, a calamitous lack of verbal control. Crane, according to Horton, had been passing through a familiar period of despondent sterility, and the reviews in both kinds helped restore a portion of vitality; he was exhilarated, and at the same time he was stung, into fresh creative action.

As spring (1927) passed into summer, and despite some hectic sexual and alcoholic excursions, Crane kept remarkably busy. He revised several of the independent lyrics of the previous year ("Royal Palm," "The Air Plant," "O Carib Isle!"); drew further upon his experience on the Isle of Pines in a few new poems ("The Hurricane," "Island Quarry," and others); completed the "Harbor Dawn" and "Van Winkle" sections of *The Bridge* and wrote "The River"; and saw to the publication—often after careful re-working—of almost all the parts of his epic which had by then been written. Until well into the autumn of 1927, Crane was in every sense a practicing professional poet.

Then, somehow, his life simply seems to lose its rhythm.

Only in much larger and vaguer outlines than before, and by taking longer stretches of time and surveying his career from a greater distance, can we make out—during the last four and a half years of his life—that characteristic ebb and flow of energy, that spiritual coming and going that, up to now, had been apparent almost month by month, or anyhow season by season. When Horton tells us that prior to the end of July 1929, "for two years [Crane] had written nothing except random phrases and fragments," he is exaggerating only a little; a few unpublished poems have since turned up, but they are indeed hardly publishable. And when, in a letter to Samuel Loveman dated "Easter, '32" and inclosing the final version of "The Broken Tower," Crane himself said "here's a poem—about the first in 2 years," he was exaggerating only a trifle more; the dozen-odd lyrics Crane did compose in 1930 and 1931—about half of them still in manuscript—are so inferior to "The Broken Tower" that Crane's comment is quite justified. One can, in fact, hear very plainly the stress and exultation in his opening phrase: "here's a poem"—at last.

Apart from those two splendid periods of creativity (the summer of 1929, the winter of 1932), much, though not all, of the story of Crane's life after 1927 is a sorry and a shapeless one. In November of the latter year, and after a series of false starts and short-lived jobs, Crane went to California as a sort of intellectual companion to Herbert Wise. It was a joyless venture, relieved only by stimulating conversations with Yvor Winters, whom he now met in person for the first time. Crane resigned his position in February 1928, and went to stay with his mother and grandmother in Hollywood— only to depart in a hurry for New York at the end of May, following what appears to have been a truly hideous and irrevocable quarrel with Mrs. Crane. The summer—that normally productive season—was spent finding and quitting job after job, and consorting with the sailors he managed to pick up in the bars of Manhattan and Brooklyn. Upon the death of his grandmother later in the year, Crane received a bequest of five thousand dollars, and just before Christmas he sailed for England.

The brief stay in London was (for Crane at this stage) reasonably calm and rewarding, with only one or two really startling outbursts. But in France, and especially in and near Paris, Crane was introduced into an overwrought atmosphere of artistic frenzy and sexual aberration, and he joined the fray with furious enthusiasm. He was writing some, but not enough; and "each week-end," Horton says, "he drowned his [poetic] conscience in a drunken whirl of excitement." Most of those weekends, in fact, were spent in an old re-modeled mill at Ermonenville, just outside Paris, belonging to Harry and Caresse Crosby, owners of the Black Sun Press. The Crosbys were enormously taken with what they had read of *The Bridge,* and the bizarre hope they shared with Crane was that he might complete the epic amid the uproar of "Le Moulin." The "mobs" of "poets and painters and pederasts and lesbians" whom Harry Crosby describes in his diary as typical week-end visitors [1] made it, of course, impossible for Crane to do any sustained writing; indeed, he clearly contributed more than his share to the turmoil. He did compose a couple of desultory lyrics, one of which— "I Rob my Bread to Reach those Altitudes"—leads from a visit to the Eiffel Tower (presumably the altitudes in ques-tion) on to patriotic reflections about the shape and promise of American culture:

> My countrymen—give form and edict
> To the morrow. You shall know
> The harvest as you have known the spring. [2]

The lines are as prefunctory as may be, and the Whitmanian posture is not, in this instance, persuasive; but the poem suggests that Crane's imagination was slowly re-awakening to his major enterprise. The subdued and prosy hint of

---

[1] Quoted by Horton, *Hart Crane,* p. 257.
[2] Handwritten; in the Special Collections of the Columbia Uni-versity Library.

confidence in the future of America implied, as always, the least glimmer of a returning confidence in himself—as was shown in the sequel. For although Crane added little to the manuscript of *The Bridge* during the months in France, he settled down to it almost immediately upon his return to America in late July (1929). At Columbia Heights in Brooklyn and then back in Patterson, Crane experienced the last of "these fevers of work" (as he himself put it) from which *The Bridge* had fitfully emerged. By Christmas, as we have seen, he sent Caresse Crosby the final version of "Quaker Hill" and declared the poem finished.

It has not been my purpose to trace Crane's biography here or in any other moment of his career. This has been done admirably by others, and it is being done once more, down to the smallest accessible detail, by Professor Unterecker. My own biographical jottings and my insistence on relative dates are intended merely to serve one or two critical observations. For one thing, a great deal of Crane's most bellicose and disconcerting behavior occurred *after* that curious but no doubt inevitable loosening of the seams in late 1927. One should avoid what seems to me to be the continuing error of reading back (chronologically) from the life into the poetry—that is, into the poetry so much of the best of which was written *before* the time we are now concerned with. Edward Dahlberg, for example, has spoken recently—and was strongly supported by Kay Boyle for doing so—of the "bedlamite shrieks of a soul sunk like Atlantis" that are allegedly audible in Crane's verses.[3] Mr. Dahlberg and Miss Boyle are among the most acute and literarily knowing members of the American world of letters, and they were (I gather) well acquainted with Hart Crane in the post-1927 period. But they have, to borrow a phrase from Whitman, given voice to the usual mistake. Whatever roars of outrage or exuberance Crane may have uttered in the din of Ermenonville, or cavorting in the taverns and reeling

[3] *New York Review,* January 20, 1966. Miss Boyle's letter appeared in the March 31 issue of the same periodical.

down the streets of New York, "bedlamite shrieks" are scarcely the defining attribute of poems like "Repose of Rivers" or "Voyages" or "Emblems of Conduct" or "Recitative" or "At Melville's Tomb"—or of any part of *The Bridge* and most emphatically not of "Atlantis." "Bedlamite shrieks" may, I realize, be a form of praise; the image of Crane in constant eruption—shouting back with courage and wild beauty at an appalling and destructive world—has been fostered by his admirers and emulators, too. But the image, though it may be dramatic and in certain moods appealing, will not survive a fair reading of Crane's poems. The soul that informs those poems was not "sunk like Atlantis," however tormented his friends may have assumed the man to be in the later years.

Conversely, the assumption about Crane's psychological condition in those years has led to a decidedly arguable verdict on the sections of *The Bridge*—"Cape Hatteras," "Indiana," and "Quaker Hill"—which Crane wrote in the very middle of them. Since Crane had given in to his most disorderly impulses (so the almost unconscious argument runs), these poems must be outright failures that do irreparable damage to the epic; they are indeed (so the argument doubles on itself) clear evidence of his moral and psychological and (hence) artistic collapse. "Indiana" is without question far below the best level of *The Bridge,* though it struggles to achieve its necessary place in the scheme. But "Quaker Hill," while seriously flawed, has its compelling moments; and, more important, it gives graver and more poignant tone to the consciousness of death with which the poem is being gradually permeated. And "Cape Hatteras"—once it is understood that the "nasal whine of power" passage is the most artful self-parody—can be seen as one of the astonishing triumphs of modern poetry.

Throughout the year 1930, Crane pursued a restive and generally aimless course, not so much alternating as plunging back and forth between Manhattan and Patterson. Nor were the ever-increasing and ever-more violent escapades in the city—which now terminated all too often in a severe beating or roughing-up by sailors or policemen—matched as before by periods of pastoral recuperation and fresh creative efforts. The year was not literally barren. One morning, after (as it seems) a night-long homosexual session, Crane hurried off a three-stanza poem conceived, the title suggests, as a "Reply" to his still sleeping companion, and which oddly mingles the sense of shame and a poet's pride:

Go then, unto thy turning and thy blame.
Seek bliss then, brother, in my moment's shame.
All this that balks delivery through words
Shall come to you through wounds prescribed by swords. . . .

So sleep, dear brother, in my fame, my shame undone.

And following the suicide of Harry Crosby in the winter of 1930, Crane wrote an elegy for his friend—"To the Cloud Juggler"—which assembled many of Crane's favorite vocables (cluster, vision, rainbow, azure, moon, dawn, floating), but which even his real grief and even perhaps his dark empathy could not stir into imaginative life. In July, Crane composed a nine-line lyric, only recently published, called "The Alert Pillow"; and this, as it manipulates the viable theme of awakening and of adjusting one's dream-vision to the challenge of reality, is at least Crane at his second best.[4] But by and large the year was a wasteful and, for the reader, a depressing one.

Yet perhaps we demand too much. Crane was suffering a normal reaction to the publication of his long-delayed epic (it appeared in France, we recall, in February, and in New York in April); and the reviews of it deepened Crane's mood of exhausted and occasionally frenetic gloom. For in addition to the misunderstanding and disbelief with which his poetry had always been greeted, such highly honored

[4] Published, with critical analysis, in the pamphlet "Hart Crane: a Conversation with Samuel Loveman" (Interim Books, 1964).

critics and poets as Yvor Winters and Malcolm Cowley and Allen Tate—in distinctively different tones and terms—now joined the choral indictment not only of *The Bridge* but of the whole tenor, and the accompanying technique, of Crane's Romanticism, of his guilty poetic association with Emerson and Whitman. These were the reviews that established the stereotype judgment on *The Bridge* as a failure, even though (and the enlarged cliché is the more tedious) possibly a magnificent failure. Meanwhile, however, Crane answered private messages of praise with sweet-tempered appreciation; and his more defensive letters—for example, the letter to Tate of July 13, 1930, to which we shall return— reflected something of the staunchness, of his irreducible conviction about the rightness of his poetic path, that had characterized him in earlier days.

In almost every period of Crane's career there was a saving instant of sorts, and in 1930 it was what turned into a three-month visit, beginning in late December, with his father and stepmother (Clarence Crane's third wife) at Chagrin Falls, Ohio. Crane was already fond of his stepmother, and he now grew closer to his father than he had ever been before. It was more than a reconciliation; it was something like an affectionate intimacy; a developing relationship which had begun in 1927—when Mr. Crane, evidently bent on rediscovering his son, settled a small sum per month on him— and which had progressed further, one assumes, after the dreadful break between Crane and his mother. The new warmth was helped by the almost complete sobriety which, astonishingly, Crane was able to sustain during the entire visit; in this physical regard, at least, the months in Chagrin Falls had the curative value of other rustic removals. Nothing creative was forthcoming, however: "No writing is being done yet," Crane wrote Solomon Grunberg in January; and to Waldo Frank in February, he reported that he had been "on the water wagon two months now," but added with witty bitterness (as though parodying the typical charge of his critics) that "if abstinence is clarifying to the vision, as they claim, then give me back the blindness of my will. It needs fresh baptism." An occasion for fresh alcoholic baptisms was soon afforded. In March 1931, he received notice that he had been granted a Guggenheim Foundation fellowship—for the study of "European culture," and especially French literature, with the eventual aim (in the words of his application) of comprehending "the emergent features of a distinctive American poetic consciousness." If the phrase sounds familiar, it is because one has often read it—one has even perhaps written it—in critical studies of Crane; needless to say, Crane himself never made the slightest gesture toward such a study. But he came back to New York to celebrate the fellowship in a round of drinking bouts. Then, at the last minute and for reasons that remain unclear, he switched his plans from Europe to Mexico; and in early April, he sailed on the S. S. *Orizaba* for Mexico City.

Crane's year in Mexico has, thus far, been considerably blurred in the telling, mainly because the shadow of his death looms at the end of it. Horton, noting that the ship on which Crane sailed south was the same as that from which he disappeared, sailing north, in April 1932, sees the Mexican experience as an uninterrupted journey toward death: "From the moment he set staggering foot aboard" the *Orizaba,* Horton says, "the story of [Crane's] life is also, almost exclusively, the story of his death." This we beg leave to doubt, until or unless certain facts are better determined than they are at present. During most of the balance of the year (1931), Crane stayed with or near his "old and wonderful friend" Katharine Anne Porter, herself the recipient of a Guggenheim fellowship; and Miss Porter's account (transmitted by Horton and Weber) of Crane's fantastic drunken melodramatics—his bellowings about suicide, but also the subsequent shout of self-directed laughter—is well known. But Crane's letters, which so frequently belie a little the customary picture of him, suggest a way of life not devoid of purpose and satisfaction, one given over largely to energetic and enthusiastic explorations of Mexican culture—of art and architecture and local habits and religious rituals. And over the year, Crane managed about a poem or a poetic fragment a month: ranging from the random couplet "Hieroglyphic"

> Did one look at what one saw
> Or did one see what one looked at [5]

through a cluster of poems about the Mexican Indians ("The Circumstance," the more hasty and teasing "They Were There Falling," and others) to "Purgatorio," a stammering twenty-one-line piece bespeaking, not without pathos, a sense of utter isolation and creative paralysis. No one of these even approaches the first-class Crane, but several have a certain salvageable value; and Crane had reason to feel that he might, just possibly, be on the verge of a new visionary threshold.

He arrived at that threshold soon after the first of the year, 1932, when he began to write what, in retrospect, is one of his two or three finest lyrics, "The Broken Tower." On the most personal level, the poem arose from his recently quickened love for Peggy Baird, an old friend whom he had re-encountered in Taxco. It was probably the first and certainly the only genuine heterosexual relationship of his life, ringed around as it may have been with other impulses and recurring explosions. It was Miss Baird (again, on the personal level) "whose sweet mortality stirs latent power," in the words of the poem, and who was the immediate source of the new spiritual health and the beautifully recovered vision which the poem quietly and intricately celebrates. Crane worked on "The Broken Tower" for more than two months, completing it toward the end of March. By this time he was arranging to return to the United States, to sort out the exasperating confusion attendant upon a large legacy from his father (who had died the previous July). He sailed with Peggy Baird on April 24.

[5] In a letter to Irita Van Doren, March 4, 1932; Special Collections, Columbia University Library.

Crane disappeared over the side of the *Orizaba* around noon on April 27, 1932. So much seems to be incontestable fact, though his first two biographers give very slightly different dates, and Miss Baird in her memoir speaks of leaving Vera Cruz on a hot day "in July." [6] But whether he jumped or fell or simply reeled over backwards—whether, in short, his death was a deliberate suicide or a brutal mishap or something in between, at once willed and accidental— this will probably never be cleared up beyond all reasonable doubt. Crane had been drunk and belligerent the night before, and on the morning of his death he told Peggy Baird that he felt "utterly disgraced." He had lost his pocketbook, containing all his money, but, as Miss Baird says, though this was embarrassing it was "not too serious." The assumption of suicide rests, of course, not upon verified facts and convincing eyewitnesses, but on the belief that literal self-destruction was implicit in the whole pattern of Hart Crane's career and in the whole emotional and psychological tendency of his poetry.

The developing legend required so tragically symmetrical an ending, just as the cultural scene demanded a poet-hero of tragic dimensions—though this is not at all to say that *because* of its dramatic contours, the legend is unfounded. But as I have constantly insisted, I do not myself find a suicidal urge—a "bias towards death"—unequivocally expressed, or anything like a dominant note, in either *White Buildings* or *The Bridge*. There is an undeniable air of self-*consumption* in Crane's assault upon experience, and in the sometimes stupendous display of energy, of the prehensile imagination, in his poetry; but this is not at all the same thing, psychologically, as the impulse to self-*destruction,* and the poetry resulting expresses rather the creative wish than the so-called death-wish. [7] And though a different reading of "The Broken Tower" is possible, as we shall see, the

[6] "The Last Days of Hart Crane," *Venture,* Vol. 4, No. 1 (1961).
[7] Glauco Cambon, who has written penetratingly about Hart Crane in *The Inclusive Flame* (1963), has been most helpful, in conversation, in refining this important distinction.

poem in my view moves through pain and doubt to a peace-
fully confident sense of renewed life and love and poetic
power. Crane did indicate some uncertainty about the poem
in a letter to Malcolm Cowley, though he also admitted
that he was "getting too damned self-critical to write at all
any more"; but in the same mail, he dispatched a letter to
Samuel Loveman charged with a gay excitement about life
("Happiness continues, with also all of the gay incidentals
of a Mexican Easter—exploding Judases, rockets . . . flowers
galore and a sky that carries you ever upward") which
seems unmistakably, in its very wording, to reflect an excitement about his latest poetic achievement.

As to the fact, Miss Baird says somewhat obscurely that
Crane was "driven to this end which surely he never meant."
The dire intention he had announced to her had, she believed, like his other suicidal proclamations, only "been a
threat—to get a reaction." Crane's relatives in Ohio, not at
all surprisingly, refuse to this day to believe that he killed
himself. On his father's gravestone in Garretsville they in-
scribed his full name, Harold Hart Crane, his dates, and the
phrase "Lost At Sea." That too is an incontestable fact;
Crane's fabulous shadow, like that of Melville in the elegy,
only the sea keeps.

·II·

Of the independent lyrics written just before and during
the *mensis mirabilis* in 1926 but not included in *White Buildings,* at least three reward attention: "O Carib Isle!", "Royal
Palm," and "The Air Plant." The first of these, one of
Crane's most compelling and arduous poems, is a companion-
piece to "Repose of Rivers"; it was written in the same few
days (on a trip to and from the Grand Cayman), and in
carefully dragging rhythms it deals with much the same
theme—the felt loss of vision ("the eyes' baked lenses")
and of the poetic capacity. Like "Repose of Rivers," that is,
"O Carib Isle!" (originally called "Kidd's Cove") expresses
the mood conveyed in the letter to Waldo Frank on June

19, where the two poems were first mentioned: "At present—
I'm writing nothing. . . . *The Bridge* isn't very flamboyant
these days," and one cannot "build out of an emptied
vision." [8] But "O Carib Isle!" goes beyond "Repose of Rivers": here, if anywhere, the desire for an instant escape into
nothingness really does seem to be suggested:

> Under the poinciana, of a noon or afternoon
> Let fiery blossoms clot the light, render my ghost[,]
> Sieved upward, white and black along the air
> Until it meets the blue's comedian host.

Yet even here, the strangely colorful death-wish (if such it
be) encounters a stealthy and ambiguous resistance.

"O Carib Isle!" is indeed a complex of skillfully modulated
and, one should also say, graduated themes, with more than
one turn in its brooding argument. At the outset, we observe
the indifference of the natural world before the visible fact
of death. Confronted by "the dead"—dead sea-creatures, I
suppose, lying on the beach—"nothing here . . . mourns":
neither the tarantula, nor the crabs the word for whom
"shift[s]" and "anagrammatize[s]" the name ("Carib") of
the isle,[9] nor anything else. But the poet has, or rather he
meditates having, the power to shift and convert the names
of death into the names of life. By forthrightly acknowledging and articulating the reality of death—by "count[ing]
these nacreous [shell-like] frames of tropic death"—he might
be able to "gainsay death's brittle crypt," to

> speak a name, fertile
> Albeit in a stranger tongue. Tree names, flower names. . . .

[8] The letter to Frank also mentions a third work ("the Mango
poem") which with the other two he planned to publish "under
the common title of 'Grand Cayman.'" "The Mango Tree," as it
appears in *Key West*, is a clotted little prose poem of vaguely Joycian
character ("Up jug to musical hanging jug just gay spiders yoked
you first"), sounding a note of antic and rummy cynicism—no doubt
about the entire creative enterprise.

[9] Unless Crane means that the entire phrase "fiddler crabs" shifts
and anagrammatizes the name of the poem's setting, "Kidd's Cove."

The stranger tongue is the English as against the Spanish language; and it is the language of poetic transfiguration. But then, "meanwhile," and as in the earlier poem "Passage," the inspiring wind "coils and withdraws"; energy fades; and the names of rebirth do not get uttered—"so syllables want breath."

Given this abject failure of poetic speech, the poet—or "the pilgrim" as he insinuatingly calls himself—virtually prays for an immediate obliteration of his "ambushed senses"; he consigns himself not only to the indifference but to the derision of the natural world—to "the blue's comedian host." He is once again the "derelict and blinded guest" of "Voyages VI," but the guest this time of a far less salutary "host." And he thus hopes bleakly to die *at once* rather than to suffer the "slow evisceration" undergone by the huge turtles he sees bound and helpless on their backs each morning along the wharf: "still undead," in an earlier version; their eyes "brine-caked" like his own; "such thunder" in their straining futile efforts to free themselves; their "clenched beaks"— in a line omitted from the published poem, but one which thickens the feared analogy—"coughing for the surge again." [10] Longing to escape that hideously drawn-out death-process, the poet nevertheless—and it is an appalling, almost an unendurable image—feels his spirit slowly congealing through long and vacant afternoons.

But much depends, for an assured critical assessment of "O Carib Isle!", on one's sense of the last two lines:

You have given me the shell, Satan,—carbonic amulet
Sere of the sun exploded in the sea.

Weber (who quotes a slightly different earlier version) [11] takes the lines as simply the climax of the death-wish, and

[10] This fifth line of the penultimate stanza in every version except the one in *The Complete Poems* was, I suspect, omitted from the latter by editorial mistake.

[11] You have given me the shell, Satan,—the ember Carbolic, of the sun exploded in the sea.

sees in "the symbolic explosion of the life-radiating sun in the death-dealing sea. . . . the coveted extinction of light in dark waters." He may well be right; "O Carib Isle!" is perhaps the most death-burdened of Crane's poems. But the issue turns on the identity of Satan. This is the name ascribed, at the end, to the mysterious figure, the deadly force, alluded to in the serial questions of stanza five. *Satan* is "the Captain of this doubloon isle / Without a turnstile"—he is the presiding power in the land of death, from which there is no return; he is "Commissioner of the mildew throughout the ambushed senses"—the source of that decay that has fatally afflicted the poetic capacity; and his are the "Carib mathematics" that "web the eyes' baked lenses"—he is the agency of all those multiple deaths and modes of death the poet would seek to "count." He is everything that resists, diminishes, destroys—everything that, in the phrases from *Moby-Dick* (which Crane was then re-reading), cakes the brain and cracks the sinew. But he is also, I venture, one of the Satans of William Blake: specifically the Satan addressed contemptuously by Blake in the epilogue to "The Gates of Paradise" as "the Accuser who is the God of this World."

Crane cited this remarkable little poem in one of the fragments for a review—which he was writing at the time of his death—of Phelps Putnam's volume of poems, *The Fifth Season.* Putnam's very title, Crane remarked, suggested a time beyond time, the season properly inhabited by poetry; and as such, it was a symbol of that "dire immortality which is implicit in Blake's enigmatical and gorgeous address 'To Satan Who is Lord of this World.'" Blake's actual title is more ironic than Crane's emendation, with an irony nobly amplified in the second of the poem's two stanzas:

> Tho' thou art worshipped by the names divine
> Of Jesus and Jehovah, thou art still
> The Son of Morn in weary Night's decline,
> The lost traveller's dream under the hill.

Lucifer's day is waning; the harsh pieties of latter-day Christianity are losing their power; the accusing deity—worshipped as Jesus and Jehovah but conceived as a kind of Manichean devil—is no more than the false dream of the spiritually lost pilgrim; and a morning of true revelation is at hand. If, as I suspect, Crane's Satan in "O Carib Isle!" brings something of this Blakeian attitude into the poem, the final lines half-conceal a striking though still ambiguous twist. The shell of death Satan has given, or forced upon, the poet-pilgrim is an "amulet": that is, a magic charm *against* evil, spiritual failure, death. What may be happening is what the poet supposed might happen. By naming the "nacreous frames," the signs and symptoms of death upon the island, the poet may have found the necessary protection against his own death; and he can even taunt a little the Satanic source of death—and hence of the amulet—in the island world, the human world.

But I have no wish to exaggerate this aspect of the poem. "O Carib Isle!" has a good deal of the enigmatical as well as a little of the gorgeous quality Crane attributed to Blake. Like "Repose of Rivers," the companion poem closes with an admission of the death of vision which, at the same time, contains a hidden and perhaps not wholly realized belief in a renascence of some sort. Here as before it is a matter of hope dimming to despair and of despair gleaming faintly with hope.[12] At the depths of Crane's most sombre apprehensions, there lurked the conviction expressed by Blake in the "Introduction" to *Songs of Experience,* in lines Crane appropriated as the epigraph for *Key West* (and which inevitably color our interpretation of the poems in that collection)—the conviction that however dark and long the spiritual night, "the morn / Rises from the slumberous mass," and that during the night:

---

[12] If so, the word "sere"—apparently added the following year, and presumably at a less dejected moment—may contain its virtual opposite; shift and anagrammatize it only a trifle, and it becomes "seer."

The starry floor,
The wat'ry shore,
Is giv'n thee till the break of day.[13]

Although "Royal Palm" and "The Air Plant" are initially what might be called nature poems—they are compact and brilliantly precise descriptions of a palm tree and a curious little tuft-like plant—they are also variations on the theme of vision and visionary utterance, as might be expected of poems written during the great month. The royal palm so closely observed (it looks like "a fountain at salute") is at the same time a paradigm of the ascent of the imagination to an utterly unimpeded, an all-transcending vision of absolute reality; the poem about it declares Crane's persisting attitude toward such absolute vision and should be kept in mind when we come to "The Broken Tower." As the palm tree climbs ever skyward ("year on year"), it is distinguished at every turn from things earthly, human, mortal. The actual world is troubled by "noontide's blazed asperities," but "Green rustlings. . . . Drift cooly from that tower of whispered light." The palm possesses itself in total solitude— it is a "gracious anchorite," communing in an unpeopled world only with transcendent truth; it soars unreachably beyond the heated and the fatal thickets of human love—

> beyond that yield
> Of sweat the jungle presses with hot love
> And tendril till our deathward breath is sealed—
> It grazes the horizons, launched above
>
> Mortality. . . .

[13] One must be cautious in speaking, as I do here, about "the poems in that collection"—i.e., *Key West*. The latter was the phrase (followed by: "An Island Sheaf") Crane had chosen at some indeterminate date—probably in the late 'twenties—as the title for an indeterminate group of poems. Professor Unterecker's best guess is that it would have been the title of only one portion of a later volume of lyrics; it was Waldo Frank, in *The Collected Poems* of 1933, who gave it its overall application. I assume, incidentally, an allusive pun on the place-name—evoking again Blake's "Western Path" of pity as the key to visionary understanding.

The royal palm represents, of course, the visionary thrust away from the crowded noonday heat and the "things irreconcilable" and toward the "virginal" and the "cool" in "Faustus and Helen I," and the comparable urge toward a spiritual realm "High, cool, / wide from the slowly smouldering fire / Of lower heavens" in the first of the "Three Songs." But in the key phrase that stands out sharply at the head of stanza three, the royal palm is "forever fruitless." It begets nothing; it ascends in vain. The visionary process it represents is too completely dissociated from actuality; it does not—as in "Faustus and Helen" and "Three Songs"—return to mingle with and to disclose an ideal radiance within the mortal and the temporal. Its rustlings, whispers, and signs do not arrive at the condition of poetry. The palm and what it symbolizes—the "unshackled" vision—have an undeniable magnificence; but it is a magnificence beyond the boundaries within which human vision gives rise to poetry.

The air plant is a species of bulbous and spreading tuft, with soft upward-stretching tentacles, which Crane had seen growing, parasitically, on the trunk of a palm tree near Kidd's Cove on the Grand Cayman. The physical imagery of this dense and orderly lyric is even more exact than that of "Royal Palm": Crane watches

> the wind that jars
> Its tentacles, horrific in their lurch;

and he notices how

> The lizard's throat, held bloated for a fly,
> Balloons but warily from this throbbing perch.

The air plant is indeed more palpably rendered, it occupies more of its poetic space, than the royal palm. It is not so much a symbol of the active imagination as it is a phenomenon which, so to speak, "makes you think" of the imagination. For the latter, too, is a parasite; it is engrafted upon the actual but not itself rooted in actuality; it responds to the visitations of the inspiring wind, but often does so awkwardly, lurchingly. It is, as Crane had learned, an exceedingly precarious and unstable instrument. The skylark's song it strives to utter may at times sound like the nervous twittering of a less melodious bird ("A bird almost—of almost bird alarms"). Yet it gives voice to nature: it invests air and sky with its own verbal music ("Ventriloquist of the Blue!"); the theme of "Sunday Morning Apples" is thus belatedly and far more expressively returned to. And in a sudden and dramatic lift of poetic momentum, Crane, in the closing lines, sees both the air plant and the imagination raised by the mightiest of literal and symbolic winds to their highest power, to truly godlike force:

> While beachward creeps the shark-swept Spanish Main
> By what conjunctions do the winds appoint
> Its apotheosis at last—the hurricane!

When, in October 1926, the Isle of Pines was struck by a hurricane, Crane must have felt that nature was realizing in its own enormous and shattering manner one of his favorite symbols: that it was responding with abrupt and ultimate vehemence by providing him in very fact with that "apotheosis" of sheer energy which he had formulated in verse. This must have been one cause of the wild exuberance the experience aroused in him: when the ferociously devastating storm (which ravaged almost the entire Carribbean over a three-day period) was over, and Crane discovered that he and his friend "Aunt Sally" Simpson had survived, his first reaction (in Horton's words) was "a mood of crazy joy." Something of that seething hilarity went into the two poems Crane wrote about the event: "The Hurricane" (formerly "The Hour"), which is mainly a product of the following summer; and "Eternity," which was probably composed soon after the whirlwinds had passed by.

The poems make an odd and instructive pair. Neither is of first importance; but the relative superiority of "Eternity," as Jonathan Aaron has argued in a noteworthy discussion, is due—most untypically—to its groping after "an experience which has not settled and coalesced in Crane's mind"; Crane in this unusual instance can be observed "warily circling what he considers to be an event fraught with the stuff of poetry . . . to tame it" before converting it into his mode of visionary utterance.[14] In "The Hurricane," quite the other way, the materials have been all too thoroughly transposed and versified; the later work is a virtuoso piece, pulsating with thrilled wonder at the divine fury exemplified by the storm, but doing so in such exclamatory and out-of-date or coined language that the poem appears to be clothed in a sort of verbal fancy-dress borrowed for this one occasion:

> Thy swifting heart
>
> Naught stayeth, naught now bideth
> But's smithereened apart! [15]

The potent if indistinct analogy between the sublime destructive violence of God-in-nature and the violence of the creative imagination at its most intense gives "The Hurricane" its portion of effectiveness, and is the source of Crane's no doubt genuine excitement; few modern poets knew better than Crane that the creative talent (as R. P. Blackmur has put it) is a violence of the soul. But "Eternity"—though by contrast with "The Hurricane" it stays for the most part this side of achieved poetry—is the more authentic composition: for here the poem *rises* (to borrow from Jonathan Aaron again) from the piled-up details of the storm's aftermath—

> Wires in the streets and Chinamen up and down
> With arms in slings, plaster strewn dense with tiles,
> And Cuban doctors, troopers, trucks, loose hens . . .

[14] "Hart Crane's 'Eternity,' " an unpublished paper.

[15] The construction and idiom of the last quoted line particularly sounds like Gerard Manley Hopkins; but Horton seems to have demonstrated beyond question that Crane was unfamiliar with Hopkins' poetry until nearly a year after he wrote "The Hurricane."

—to a moment of genuine and traditional apocalyptic vision.

The end of the world, as the poet and the poem move cautiously through the wreckage, seems really to have occurred—at least the end of the local world:

> some rumor blew
> That Havana, not to mention poor Batabanó
> Was halfway under water with fires
> For some hours since.

Out of this comes the revelation of stanza five: a revelation the more impressive since it has been stirring slowly in the poet's hesitantly transfiguring survey of the actual debris, and since it is couched in language that at once grows out of and jostles incongruously with the reportorial style of that survey. It is the vision of a phantom horse: the white steed of *the* Apocalypse, an emblem of that careening force described all too breathlessly in "The Hurricane," and as such the sign of the termination of time, a glimpse of eternity itself:

> For I
> Remember still that strange gratuity of horses
> —One ours, and one, a stranger, creeping up with dawn
> Out of the bamboo brake through howling, sheeted light
> When the storm was dying. . . .
>
> There's Don—but that one,
> white
> —I can't account for him! And true, he stood
> Like a vast phantom maned by all that memoried night
> Of screaming rain—Eternity! [16]

[16] Crane has supplied the title for a great many poems, volumes of poems (*Permit Me Voyage*), essays, volumes of essays (*The Heel of Elohim, The Visionary Company*), plays (*Summer and Smoke*), works of fiction (*Such Random Consolations*) and autobiography (*Emblems of Conduct*). The superb phrase in the lines just quoted —a "gratuity of horses"—may already have been used; if not, we may expect it to be in the near future. The point is not a frivolous one. It is the quality of encompassing finality—as it were, of a tenacious seizure of reality—that marks Crane's phrase-making power, and because of which his idioms are so wonderfully apt for titular purposes.

We need not go as far as Mr. Aaron in suggesting that the white horse "represents the kind of vision [Crane] was striving to attain," while the "dazed mule" that dies by the pump in the next stanza is "Crane's enervated and beaten imagination"; because the poem itself does not go that far. The poem simply gropes upward to a moment of startling vision—of illuminating hallucination, perhaps—and then falls quickly away into the casual information and barroom gossip of the final stanza, all vision dissipated. It leaves behind an assortment of undefined images, juxtaposed without resolution. But it leaves behind, too, an example of the creative process, of the imagination struggling to beget out of calamity and wreckage some fleeting perception of the eternal.

A word, finally, on a modestly successful poem contemporary with "The Hurricane"—"Island Quarry." It is another resolute scrutiny of death, here represented by a mountain quarry where unnamed persons "saw" the marble into "Flat prison slabs," "Square sheets"—gravestones, that is, marble shrouds for the dead. With a kind of obvious adroitness and in elusively Biblical tones, Crane contrasts two roads as two responses to mortality: the path that curves "quivering" around the mountain and leads on to "tears and sleep" (useless lament and psychological evasion); and the "straight road" that heads directly into the mountain and "into marble that does not weep." But "Island Quarry" is not, to make the necessary distinction, about the determination to die. It is about *looking at* death, acknowledging the irremediable fact. It is the poet's "eyes"—not his private inclinations—which, sometimes at dusk on the Isle of Pines:

> burned hard and glad
> And did not take the goat path quivering to the right.

Few modern poets have so decidedly earned the right to that tough-spirited gladness, or to the vision of loveliness which the acceptance of death's reality gives rise to—a vision of "this island lifted, floated / In Indian baths. . . ."

·III·

Among the sporadic poems and fragments Crane wrote in Mexico, several reflected on the present condition and the evil history of the Mexican Indians. Crane studied the actual Indians with fascination, caution, and compassion; but in his imagination, they sometimes mingled, not unnaturally, with the legendary American Indians of *The Bridge*. "The Circumstance," occasioned (I take it) by the statue of an old Indian god named Xochipilli—"a god of flowers in statued / Stone . . . of love—" is an echo, almost a plagiarism, of "The Dance," as it meditates on "the coruscated crown" and "the drastic throne" of the divine authority over a long since "dismounted people." Like Maquokeeta, Xochipilli too, in this brief and resistant lyric, seems at once to have vanished into the ages and to live forever, peering out over his own Mexican "bivouacs" of "angered slain." He combines indeed the royalty of Maquokeeta with the devotion and smiles of Pocahontas. And as his enduring statue "drink[s] the sun," a force "stronger than death smiles in flowering stone"—a triumph over time, the last murky phrases imply, and an insight into its mystery.

In a related poem called "They Were There Falling," Crane playfully attributes to the contemporary Mexican Indians the same kind of natural understanding—knowledge gained not from doctrinal instruction but from observing the life of nature—that he had observed in the vagrants of "The River," and that, very greatly heightened, became the mythic imagination of the Indians in "The Dance." These "displaced Indians," Crane remarks,

> scan more news
> On the hind end of their flocks each day
> Than all the tourists bring their way,

and "all that the missions and votaries / dispense. . . . doesn't confuse these Indians." [17] But in "The Sad Indian," Crane

[17] Special Collections, Columbia University Library.

turned away from these attractive fantasies to admit the grim truth—that the "keen vision" of an earlier Indian epoch had been warped and stunted by the long history of savage oppression:

> the lash, lost vantage—and the prison
> His fathers took for granted ages since.

The "sad heart" of the contemporary Indian is no longer able to "count / Hours, days—and scarcely sun and moon." Whether Crane was or was not still considering, as at one time he had, a long poem about the conquest of Mexico by foreign invaders (alluded to in "The Circumstance" as "a bloody foreign clown"), a characteristic theme is detectable somewhere in these blunted bits and pieces—the contrast between past visionary grandeur and present visionary enslavement, with the usual hint of a transformation scene at the far edge of possibility.

But other poems of this period return to the (for Crane) engrossing if troubled theme of the poetic self, and two of these may be mentioned as prologue to Crane's final masterpiece, "The Broken Tower." In "Reliquary," Crane—after some jerky and all but incomprehensible references to a pillow and a ditch, to Apollo and Sagittarius—raises the issue of his own artistic (and presumably sexual) heresies, and goes on to ask who, if anyone, will be his poetic beneficiary and successor. It is not a very attractive work, but it contains a valuable statement of Crane's consciousness of himself within a (then) unfashionable and yet, Crane believed, by no means exhausted tradition. "Reliquary" is, indeed, an elliptical version of some remarks Crane had made to Allen Tate in the letter of July 13, 1930; the poem may even date from that period, though such skimpy evidence as there is seems to place it a year or so later.

"The fact that you posit *The Bridge* at the end of a tradition of romanticism," Crane wrote, alluding to Tate's review of the epic, "may prove to have been an accurate prophecy, but I don't yet feel that such a statement can be taken as a foregone conclusion." Indulging in what was to prove an incomparably more accurate prophecy, Crane continued: "A great deal of romanticism may persist—of the sort to deserve serious consideration, I mean." This was the basis of his hope that *The Bridge* might serve "as at least . . . a link connecting certain chains of the past to certain chains and tendencies of the future." Crane felt the more strongly about this since such linkage had just been flatly denied by Genevieve Taggard in a review of Stanley Kunitz's first volume of poems. Kunitz's poetry, Miss Taggard declared, put an end once and for all to the kind of writing that had flourished for some years—"the cloudy and pretentious writing" the reviewer attributed to Crane, to Tate and Winters and also (ever more surprisingly) to Louise Bogan and Leonie Adams. These poets, according to Miss Taggard, had survived on the sheer blind faith of their admirers, a faith which "is sometimes very bad for an artist—and it has been bad, undoubtedly, for Hart Crane, who tends to stir up because he cannot clarify." Though hurt by these familiar accusations, Crane was willing to believe that Kunitz was "evidently an excellent poet," partly because of the promise of Kunitz's title—*Intellectual Things*—which derived from the same passage in Blake's "I Saw a Monk of Charlemagne" which Crane had drawn upon in "The Wine Menagerie" and had held up as a key example of the logic of metaphor in his letter to Harriet Monroe.

Crane's conclusion was that of a poet matured and battle-scarred by experience: "I can't help thinking that my mistakes may warn others who may later be tempted to an interest in similar subject matter." But the tone of "Reliquary" is more defiant, as Crane locates himself among those "who, somehow, do not follow," "who are variants," who "refuse the clinch / With desperate propriety." The latter phrase defines, with a certain animation, the poem's chief tension—between the soundness of his poetic commitment and the fierce critical hostility it had aroused. (Again, along with "poetic" read also "sexual.") But the poet in "Reliquary" stands by his singularity, and dares wonder who will come after him to give fresh utterance and new imaginative twist to the same heretical impulses:

> Who is now left to vary the Sanskrit
> Pillowed by

> My wrist in the vestibule of time—Who
> Will hold it—wear the keepsake, dear, of time . . . ?

The word "my" stands out with unexpected bravado. Crane is here taking to himself that "Sanskrit charge"—that capacity to "conjugate infinity"—discerned in the "wrist" of the "Falcon-Ace" of "Cape Hatteras"; but almost four decades later, Crane's question remains to be answered.

"Purgatorio" is a heavyhearted expression of isolation and guilt. In phrases that tremble and break, Crane speaks of being "apart" from his country and his friends—not so much physically separated, as an American in Mexico, but cut off from the sources of creativity and transported into a nightmare "landscape of confession," where "absolution" seems at best problematic. Exile of this kind "is thus purgatory"; but not a *Purgatorio* (a purging and purifying experience) "such as Dante built." [18] It is rather a condition of being smothered in his own inertia—"And I have no decision," no strength of will, no power of determination among poetic options. The final lines introduce a portion of the theme and symbolism that Crane would shortly develop with an extraordinary reversal of mood in "The Broken Tower":

> I am unraveled, umbilical anew,
> So ring the church bells here in Mexico—
> (They ring too obdurately here to need my call)
> And what hours they forget to chime I'll know
> As one whose altitude at one time, was not so.

[18] It was in Mexico, in 1931, that Crane read *The Divine Comedy* for the first time.

This is not much more than rhymed muttering; but through it one hears the poet reminding himself that he, once, entertained a far loftier vision than any he can now summon up—the vision of a world beyond the hours announced by the church bells, though those same bells intone a reality beyond the reach of and indifferent to his own diminished voice.

·IV·

In "The Broken Tower," every word not only counts, but counts for double and triple; never did the connotations of Crane's language interact to greater ranges of beauty and meaning—ranges beyond anything the present context permits me to arrive at. The poem consists of ten four-line stanzas of closely worded iambics and with quiet but steadily audible alternating rhymes. "Alternation," in fact, at once describes the poetic technique and in part, as we shall see, identifies the developing theme of the work. It is, one might say, the most antiphonal of Crane's lyrics, rising as it does from the alternating sound, the sonorous ding-dong, of church bells (like those in "Recitative") heard at dawn:

> Have you not heard, have you not seen that corps
> Of shadows in the tower, whose shoulders sway
> Antiphonal carillons launched before
> The stars are caught and hived in the sun's ray?

As stanza follows stanza, alternating words and sounds, phrases and figures, build into the fluid pattern which is the symbolic tower, the achieved vision, of the poet's imagination. Among them: "gathers" (*God*) and "dispatches" (*me*); "have you not heard," and "have you not seen"; "outleaping" and "prostrate"; the "tribunal monarch of the air," and the "she" of "sweet mortality"; "lift down the eye" and "lifts love [by implication, "up"] in its shower"; along with a number of near repetitions and internal rhymes which thicken the poem's texture: "I know not where. . . . I know not wither," "strikes. . . . strokes," "hold. . . .

healed," and so on. But the poem, energized by these verbal antiphonals, reaches toward much larger alternations yet.

One way to perceive the latter—to define, as it were, the essential creative duplicity of the poem—is to observe that "The Broken Tower," as I have said before, recapitulates Crane's poetic career very near the end of it in just the way "Repose of Rivers" did six years earlier, at something like its mid-point. We notice here again echoes and reminders of other poems, of other poetic moments and visionary achievements: of "Recitative," most obviously, in the stanza just quoted, but also of various phases of *The Bridge*—of the dawn, of vision receding and of the pivoting gulls of "Proem," and (in references to "canyons" and "banked voices slain") of the extreme visionary intensity of "The Dance." The dance motif recurs in the swaying "shoulders" of the bells—the latter allusion being reminiscent, too, of the sea's "turning shoulders" which "count the hours" in "Voyages II"; and the marriage of sky and earth here compares with that of sky and sea in "Voyages III." Less overtly but by no means less importantly, the poem recalls to itself, as its own abiding principle, the grand climactic imperative of "Faustus and Helen III":

> Distinctly praise the years, whose volatile
> Blamed bleeding hands extend and thresh the height
> The imagination spans beyond despair,
> Outpacing bargain, vocable and prayer.

And throughout this sustained act of personal poetic recollection, there seems perhaps to be a sense of crucial alternation—eventually, as it may be, of fundamental contrast—of special urgency for Crane: namely, between the constrained lyrical manner of *White Buildings* and the expansive epical ambition of *The Bridge*. The hypothesis is, at least, worth pursuing.

In the letter to Allen Tate of July 13, 1930, responding to what Crane (who had not read it) called Tate's "admirable review of *The Bridge*" and going on to talk about poetry that does not, didactically, attempt "to sum up the universe in one impressive little pellet," Crane remarked:

> I admit that I don't answer the requirements. My vision of poetry *is* too personal to "answer the call." And if I ever write any more verse it will probably be at least as personal as the idiom of *White Buildings* whether anyone cares to look at it or not.

One should as always take note of the date. This letter was written during the summer of Crane's most radical discontent, and the statement need no more be taken as final than the disheartened report about *The Bridge* in June 1926—or than any other statement Crane made, or any vision he articulated; finality was an often stunning quality in his rhetoric (he was, as we have noted, a great poet of "ultimate" phrases), but it was not an element of his consciousness. Still, in the long and sometimes tiresome debate as to whether Crane's lyric poems are somehow "better" than his epic, it has been argued that the passage above represents Crane's settled conviction after completing *The Bridge:* that he had now decided that what he had attempted there was beyond his capacities and perhaps beyond those of poetry itself; that he therefore accepted the limitations of his incorrigibly personal idiom; and that this conviction provides the basis and most of the content of "The Broken Tower."

This argument has been put forward by Marius Bewley, in the course of an uncommonly astute reading of the poem.[19] Bewley's remarks are worth quoting as we near the end of Crane's long and often painful but no less often intoxicated poetic journey; for they state a familiar case as keenly and sympathetically as any discussion of Crane that comes to mind, and they thus provide a last chance to clarify what is probably the key aspect of Crane's poetry (that is, of course, to clarify my own opinion on that aspect). "The Broken Tower," Bewley writes, is "an objective

[19] "Hart Crane's 'The Broken Tower,'" *Accent* (Spring 1959).

and deliberately thought out expression of Crane's literary faith in his last months, and it expresses what he had learned of his own limitations by writing *The Bridge*." Bewley quotes both the letter to Tate and the final lines of "Faustus and Helen" as instances of Crane's all too infrequent clarity of poetic purpose; and after a detailed examination of the first six stanzas of "The Broken Tower," he arrives at the following summary. "The poet, dedicated to an absolute, a Platonic vision, must necessarily fail to achieve it in his art. Crane had learned that the tower of absolute vision was much too high to climb in his poetry." And so, Bewley continues, Crane's last poem records a turning away from the supreme visionary effort symbolized by an Apollo-like figure ("that tribunal monarch of the air") to the more modest poetry of "sweet mortality," toward which he is beckoned by a female symbol of "the very centre of Crane's own being"—of his own truest capabilities. In the closing stanza, according to Bewley, Crane beautifully announces his understanding that "absolute vision" (represented by the masculine tower) "can be approached only through the limiting and distorting perspectives of mortal vision" (represented by the feminine lake).

This is all very well said. My own view, nonetheless—the one I have pressed repeatedly—is that everything Crane wrote from "Faustus and Helen" onward announces and enacts the exact same understanding Bewley attributes almost uniquely to "The Broken Tower." Similarly, my view of "The Broken Tower" is that—although it is undoubtedly an expression of Crane's literary faith, and although its tone for the most part is wiser and sadder than the earlier poems on this theme—it is *not* a new and, at the last, an authentic appraisal by Crane of his creative powers and of the boundaries of poetry. It is, I believe, in the deepest sense autobiographical, a retracing of the particular visionary path he had been ardently and desperately following for more than a decade. What is new is the pattern of ingredients—a freshness of idiom, an originality (for Crane) of symbol, a new melodic structure, and as it were a newly contrived dialectic.

Consequently, the grand alternation which gives the poem its momentum is not precisely between two modes of poetry Crane had sought to practice, one to fine effect and the other with a kind of disastrous wrong-headedness. Two modes of poetry are certainly contemplated; but one of them, so the poem declares (not without profound regret or even, if you will, anguish), had never been accessible to the poet. This is poetry which, if it were possible for mortal man to compose it, would rehearse the phenomenon described in the first two and a half stanzas—a genuine religious process, with supernatural energies genuinely at work in it. For the first thing to say about the bells that ring in those stanzas is that they are the real bells of a real church: the bells, in fact, of the village church in Taxco which Crane helped the sexton ring one morning in late January 1932. "The sublimity of the scene and the thunder of the bells," as Crane's friend Leslie Simpson recalled, "woke in Hart one of those gusts of joy of which only he was capable." [20] The ensuing poem is swept back toward a joy peculiar to Crane; but at its beginning, it presents us with an immense and chilling contrast:

> The bell-rope that gathers God at dawn
> Dispatches me as though I dropped down the knell
> Of a spent day—to wander the cathedral lawn
> From pit to crucifix, feet chill on steps from hell.

The bell-rope that draws together the faithful by the very act of intoning the imminent visitation of God among them: this bell-rope at the same time "dispatches" the poet; it sends him down in his imagination to the domain of his own poetry—where, by comparison, instead of bells at dawn there resounds the death-knell of the spent or dying day; and where, instead of envisioning the heavenly kingdom, he had been exploring a temporal and fallen world which

[20] Quoted by Horton, *op.cit.*, p. 292.

(again by comparison) seems to be a species of hell, a place of torment and the abyss. Here lies the first fundamental contrast of "The Broken Tower": between a true, direct and as it were real-life experience of God, and the loftiest religious experience that purely human poetic resources can aspire to. The virtues of such purely human efforts, Crane may be heard saying in an adaptation of St. Augustine, are no more than shining sins.

The contrast continues and enlarges. After the second stanza—an expression of astounded excitement over the magnificence of the religious accomplishment, with an image of the stars as what Crane elsewhere calls "the bees of Paradise"—the poem reaches its first turn:

> The bells, I say, the bells break down their tower;
> And swing I know not where. Their tongues engrave
> Membrane through marrow, my long-scattered score
> Of broken intervals . . . And I, their sexton slave!

These bells, these agencies of supernatural power—and the reference is still to the bells of Taxco—break down their confining context; their music bursts beyond the actual setting, the actual tower, and, carrying the faithful in spirit with them, it echoes within some dimensionally superior reality—the realm of a God which the poet can never fully know, can never literally enter in his poetry. For the contrast has made him aware of a different kind of shattering, of a different tower differently broken; the tongues of the bells "engrave" (punningly, they *bury* within his consciousness) his own poems, all of which—though only for the moment—seem to him a "long-scattered score / Of broken intervals"; and though he longs to be "their sexton," to ring comparable bells to comparable effect in his poetry, he remains enslaved within the boundaries of mortality. It is that periodic moment of seemingly unassuageable despair that the Romantic imagination always passes through, and which Crane had passed through in "The Tunnel" en route to a vision of sublimity.

It is within this perspective that, in the fourth stanza, Crane surveys his greatest poetic efforts and finds them a series of splendid thrustings toward a transcendent reality which nevertheless have fallen back calamitously into the temporal:

> Oval encyclicals in canyons heaping
> The impasse high with choir. Banked voices slain!
> Pagodas, campaniles with reveilles outleaping—
> O terraced echoes prostrate on the plain! . . .

Though the logic of metaphor is here stretched to the utmost, this awesomely packed stanza is brilliantly successful. Crane's poems, so he tells us, may have been intended as "encyclicals," as messages of authoritative religious instruction which compose a "choir" and ring from their own bell-tower ("campaniles"). They may have been intended as "banked" and "terraced" structures—graduations of the spirit, that is, toward the godhead—which finally outleaped the entire world of the actual. It had been a mighty creative struggle; but the battle had ended with, as it were, the corpses of poems (of slain voices) blocking the entrance to the canyon, piled up at the very threshold of vision; by one of Crane's most serious puns, the metaphorical mountain pass becomes that which obstructs it, an "impasse."

That is one perspective: a perspective in which Crane measures his poetry against a true experience (as the saying goes) of the absolute and, by extension, against a hypothetical poetic creation which would contain and make palpable such an experience. But he then moves on (it is the poem's second significant turn) to remember what he had in fact all along attempted to do. If, like Whitman at one moment in "Crossing Brooklyn Ferry," Crane could say that the best he had written seemed to him blank and suspicious, a dismal failure, he could also, like Whitman in that same poem, progress to a healthier and ultimately a more ecstatic sense of what he had done and was still doing.

And so it was I entered the broken world
To trace the visionary company of love, its voice
An instant in the wind (I know not whither hurled)
But not for long to hold each desperate choice.

No more precise and richly compressed account of Crane's poetic career can be imagined. Not only did Crane enter in consciousness and time and again re-enter what he had for years referred to as "the broken world"—this fallen and fragmented world which he had traversed at greatest length in the bars and powerhouses and burlesque theaters and country clubs and subways of the later portions of *The Bridge*. Not only had he done so with the unflagging determination to trace *within it* the visionary company of love—by an act of poetic transfiguration, to make evident a condition of wholeness and harmony and thus metaphorically to redeem it. Not only had he made the voice of vision and of love audible on those occasions when he had been enlisted in the service of the inspiring wind, his poetic muse. But also—and how often have we observed it—the vision begotten out of the almost intractable materials so desperately yet necessarily chosen had never endured for more than "an instant."

Doubts and queries persist yet a little longer, as Crane searches further into his creative past:

My word I poured. But was it cognate, scored
Of that tribunal monarch of the air
Whose thigh embronzes earth, strikes crystal Word
In wounds pledged once to hope—cleft to despair?

Bewley is probably right in identifying the "monarch of the air" as Apollo, or some mythological deity invoked to symbolize a godlike vision—a symbol then transformed at one verbal jump into the figure of Christ, as the thigh that embronzes earth becomes the wounded thigh of the Word made flesh and dying upon the cross that human despair might be lifted by a pledge of redemption. Poetry "cognate" with those divine beings would indeed be a poetry of absolute vision; but Crane knows that the word at the heart of his own poems had never been "scored" of that "crystal" (that is, Christian) Word, and he says so in questions that turn smoothly into ever-more serenely confident answers:

> The steep encroachments of my blood left me
> No answer (could blood hold such a lofty tower
> As flings the question true?)—or is it she
> Whose sweet mortality stirs latent power?—

Those steep encroachments are not primarily Crane's personal excesses or debauches. It is not a private but a universally human limitation, that of a mortal man of flesh and blood, that forbids any answer but the self-answering question. The poet is by nature caught within what, in "Royal Palm," he had called the human "jungle" of "hot love," above which the visionary palm tree—carefully distinguished from the thrust of human poetry—"soared suchwise through heaven": as here, in a nearly identical image, the "lofty tower . . . flings the question true."

And so, having submitted himself and his writing to these formidable challenges, Crane has won through to a final surmise which evolves into an utterly invulnerable affirmation:

> or is it she
> Whose sweet mortality stirs latent power?—

> And through whose pulse I hear, counting the strokes
> My veins recall and add, revived and sure
> The angelus of war my chest evokes:
> What I hold healed, original now, and pure. . . .

These are the different strokes of a different and interior bell: the bell-like pulsations in his veins and that of his beloved, sounding the evening angelus of peace and an end to the creative battle implicit in the military imagery of the fourth stanza. The angelus is not only "sure," it is "revived": it is rung again, as it has so frequently rung before, bestirred by the female figure who is at once, as Bewley puts it, "an emblematic concentration" of certain qualities in Crane's own nature and the particular human being (Peggy Baird) whose love has re-animated those qualities. Creative energy seeps back into him; and what he now holds—as against what his blood could not even try to hold—is a healed and purified imagination.

We come to the last stanzas and a hauntingly lovely description of the creative act which brings "The Broken Tower" to a climax scarcely matched elsewhere even by this master of climactic language:

> And builds, within, a tower that is not stone
> (Not stone can jacket heaven)—but slip
> Of pebbles,—visible wings of silence sown
> In azure circles, widening as they dip
>
> The matrix of the heart, lift down the eye
> That shrines the quiet lake and swells a tower . . .
> The commodious, tall decorum of that sky
> Unseals her earth and lifts love in its shower.

One hesitates to touch it, since if one is to say anything, one wants to see and to say everything, as though it were possible to be the angelic critic Crane's poetry seems to demand. Let us content ourselves with the obvious: that here the author of *White Buildings* is bringing into view the most perfect building, the most sublime poetic construct, his imagination can design. This tower—this "loft of vision," to borrow from "Atlantis"—is built *within* the human spirit. It is not a thing of frozen stone (which, Crane now says with a kind of earned arrogance, could never encompass the heaven of the creative imagination). It is rather a spiritual flowing, like a shower of pebbles (we recall the "bright stones" of metaphor "wherein our smiling plays" in "Possessions"); or it is like the dipping and circling flight of the sea gulls which, in "Proem," represented the harmonious vision—gulls which are visible and yet silent with that so highly communicative silence that marked the ending of Crane's other great poetic inquiries.

This is the vision that enlarges the very heart of the heart; and in an enchanting oxymoron it "lift[s] down the eye." Love and perception are again united: but a perception proper to human poetry, working within the broken world, seeking to transform it. In the Emersonian manner to which Crane had so long been attached (and in Emerson's words), it is a vision that "finds beauty and holiness" in natural facts, and raises them "to divine use": it *"shrines* the quiet lake"—another and happier way of envisioning our actual world—and by doing so it "swells a tower" of poetry. The heaven created in poetry and by poetry is not the heaven bespoken by the bell-rope of the first stanza; but it releases the music of the realm of man, and love surges within it. Neither here nor anywhere else was Crane attempting to articulate an absolute vision; he was striving to show the familiar world transfigured and enshrined and so, poetically speaking, redeemed—yet still familiar, still our world. But surely, as he was writing "The Broken Tower," Crane must have heard that "absolute music in the air again" to which he listened in the extraordinarily fertile summer of 1926.

Index of Crane's Writings

General Index

PS
3505
.R272-
Z74
1978

Date Due
